SHONEN JUMP MANGA EDITION

Muhyo & Roji's Bureau of Supernatural Investigation BSI

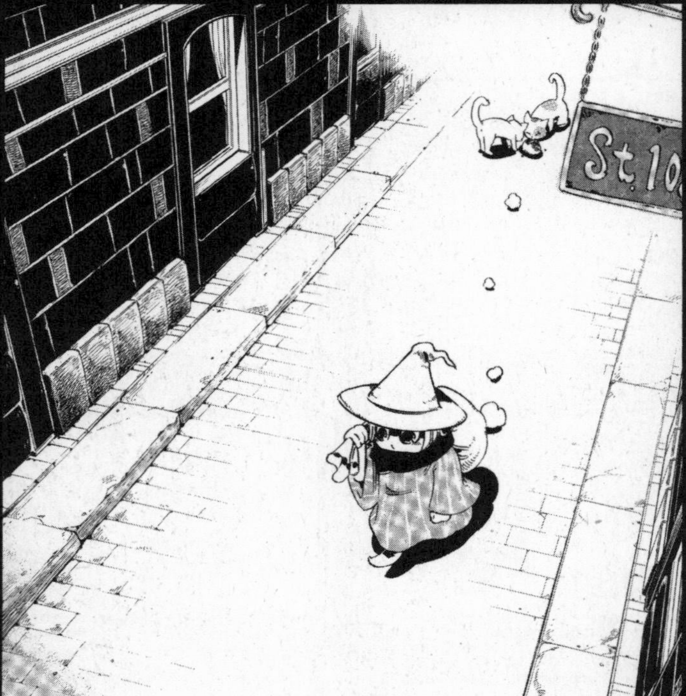
St.10

Vol. 7 Trials & Tribulations

Story & Art by **Yoshiyuki Nishi**

Dramatis Personae

Jiro Kusano (Roji)

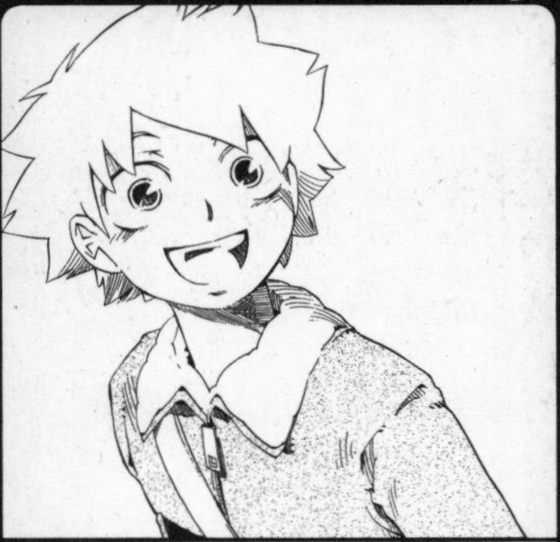

Assistant at Muhyo's office, recently promoted from the lowest rank of "Second Clerk" to that of (provisional) "First Clerk." Roji has a gentle heart and has been known to freak out in the presence of spirits. Lately, he has been devoting himself to the study of magic law so that he can pull his own weight someday.

Toru Muhyo (Muhyo)

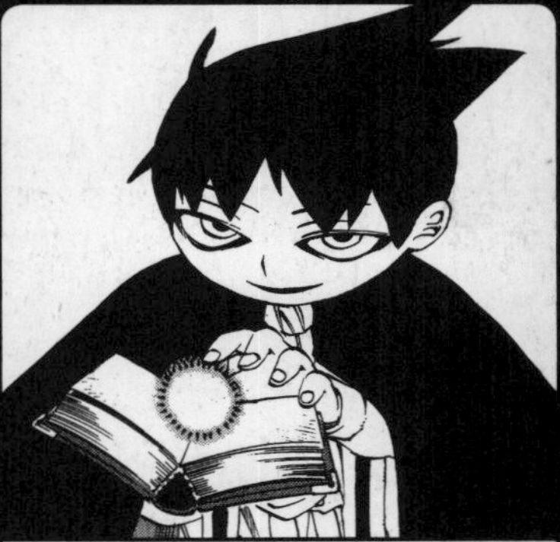

Young, genius magic law practitioner with the highest rank of "Executor." Always calm and collected (though sometimes considered cold), Muhyo possesses a strong sense of justice and even has a kind side. Sleeps a lot to recover from the exhaustion caused by his practice.

Yu Abiko (Biko)

Muhyo's classmate and an Artificer. Makes seals, pens, magic law books, and other accoutrements of magic law.

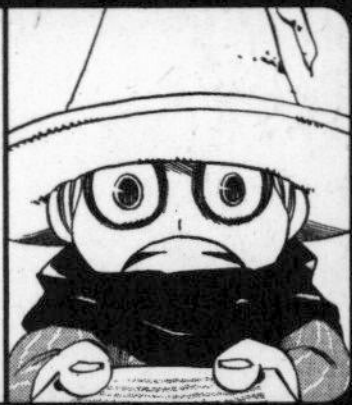

Yoichi Himukai (Yoichi)

Judge and Muhyo's former classmate. Expert practitioner of all magic law except execution.

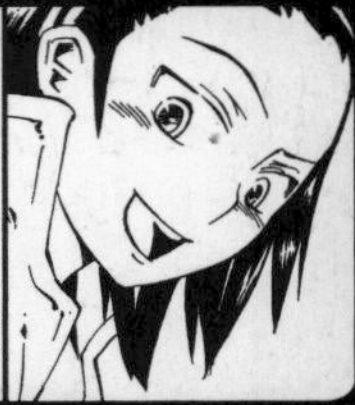

Rio Kurotori (Rio)

Charismatic Artificer who turned traitor when the Magic Law Association stood by and let her mother die.

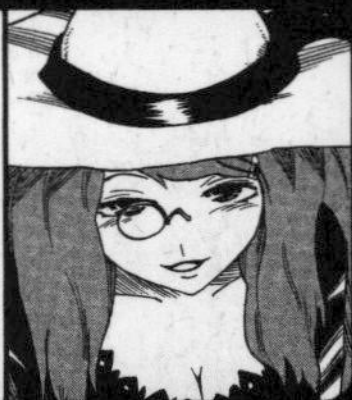

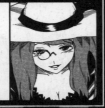

Soratsugu Madoka (Enchu)

Muhyo's former classmate and Executor-hopeful until one event turned him onto the traitor's path.

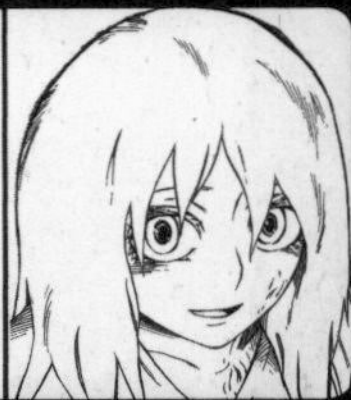

Hanao Ebisu (Ebisu)

Judge and Goryo's former underling, fired after his failure during the showdown against Muhyo at the haunted apartments.

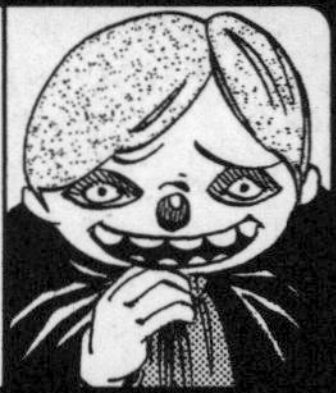

Page Klaus

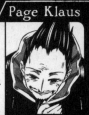

Chief Investigator for the Magic Law Association and Headmaster of the Magic Law Academy. Executor and Yoichi's supervisor.

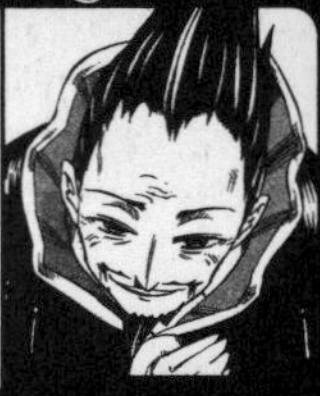

Reiko Imai

Brave Judge who joined Muhyo and gang during the fight against Face-Ripper Sophie.

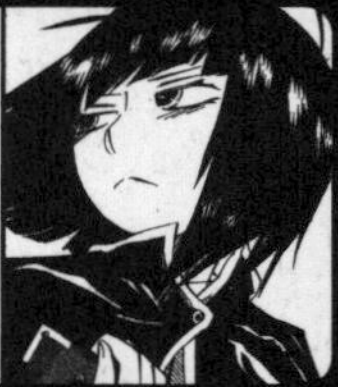

Lili & Maril Mathias

Twin sister and brother who are taking the magic law examinations. They join Roji on the special magic law retreat.

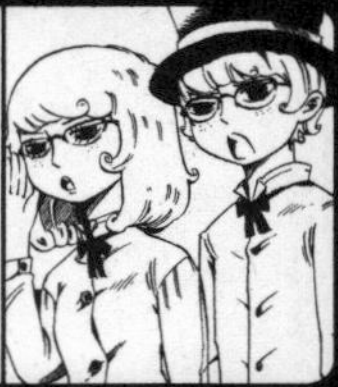

The Story

Magic law is a newly established practice for judging and punishing the increasing crimes committed by spirits; those who use it are called "practitioners."

With his office at stake, Muhyo's victory in a contest against Goryo is clear—until Muhyo declares his own defeat and puts Roji on indefinite leave. Muhyo sets off alone to prepare for the coming battle against the practitioners of forbidden magic law by forming a contract with the underlord Pluto himself. Meanwhile, a despondent Roji decides to take the magic law examinations to find out why Muhyo chose him as his assistant in the first place. However, the examinations turn out to be a selection for Page's special magic law retreat—a retreat that promises to be terrifyingly educational.

Nana Takenouchi (Nana)

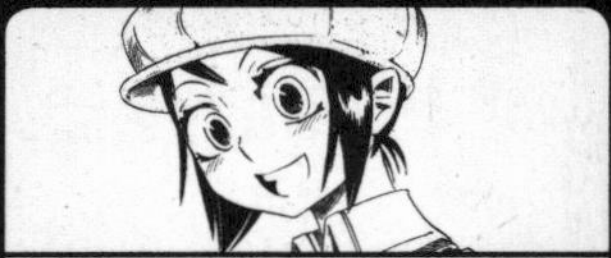

High school student and aspiring photographer. She's also a spirit medium, which gets her into all sorts of trouble...

Daranimaru Goryo (Goryo)

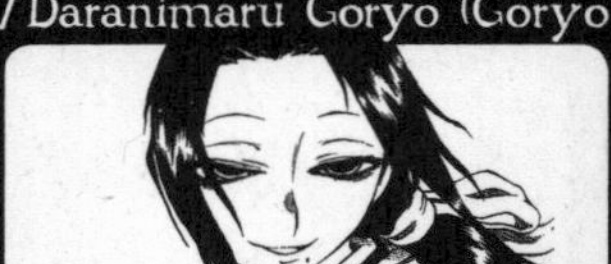

An Executor and gifted strategist who considers Muhyo his rival. Head of the Goryo Group syndicate.

Teeki

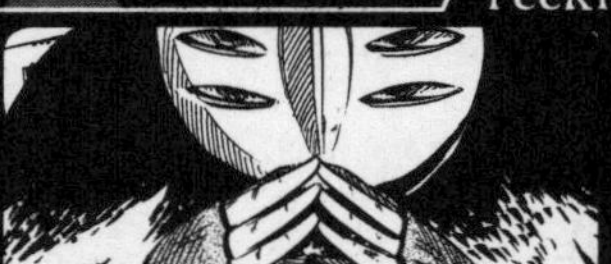

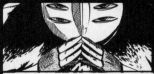

Dangerous entity marked as a traitor to the Magic Law Association for 800 years.

Muhyo & Roji's Bureau of Supernatural Investigation BSI

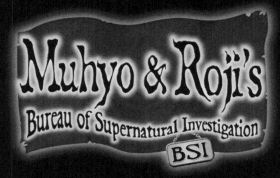

CONTENTS

7

ARTICLE 51
TRIALS & TRIBULATIONS

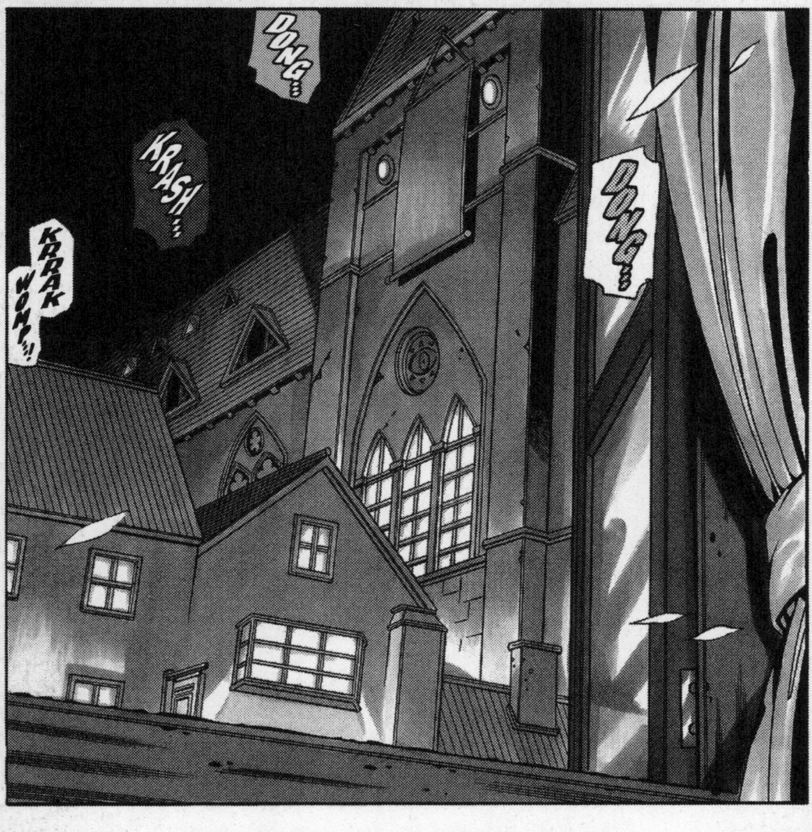
DONG...
DONG...
KRASH...
KRRAK
WOMP...!

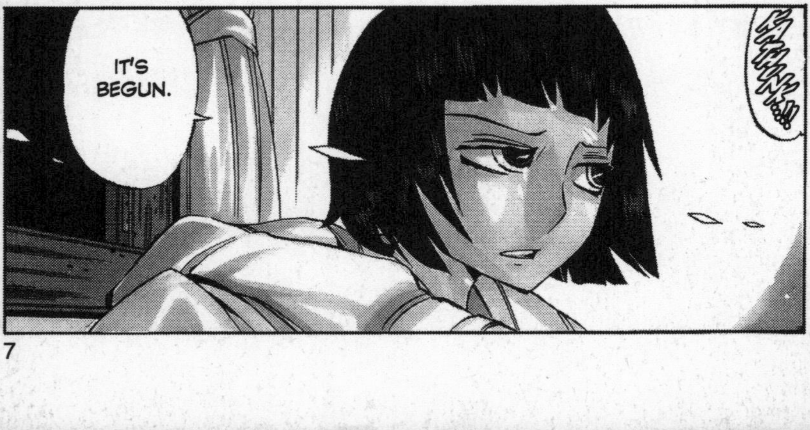
KA-THUNK...!!
IT'S BEGUN.

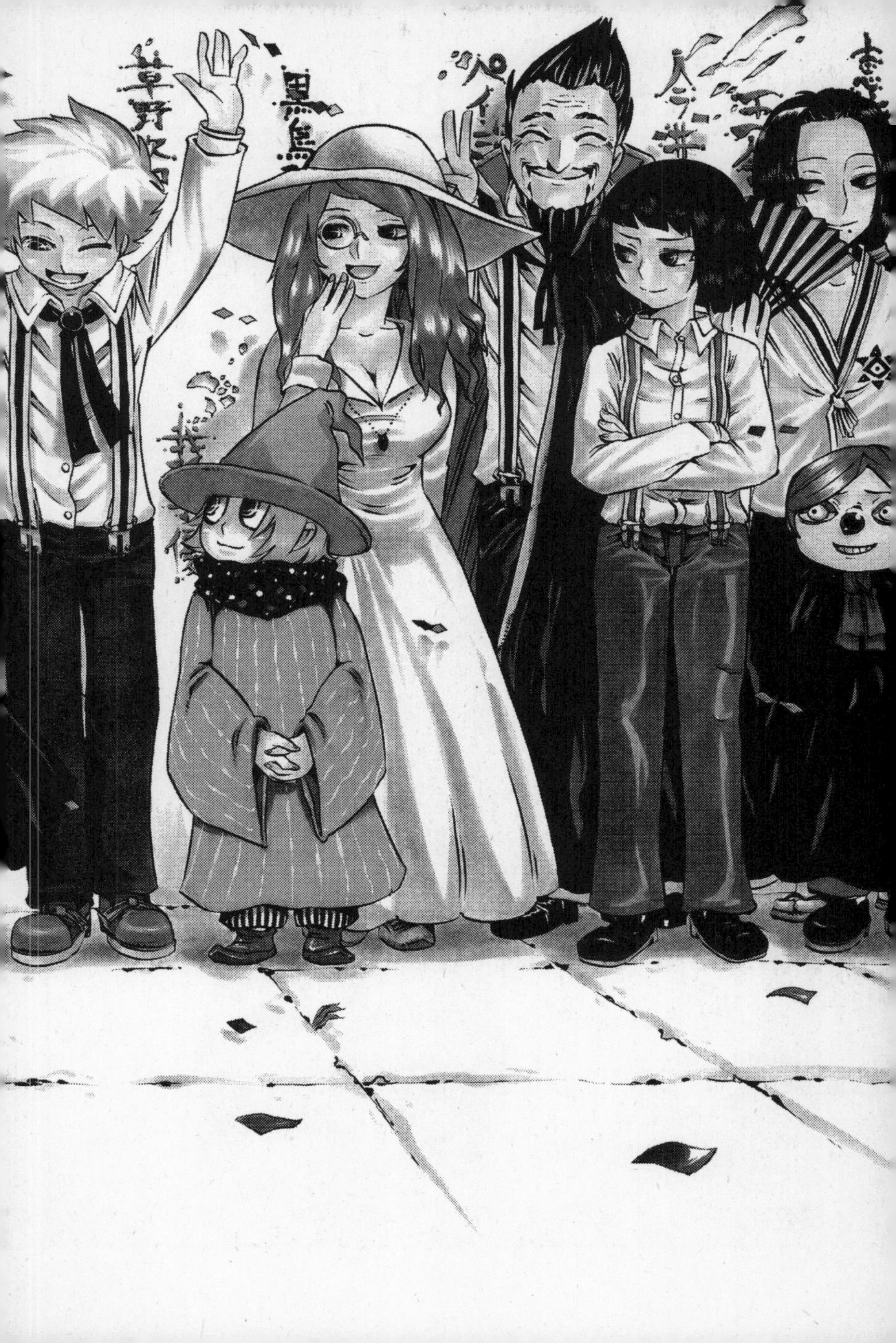

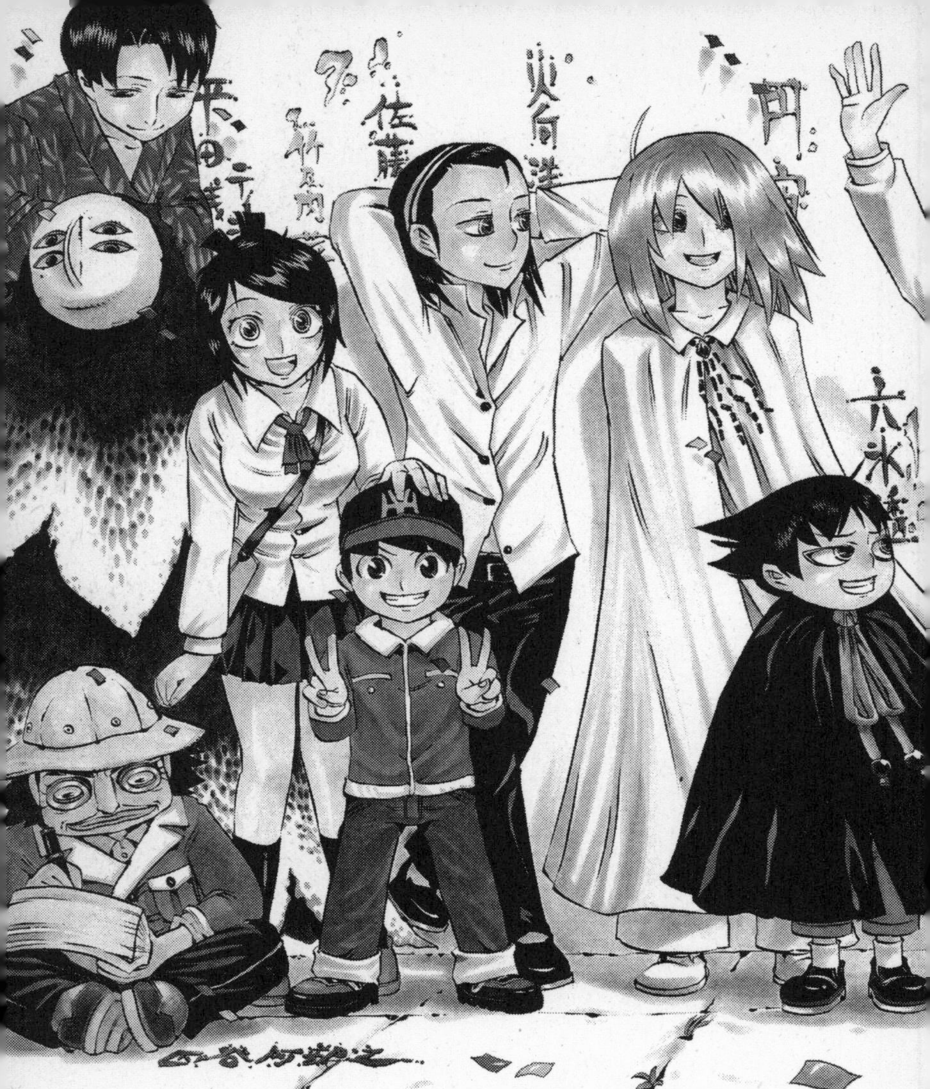

ARTICLE 51
TRIALS & TRIBULATIONS

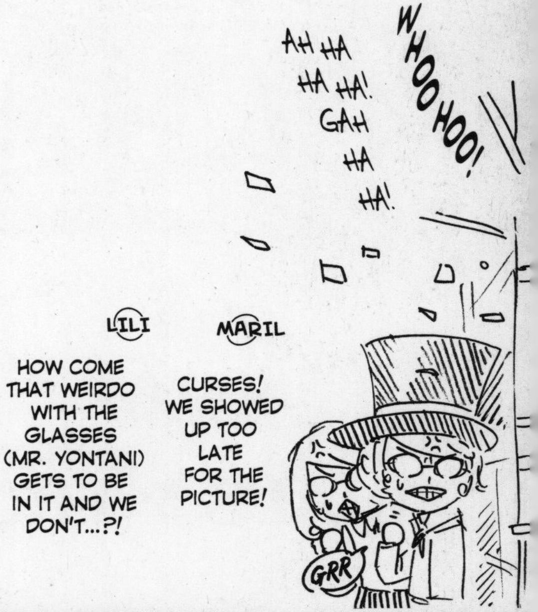
WHOO HOO!
AH HA HA HA! GAH HA HA!
LILI
HOW COME THAT WEIRDO WITH THE GLASSES (MR. YONTANI) GETS TO BE IN IT AND WE DON'T...?!
MARIL
CURSES! WE SHOWED UP TOO LATE FOR THE PICTURE!
GRR

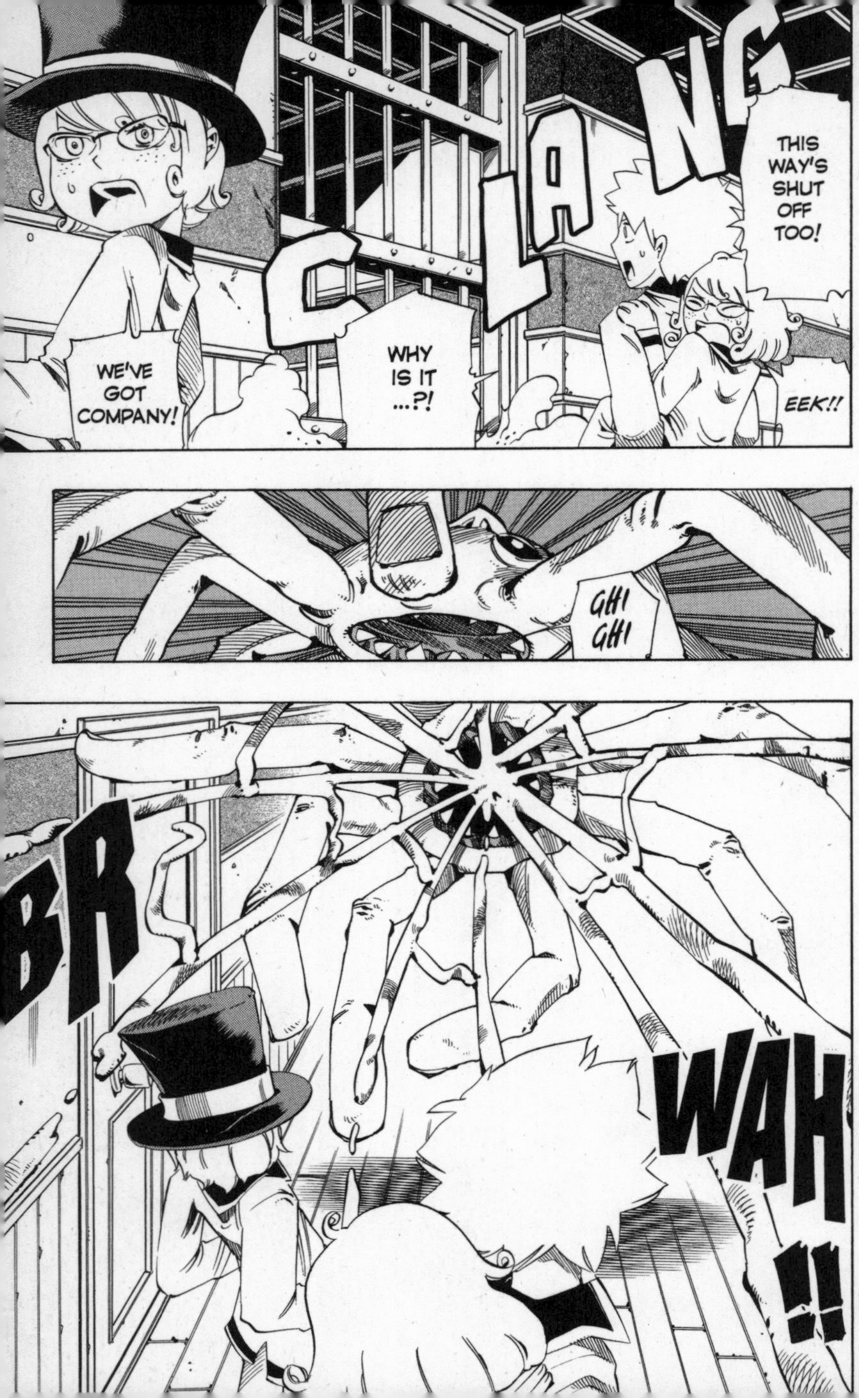
THIS WAY'S SHUT OFF TOO!
EEK!!
CLANG
WHY IS IT ...?!
WE'VE GOT COMPANY!
GHI GHI
WAH!!
BR

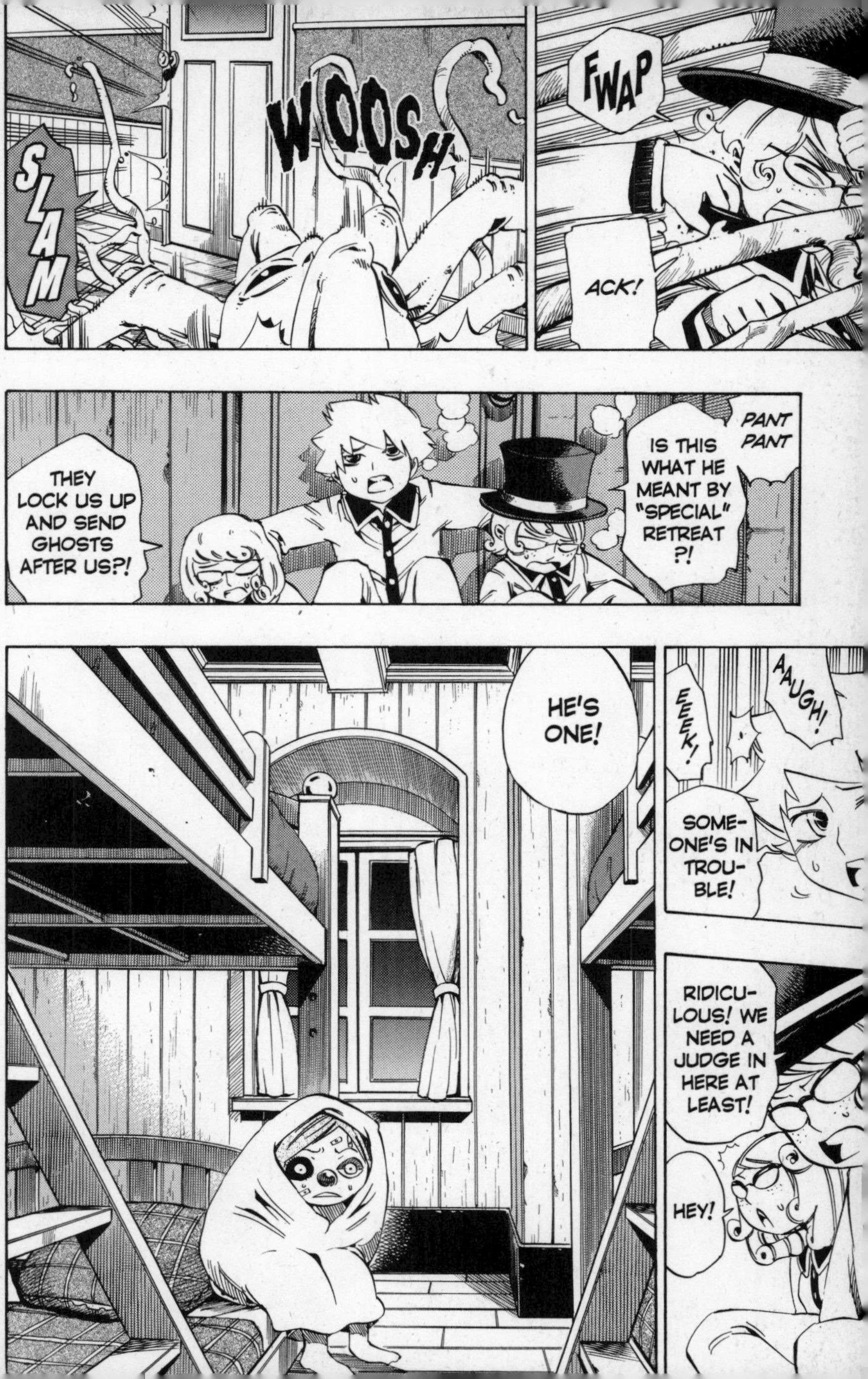
FWAP
ACK!
WOOSH
SLAM
PANT PANT
IS THIS WHAT HE MEANT BY "SPECIAL" RETREAT?!
THEY LOCK US UP AND SEND GHOSTS AFTER US?!
AAUGH!
EEEK!
SOME-ONE'S IN TROU-BLE!
RIDICU-LOUS! WE NEED A JUDGE IN HERE AT LEAST!
HEY!
HE'S ONE!

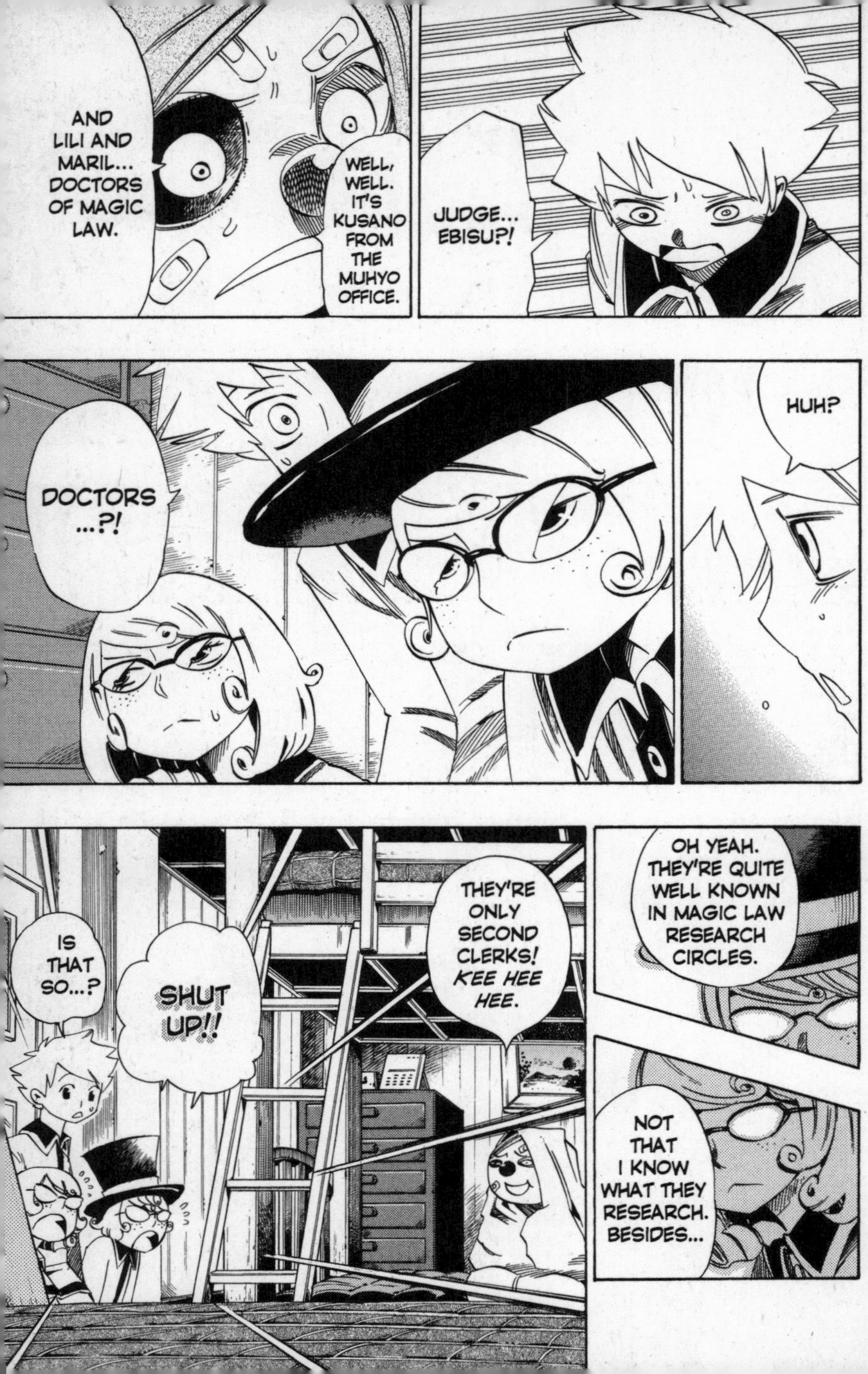
JUDGE... EBISU?!
WELL, WELL. IT'S KUSANO FROM THE MUHYO OFFICE.
AND LILI AND MARIL... DOCTORS OF MAGIC LAW.
HUH?
DOCTORS ...?!
OH YEAH. THEY'RE QUITE WELL KNOWN IN MAGIC LAW RESEARCH CIRCLES.
NOT THAT I KNOW WHAT THEY RESEARCH. BESIDES...
THEY'RE ONLY SECOND CLERKS! KEE HEE HEE.
SHUT UP!!
IS THAT SO...?

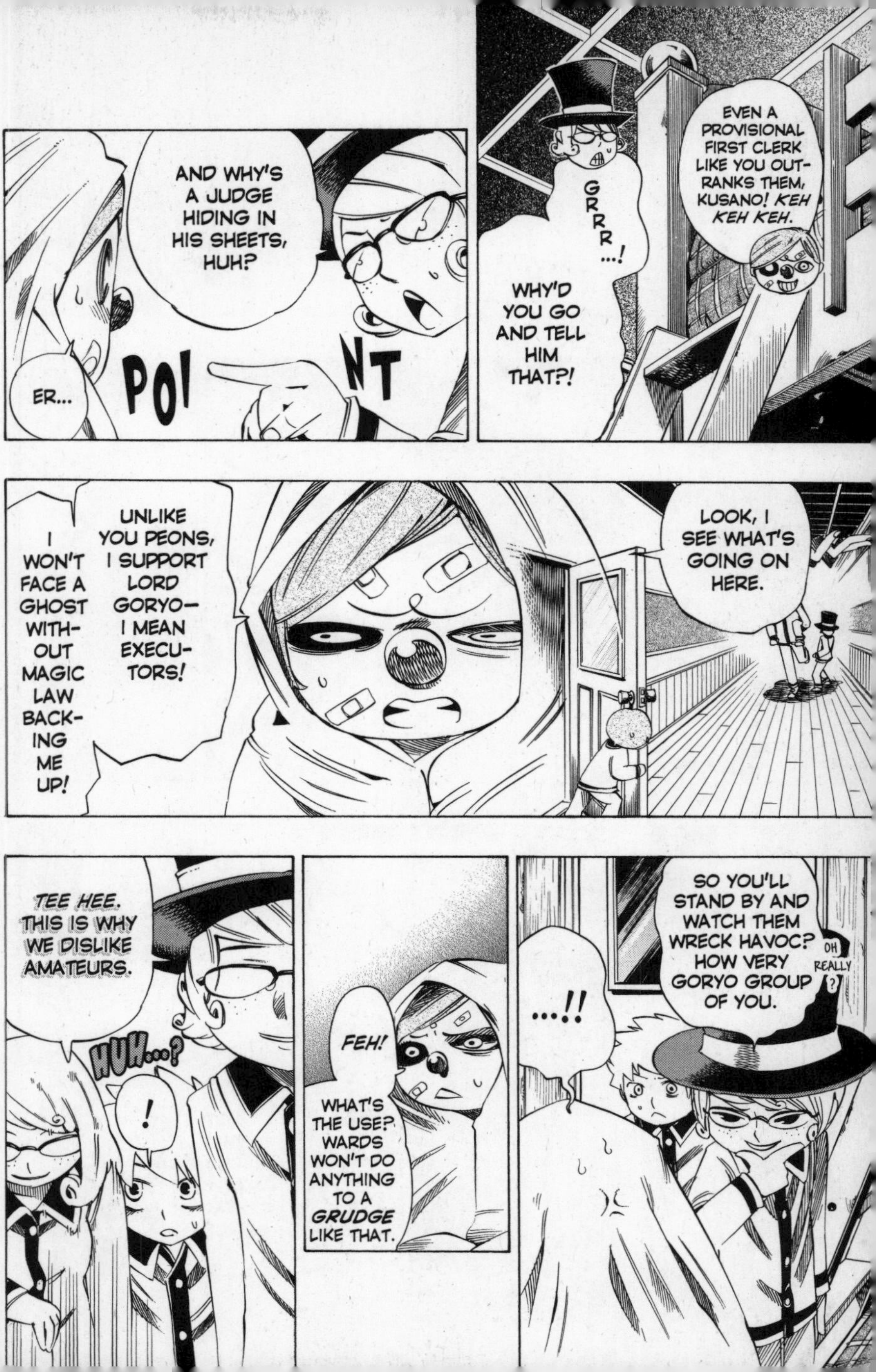
EVEN A PROVISIONAL FIRST CLERK LIKE YOU OUT-RANKS THEM, KUSANO! *KEH KEH KEH.*
GRRR...!
WHY'D YOU GO AND TELL HIM THAT?!
AND WHY'S A JUDGE HIDING IN HIS SHEETS, HUH?
POINT
ER...
LOOK, I SEE WHAT'S GOING ON HERE.
UNLIKE YOU PEONS, I SUPPORT LORD GORYO— I MEAN EXECUTORS!
I WON'T FACE A GHOST WITHOUT MAGIC LAW BACKING ME UP!
SO YOU'LL STAND BY AND WATCH THEM WRECK HAVOC? HOW VERY GORYO GROUP OF YOU.
OH REALLY?
...!!
FEH!
WHAT'S THE USE? WARDS WON'T DO ANYTHING TO A *GRUDGE* LIKE THAT.
TEE HEE. THIS IS WHY WE DISLIKE AMATEURS.
HUH...?
!

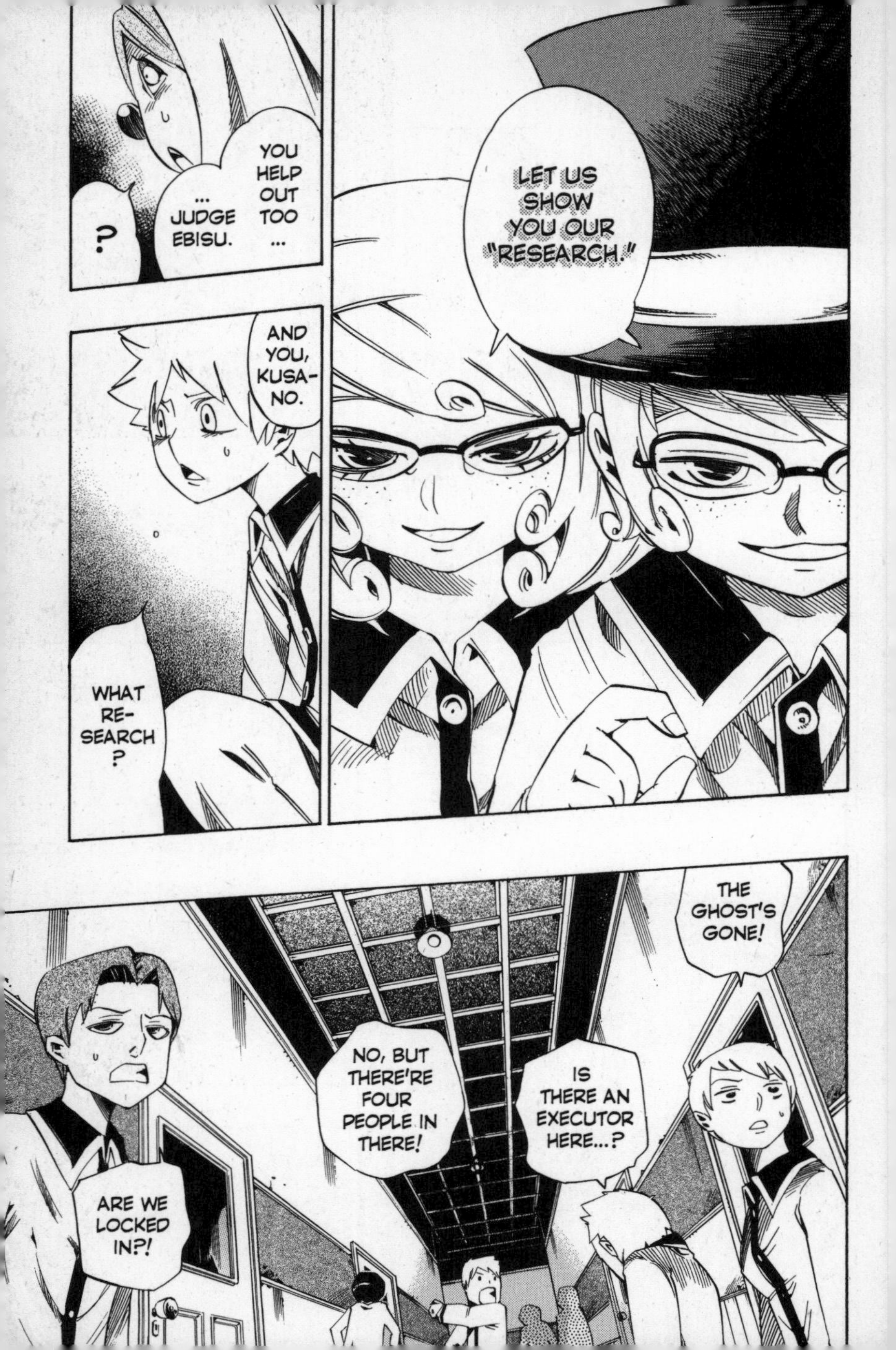
LET US SHOW YOU OUR "RESEARCH."
YOU HELP OUT TOO ...
... JUDGE EBISU.
?
AND YOU, KUSA-NO.
WHAT RE-SEARCH?
THE GHOST'S GONE!
IS THERE AN EXECUTOR HERE...?
NO, BUT THERE'RE FOUR PEOPLE IN THERE!
ARE WE LOCKED IN?!

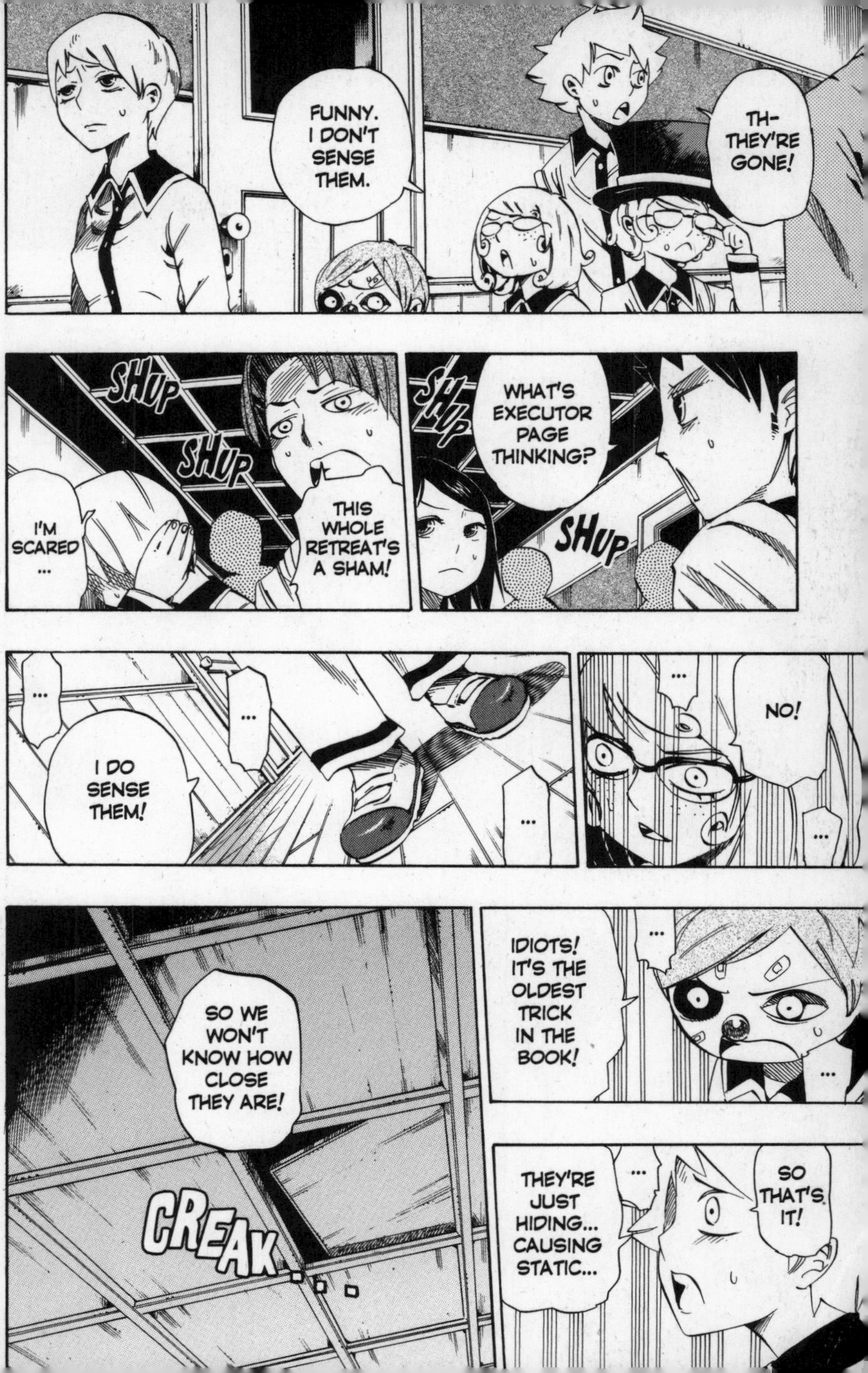

TH- THEY'RE GONE!
FUNNY. I DON'T SENSE THEM.
WHAT'S EXECUTOR PAGE THINKING?
SHUP
SHUP
SHUP
SHUP
THIS WHOLE RETREAT'S A SHAM!
I'M SCARED ...
...
NO!
...
...
...
...
I DO SENSE THEM!
...
IDIOTS! IT'S THE OLDEST TRICK IN THE BOOK!
...
SO THAT'S IT!
...
THEY'RE JUST HIDING... CAUSING STATIC...
SO WE WON'T KNOW HOW CLOSE THEY ARE!
CREAK...

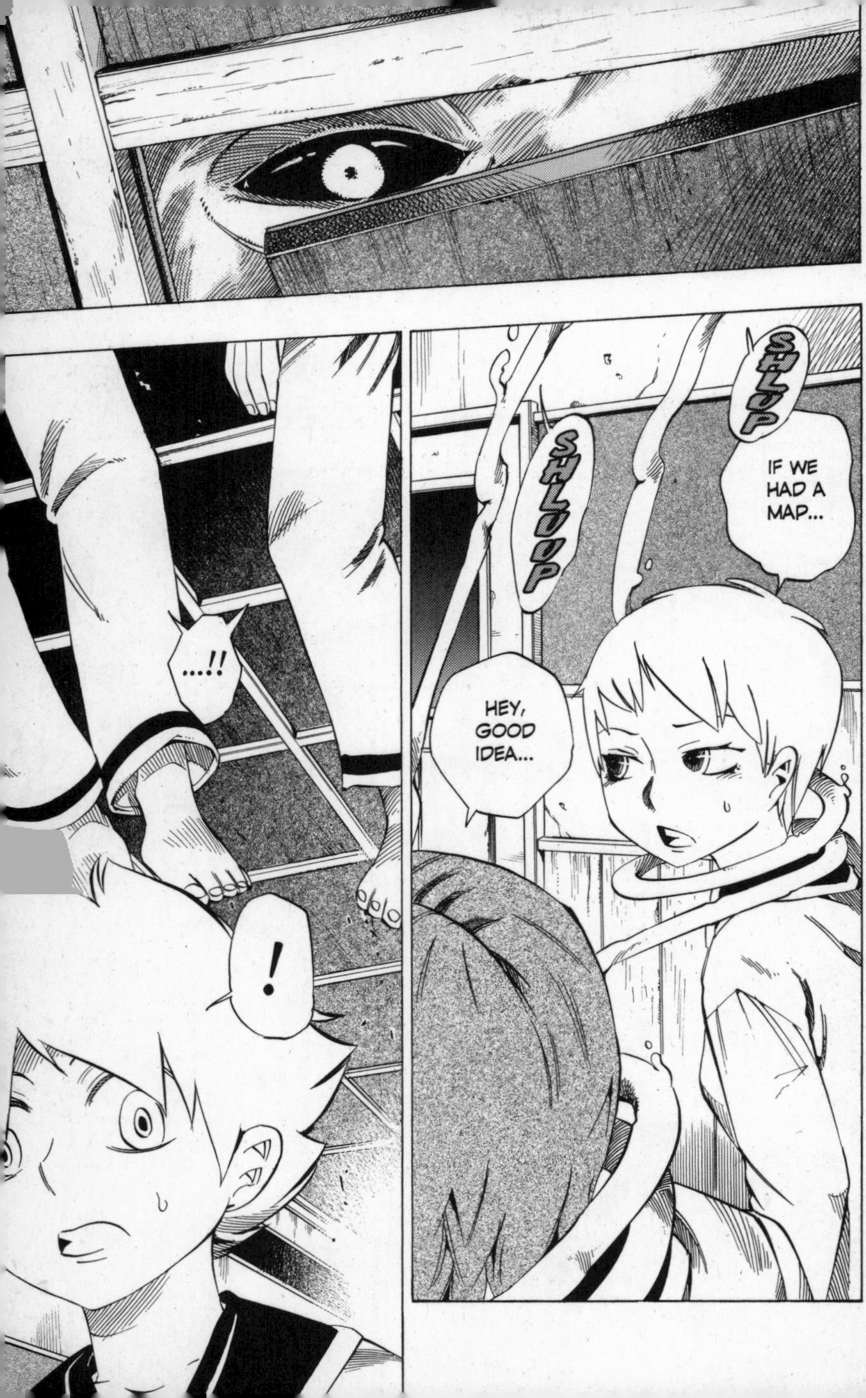
SHLUP
IF WE HAD A MAP...
SHLUP
HEY, GOOD IDEA...
...!!
!

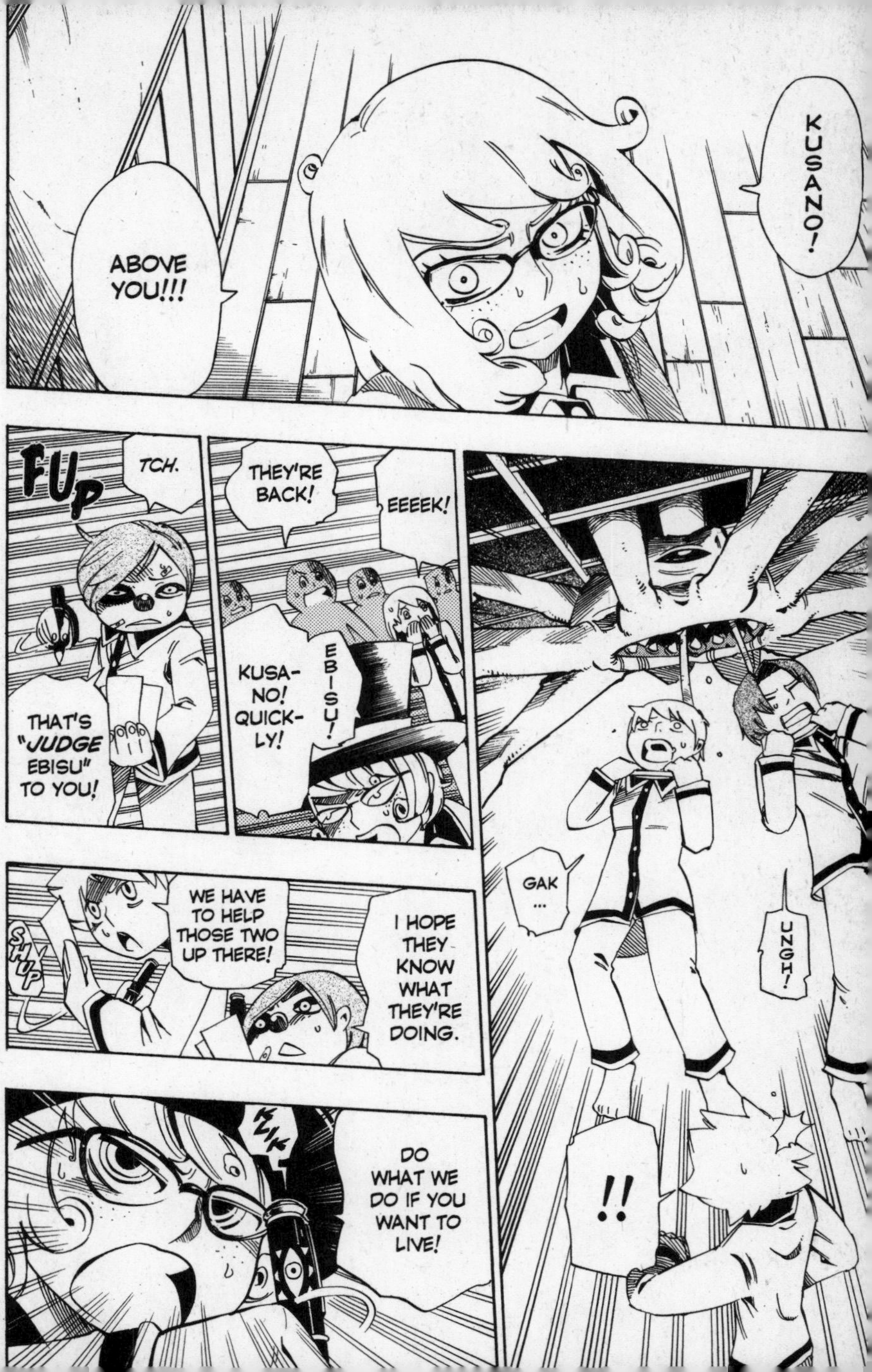

KUSANO!
ABOVE YOU!!!
UNGH!
GAK ...
!!
EEEEK!
THEY'RE BACK!
EBISU!
KUSA-NO! QUICKLY!
TCH.
FUP
THAT'S "JUDGE EBISU" TO YOU!
WE HAVE TO HELP THOSE TWO UP THERE!
I HOPE THEY KNOW WHAT THEY'RE DOING.
SHUP
KLIK
DO WHAT WE DO IF YOU WANT TO LIVE!

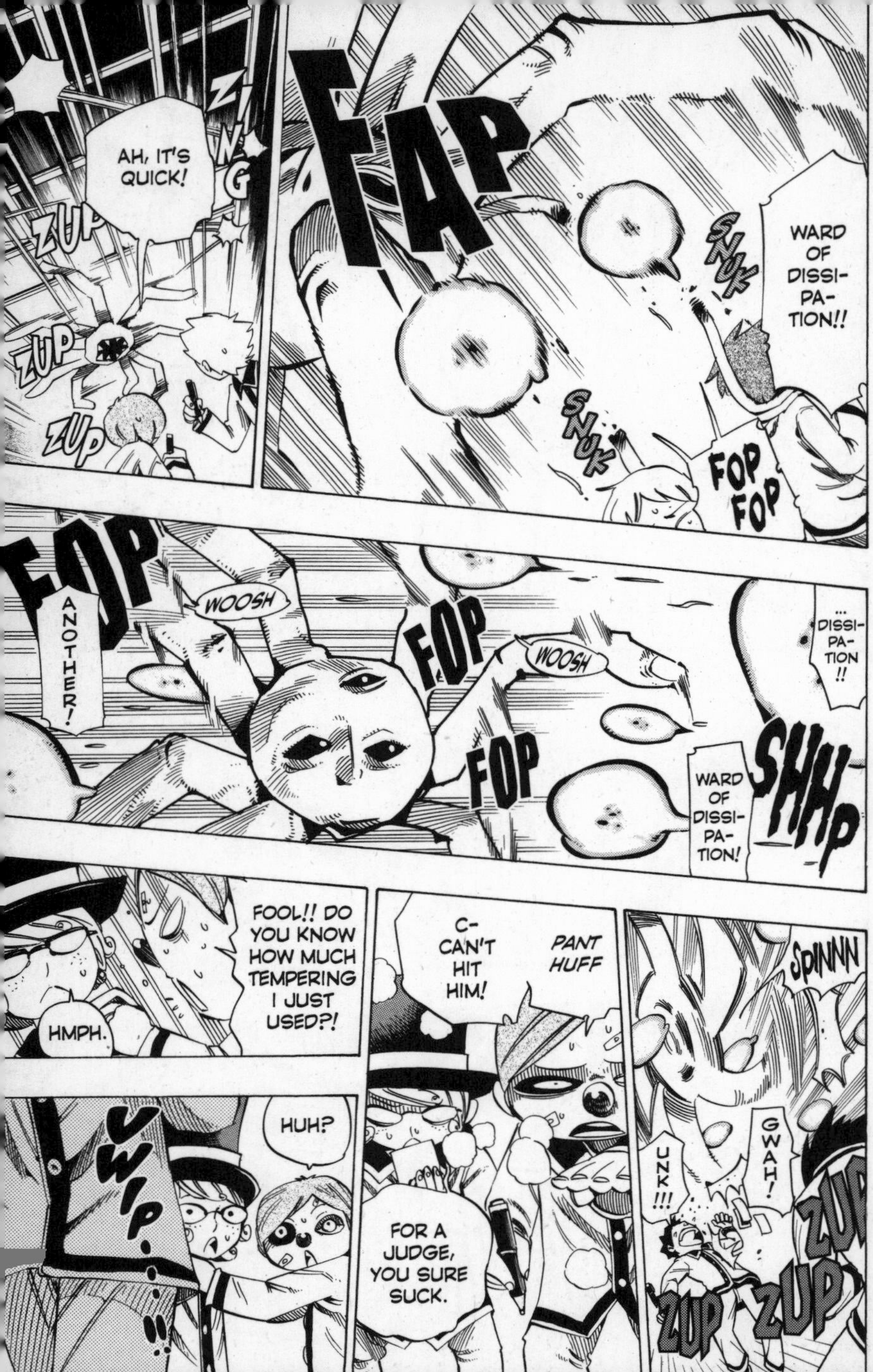
FAP
WARD OF DISSIPATION!!
SNUK
SNUK
FOP FOP
ZING
AH, IT'S QUICK!
ZUP
ZUP
ZUP
...DISSIPATION!!
SHHP
WARD OF DISSIPATION!
FOP
WOOSH
FOP
WOOSH
FOP
ANOTHER!
SPINNN
GWAH!
UNK!!!
ZUP
ZUP
ZUP
PANT HUFF
C-CAN'T HIT HIM!
FOR A JUDGE, YOU SURE SUCK.
FOOL!! DO YOU KNOW HOW MUCH TEMPERING I JUST USED?!
HMPH.
HUH?
UWIP..!!

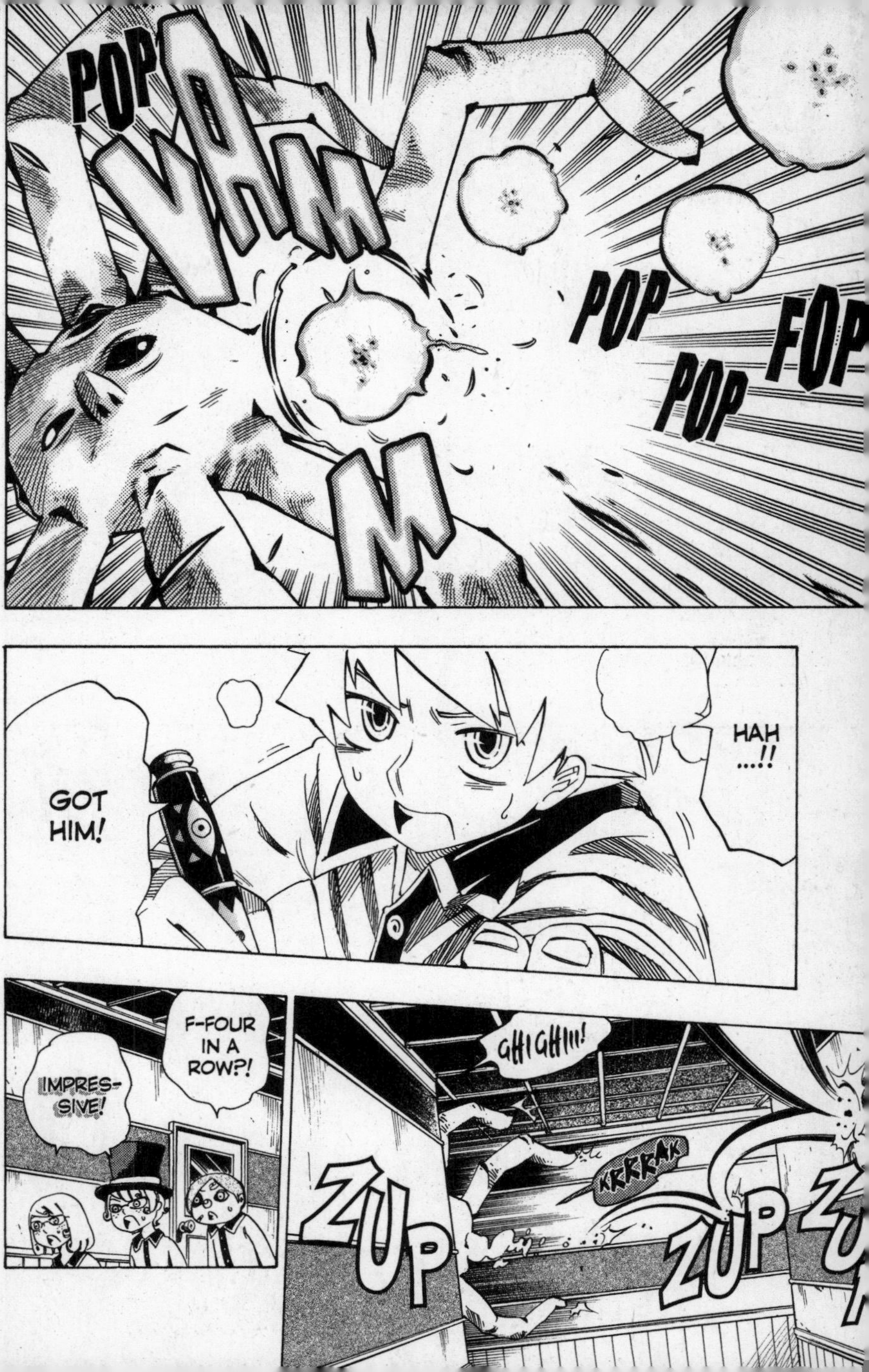
POP
VAAM
POP
POP
FOP
POP
HAH ...!!
GOT HIM!
GHIGH!!!
KRRRAK
ZUP
ZUP
ZUP
F-FOUR IN A ROW?!
IMPRES-SIVE!

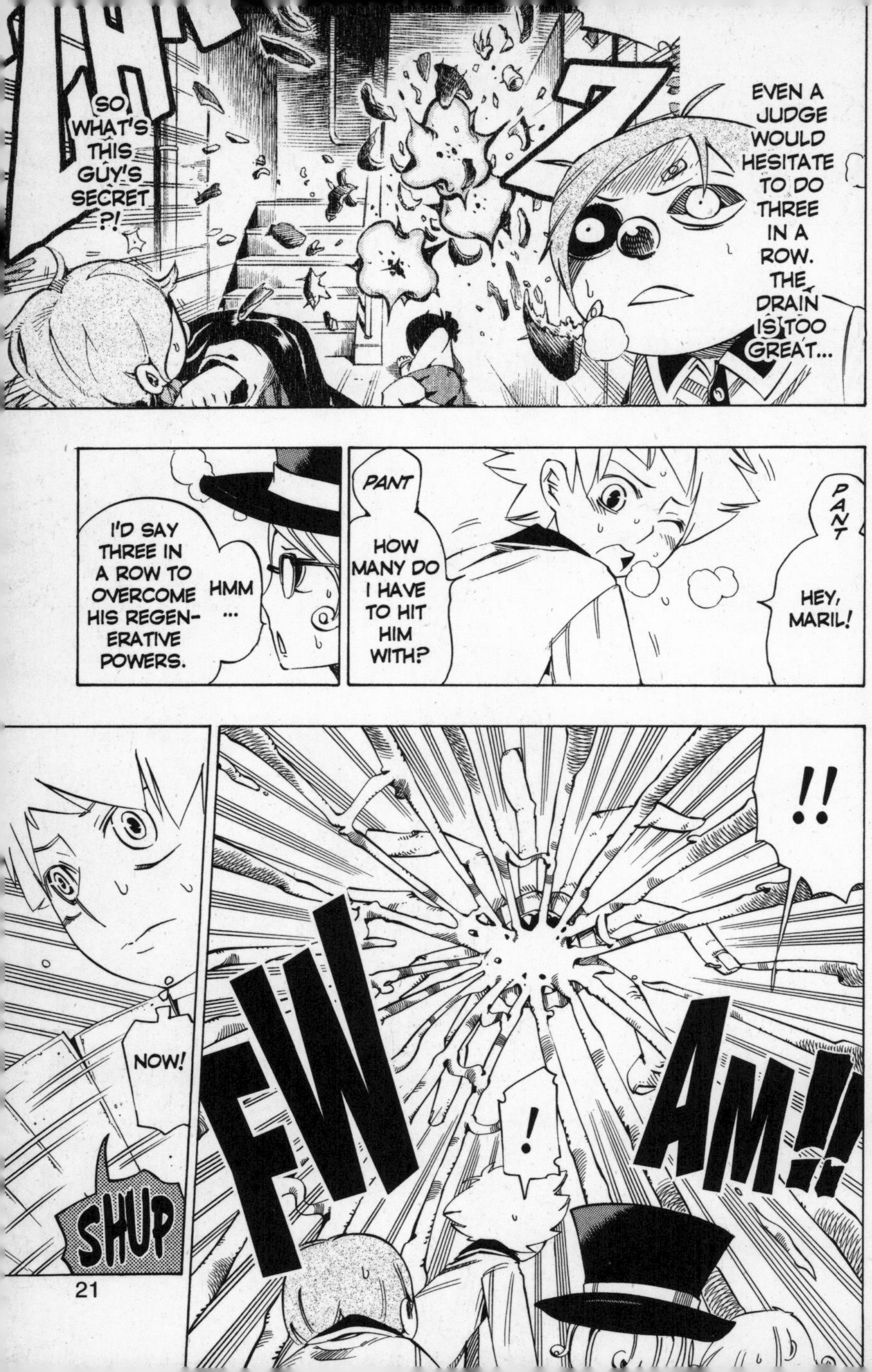
EVEN A JUDGE WOULD HESITATE TO DO THREE IN A ROW. THE DRAIN IS TOO GREAT...
SO WHAT'S THIS GUY'S SECRET?!
PANT
HEY, MARIL!
PANT
HOW MANY DO I HAVE TO HIT HIM WITH?
HMM...
I'D SAY THREE IN A ROW TO OVERCOME HIS REGENERATIVE POWERS.
!!
FWAM!!
!
NOW!
SHUP

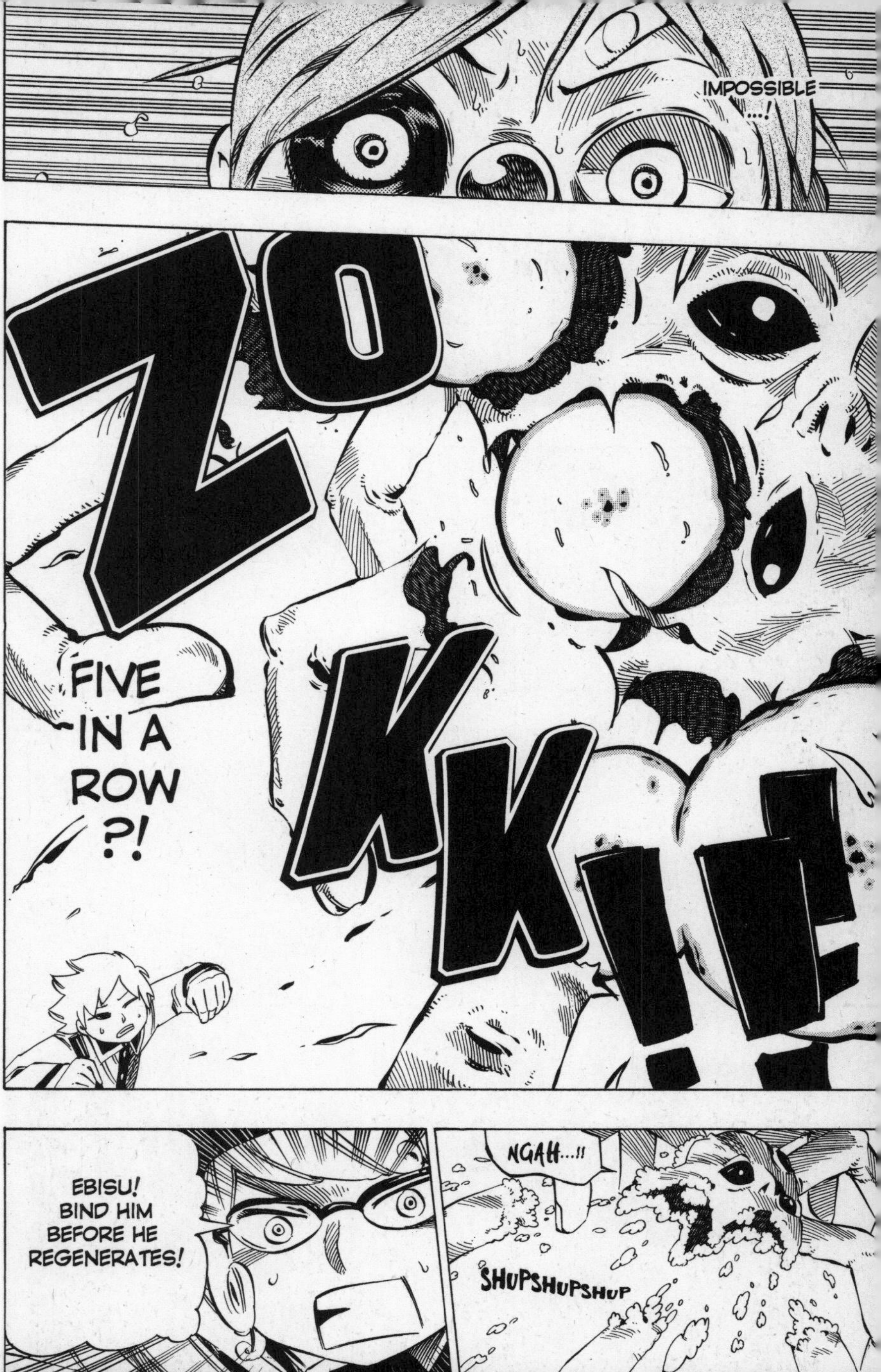
IMPOSSIBLE ...!
ZOKK!!
FIVE IN A ROW ?!
NGAH...!!
SHUPSHUPSHUP
EBISU! BIND HIM BEFORE HE REGENERATES!

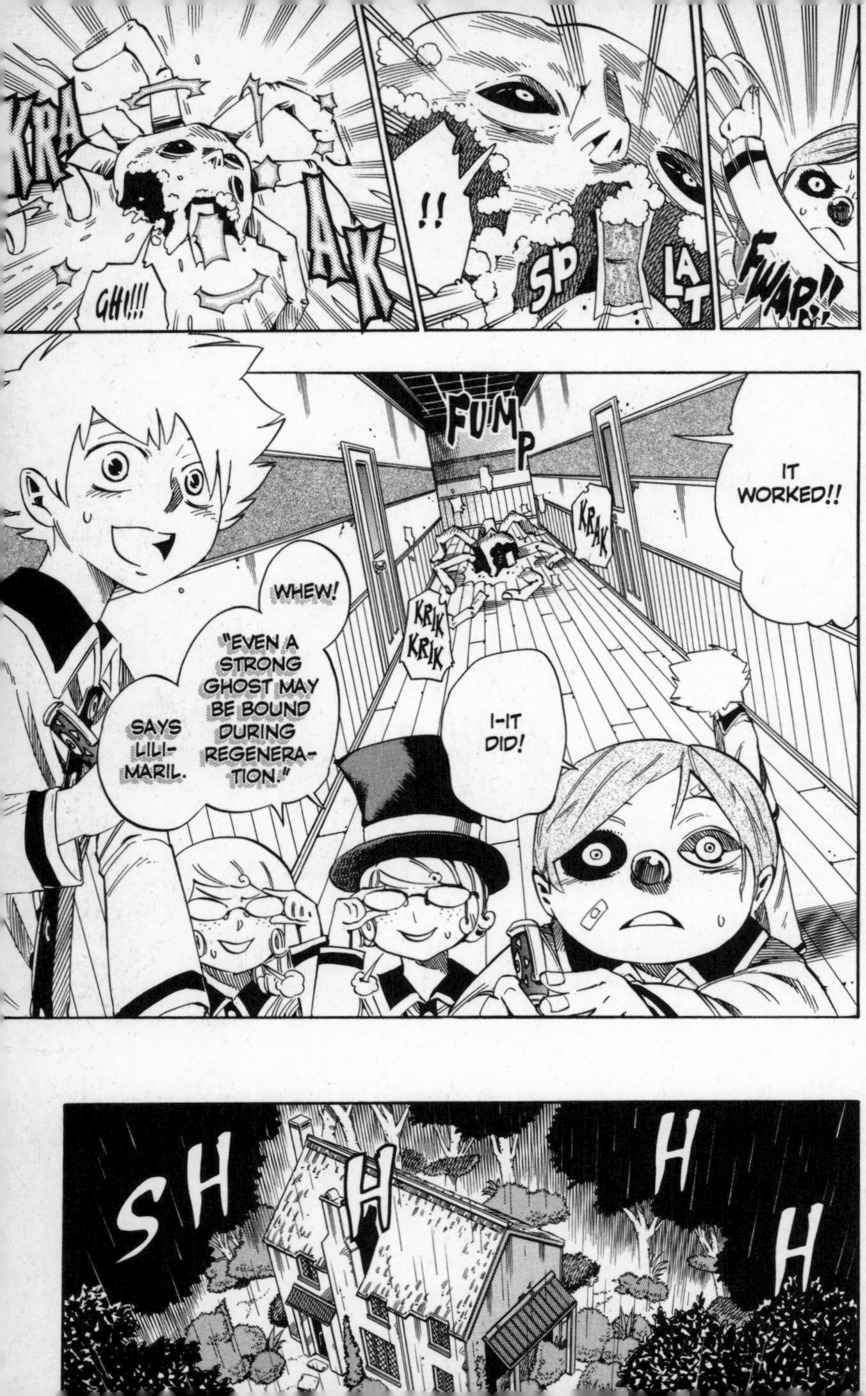
FWAP!!
!!
SPLAT
KRAAK
GHI!!!
IT WORKED!!
FUMP
KRAK
KRIK KRIK
I-IT DID!
WHEW!
"EVEN A STRONG GHOST MAY BE BOUND DURING REGENERA-TION."
SAYS LILI-MARIL.
SHHHH

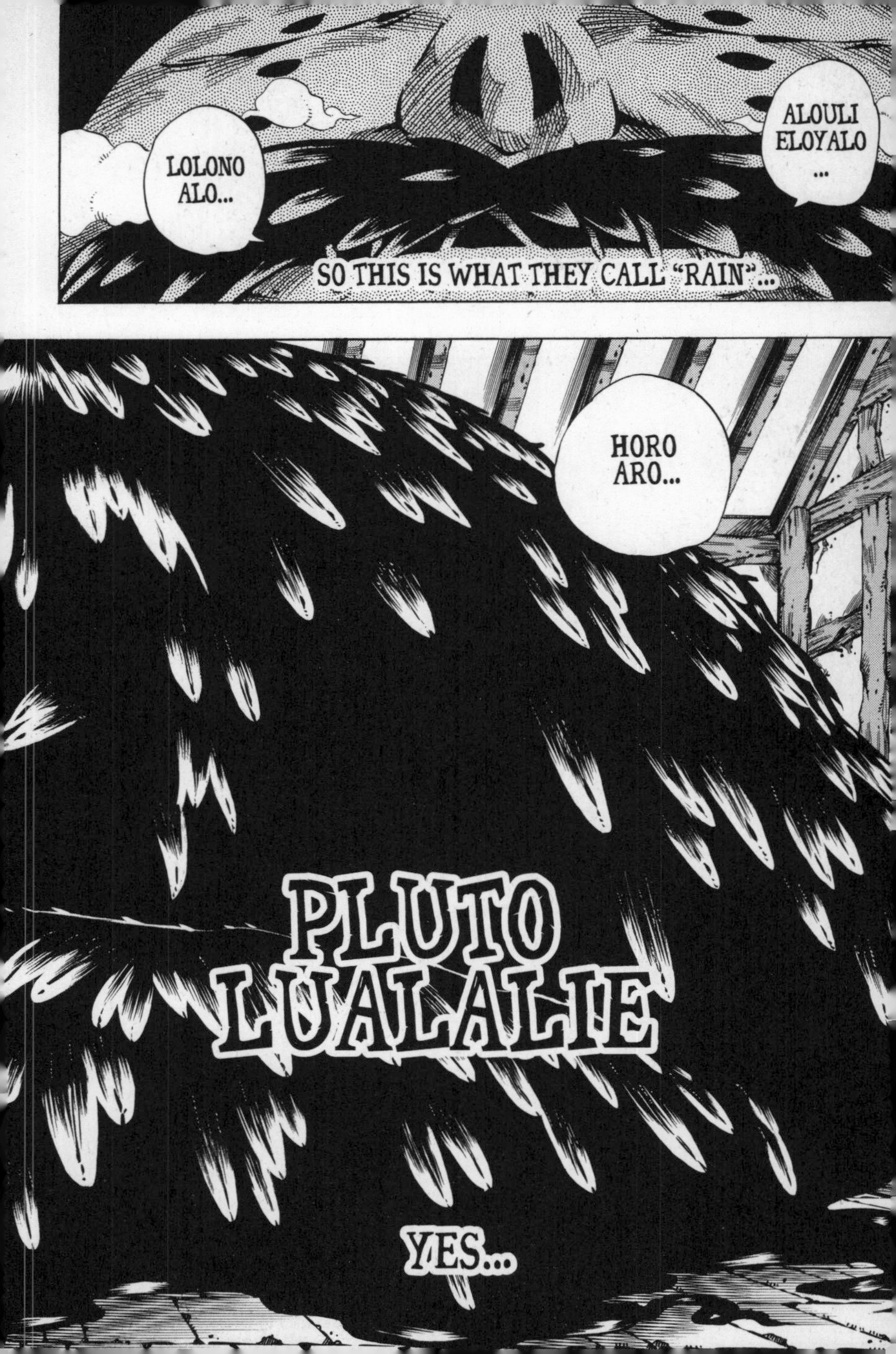
ALOULI ELOYALO ...
LOLONO ALO...
SO THIS IS WHAT THEY CALL "RAIN"...
HORO ARO...
PLUTO LUALALIE
YES...

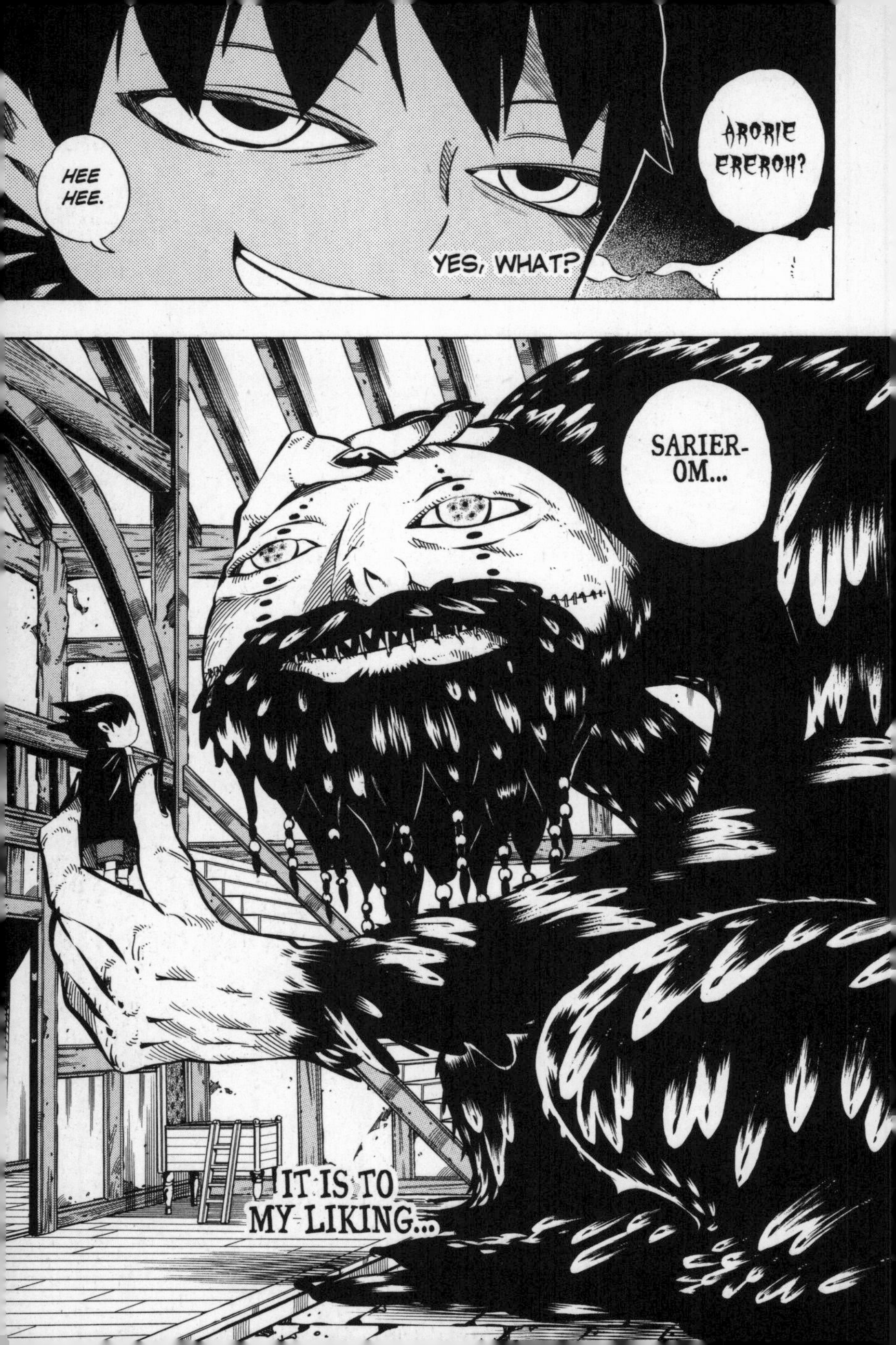
ARORIE EREROH?
YES, WHAT?
HEE HEE.
SARIER-OM...
IT IS TO MY LIKING...

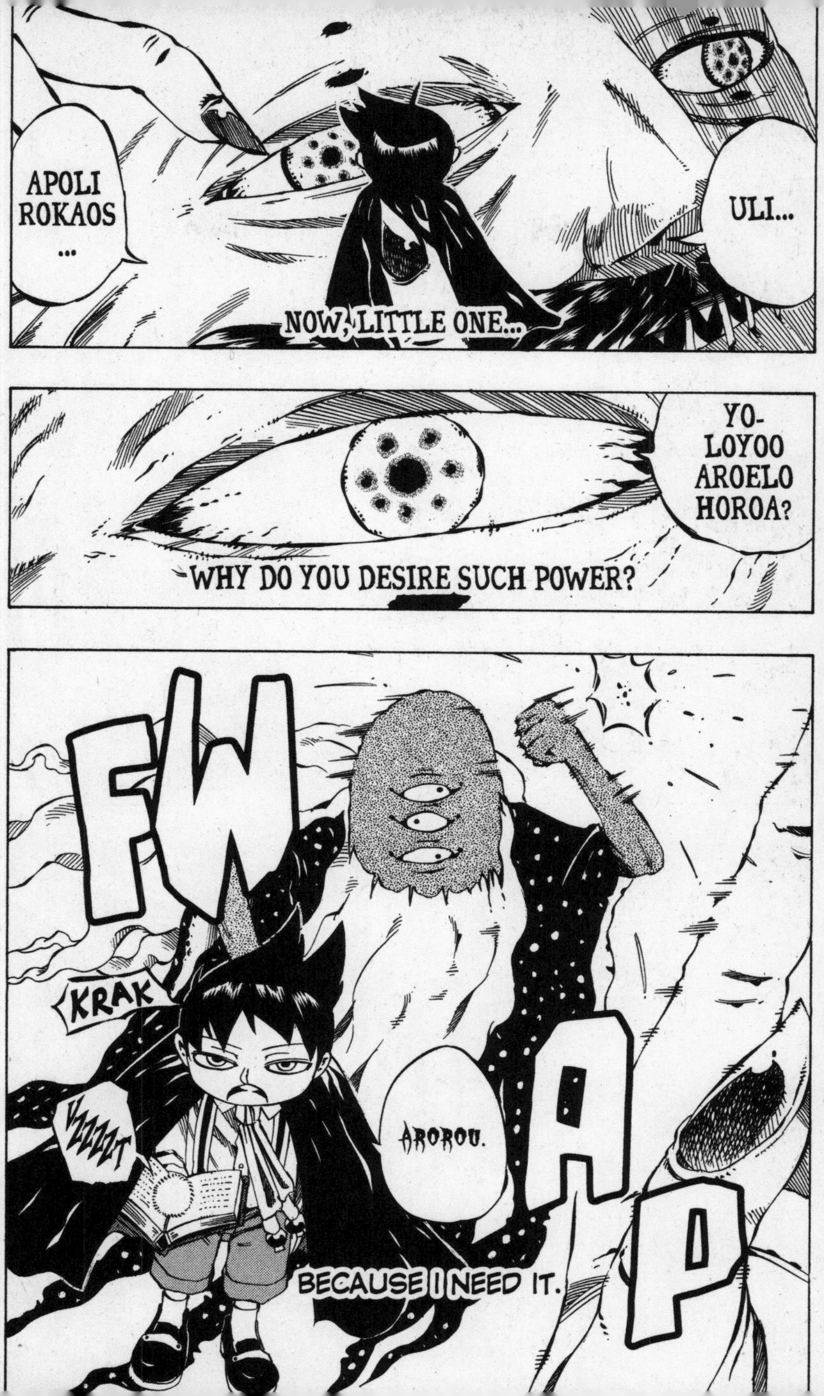
ULI...
APOLI ROKAOS ...
NOW, LITTLE ONE...
YO-LOYOO AROELO HOROA?
WHY DO YOU DESIRE SUCH POWER?
FWAP
KRAK
AROROU.
VZZZZT
BECAUSE I NEED IT.

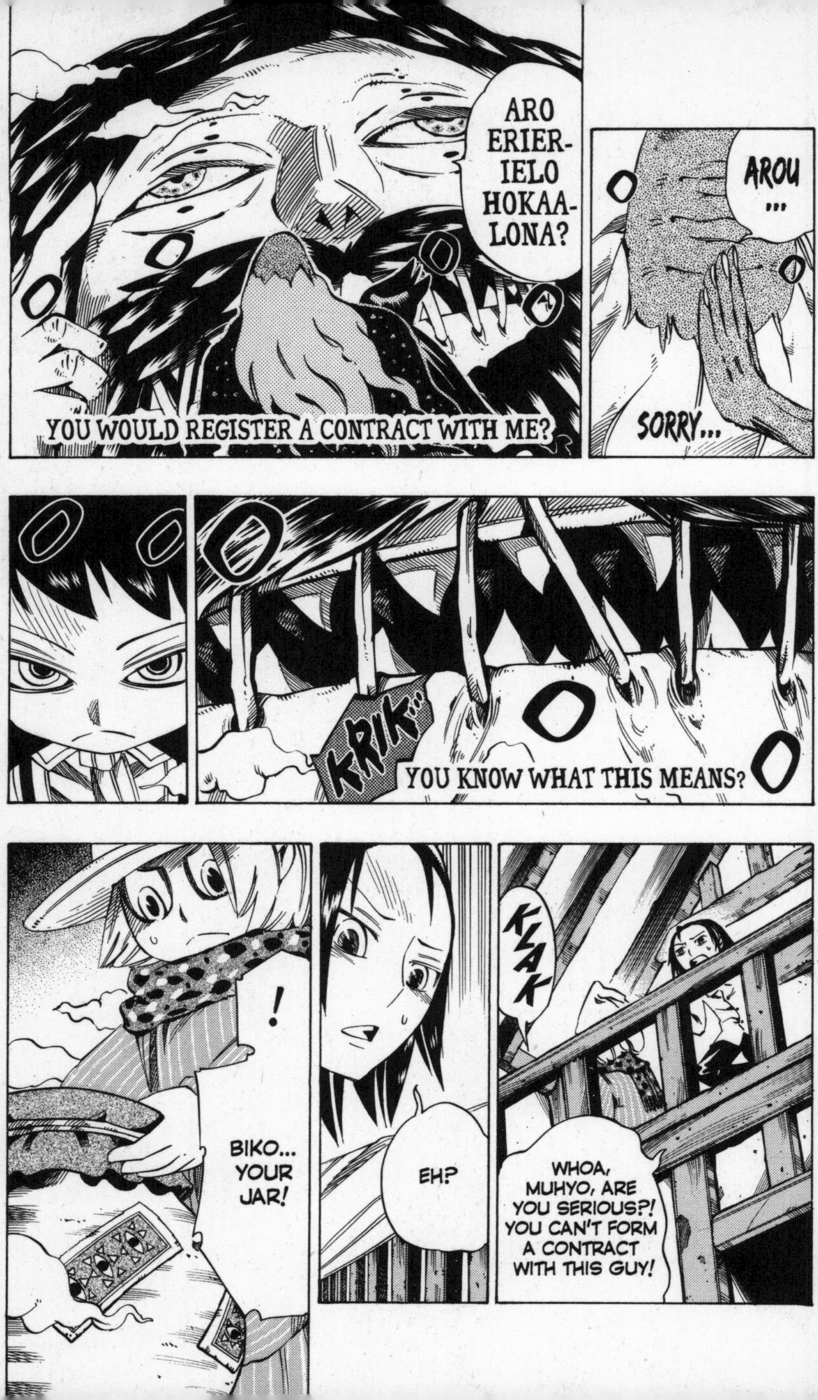
AROU ...
SORRY...
ARO ERIER-IELO HOKAA-LONA?
YOU WOULD REGISTER A CONTRACT WITH ME?
KRIK
YOU KNOW WHAT THIS MEANS?
KLAK
WHOA, MUHYO, ARE YOU SERIOUS?! YOU CAN'T FORM A CONTRACT WITH THIS GUY!
EH?
!
BIKO... YOUR JAR!

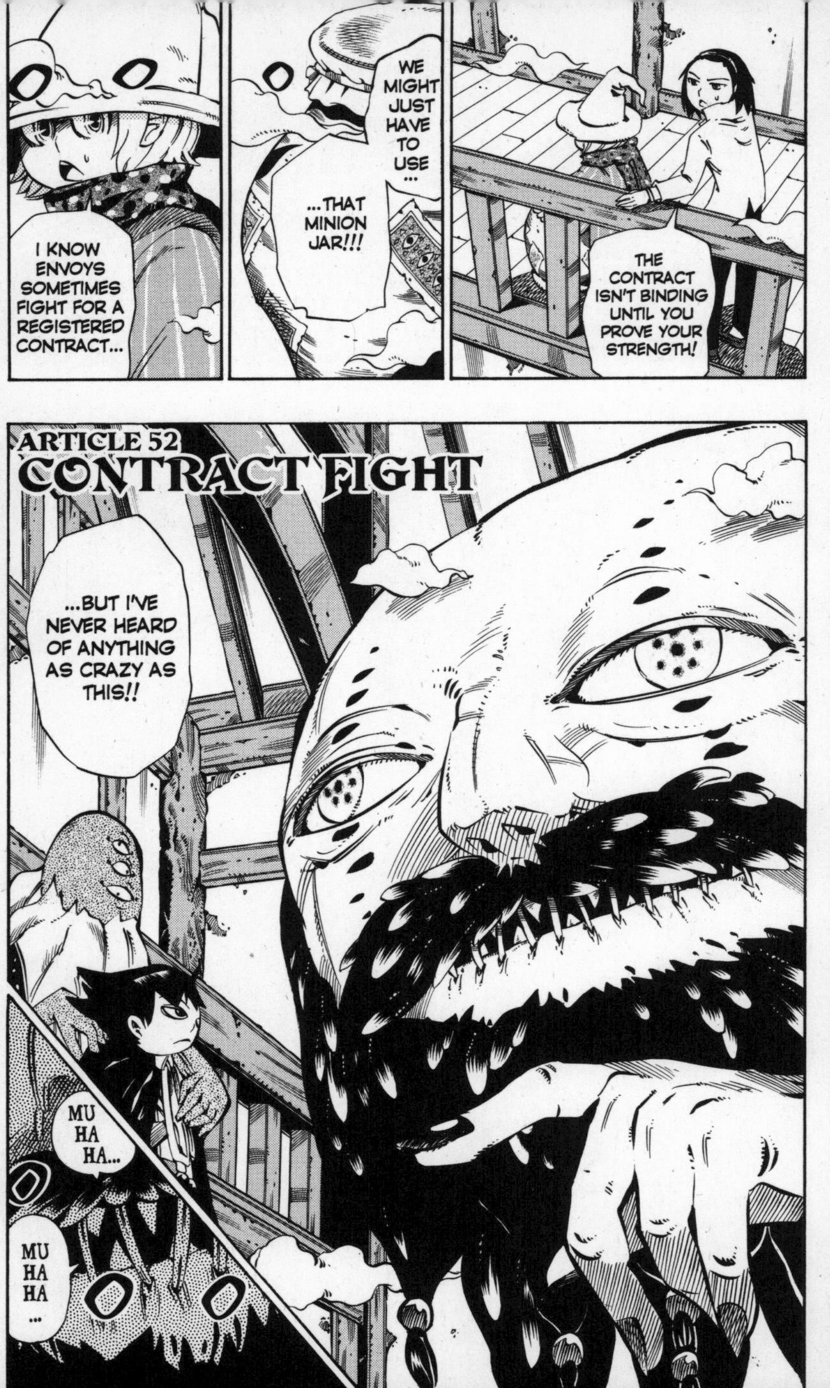
THE CONTRACT ISN'T BINDING UNTIL YOU PROVE YOUR STRENGTH!
WE MIGHT JUST HAVE TO USE ...
...THAT MINION JAR!!!
I KNOW ENVOYS SOMETIMES FIGHT FOR A REGISTERED CONTRACT...
ARTICLE 52
CONTRACT FIGHT
...BUT I'VE NEVER HEARD OF ANYTHING AS CRAZY AS THIS!!
MU HA HA...
MU HA HA ...

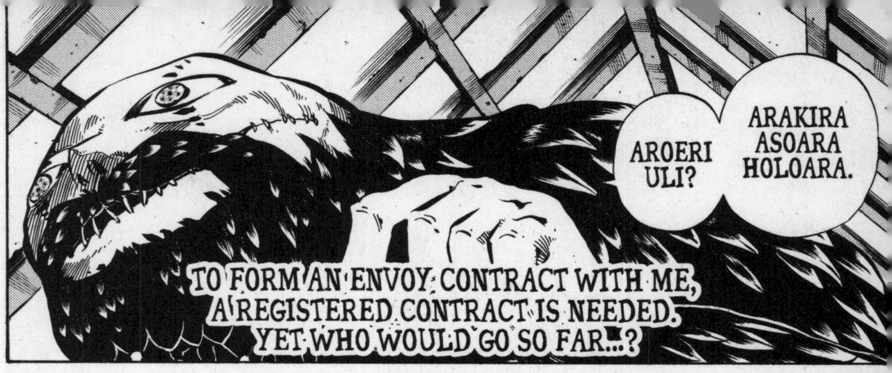
ARAKIRA ASOARA HOLOARA.
AROERI ULI?
TO FORM AN ENVOY CONTRACT WITH ME, A REGISTERED CONTRACT IS NEEDED. YET WHO WOULD GO SO FAR...?

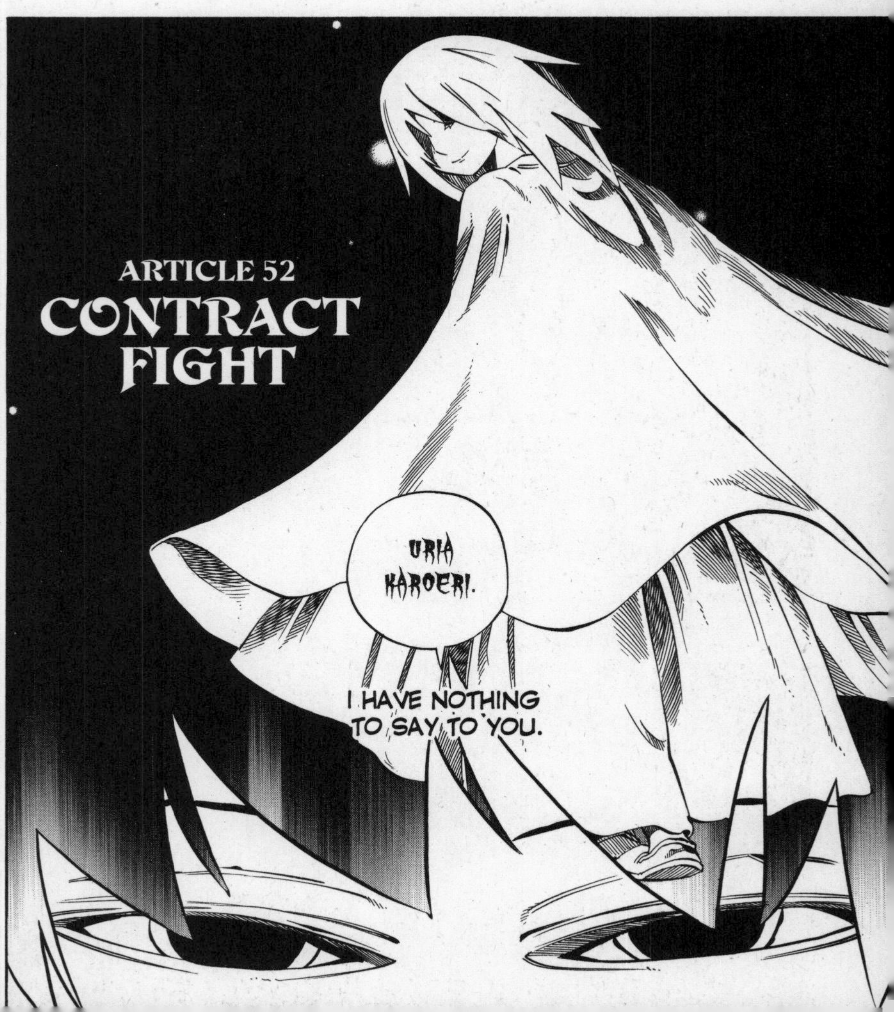
ARTICLE 52
CONTRACT FIGHT
URIA KAROERI.
I HAVE NOTHING TO SAY TO YOU.

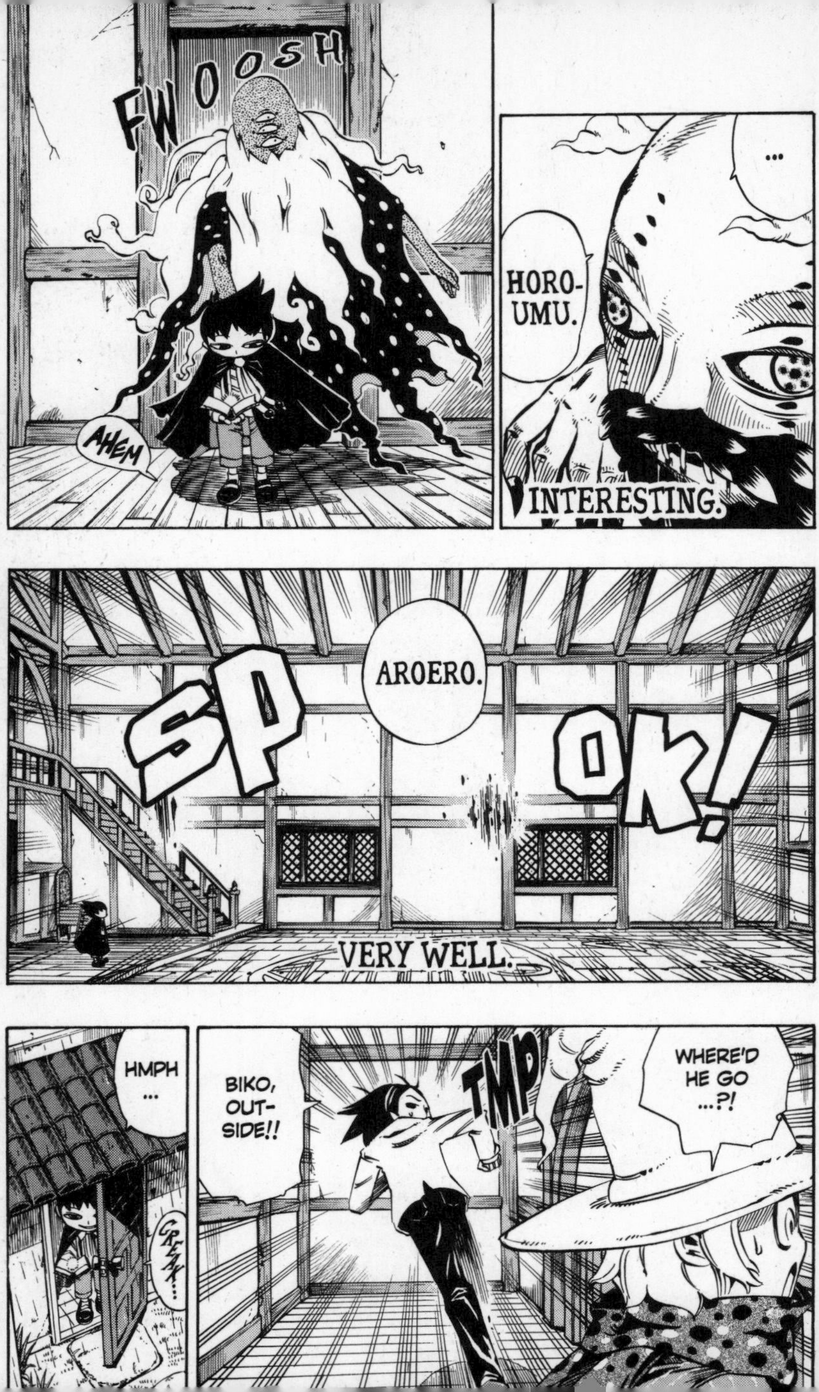
...
HORO-UMU.
INTERESTING.
FWOOSH
AHEM
AROERO.
SP
OK!
VERY WELL.
WHERE'D HE GO ...?!
TMP
BIKO, OUTSIDE!!
HMPH ...
CREAK...

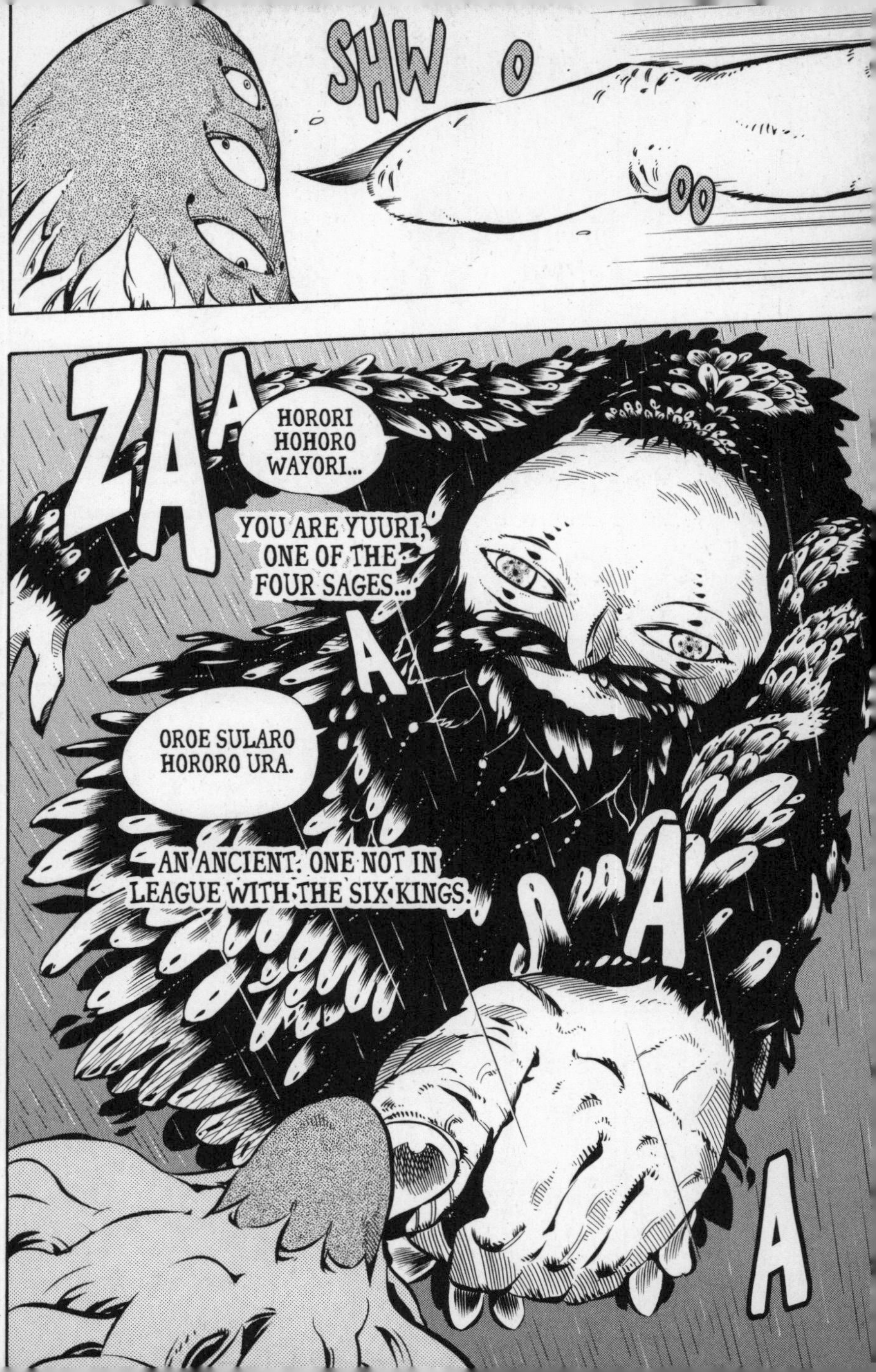
SHWOOO
ZAAAAAA
HORORI HOHORO WAYORI...
YOU ARE YUURI, ONE OF THE FOUR SAGES...
OROE SULARO HORORO URA.
AN ANCIENT: ONE NOT IN LEAGUE WITH THE SIX KINGS.

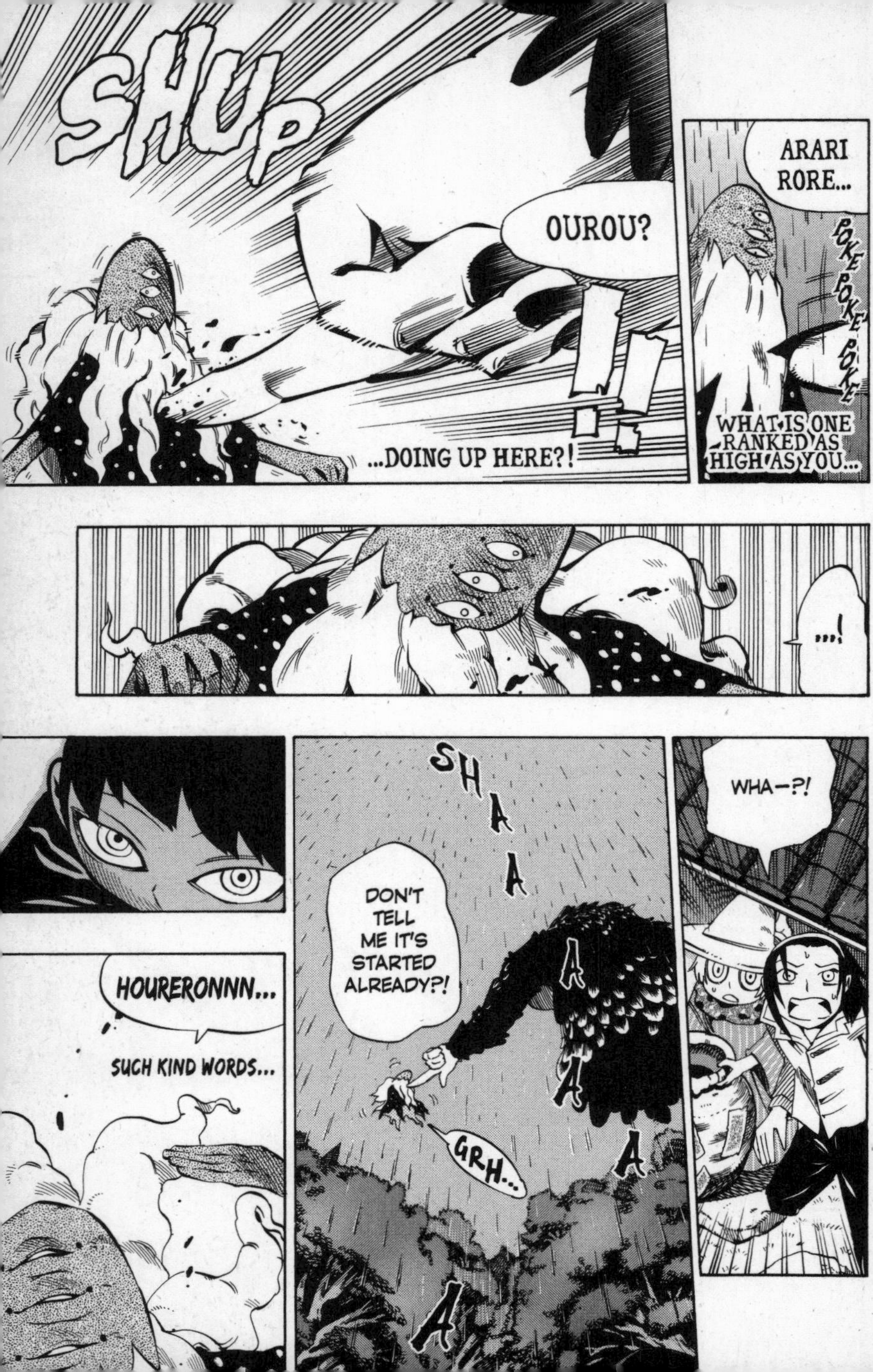
ARARI RORE...
POKE POKE POKE
WHAT IS ONE RANKED AS HIGH AS YOU...
SHUP
OUROU?
!!
...DOING UP HERE?!
...!
WHA-?!
SHAAAAAAA
DON'T TELL ME IT'S STARTED ALREADY?!
GRH...
HOURERONNN...
SUCH KIND WORDS...

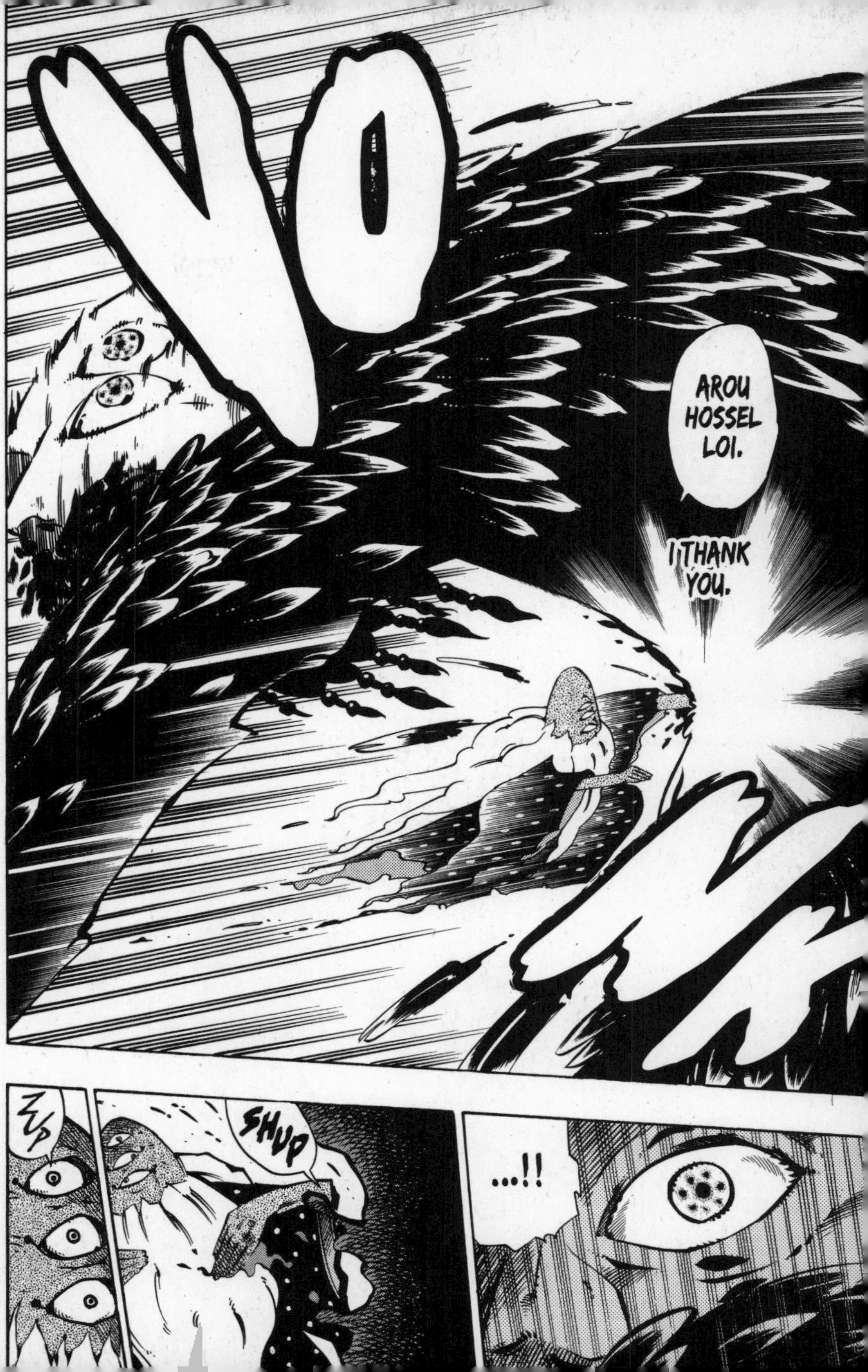
VO
AROU HOSSEL LOI.
I THANK YOU.
...!!
SHUP
ZUP

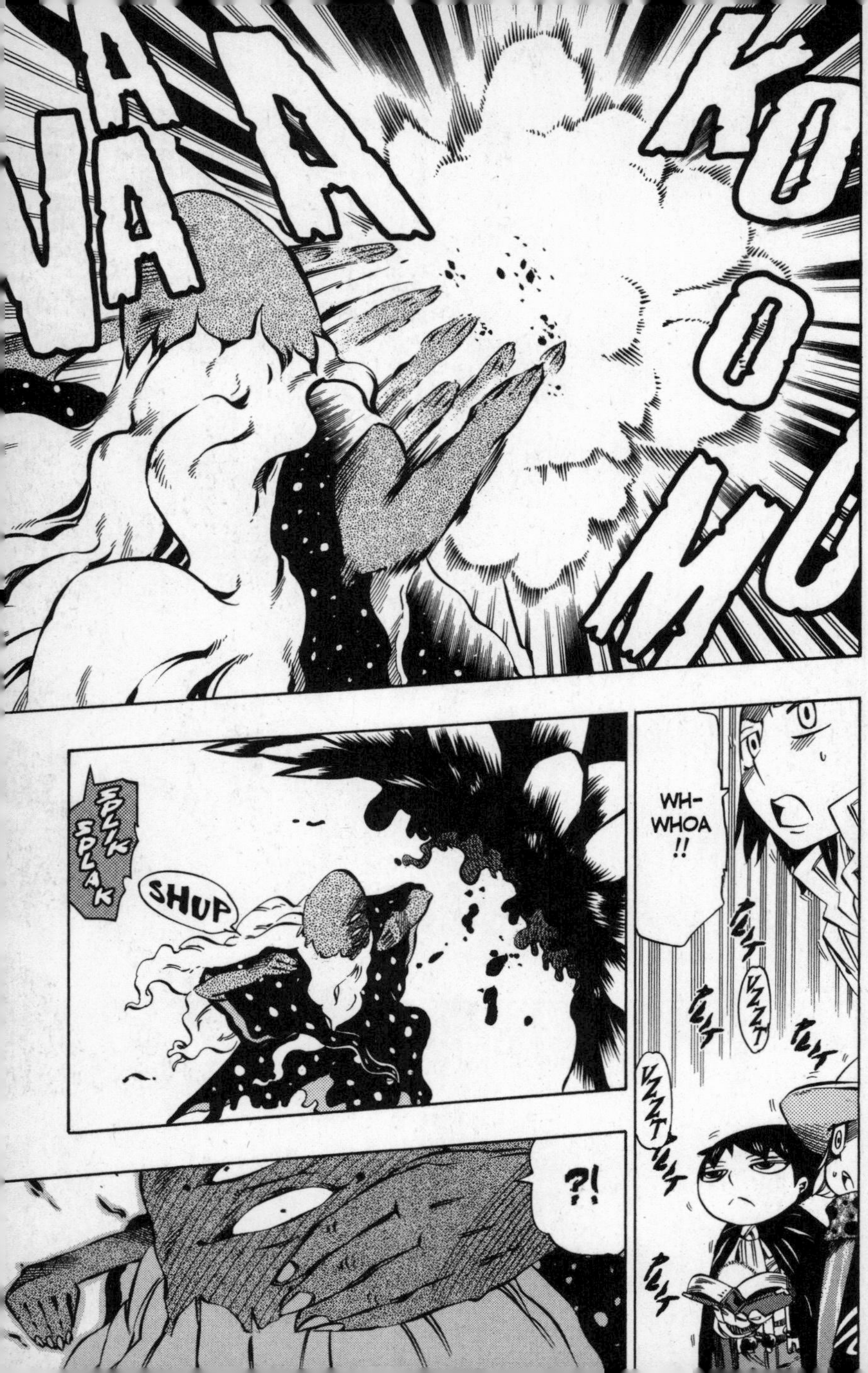
WH-WHOA!!
VZZZT
VZZZT
SHUP
SPLIK SPLAK
?!

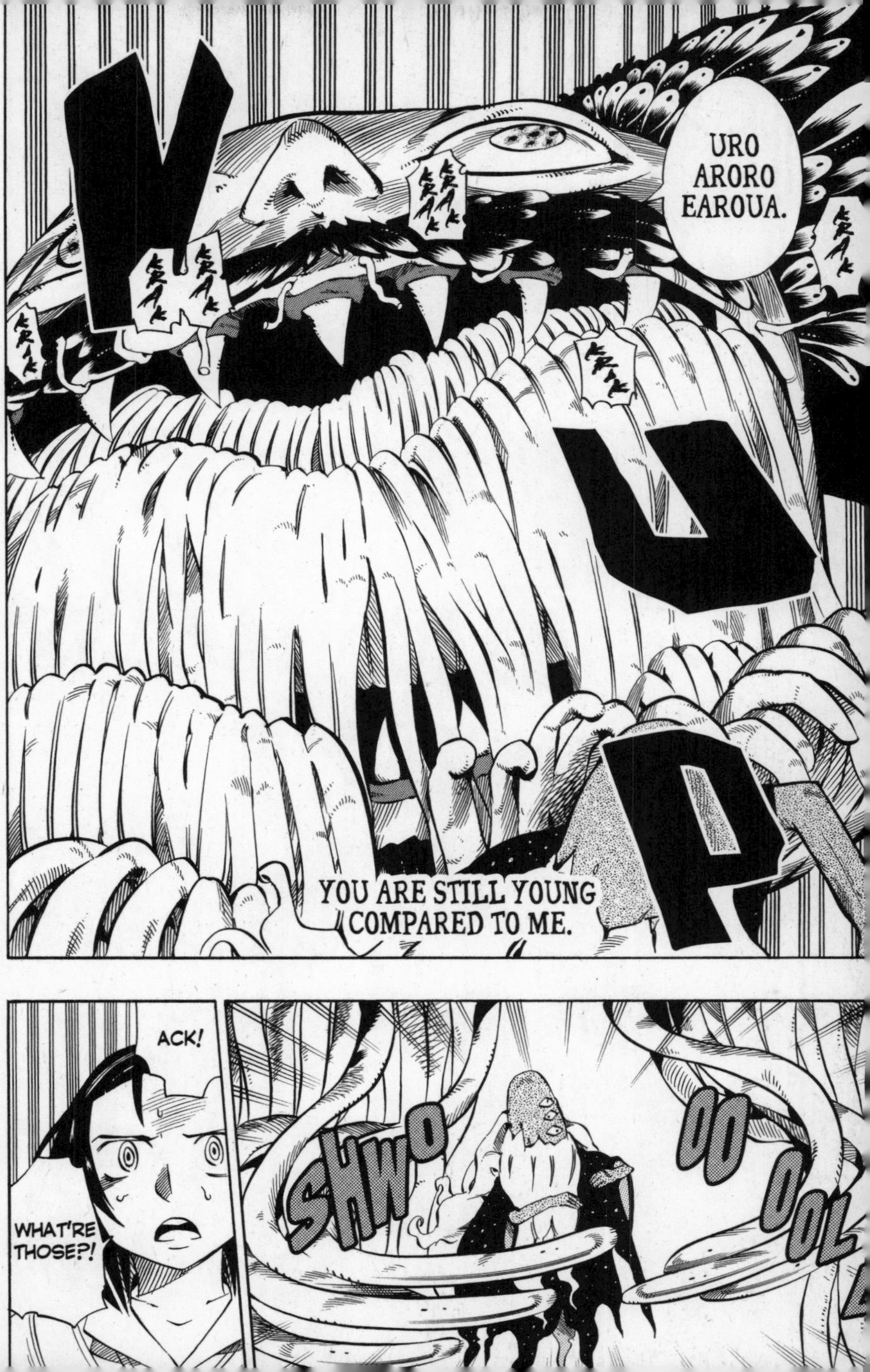
URO ARORO EAROUA.
YOU ARE STILL YOUNG COMPARED TO ME.
SHWOOOOOL
ACK!
WHAT'RE THOSE?!

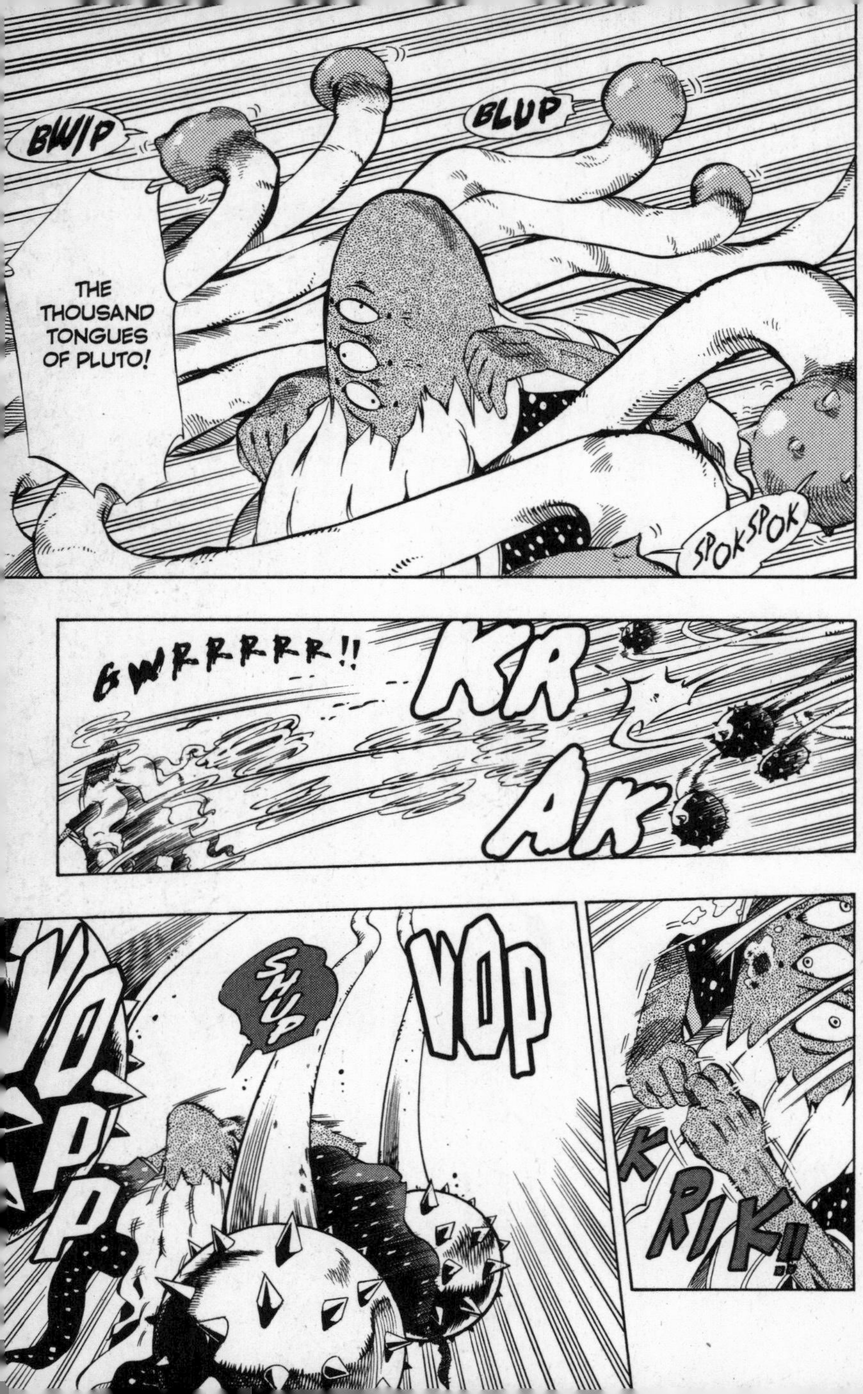
BLUP
BWIP
THE THOUSAND TONGUES OF PLUTO!
SPOKSPOK
KRAK
GWRRRRRR!!
KRIK!!
VOP
SHUP
VOPP

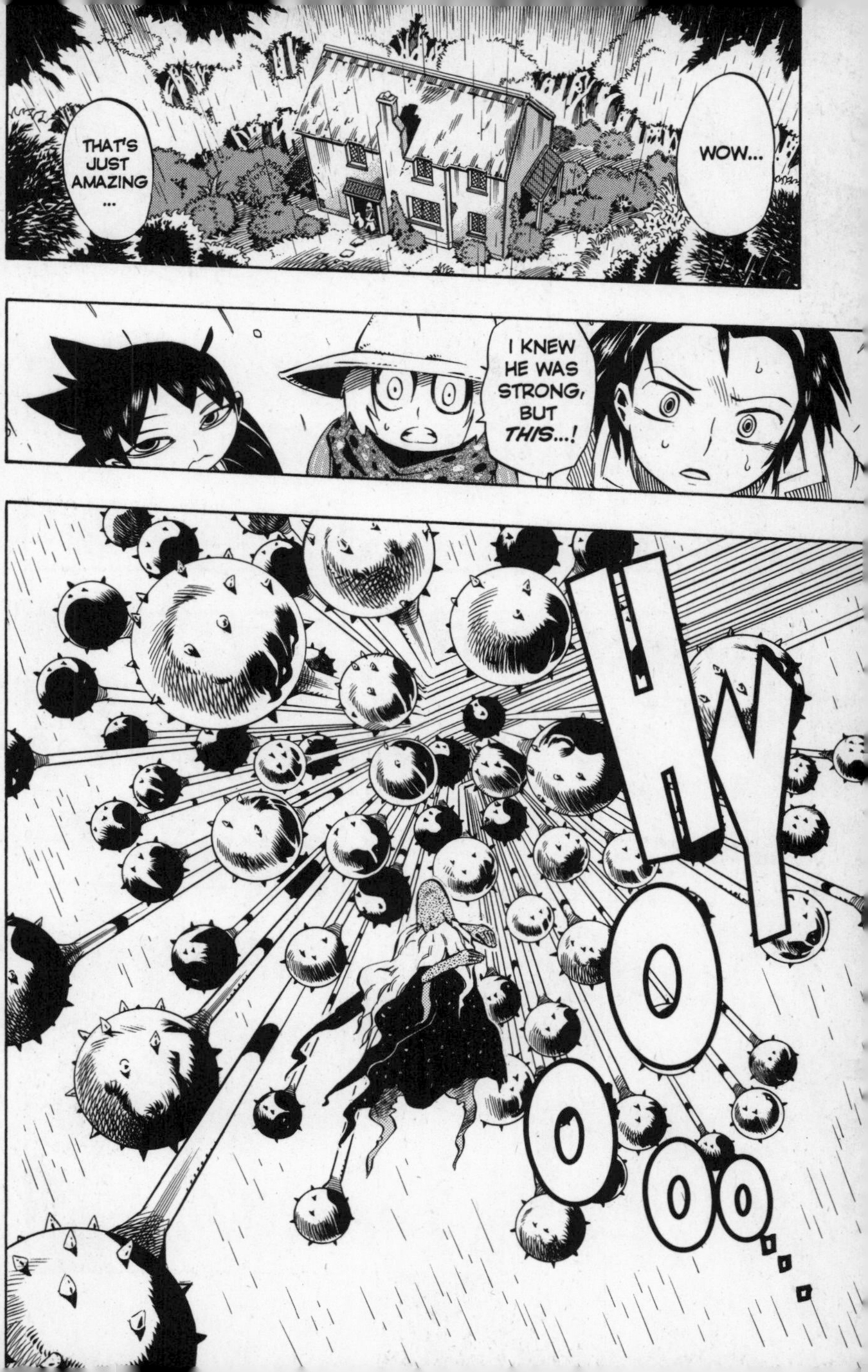
WOW...
THAT'S JUST AMAZING ...
I KNEW HE WAS STRONG, BUT *THIS*...!

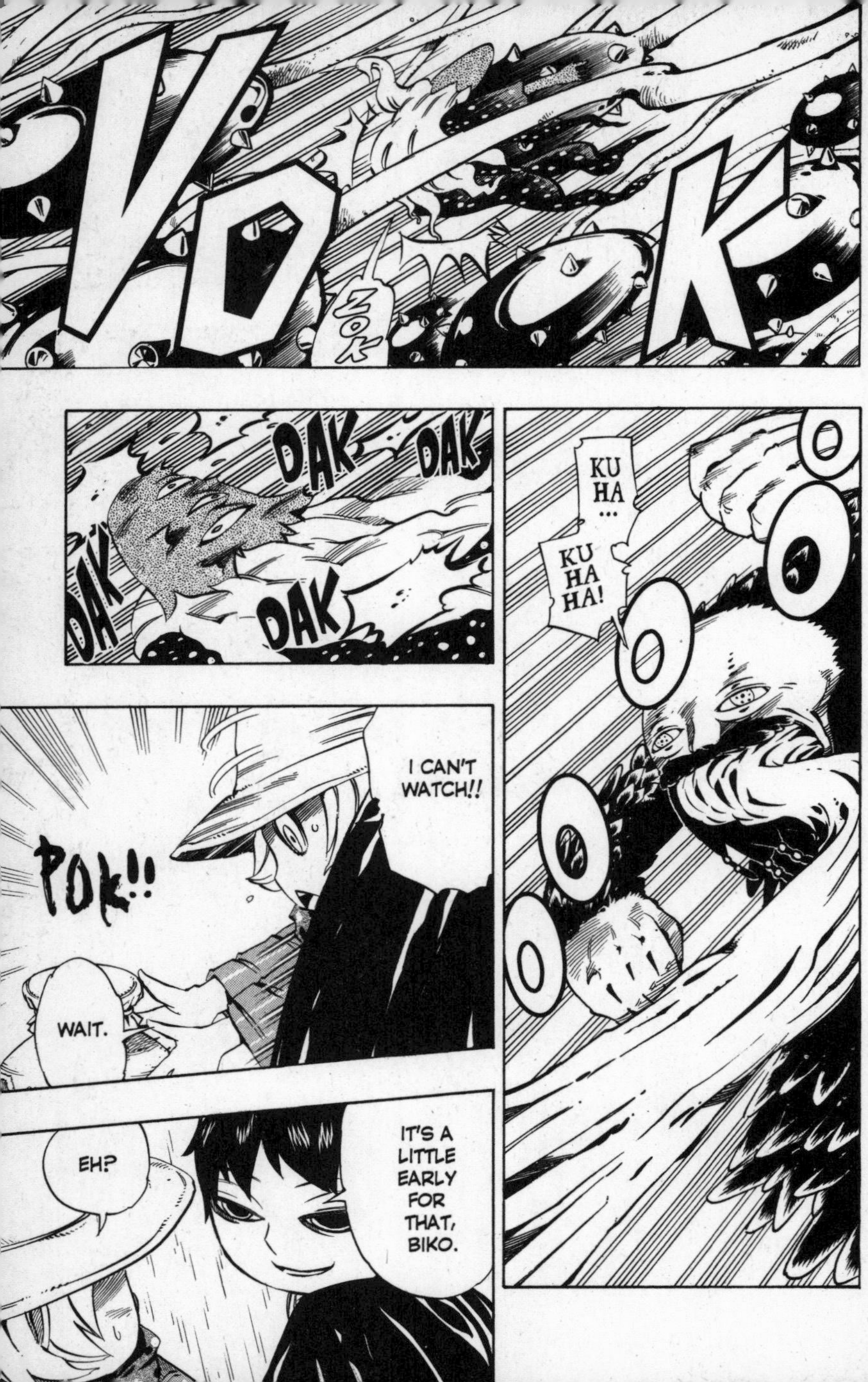
VDOK
ZOK
KU HA...
KU HA HA!
DAK
DAK
DAK
DAK
I CAN'T WATCH!!
POK!!
WAIT.
IT'S A LITTLE EARLY FOR THAT, BIKO.
EH?

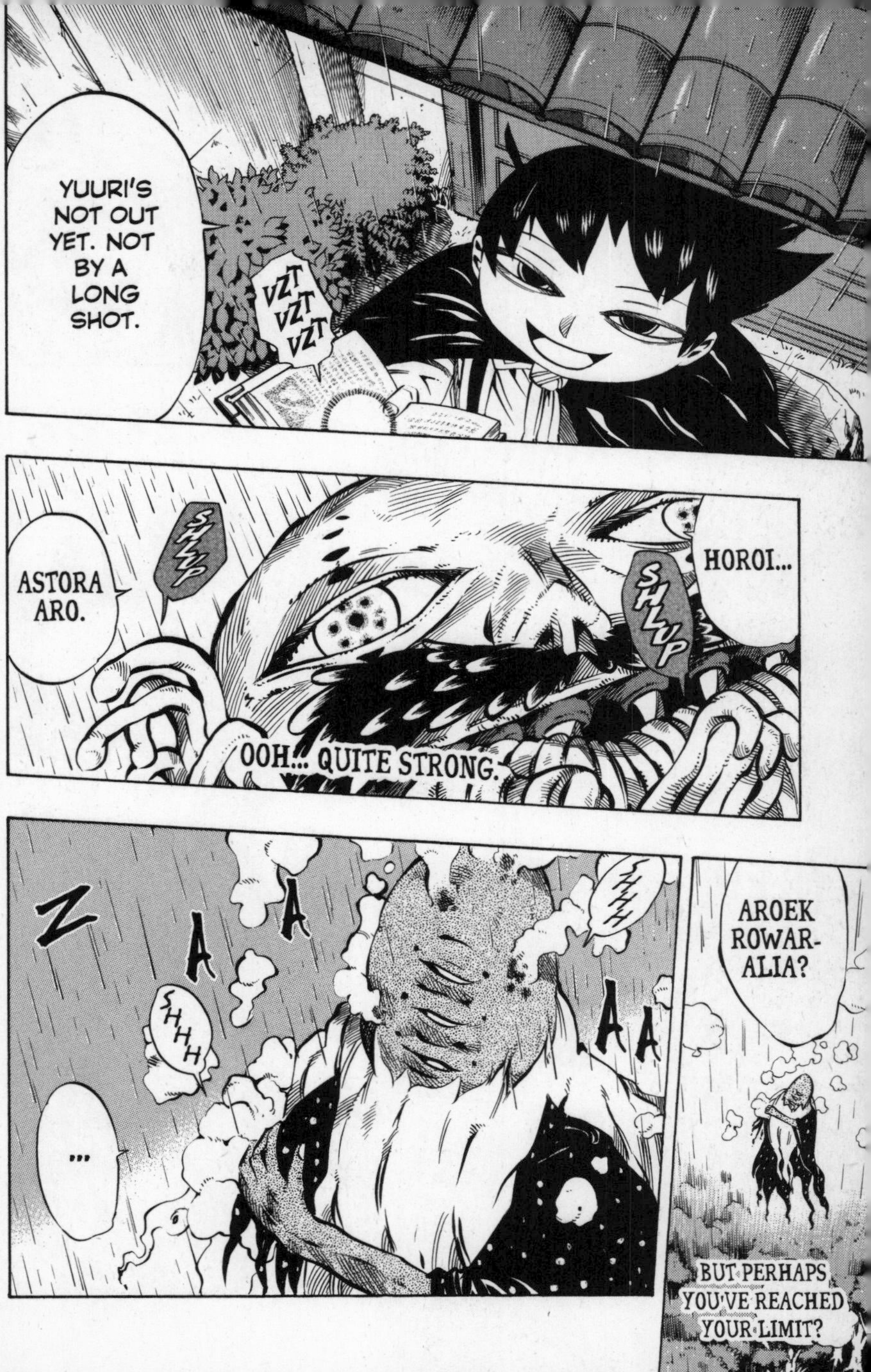
YUURI'S NOT OUT YET. NOT BY A LONG SHOT.
VZT VZT VZT
HOROI...
SHLUP
SHLUP
ASTORA ARO.
OOH... QUITE STRONG.
AROEK ROWAR-ALIA?
BUT PERHAPS YOU'VE REACHED YOUR LIMIT?
SHHH
ZAAAA
SHHH
...

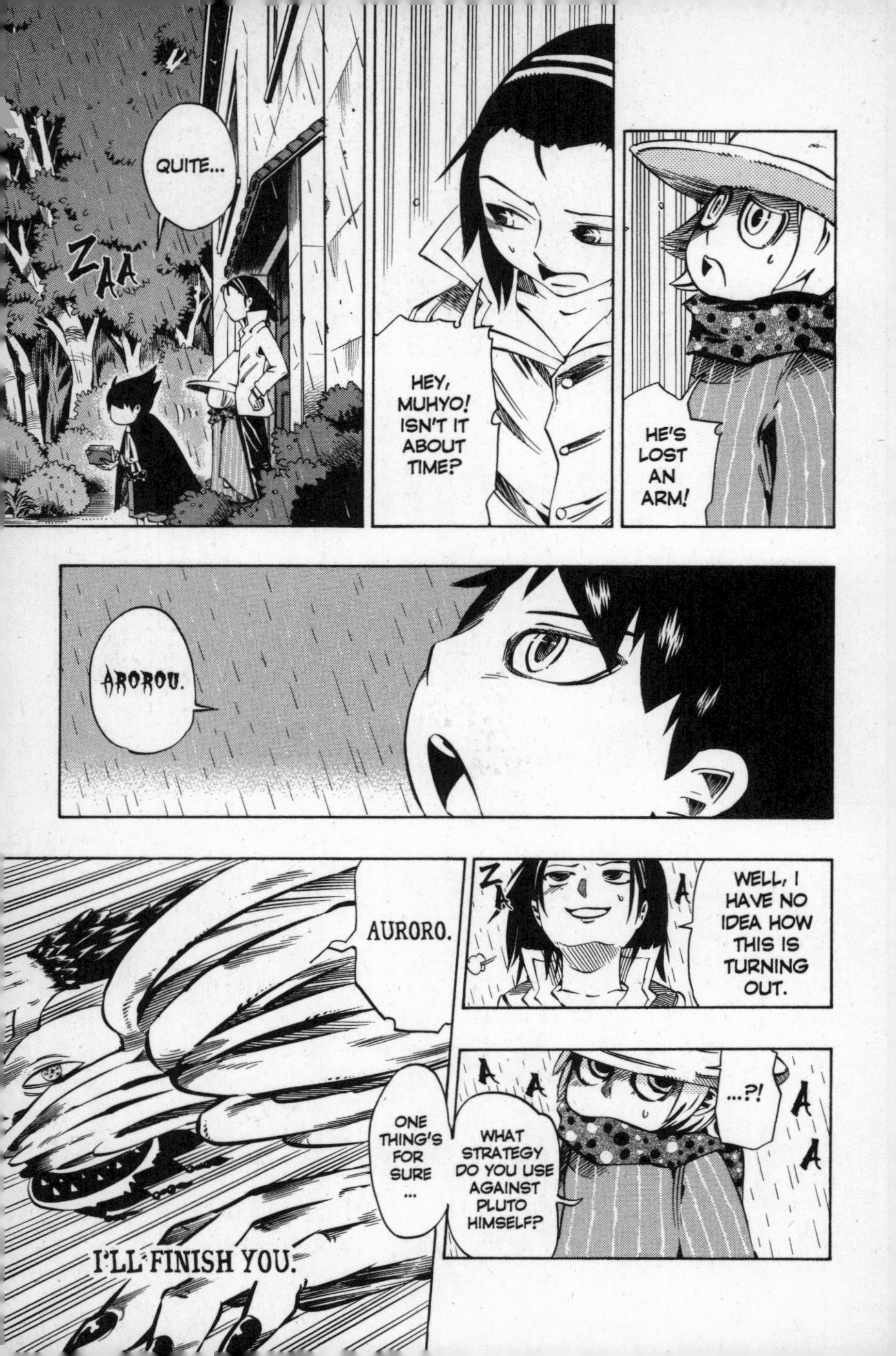
HE'S LOST AN ARM!
HEY, MUHYO! ISN'T IT ABOUT TIME?
QUITE...
ZAA
AROROU.
ZA
A
WELL, I HAVE NO IDEA HOW THIS IS TURNING OUT.
A
A
A
A
...?!
WHAT STRATEGY DO YOU USE AGAINST PLUTO HIMSELF?
ONE THING'S FOR SURE...
AURORO.
I'LL FINISH YOU.

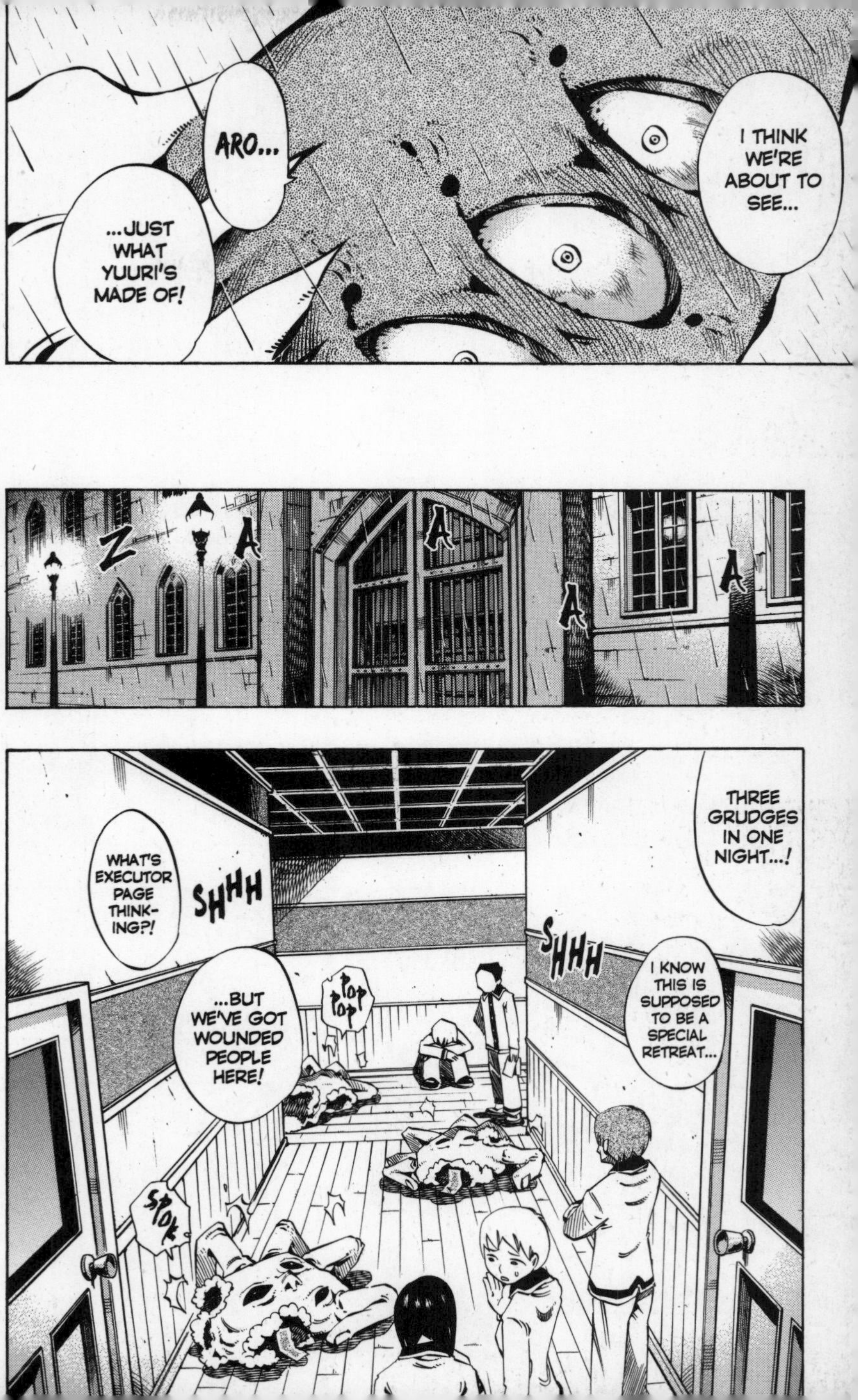
I THINK WE'RE ABOUT TO SEE...
ARO...
...JUST WHAT YUURI'S MADE OF!
ZAAAA
THREE GRUDGES IN ONE NIGHT...!
SHHH
I KNOW THIS IS SUPPOSED TO BE A SPECIAL RETREAT...
WHAT'S EXECUTOR PAGE THINKING?!
SHHH
...BUT WE'VE GOT WOUNDED PEOPLE HERE!
POP POP
SPOK

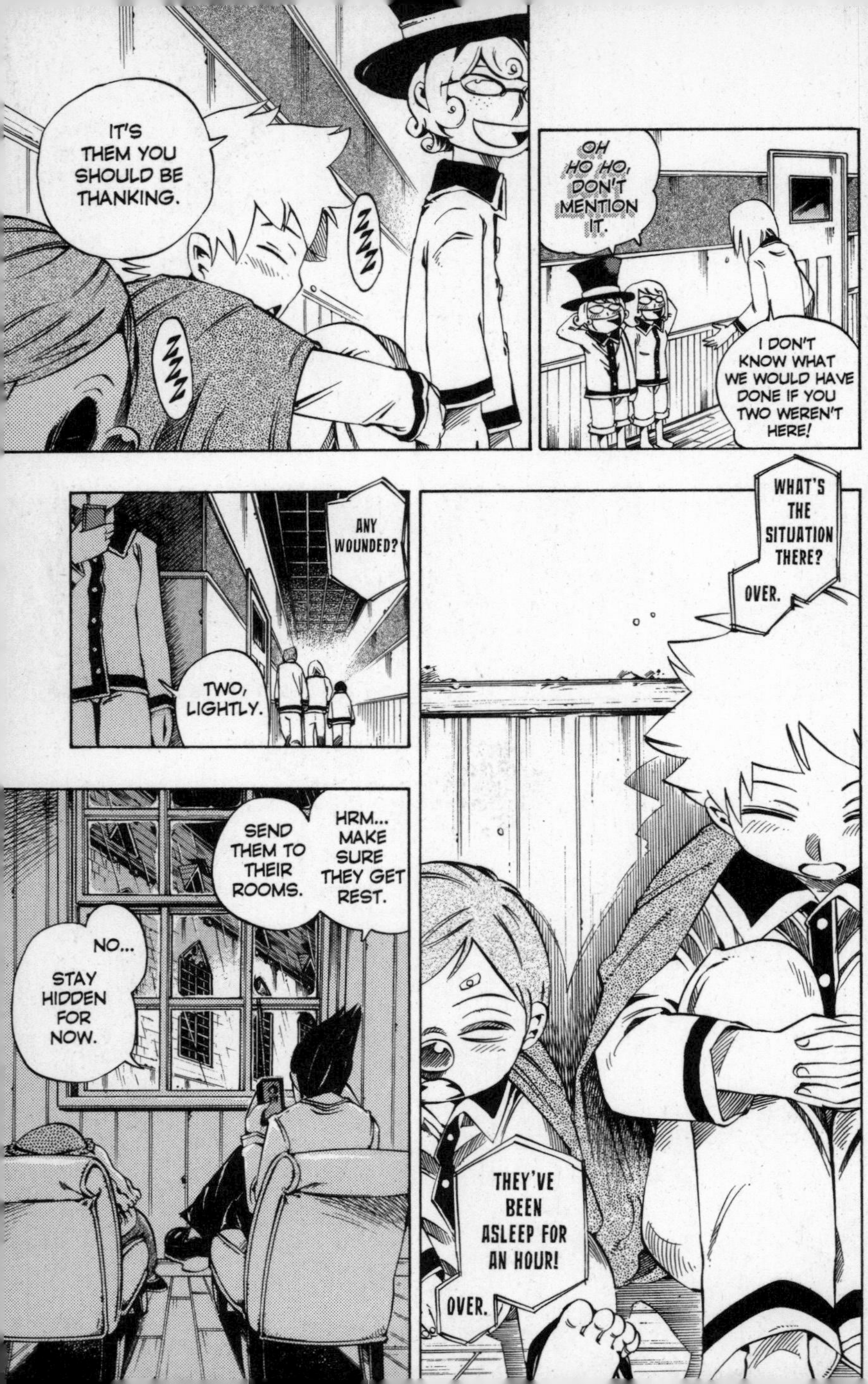
I DON'T KNOW WHAT WE WOULD HAVE DONE IF YOU TWO WEREN'T HERE!
OH HO HO, DON'T MENTION IT.
IT'S THEM YOU SHOULD BE THANKING.
WHAT'S THE SITUATION THERE?
OVER.
THEY'VE BEEN ASLEEP FOR AN HOUR!
OVER.
ANY WOUNDED?
TWO, LIGHTLY.
HRM... MAKE SURE THEY GET REST.
SEND THEM TO THEIR ROOMS.
NO...
STAY HIDDEN FOR NOW.

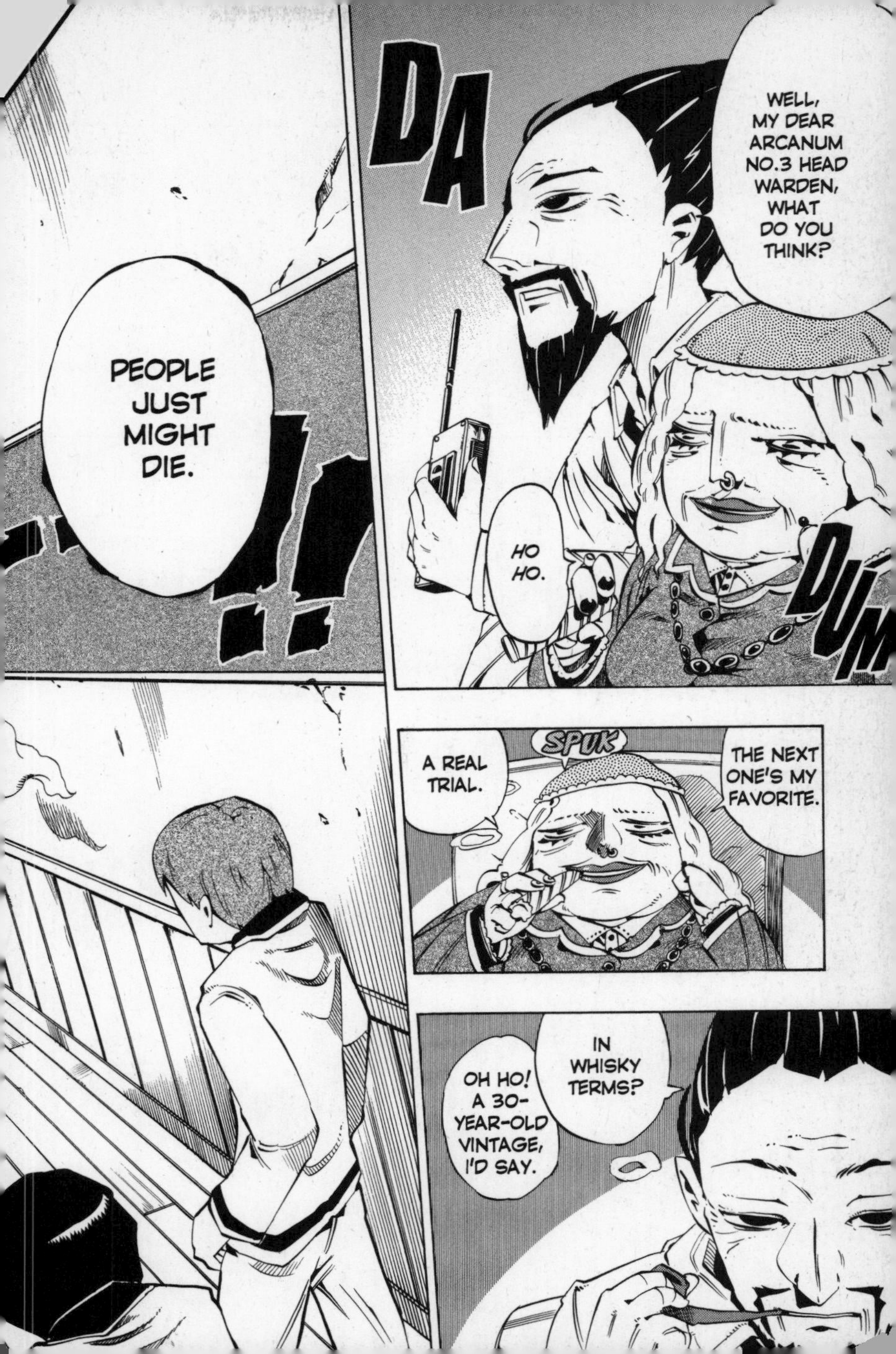
WELL, MY DEAR ARCANUM NO.3 HEAD WARDEN, WHAT DO YOU THINK?
DA
DUM
HO HO.
PEOPLE JUST MIGHT DIE.
!!
THE NEXT ONE'S MY FAVORITE.
SPUK
A REAL TRIAL.
IN WHISKY TERMS?
OH HO! A 30-YEAR-OLD VINTAGE, I'D SAY.

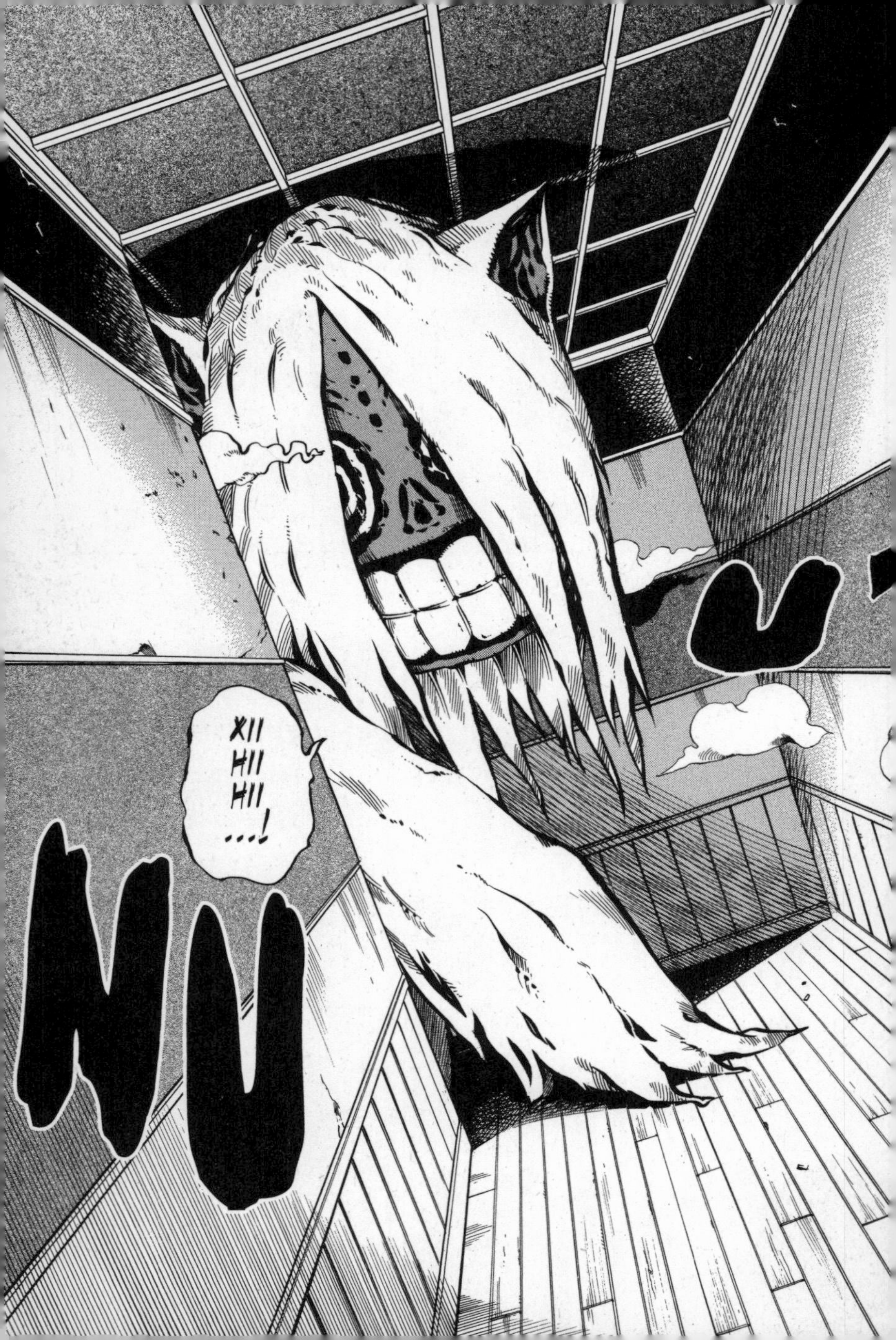
U
KIII HIII HIII ...!
NU

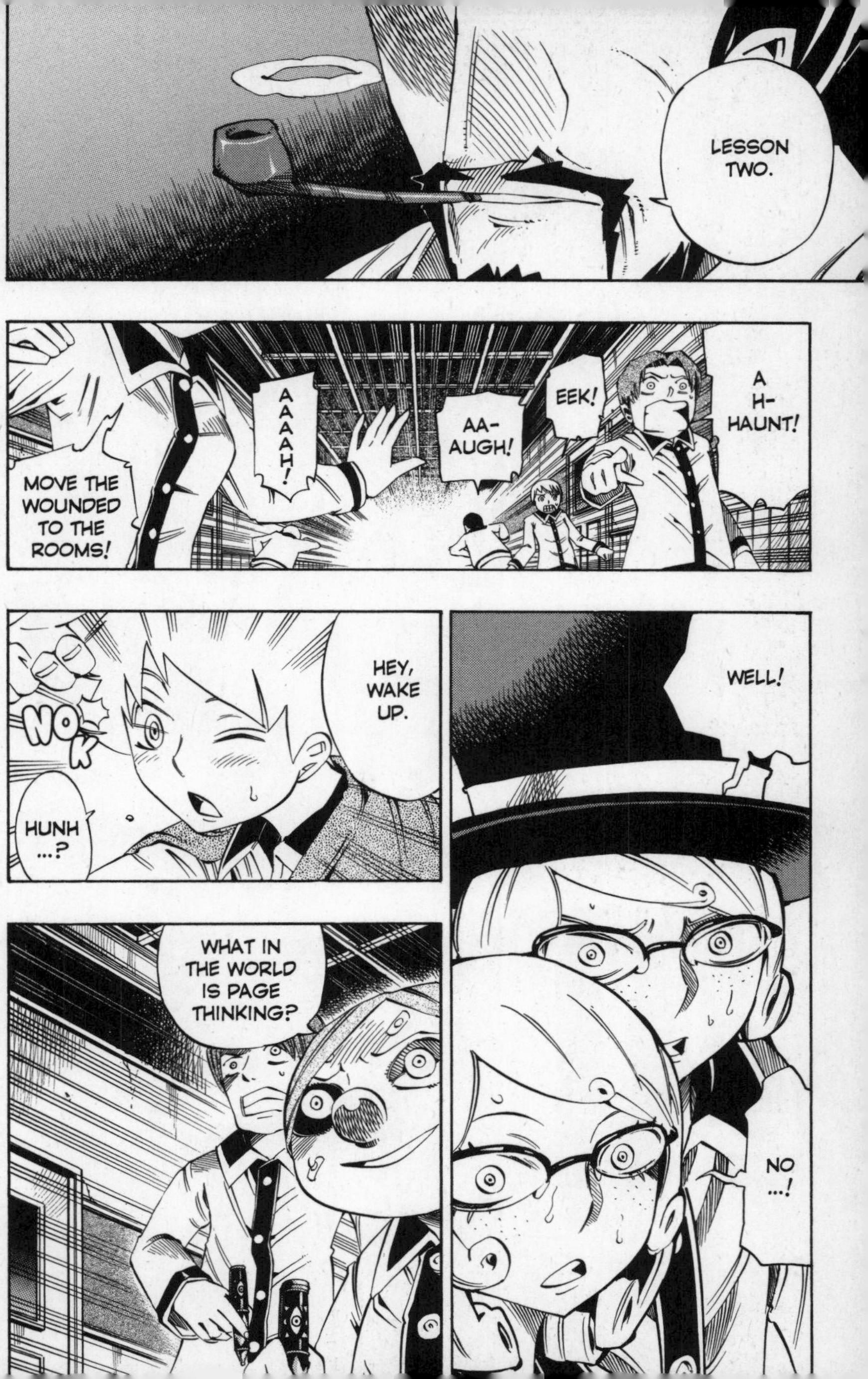
LESSON TWO.
A H-HAUNT!
EEK!
AA-AUGH!
AAAAH!
MOVE THE WOUNDED TO THE ROOMS!
WELL!
NO ...!
HEY, WAKE UP.
NOK
HUNH ...?
WHAT IN THE WORLD IS PAGE THINKING?

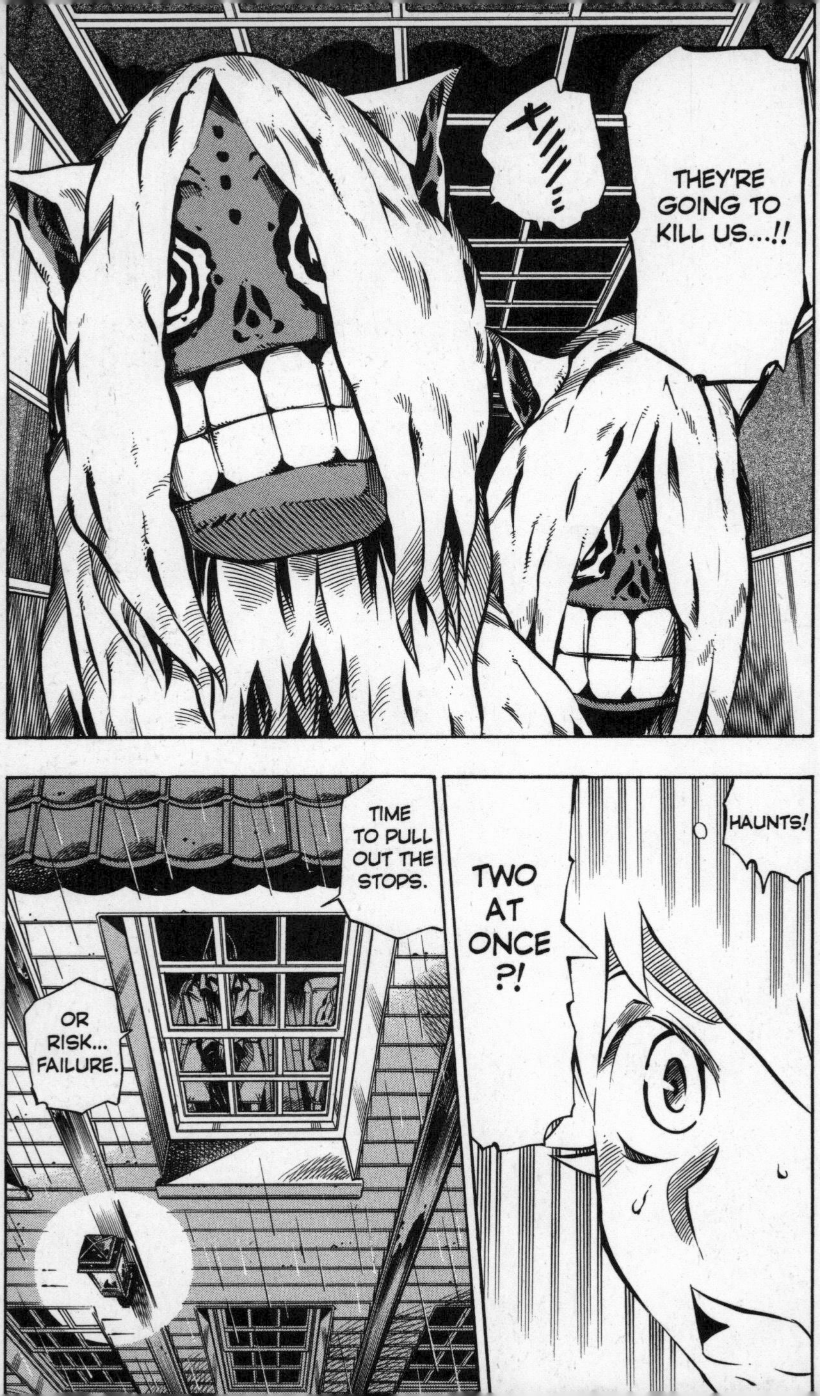
THEY'RE GOING TO KILL US...!!
HAUNTS!
TWO AT ONCE?!
TIME TO PULL OUT THE STOPS.
OR RISK... FAILURE.

Q: I NOTICED ROJI'S AND YOICHI'S PEN OF WARDS ARE SLIGHTLY DIFFERENT. IS IT BECAUSE THEY'RE DIFFERENT RANKS? OR DID YOU JUST DRAW THEM DIFFERENTLY?

-S.K., TOCHIGI PREFECTURE

A: HUH? THEY'RE DIFFERENT...? ACK!

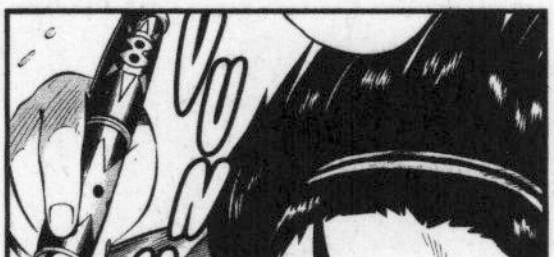

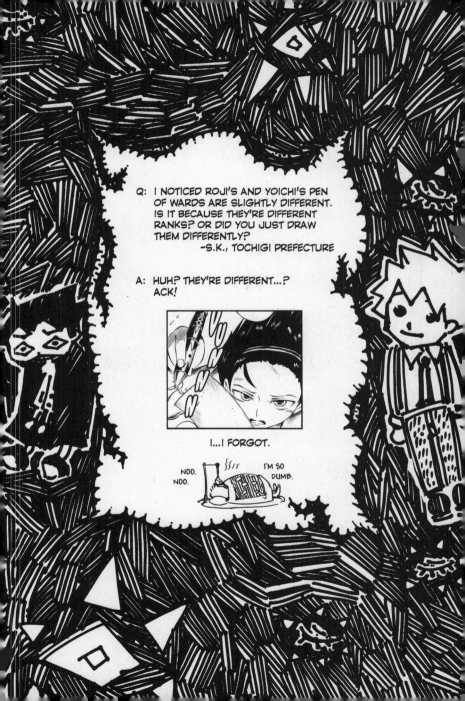

I...I FORGOT.

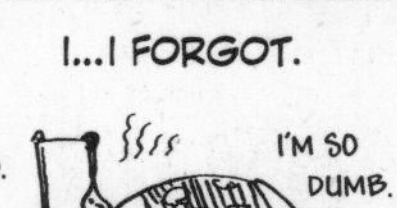
NOO.
NOO.
I'M SO
DUMB.

ARTICLE 53
THE PLAN'S END

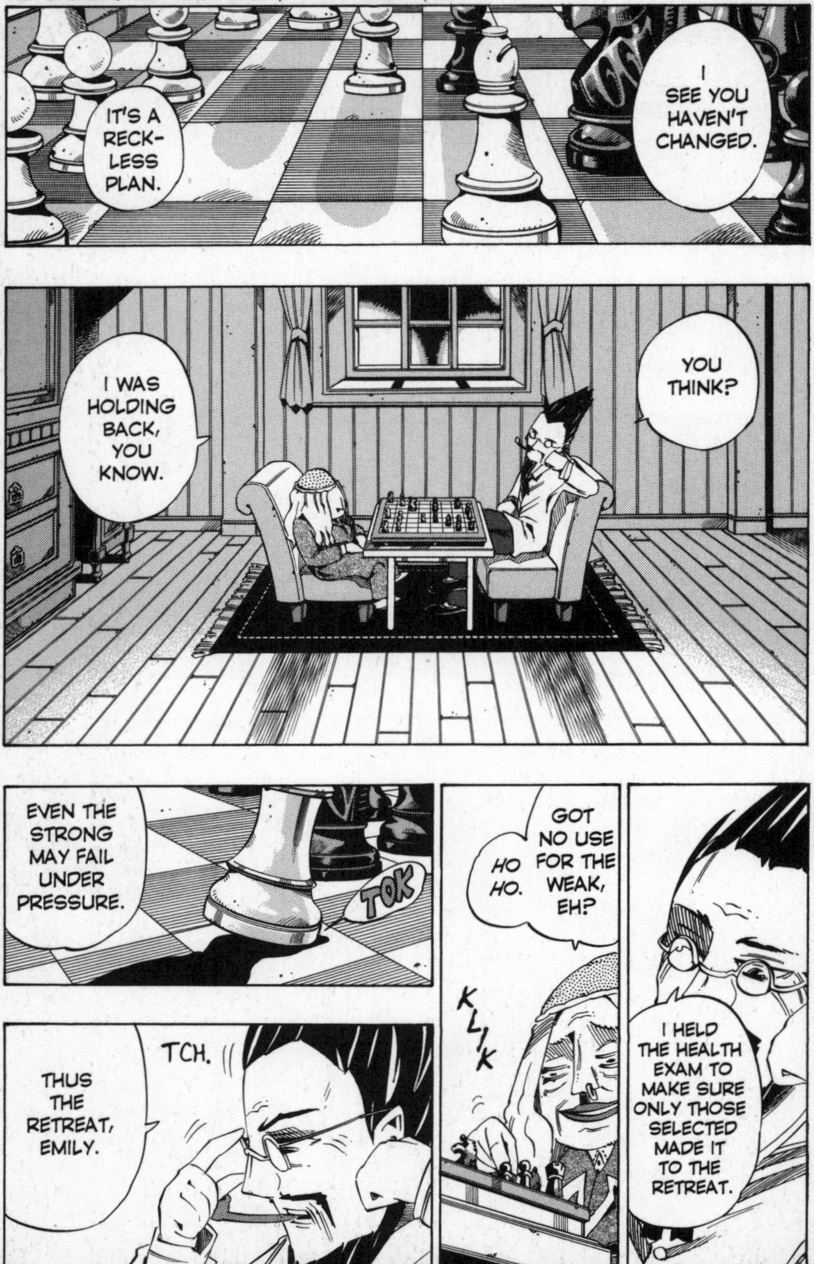
I SEE YOU HAVEN'T CHANGED.
IT'S A RECKLESS PLAN.
YOU THINK?
I WAS HOLDING BACK, YOU KNOW.
I HELD THE HEALTH EXAM TO MAKE SURE ONLY THOSE SELECTED MADE IT TO THE RETREAT.
GOT NO USE FOR THE WEAK, EH?
HO HO.
KLIK
EVEN THE STRONG MAY FAIL UNDER PRESSURE.
TOK
TCH.
THUS THE RETREAT, EMILY.

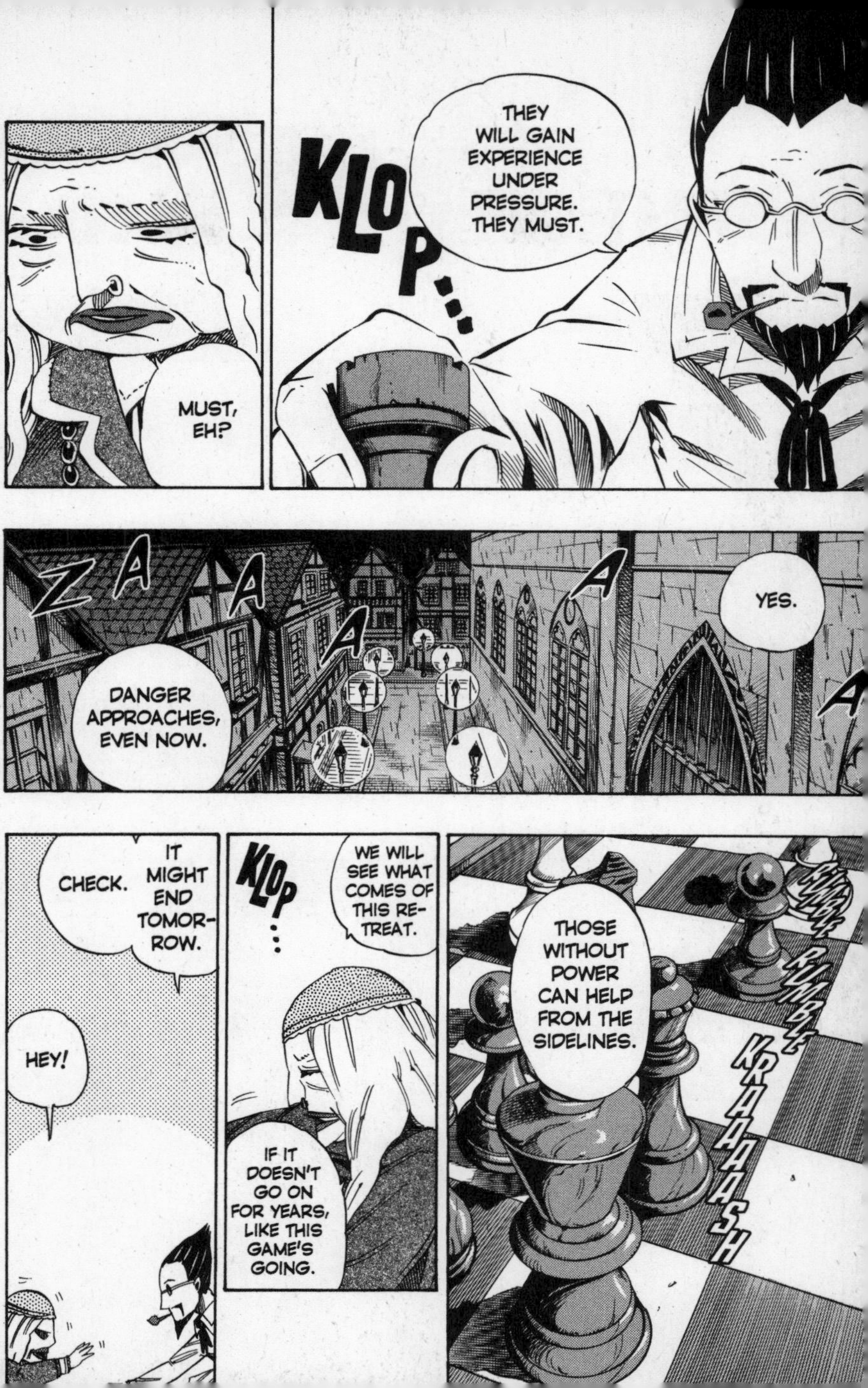
KLOP...
THEY WILL GAIN EXPERIENCE UNDER PRESSURE. THEY MUST.
MUST, EH?
ZAAAAA
YES.
DANGER APPROACHES, EVEN NOW.
THOSE WITHOUT POWER CAN HELP FROM THE SIDELINES.
RUMBLE
KRAAAAASH
KLOP...
WE WILL SEE WHAT COMES OF THIS RE-TREAT.
IF IT DOESN'T GO ON FOR YEARS, LIKE THIS GAME'S GOING.
IT MIGHT END TOMOR-ROW.
CHECK.
HEY!

ARTICLE 53
THE PLAN'S END

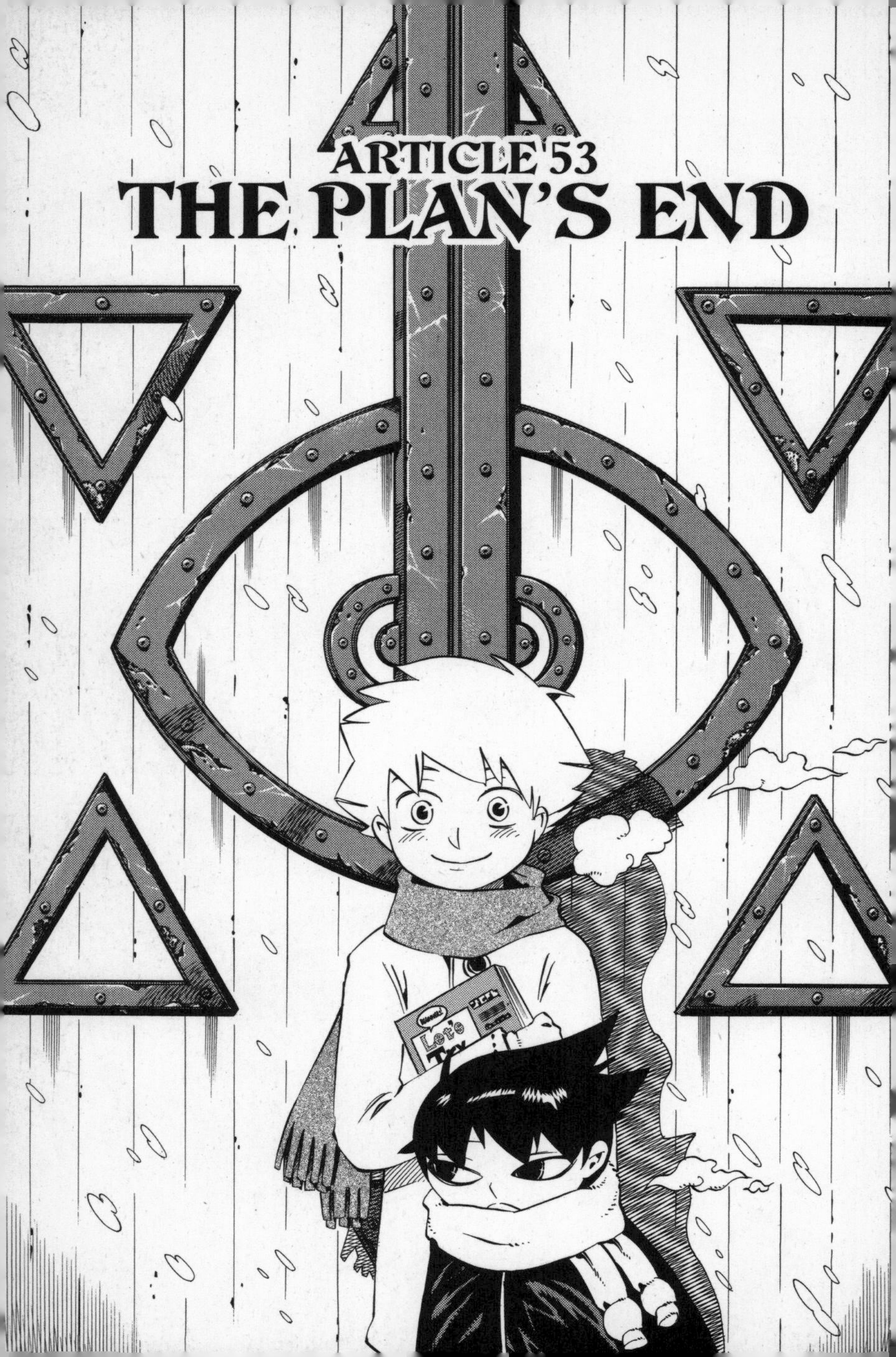
Let's Try

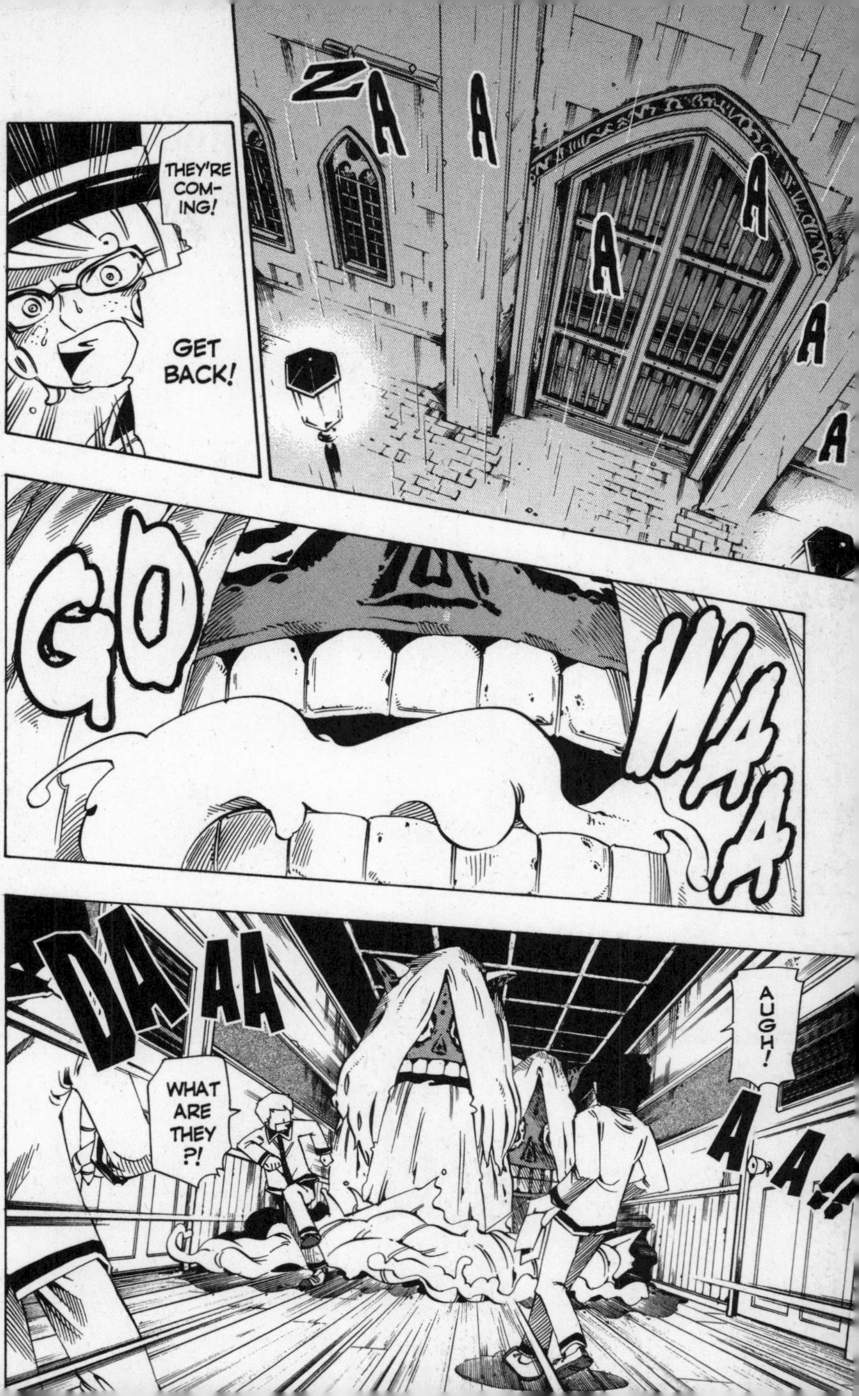
ZAAAAAAA
THEY'RE COMING!
GET BACK!
GO
WAAA
AUGH!
DAAA
AAA!!
WHAT ARE THEY?!

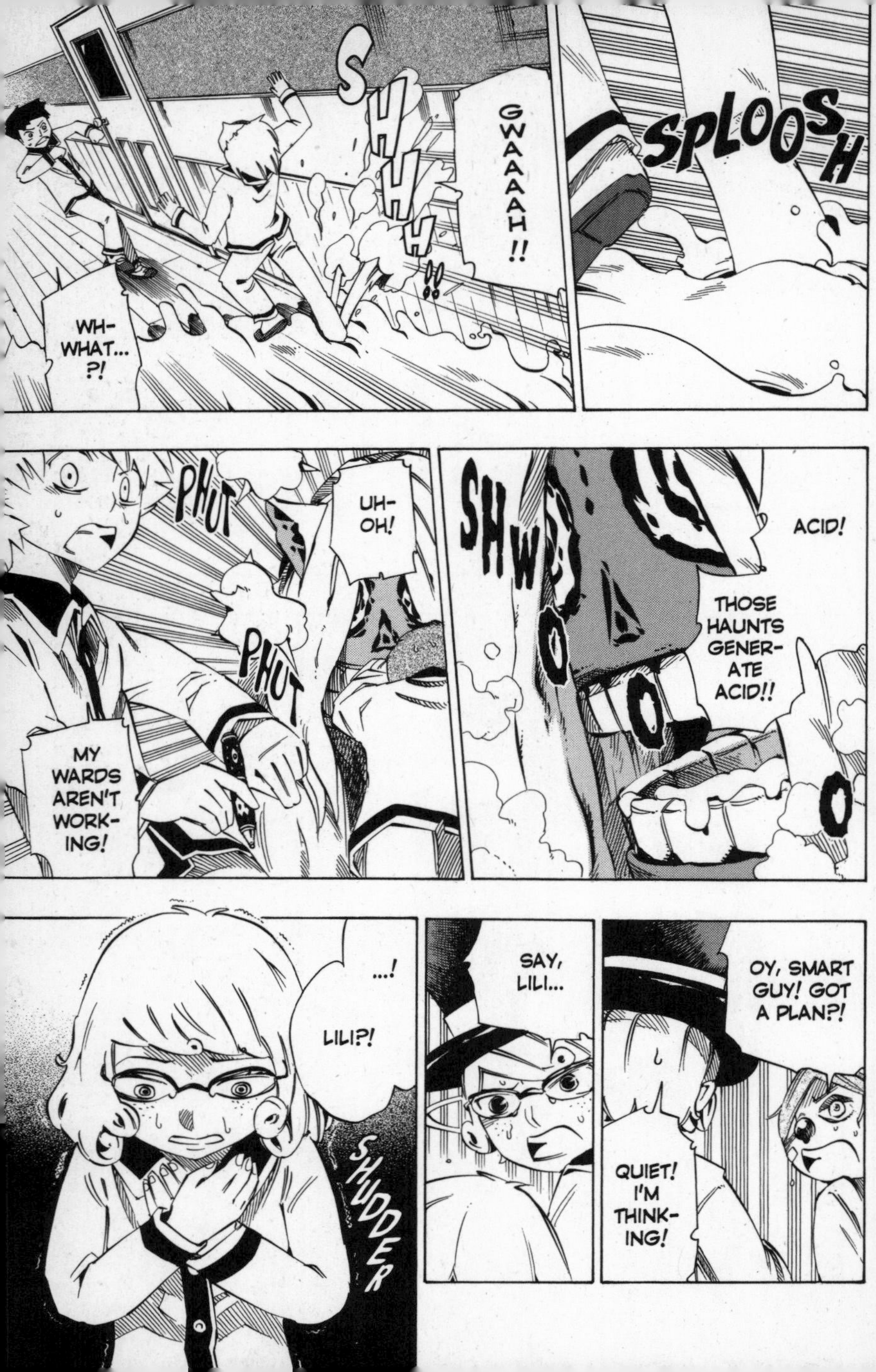
SPLOOSH
GWAAAAAH!!
SHHHH!!
WH-WHAT...?!
ACID!
THOSE HAUNTS GENERATE ACID!!
SHWOOO
UH-OH!
PHUT
PHUT
MY WARDS AREN'T WORKING!
OY, SMART GUY! GOT A PLAN?!
QUIET! I'M THINKING!
SAY, LILI...
...!
LILI?!
SHUDDER

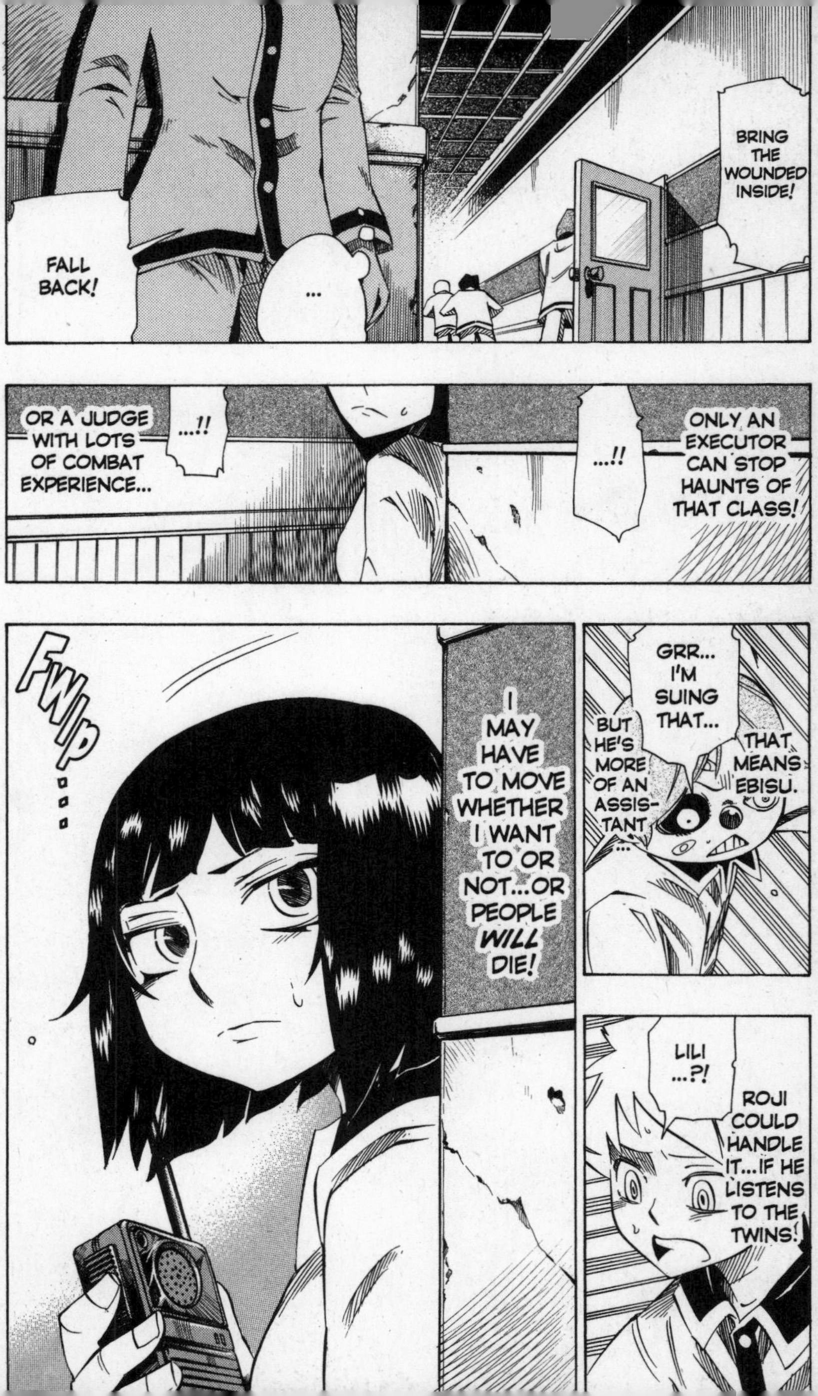
BRING THE WOUNDED INSIDE!
...
FALL BACK!
ONLY AN EXECUTOR CAN STOP HAUNTS OF THAT CLASS!
...!!
...!!
OR A JUDGE WITH LOTS OF COMBAT EXPERIENCE...
THAT MEANS EBISU.
GRR... I'M SUING THAT...
BUT HE'S MORE OF AN ASSISTANT...
LILI ...?!
ROJI COULD HANDLE IT...IF HE LISTENS TO THE TWINS!
I MAY HAVE TO MOVE WHETHER I WANT TO OR NOT...OR PEOPLE WILL DIE!
FWIP...

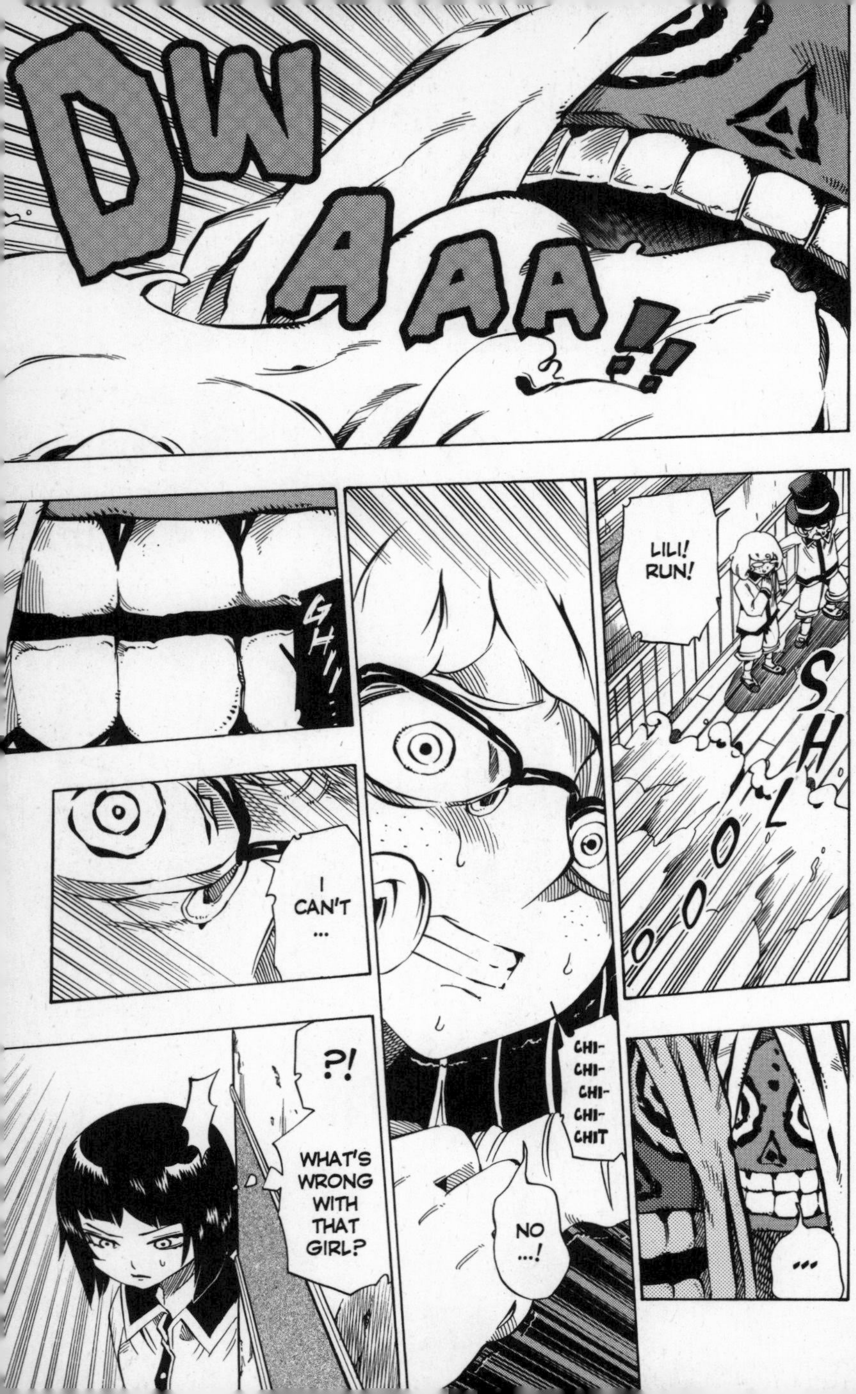
DWAAAA!!
LILI! RUN!
SHLOOOOOO
GHII
I CAN'T ...
...
CHI-CHI-CHI-CHI-CHIT
NO ...!
?!
WHAT'S WRONG WITH THAT GIRL?

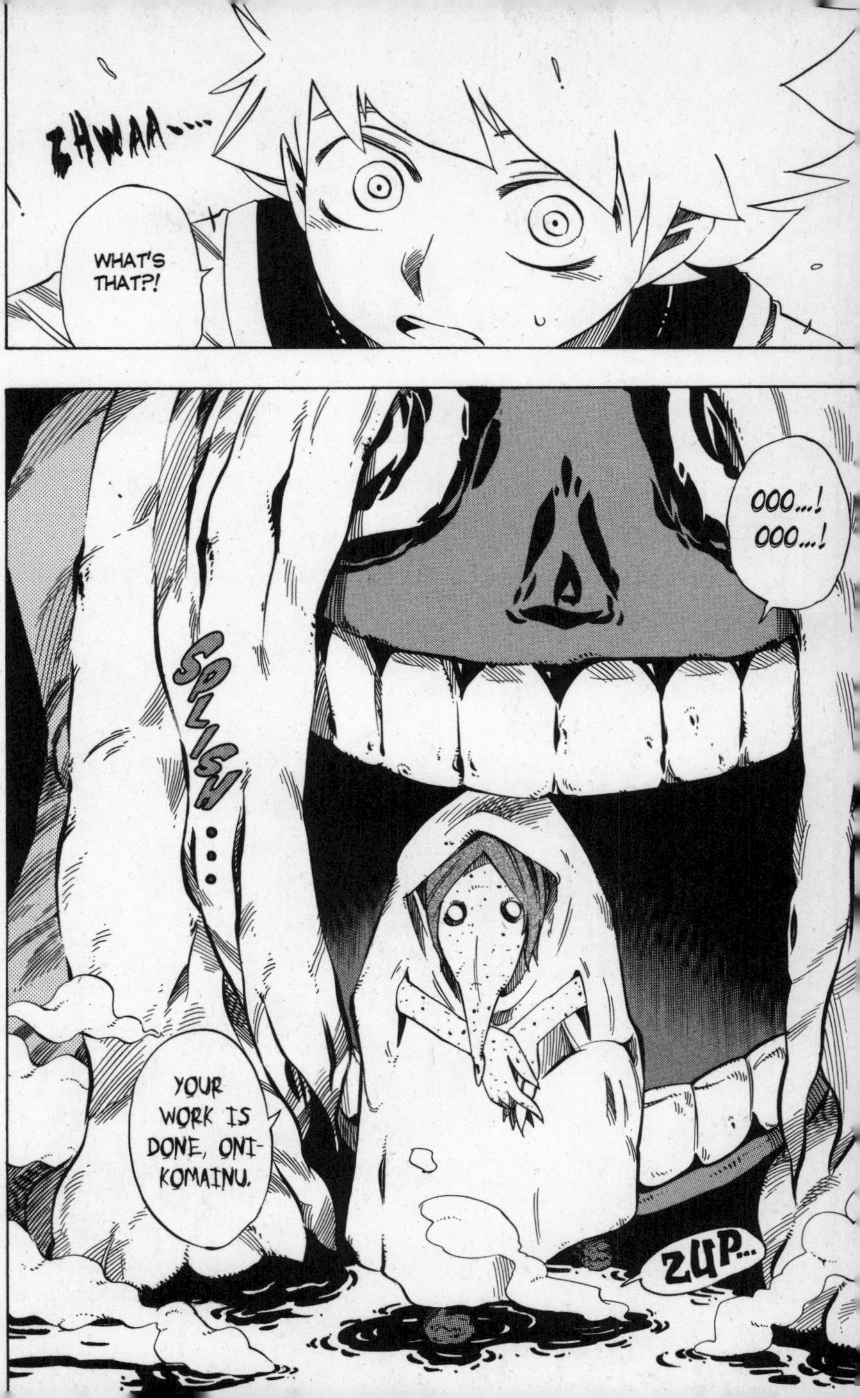
ZHWAA...
WHAT'S THAT?!
OOO...! OOO...!
SPLISH...
YOUR WORK IS DONE, ONI-KOMAINU.
ZUP...

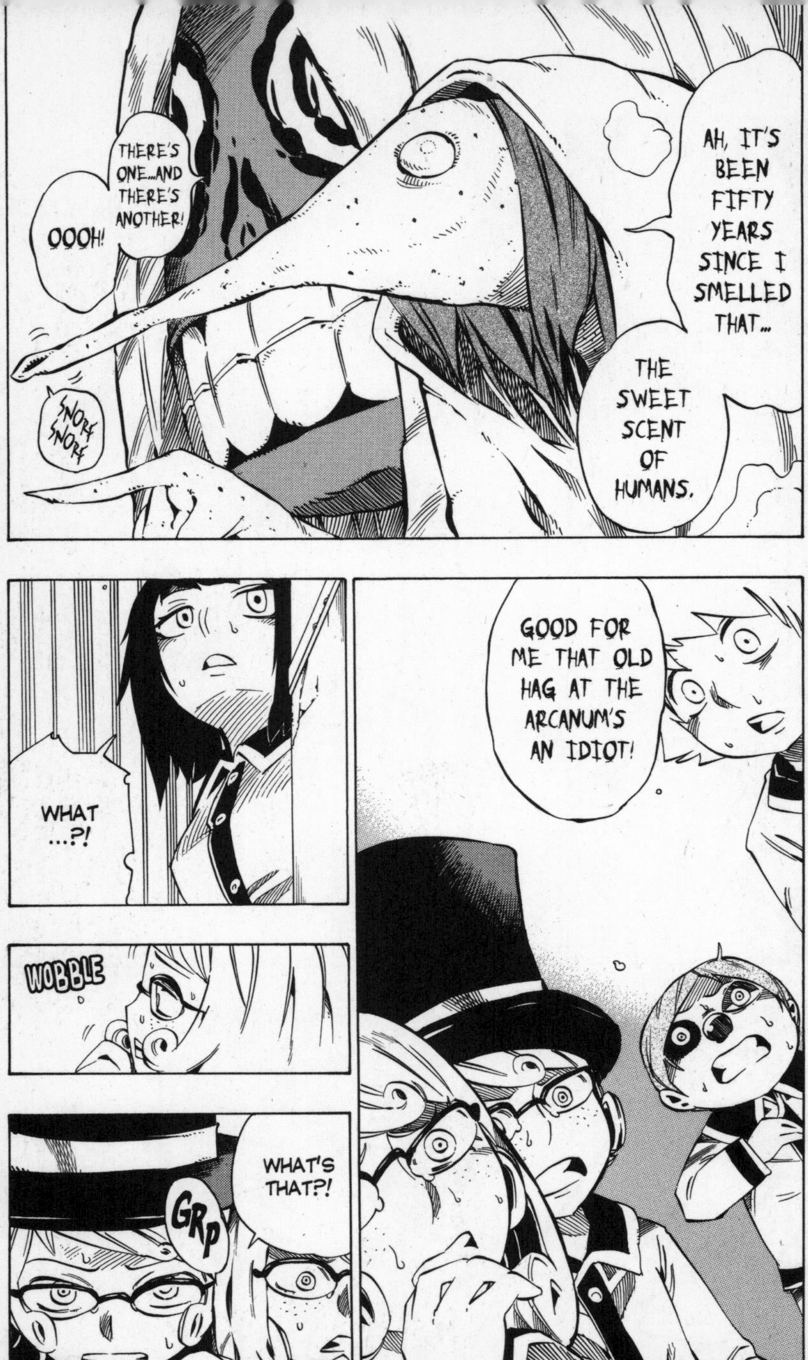
AH, IT'S BEEN FIFTY YEARS SINCE I SMELLED THAT...
THE SWEET SCENT OF HUMANS.
THERE'S ONE...AND THERE'S ANOTHER!
OOOH!
SNORF SNORF
GOOD FOR ME THAT OLD HAG AT THE ARCANUM'S AN IDIOT!
WHAT ...?!
WOBBLE
WHAT'S THAT?!
GRP

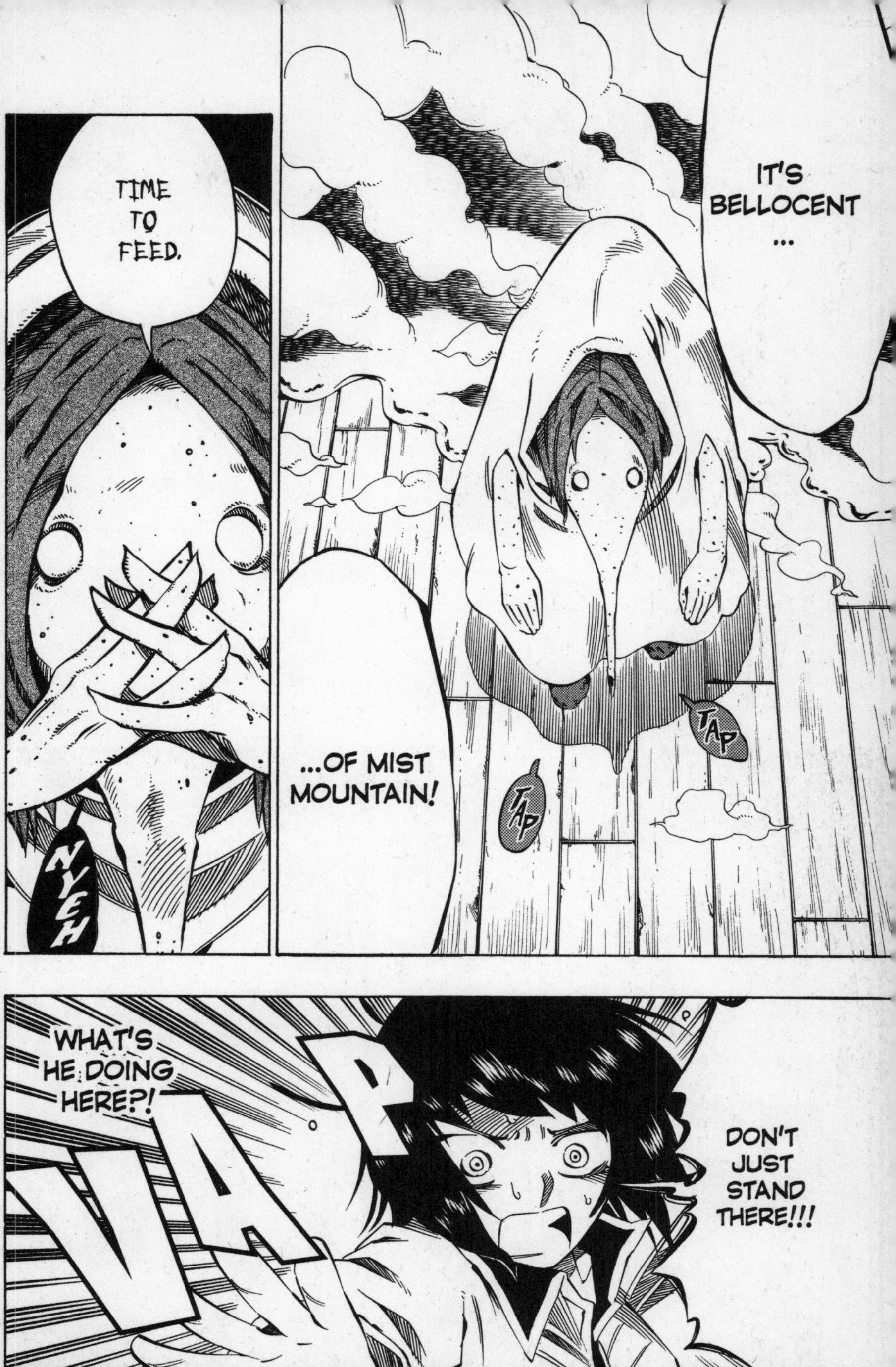
IT'S BELLOCENT ...
...OF MIST MOUNTAIN!
TAP
TAP
TIME TO FEED.
NYEH
DON'T JUST STAND THERE!!!
WHAT'S HE DOING HERE?!

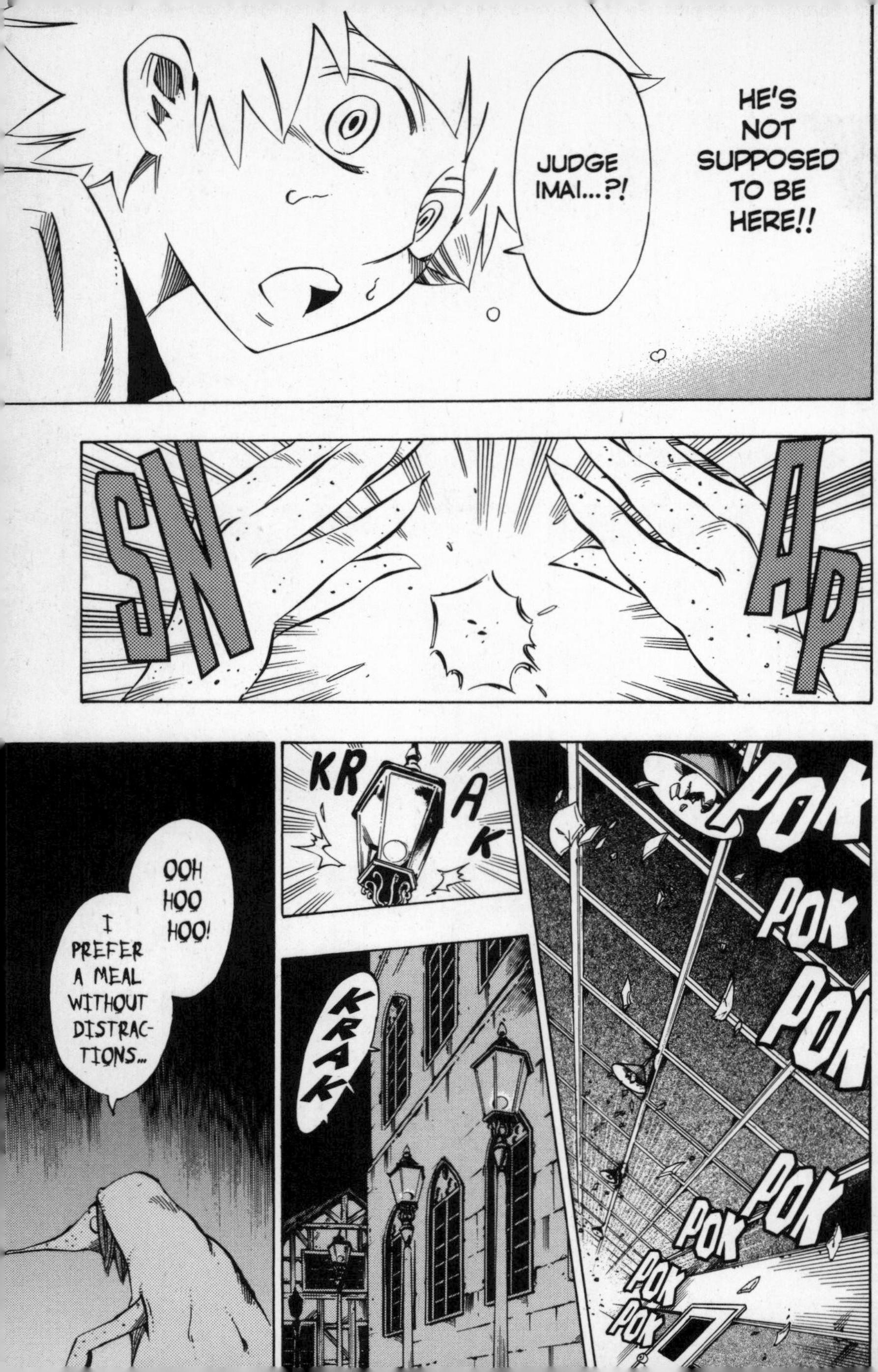
HE'S NOT SUPPOSED TO BE HERE!!
JUDGE IMAI...?!
SNAP
POK POK POK POK
POK POK POK POK POK
KRAK
KRAK
OOH HOO HOO!
I PREFER A MEAL WITHOUT DISTRACTIONS...

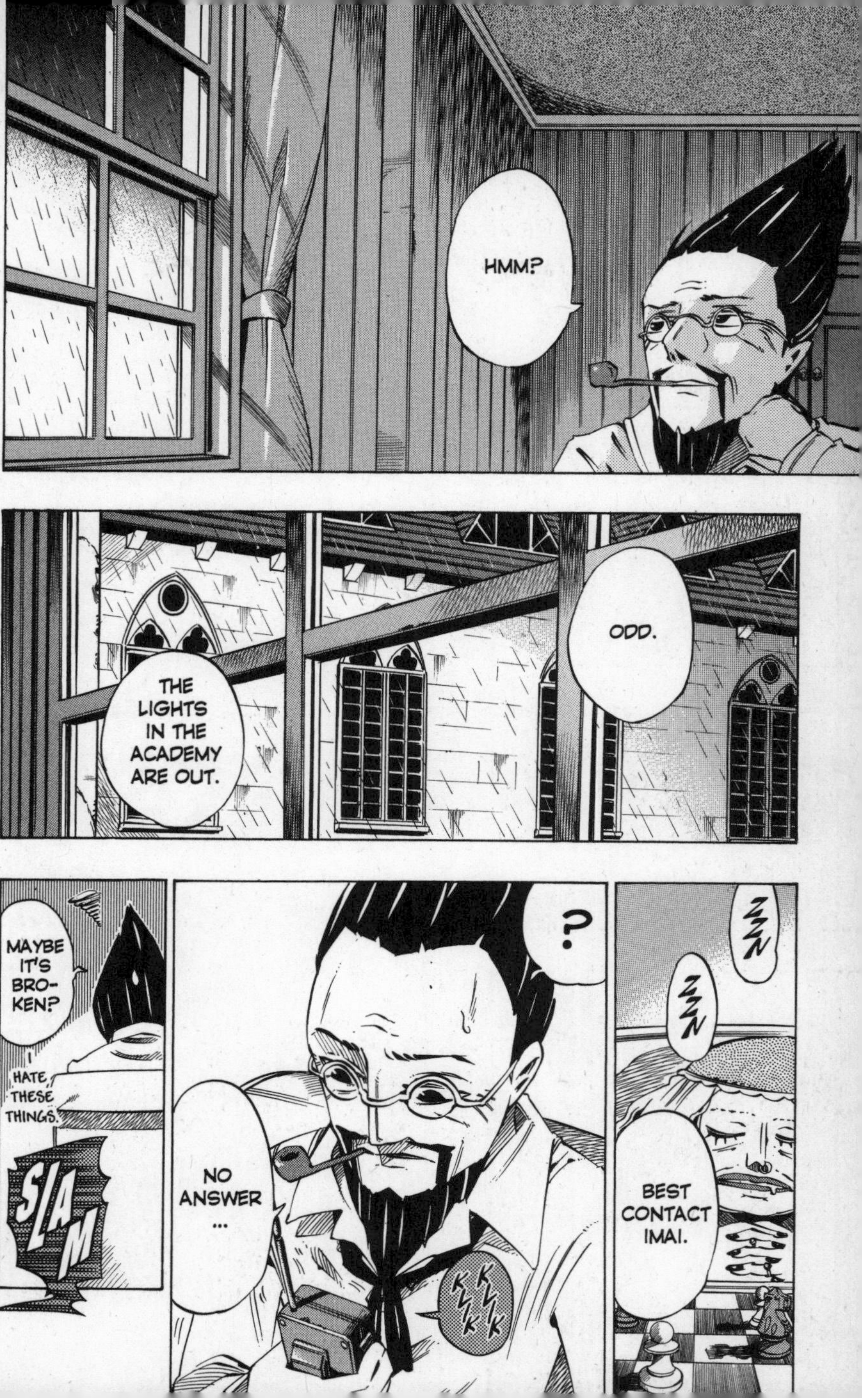
HMM?
ODD.
THE LIGHTS IN THE ACADEMY ARE OUT.
ZZZN
ZZZN
BEST CONTACT IMAI.
?
NO ANSWER ...
KLIK KLIK
MAYBE IT'S BRO- KEN?
HATE THESE THINGS.
SLAM

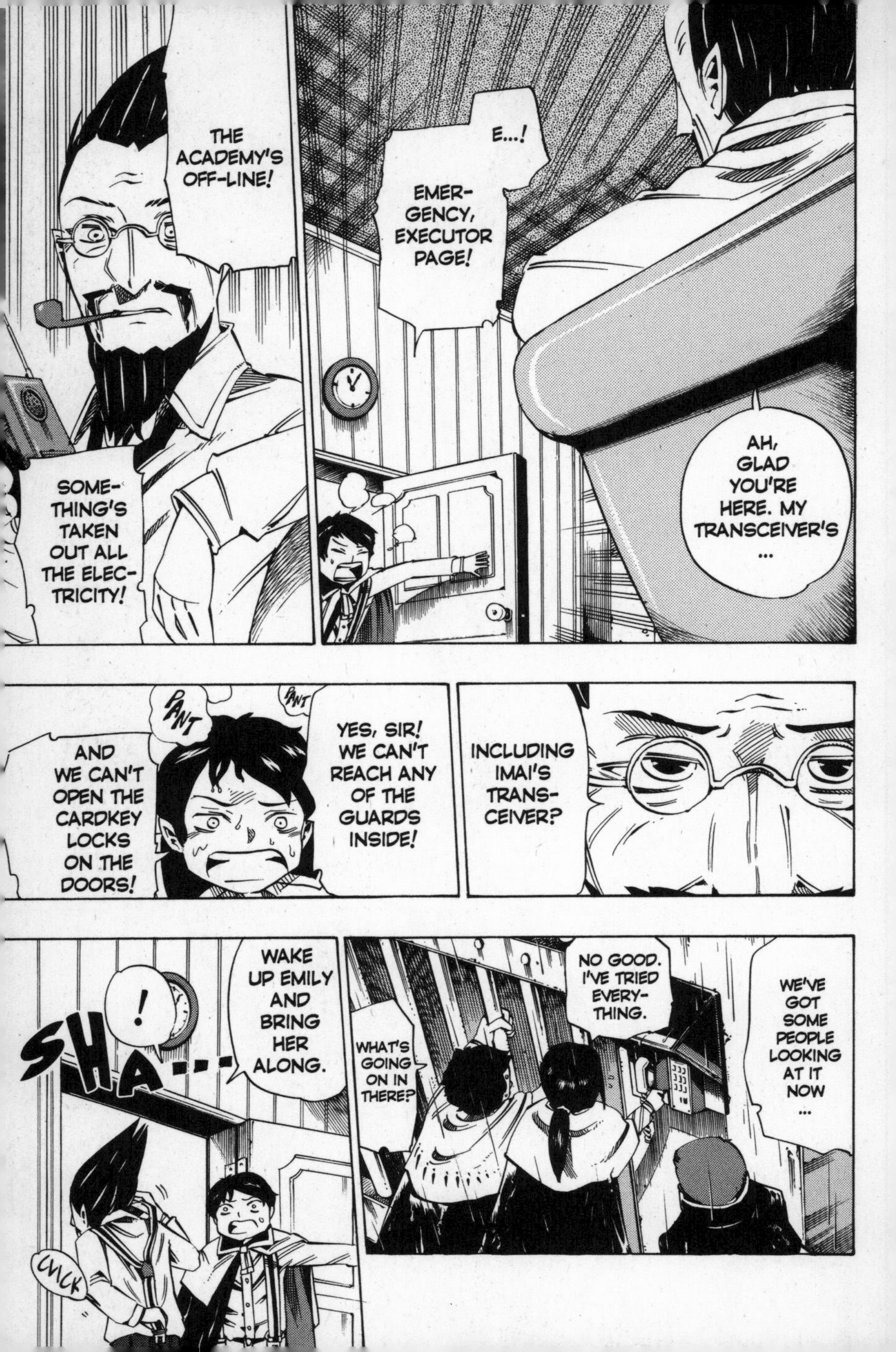
AH, GLAD YOU'RE HERE. MY TRANSCEIVER'S ...
E...!
EMERGENCY, EXECUTOR PAGE!
THE ACADEMY'S OFF-LINE!
SOMETHING'S TAKEN OUT ALL THE ELECTRICITY!
INCLUDING IMAI'S TRANSCEIVER?
PANT
PANT
YES, SIR! WE CAN'T REACH ANY OF THE GUARDS INSIDE!
AND WE CAN'T OPEN THE CARDKEY LOCKS ON THE DOORS!
WE'VE GOT SOME PEOPLE LOOKING AT IT NOW ...
NO GOOD. I'VE TRIED EVERYTHING.
WHAT'S GOING ON IN THERE?
WAKE UP EMILY AND BRING HER ALONG.
!
SHA...
CLICK

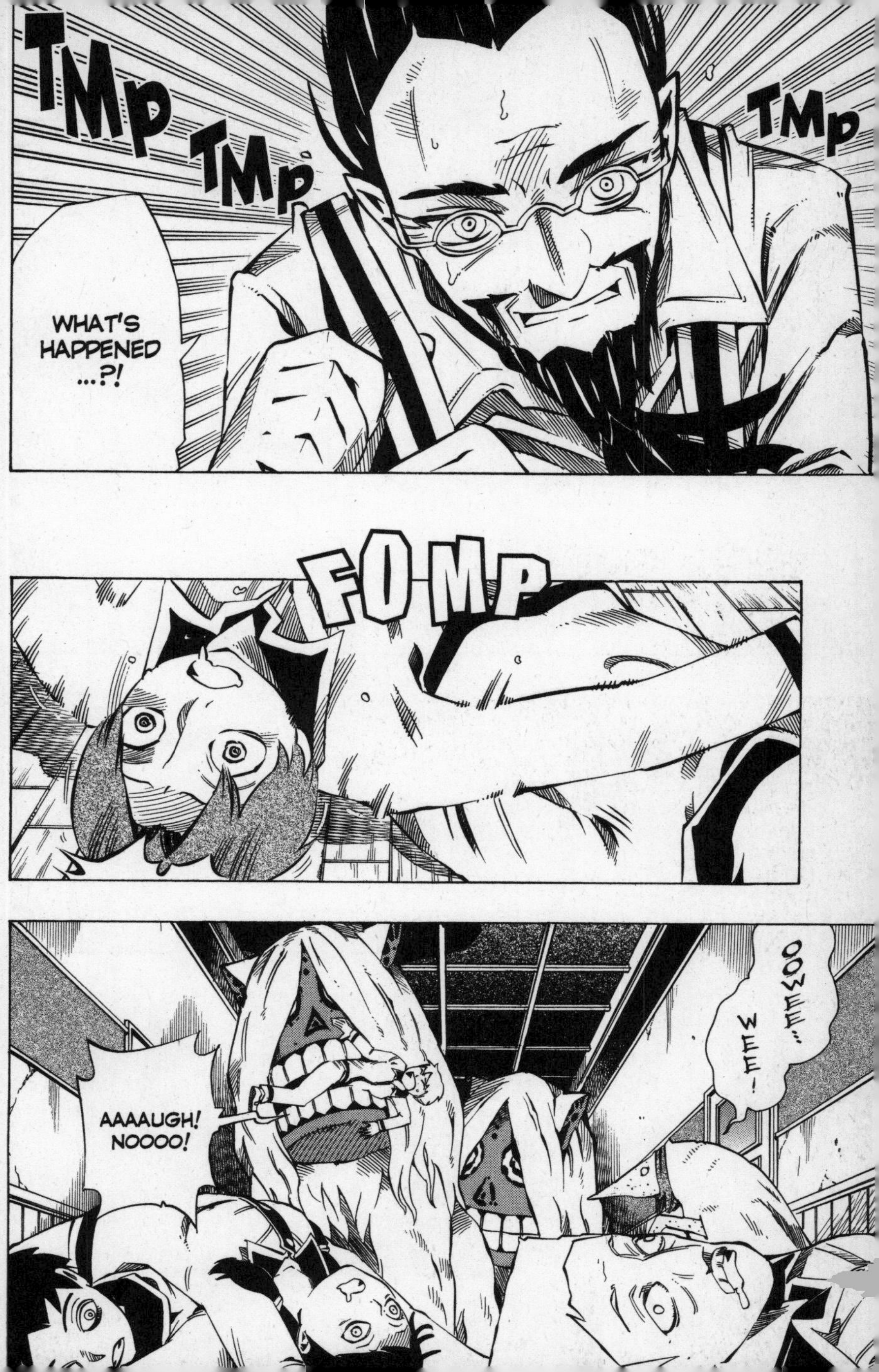
TMP
TMP
TMP
WHAT'S HAPPENED ...?!
FOMP
OOWEE... WEE!
AAAAUGH! NOOOO!

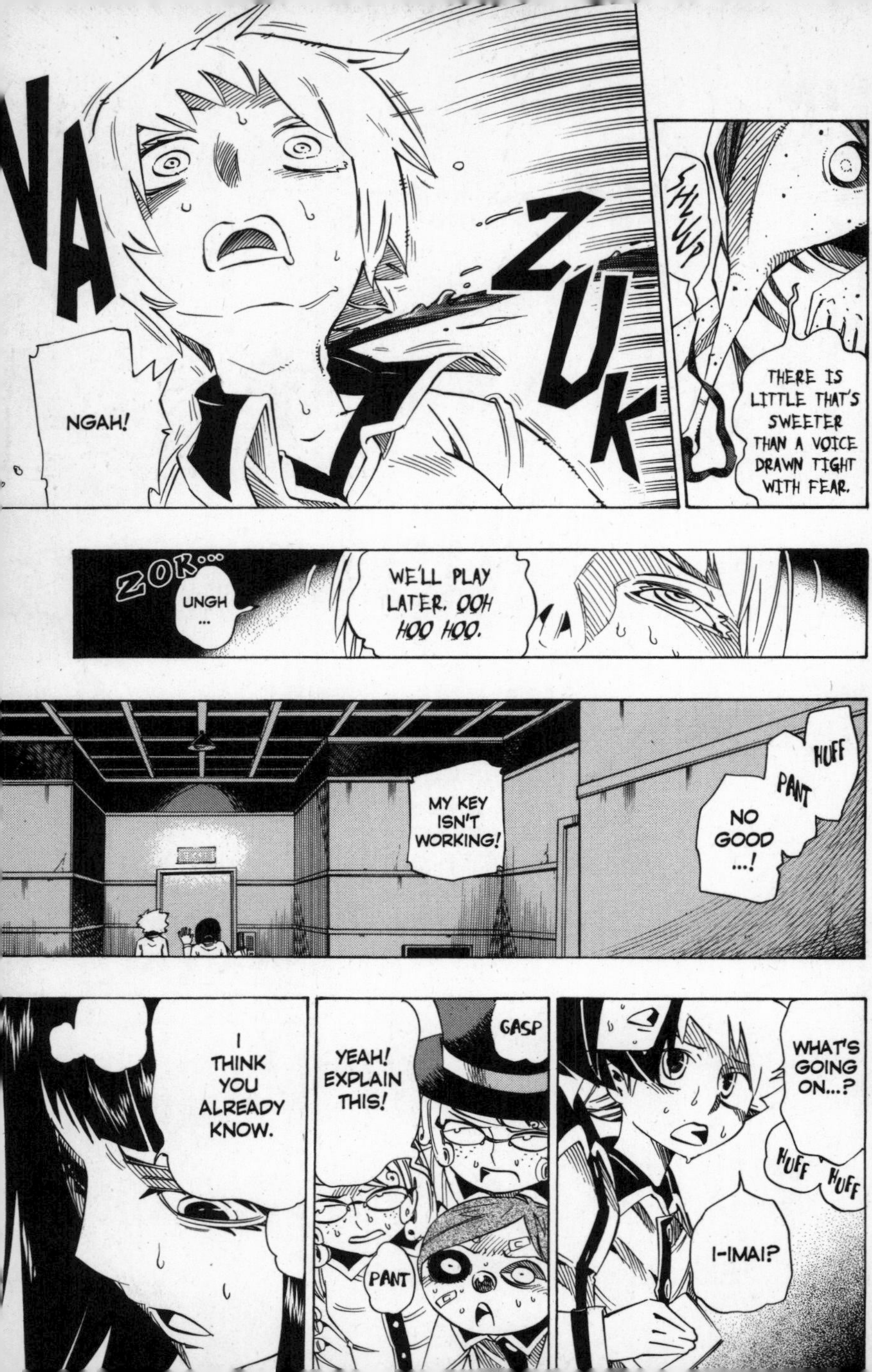
SHLUUP
THERE IS LITTLE THAT'S SWEETER THAN A VOICE DRAWN TIGHT WITH FEAR.
ZUK
VA
NGAH!
WE'LL PLAY LATER. OOH HOO HOO.
ZOK...
UNGH ...
HUFF
PANT
NO GOOD ...!
MY KEY ISN'T WORKING!
WHAT'S GOING ON...?
HUFF
HUFF
I-IMAI?
GASP
YEAH! EXPLAIN THIS!
PANT
I THINK YOU ALREADY KNOW.

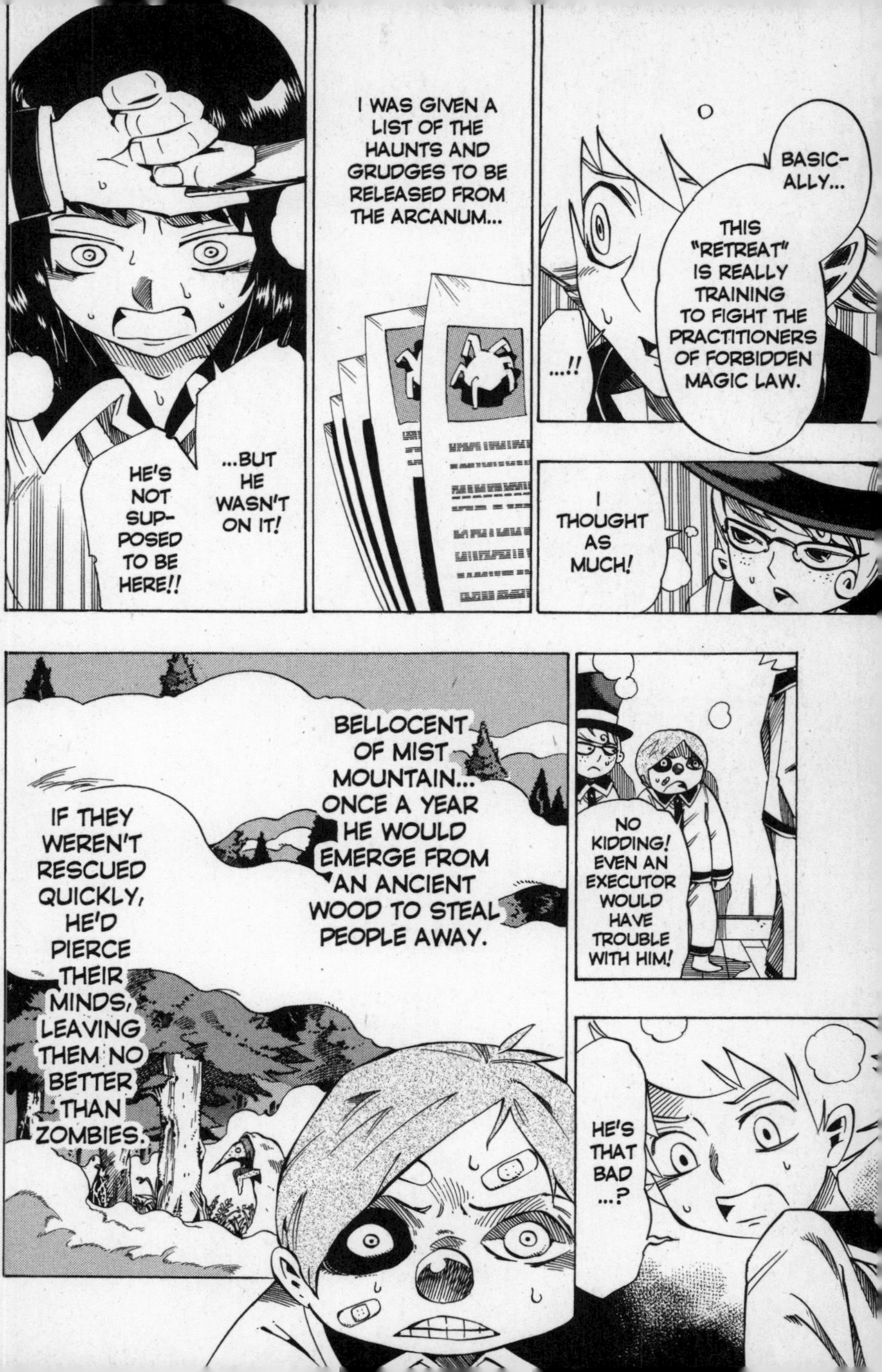
BASICALLY...
THIS "RETREAT" IS REALLY TRAINING TO FIGHT THE PRACTITIONERS OF FORBIDDEN MAGIC LAW.
...!!
I THOUGHT AS MUCH!
I WAS GIVEN A LIST OF THE HAUNTS AND GRUDGES TO BE RELEASED FROM THE ARCANUM...
...BUT HE WASN'T ON IT!
HE'S NOT SUPPOSED TO BE HERE!!
NO KIDDING! EVEN AN EXECUTOR WOULD HAVE TROUBLE WITH HIM!
HE'S THAT BAD ...?
BELLOCENT OF MIST MOUNTAIN... ONCE A YEAR HE WOULD EMERGE FROM AN ANCIENT WOOD TO STEAL PEOPLE AWAY.
IF THEY WEREN'T RESCUED QUICKLY, HE'D PIERCE THEIR MINDS, LEAVING THEM NO BETTER THAN ZOMBIES.

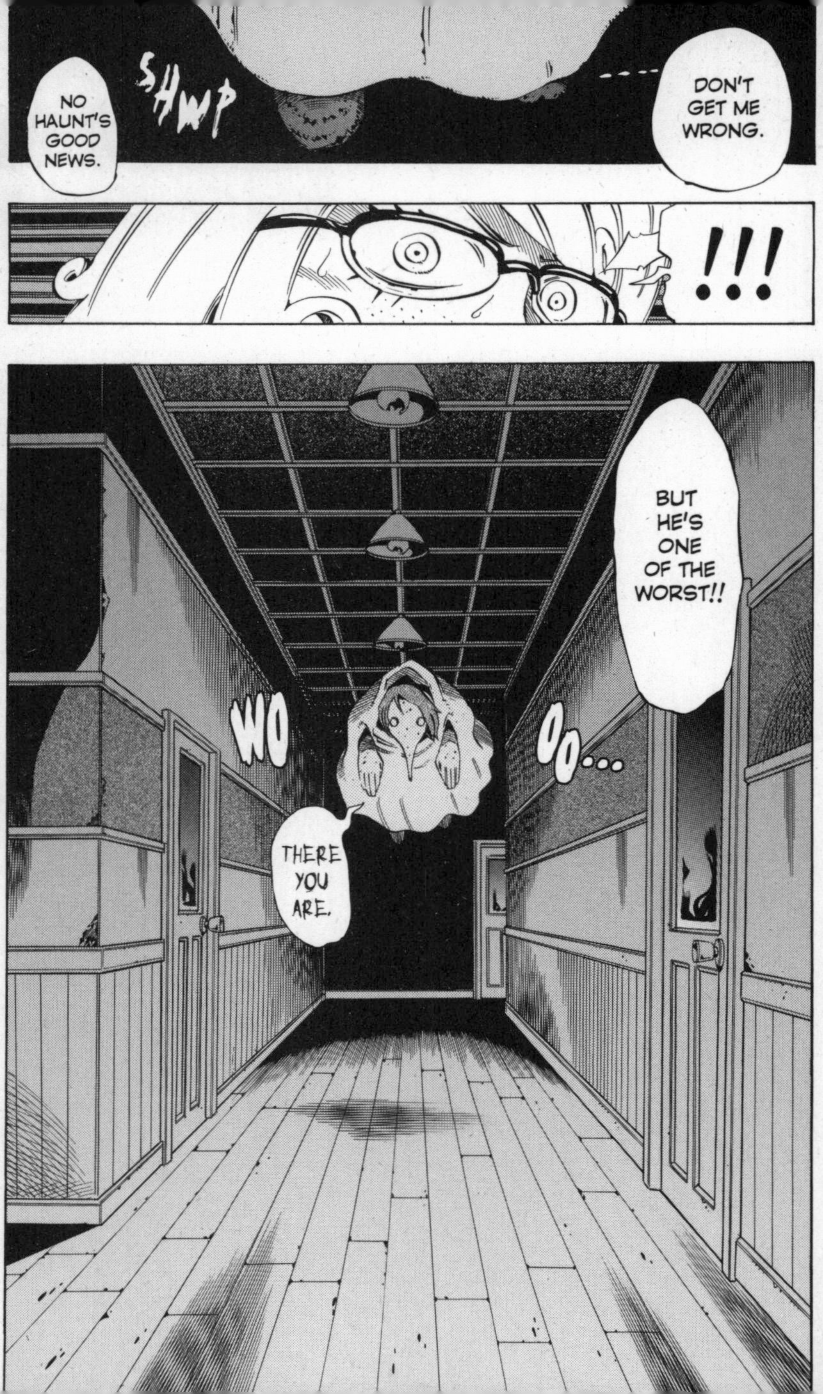
DON'T GET ME WRONG.
SHWP
NO HAUNT'S GOOD NEWS.
!!!
BUT HE'S ONE OF THE WORST!!
WO OO...
THERE YOU ARE.

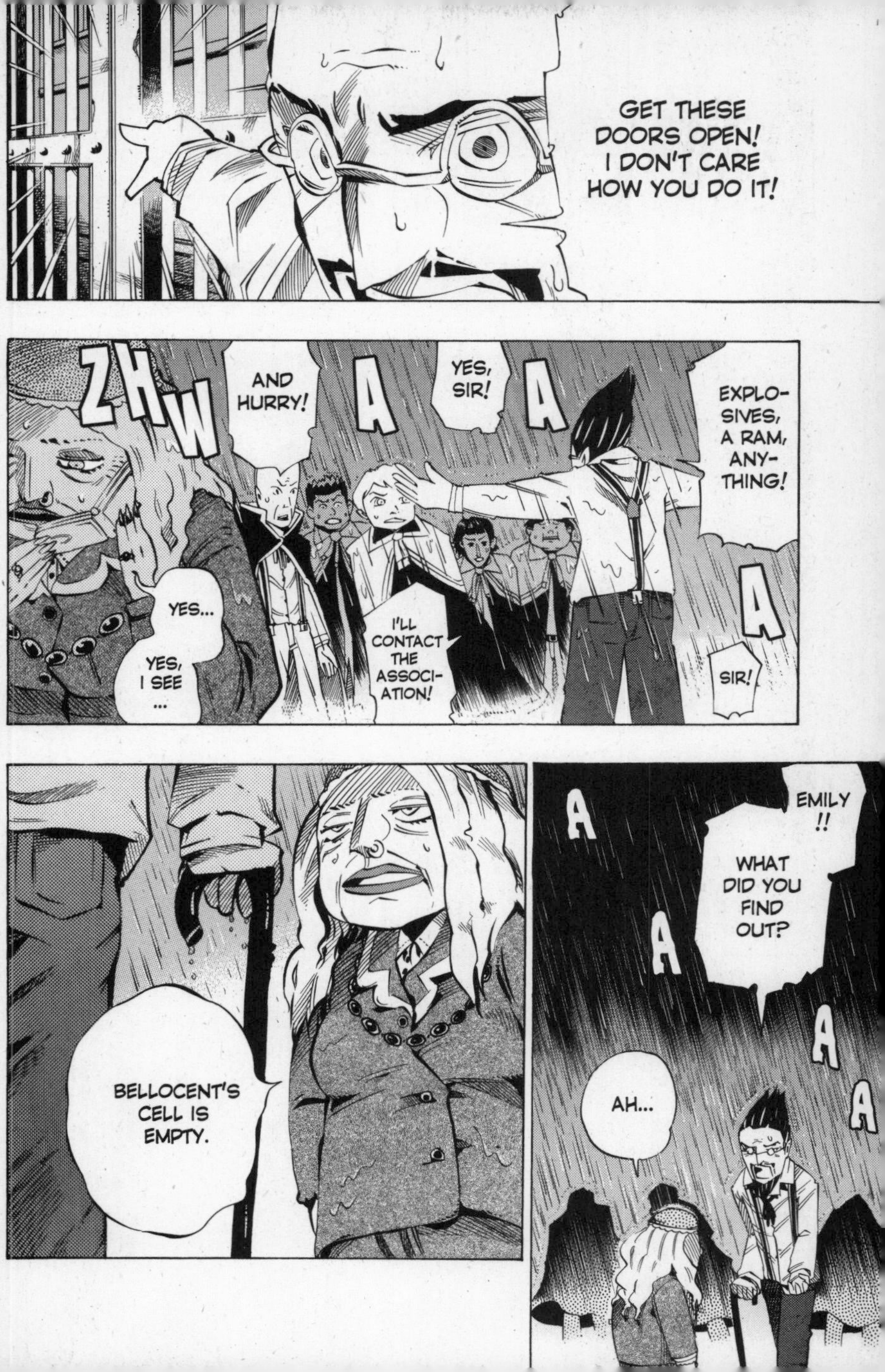
GET THESE DOORS OPEN! I DON'T CARE HOW YOU DO IT!
EXPLOSIVES, A RAM, ANYTHING!
A
YES, SIR!
A
AND HURRY!
ZHW
A
SIR!
I'LL CONTACT THE ASSOCIATION!
YES...
YES, I SEE ...
EMILY!!
WHAT DID YOU FIND OUT?
A
A
A
A
AH...
BELLOCENT'S CELL IS EMPTY.

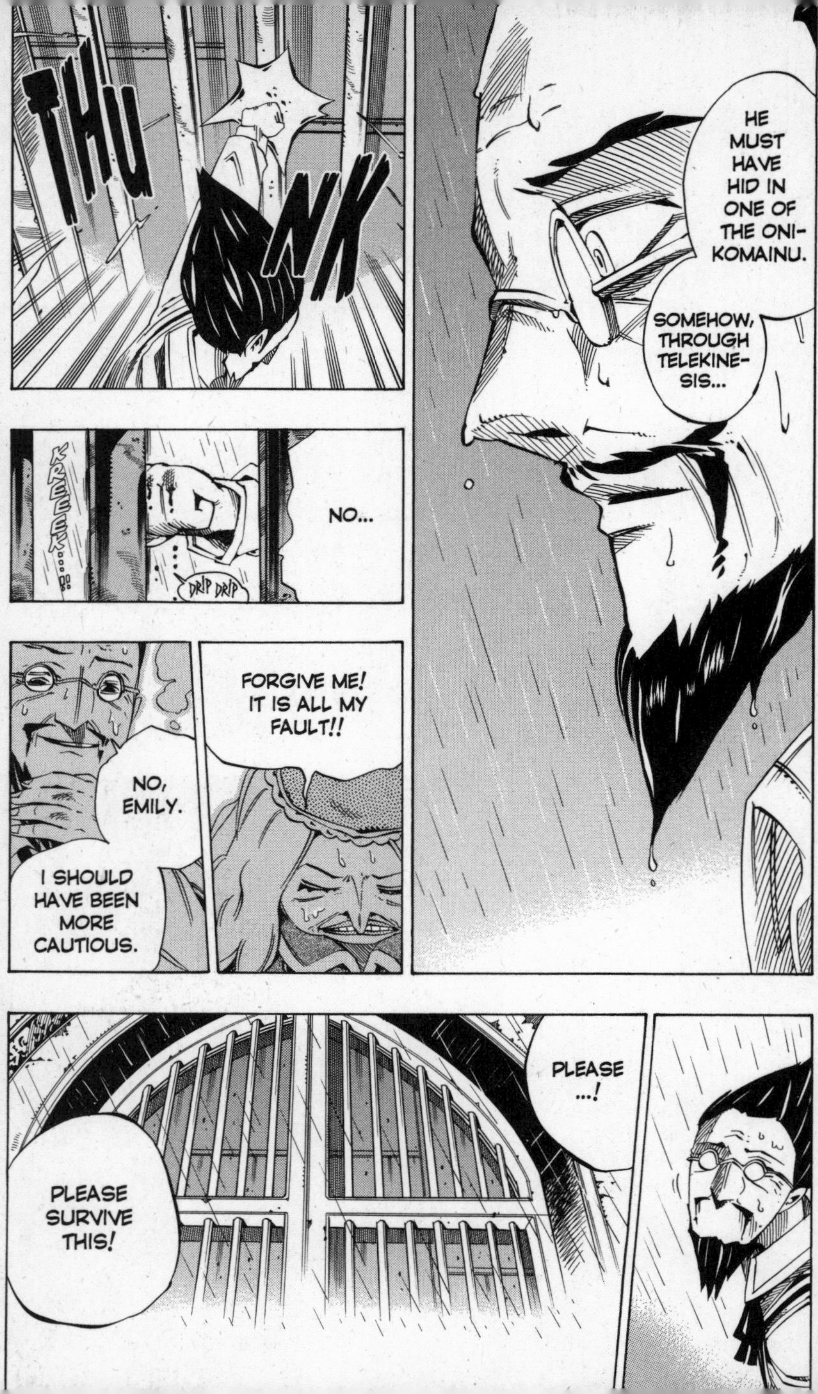
HE MUST HAVE HID IN ONE OF THE ONI-KOMAINU.
SOMEHOW, THROUGH TELEKINE-SIS...
THUNK
KREEEK...
NO...
DRIP DRIP
FORGIVE ME! IT IS ALL MY FAULT!!
NO, EMILY.
I SHOULD HAVE BEEN MORE CAUTIOUS.
PLEASE ...!
PLEASE SURVIVE THIS!

Q: OKAY, IN VOLUME 3, ARTICLE 20,
WHILE ROJI IS LOOKING UP STUFF
ON ARTIFICERS, MUHYO CHANGES
CLOTHES! HOW FAST CAN HE CHANGE
CLOTHES, ANYWAY? AND WHAT WAS
BIKO DOING, HUH?
     —Y.M., IBARAKI PREFECTURE

A: OHHHH BOY. (THIS IS A TOUGH ONE...
THEY'RE HITTING ME WHERE IT HURTS!)
AHEM. UH, WELL... I KNOW! BIKO WAS
HELPING HIM! SEE? HERE'S A DIAGRAM...

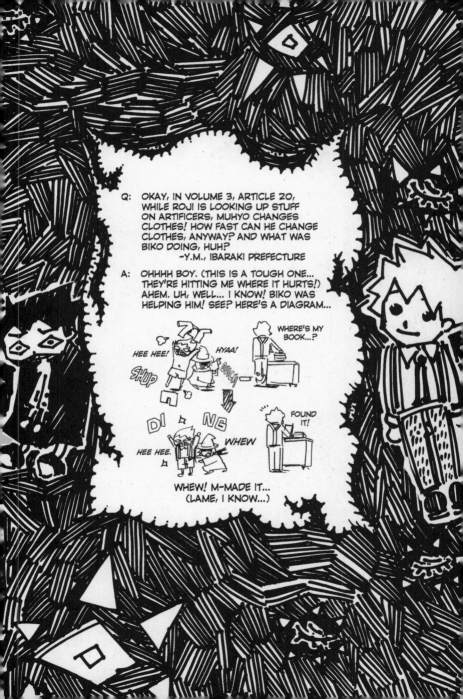

HEE HEE!

HYAA!

SHUP

WHERE'S MY
BOOK...?

DI   NE

HEE HEE.   WHEW

FOUND
IT!

WHEW! M-MADE IT...
(LAME, I KNOW...)

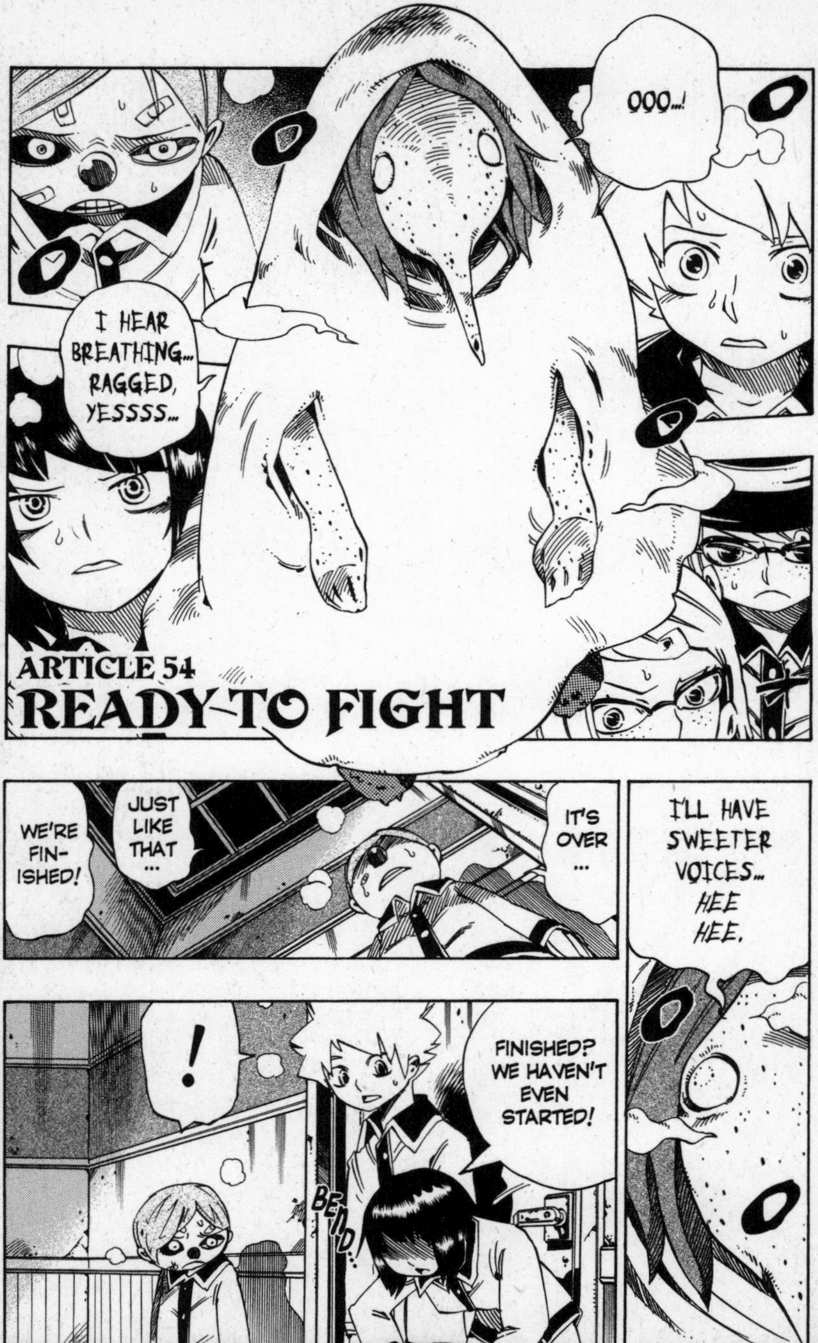
OOO...!
I HEAR BREATHING... RAGGED, YESSSS...
ARTICLE 54
READY TO FIGHT
I'LL HAVE SWEETER VOICES... HEE HEE.
IT'S OVER ...
JUST LIKE THAT ...
WE'RE FIN-ISHED!
FINISHED? WE HAVEN'T EVEN STARTED!
!
BEND

CIRCLE OF HEXI-
DIRECTIONAL
DISSIPATING
HANDS!

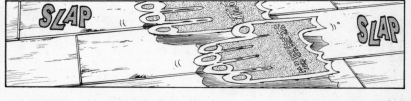

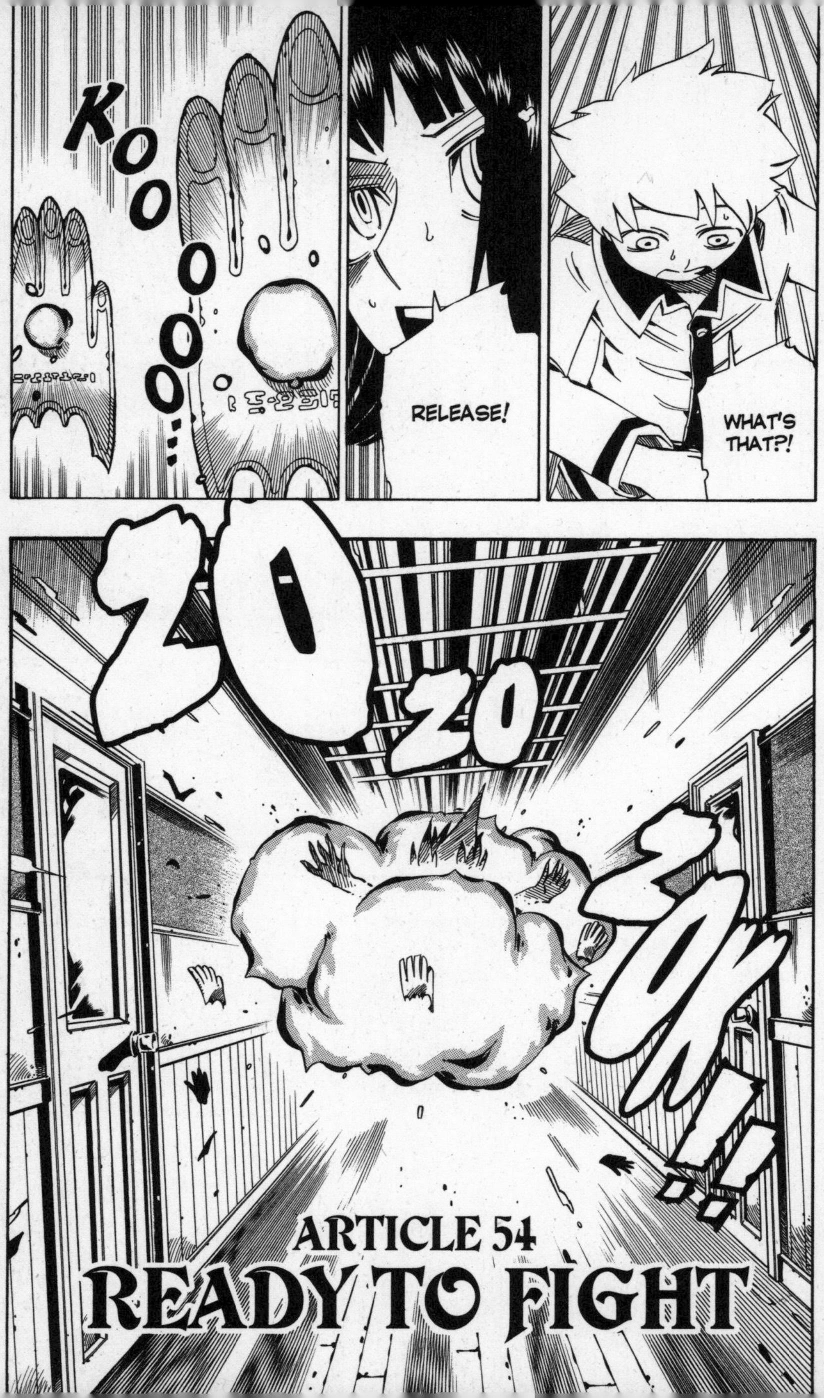
WHAT'S THAT?!
RELEASE!
KOOOOOO...
ZO
ZO

ARTICLE 54
READY TO FIGHT

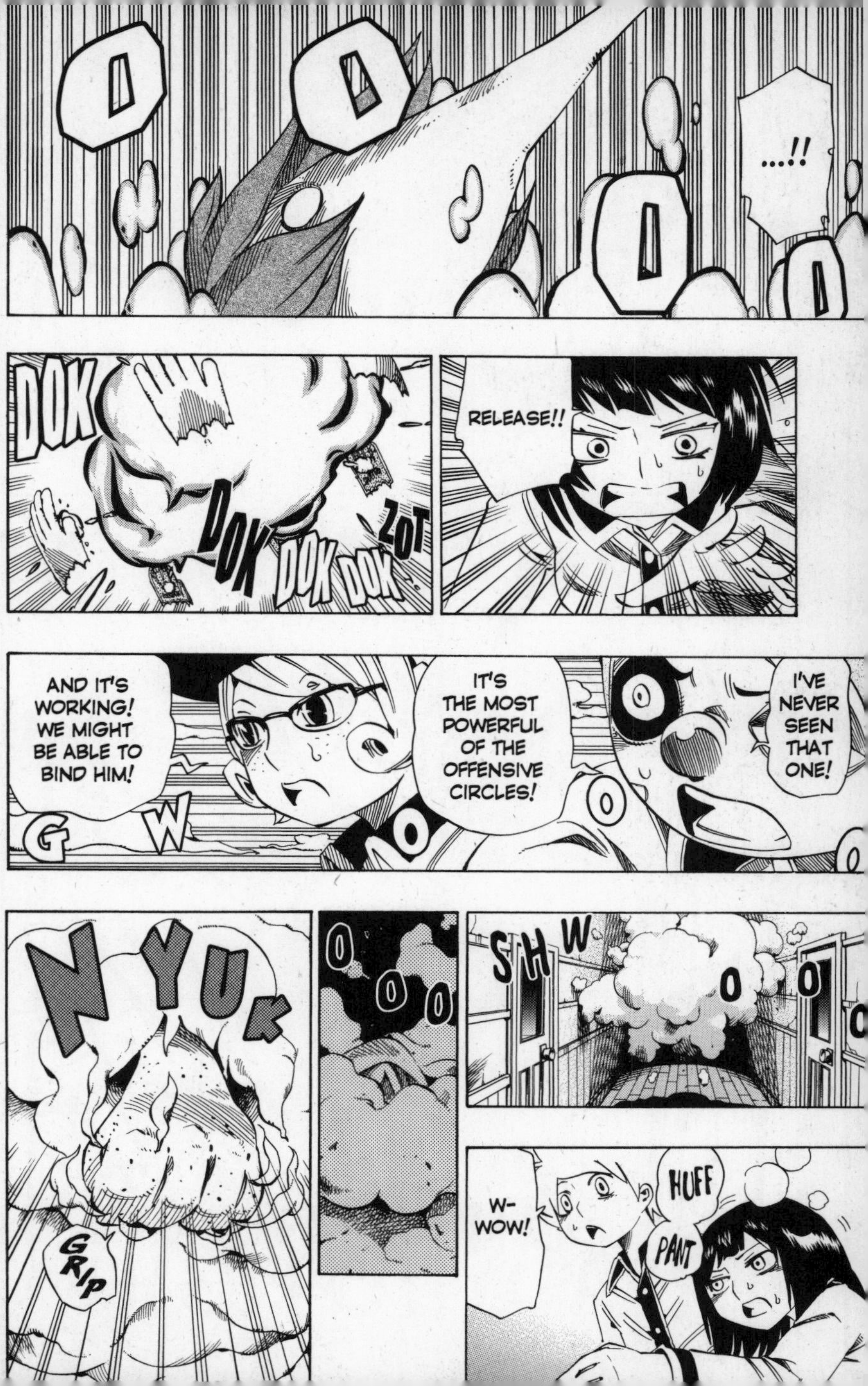
...!!
RELEASE!!
DOK
DOK DOK DOK
ZOT
I'VE NEVER SEEN THAT ONE!
IT'S THE MOST POWERFUL OF THE OFFENSIVE CIRCLES!
AND IT'S WORKING! WE MIGHT BE ABLE TO BIND HIM!
G W
SHW
W- WOW!
HUFF
PANT
NYUK
GRIP

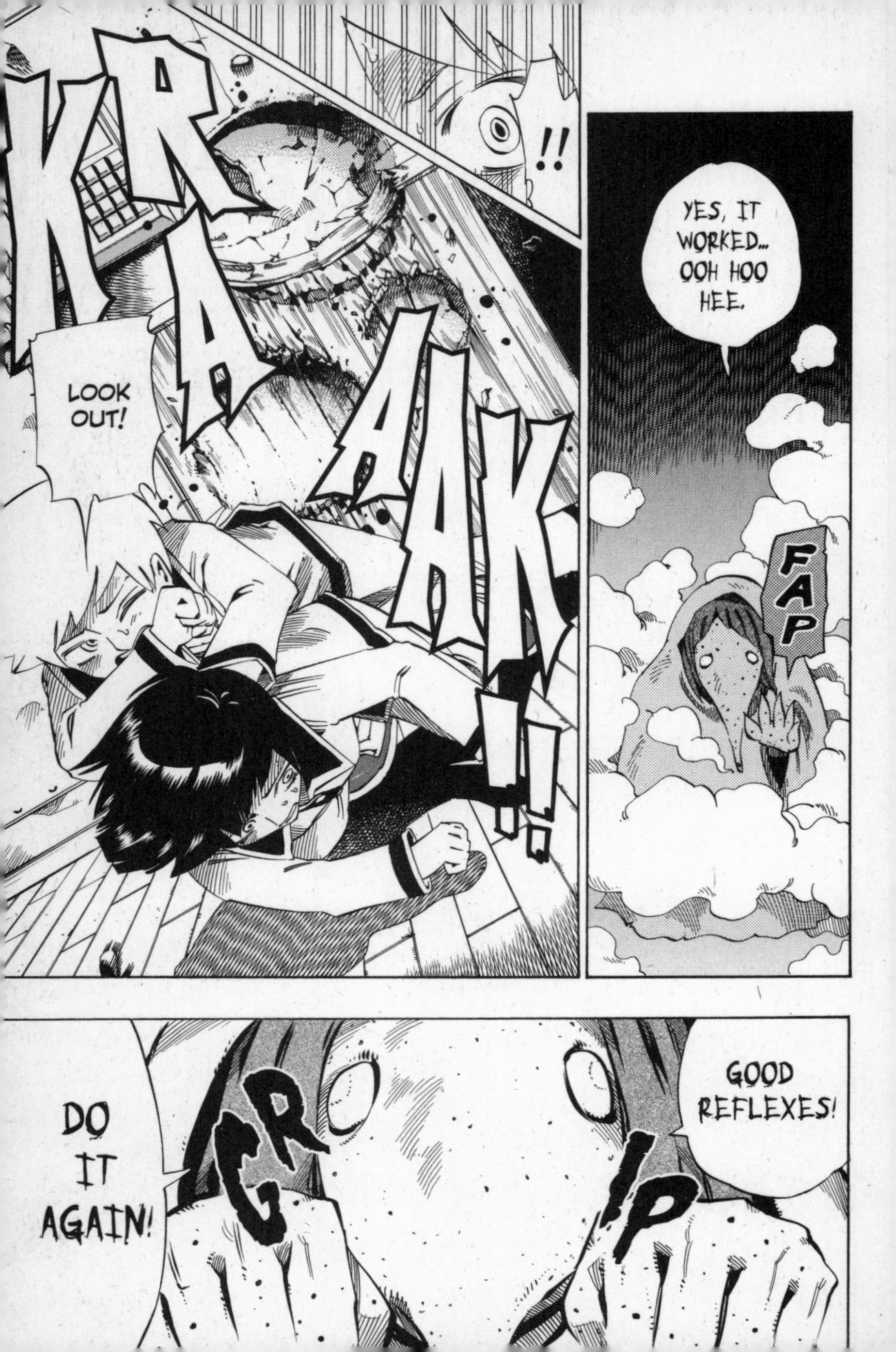
YES, IT WORKED... OOH HOO HEE.
FAP
!!
KRAAAK!!!
LOOK OUT!
GOOD REFLEXES!
GRIP
DO IT AGAIN!

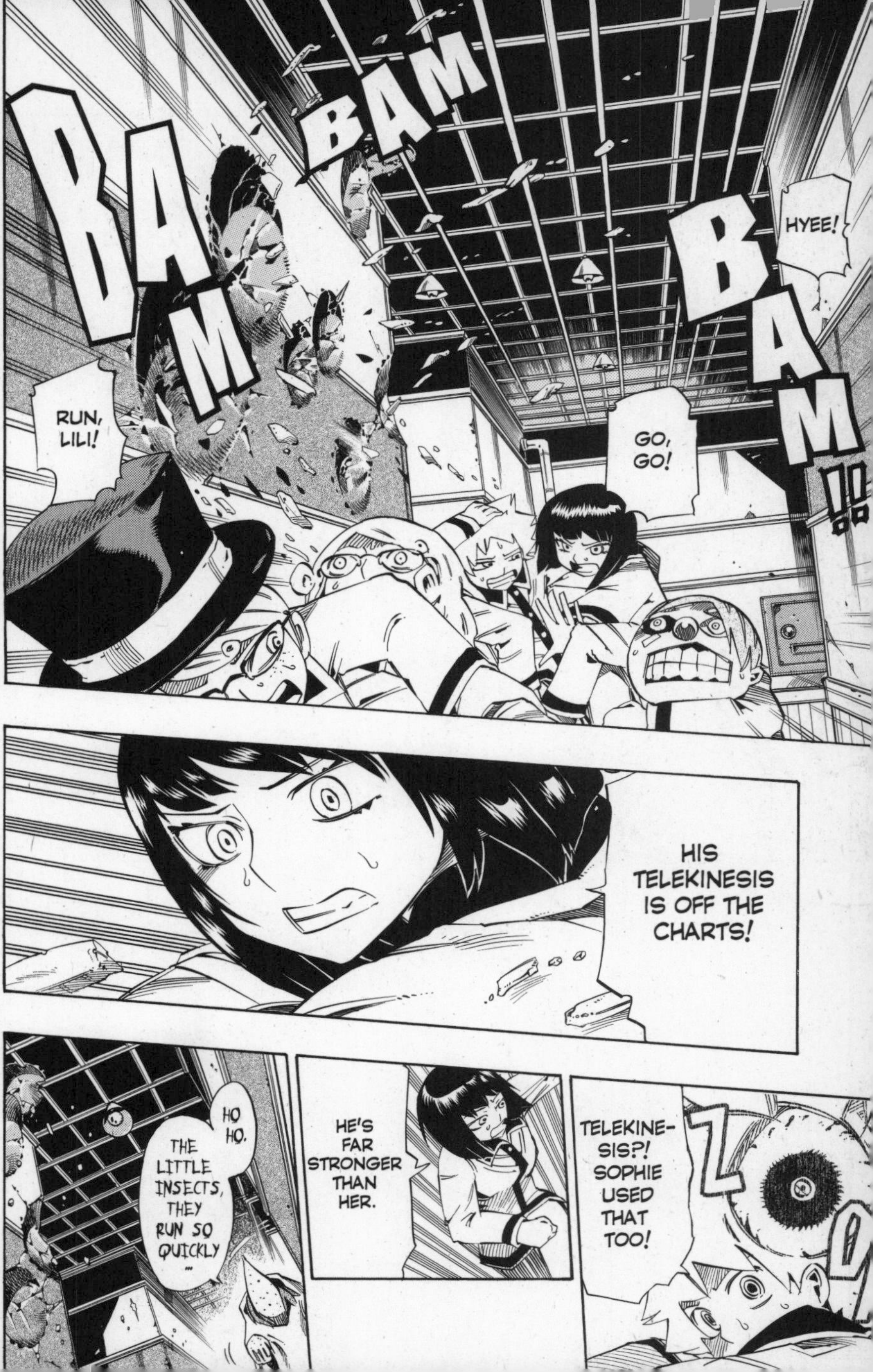
HYEE!
BAM BAM!!
BAM
GO, GO!
BAM
RUN, LILI!
HIS TELEKINESIS IS OFF THE CHARTS!
TELEKINE-SIS?! SOPHIE USED THAT TOO!
HE'S FAR STRONGER THAN HER.
HO HO.
THE LITTLE INSECTS, THEY RUN SO QUICKLY...

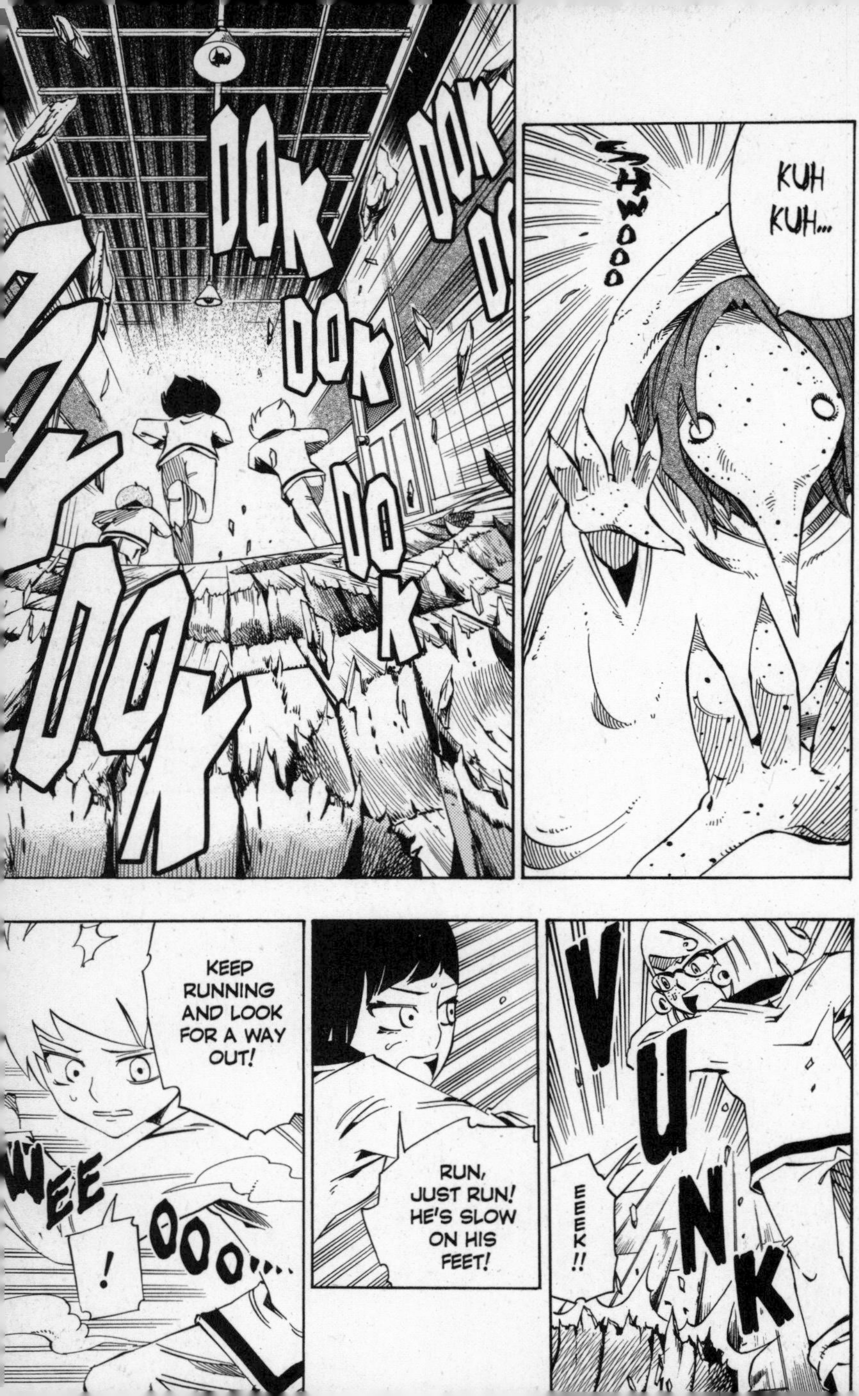
KUH KUH...
SHWOOOO
DOK
DOK
DOK
DOK
DOOK
DOK
EEEK!!
VUNK
RUN, JUST RUN! HE'S SLOW ON HIS FEET!
KEEP RUNNING AND LOOK FOR A WAY OUT!
WEE
!
OOO...

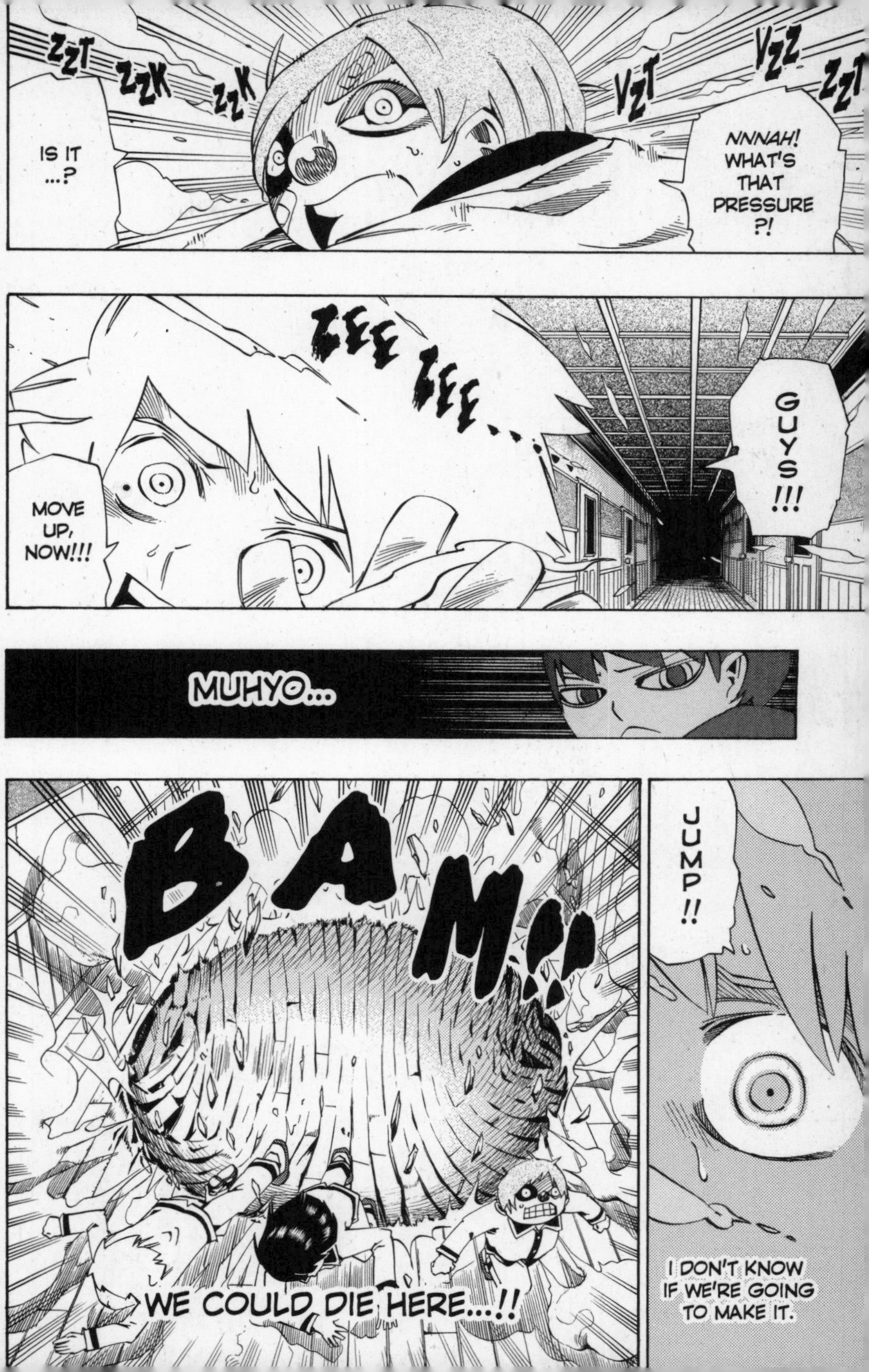
ZZT
VZZ
VZT
NNNAH! WHAT'S THAT PRESSURE ?!
ZZK
ZZK
ZZT
IS IT ...?
GUYS!!!
ZEE ZEE...
MOVE UP, NOW!!!
MUHYO...
JUMP!!
I DON'T KNOW IF WE'RE GOING TO MAKE IT.
BAM!!
WE COULD DIE HERE...!!

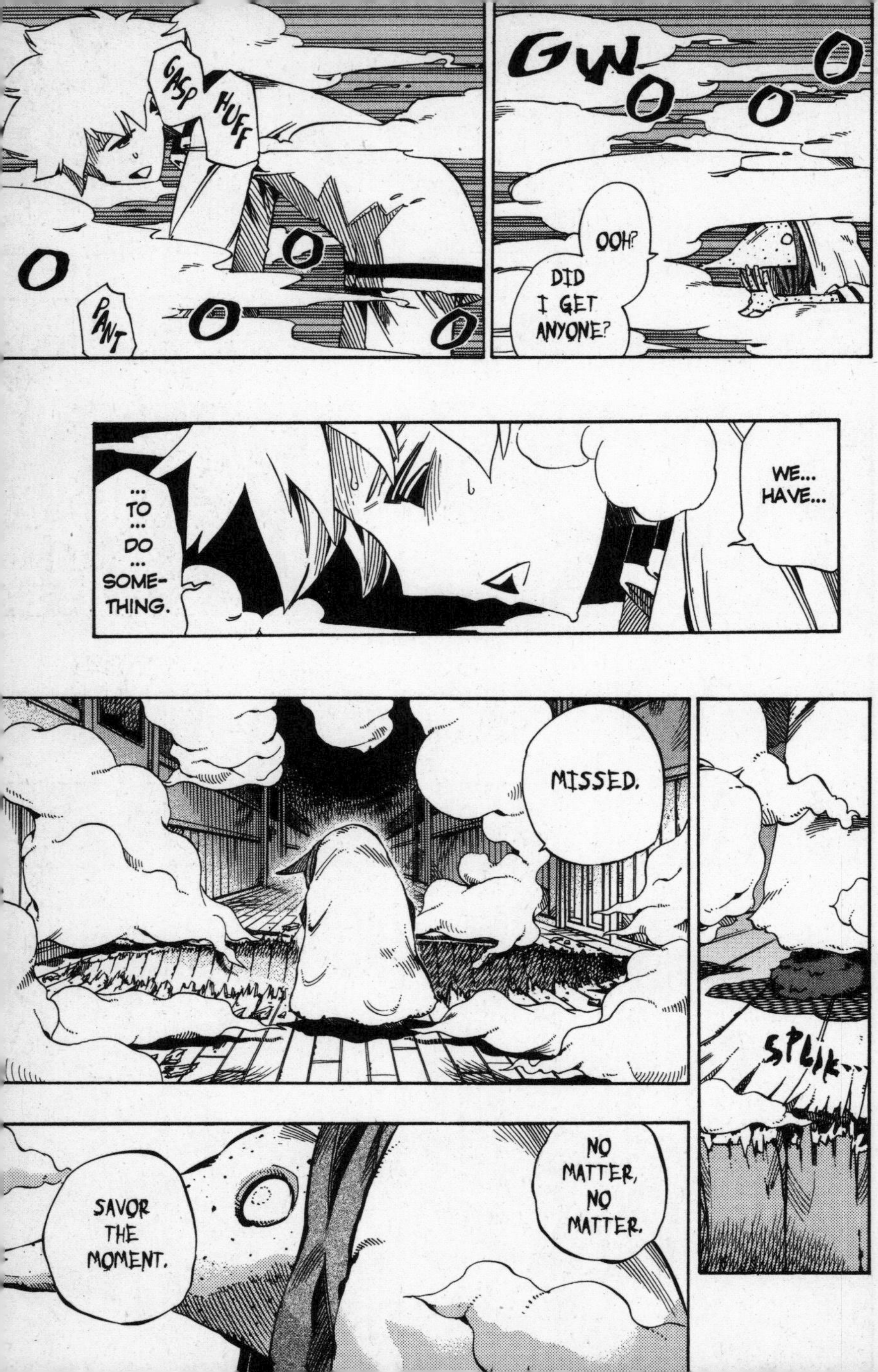
GWOOO
OOH?
DID I GET ANYONE?
GASP
HUFF
OOOO
PANT
WE... HAVE...
...TO...DO...SOME-THING.
SPLIK...
MISSED.
NO MATTER, NO MATTER.
SAVOR THE MOMENT.

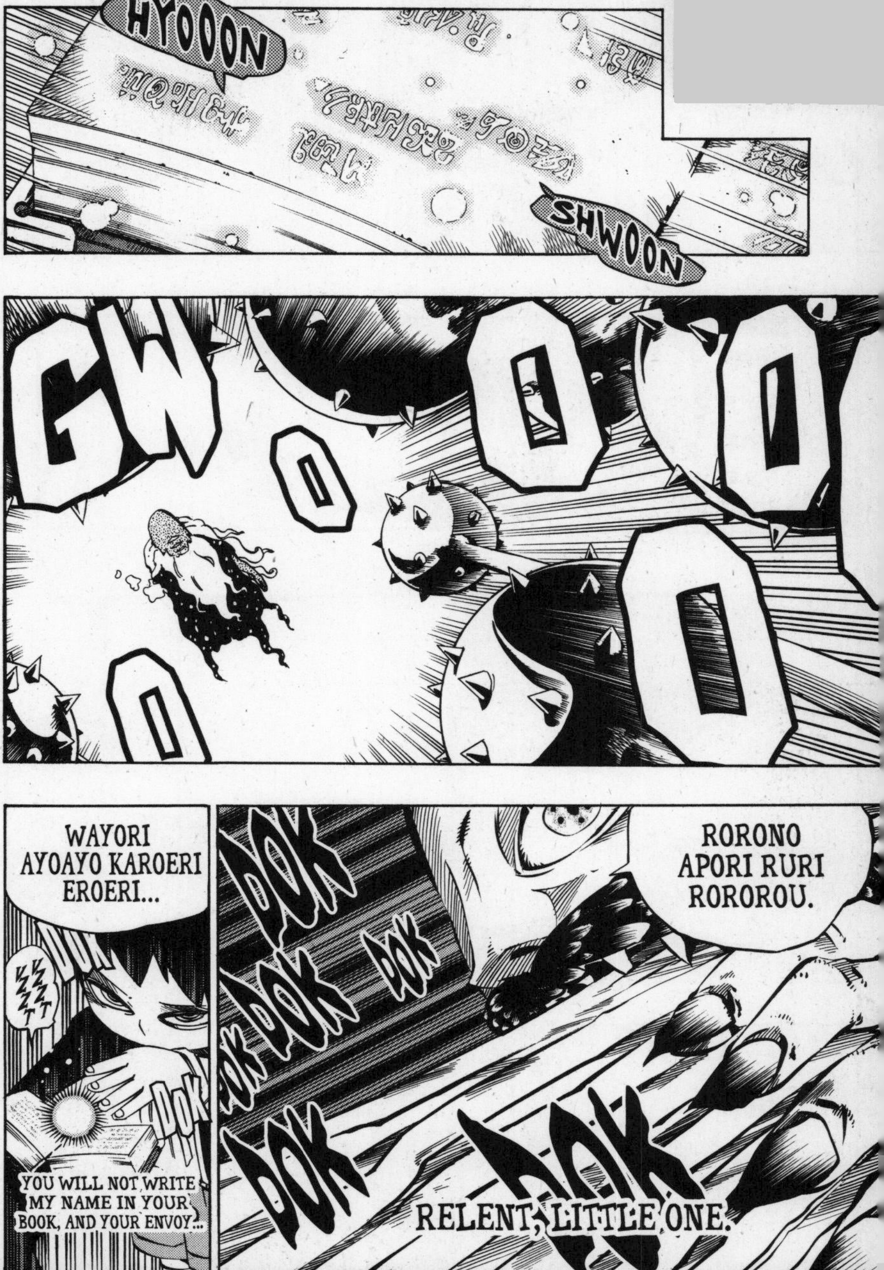
HYOOON
SHWOON
GWOOOOOO
RORONO APORI RURI ROROROU.
DOK DOK DOK DOK DOK
DOK DOK
RELENT, LITTLE ONE.
WAYORI AYOAYO KAROERI EROERI...
DOK
DOK
YOU WILL NOT WRITE MY NAME IN YOUR BOOK, AND YOUR ENVOY...

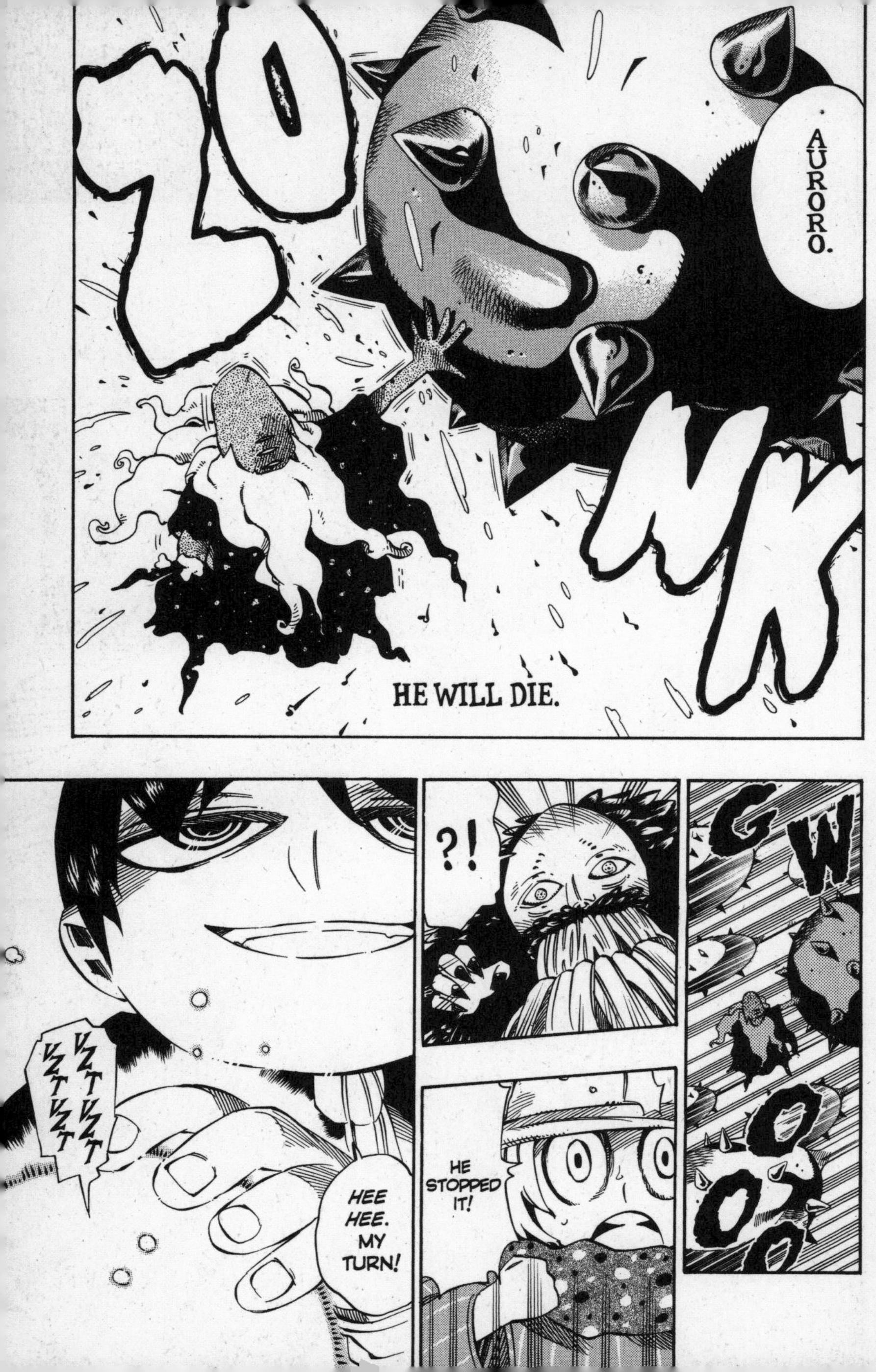

AURORO.
HE WILL DIE.
GWOOOO
?!
HE STOPPED IT!
HEE HEE. MY TURN!
VZTVZT VZTVZT

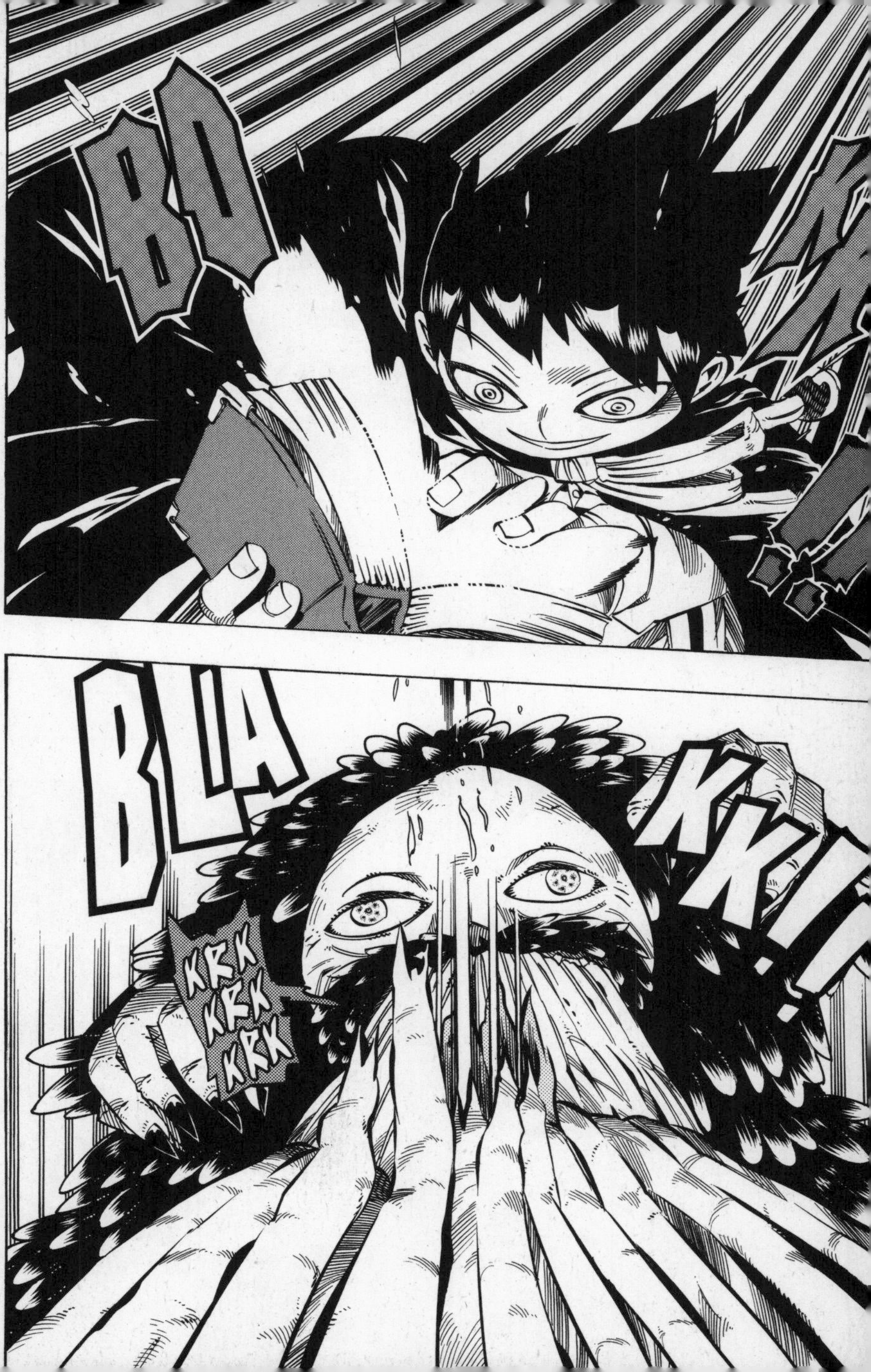
BO
BLA
KK!!
KRK
KRK
KRK

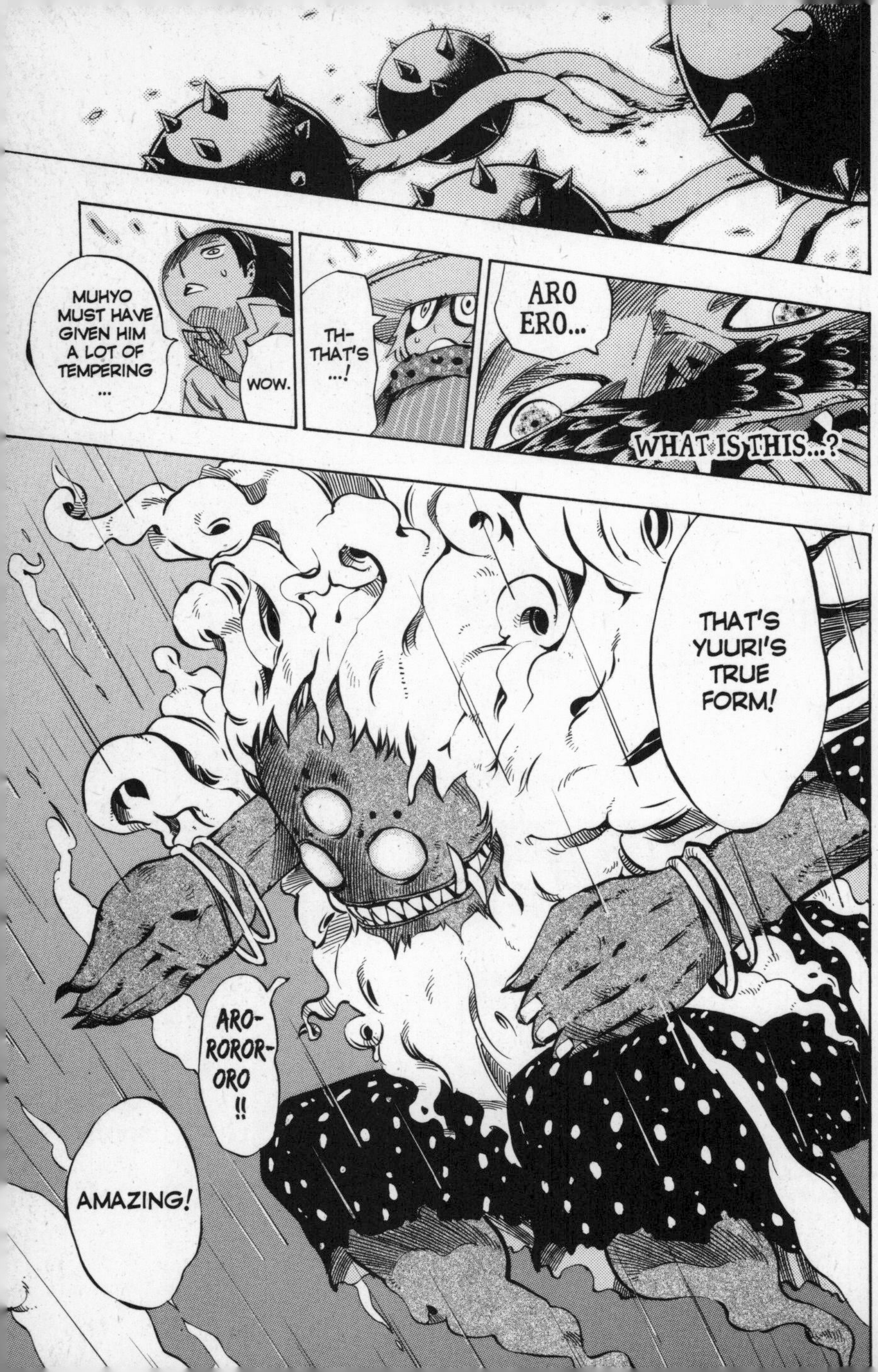
ARO ERO...
WHAT IS THIS...?
TH-THAT'S ...!
WOW.
MUHYO MUST HAVE GIVEN HIM A LOT OF TEMPERING ...
THAT'S YUURI'S TRUE FORM!
ARO-ROROR-ORO !!
AMAZING!

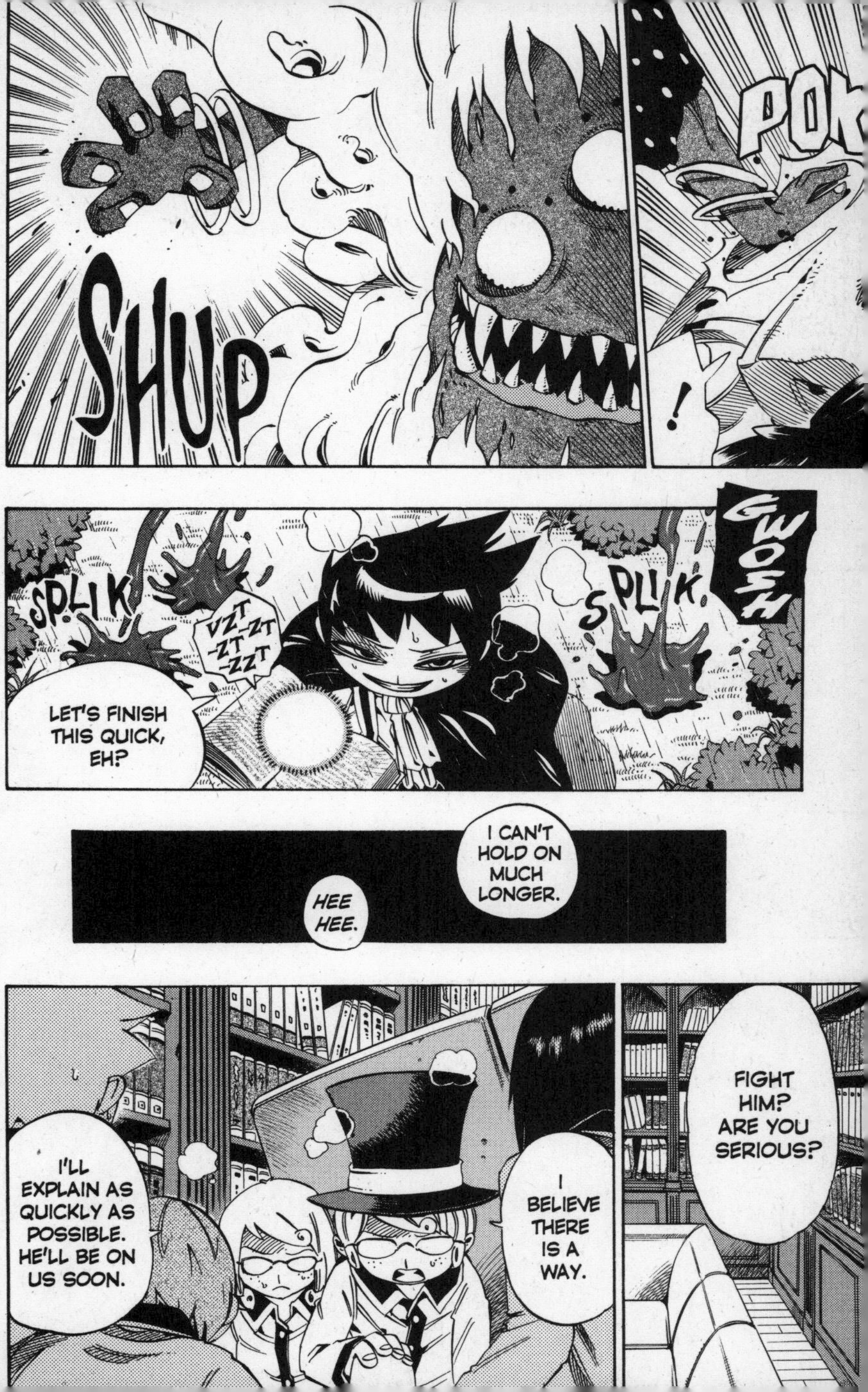
POK
!
SHUP
GWOSH
SPLIK
SPLIK
VZZT -ZT-ZT -ZT -ZZT
LET'S FINISH THIS QUICK, EH?
I CAN'T HOLD ON MUCH LONGER.
HEE HEE.
FIGHT HIM? ARE YOU SERIOUS?
I BELIEVE THERE IS A WAY.
I'LL EXPLAIN AS QUICKLY AS POSSIBLE. HE'LL BE ON US SOON.

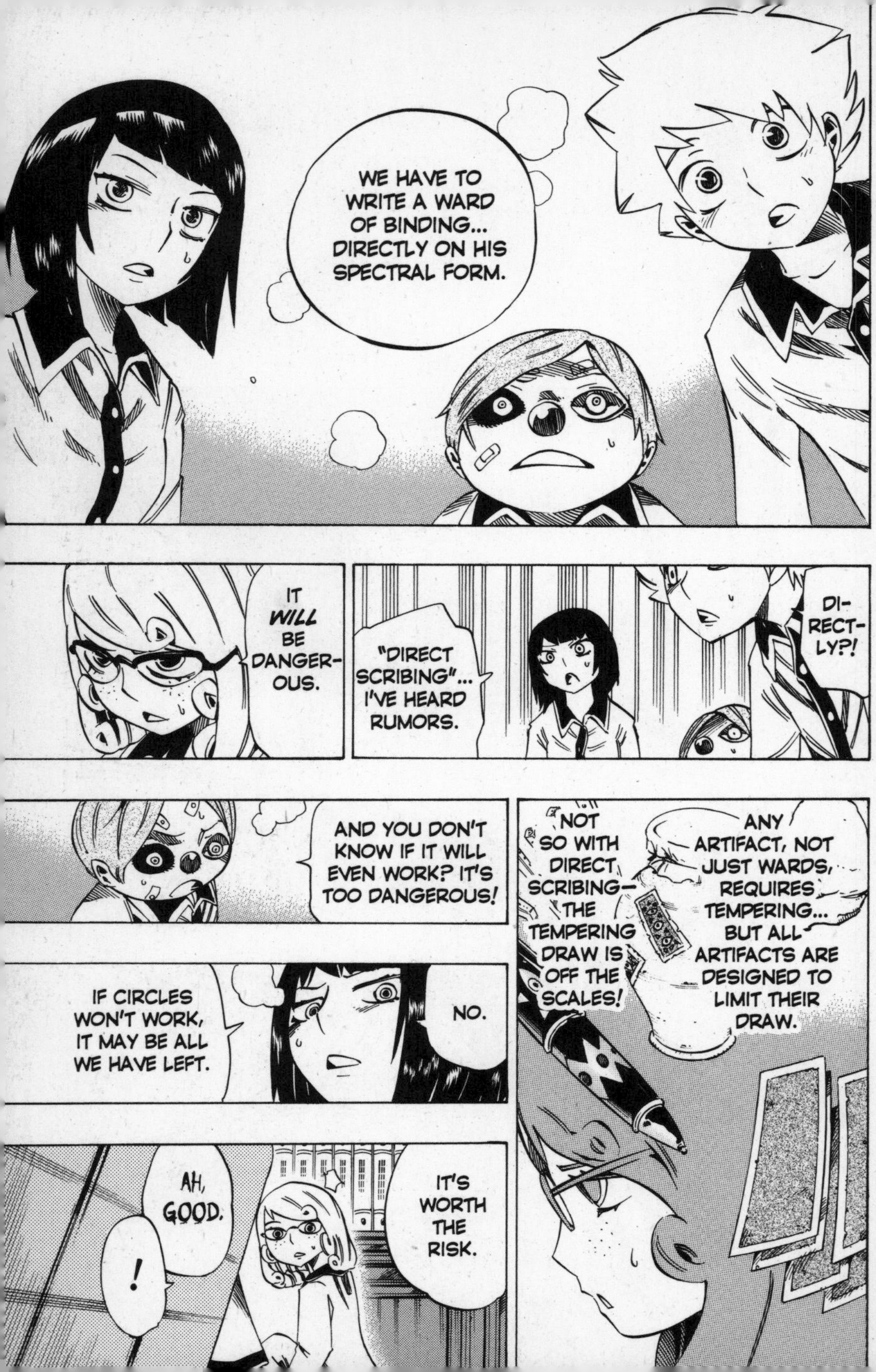
WE HAVE TO WRITE A WARD OF BINDING... DIRECTLY ON HIS SPECTRAL FORM.
DI-RECT-LY?!
"DIRECT SCRIBING"... I'VE HEARD RUMORS.
IT *WILL* BE DANGER-OUS.
ANY ARTIFACT, NOT JUST WARDS, REQUIRES TEMPERING... BUT ALL ARTIFACTS ARE DESIGNED TO LIMIT THEIR DRAW.
NOT SO WITH DIRECT SCRIBING—THE TEMPERING DRAW IS OFF THE SCALES!
AND YOU DON'T KNOW IF IT WILL EVEN WORK? IT'S TOO DANGEROUS!
NO.
IF CIRCLES WON'T WORK, IT MAY BE ALL WE HAVE LEFT.
IT'S WORTH THE RISK.
AH, GOOD.
!

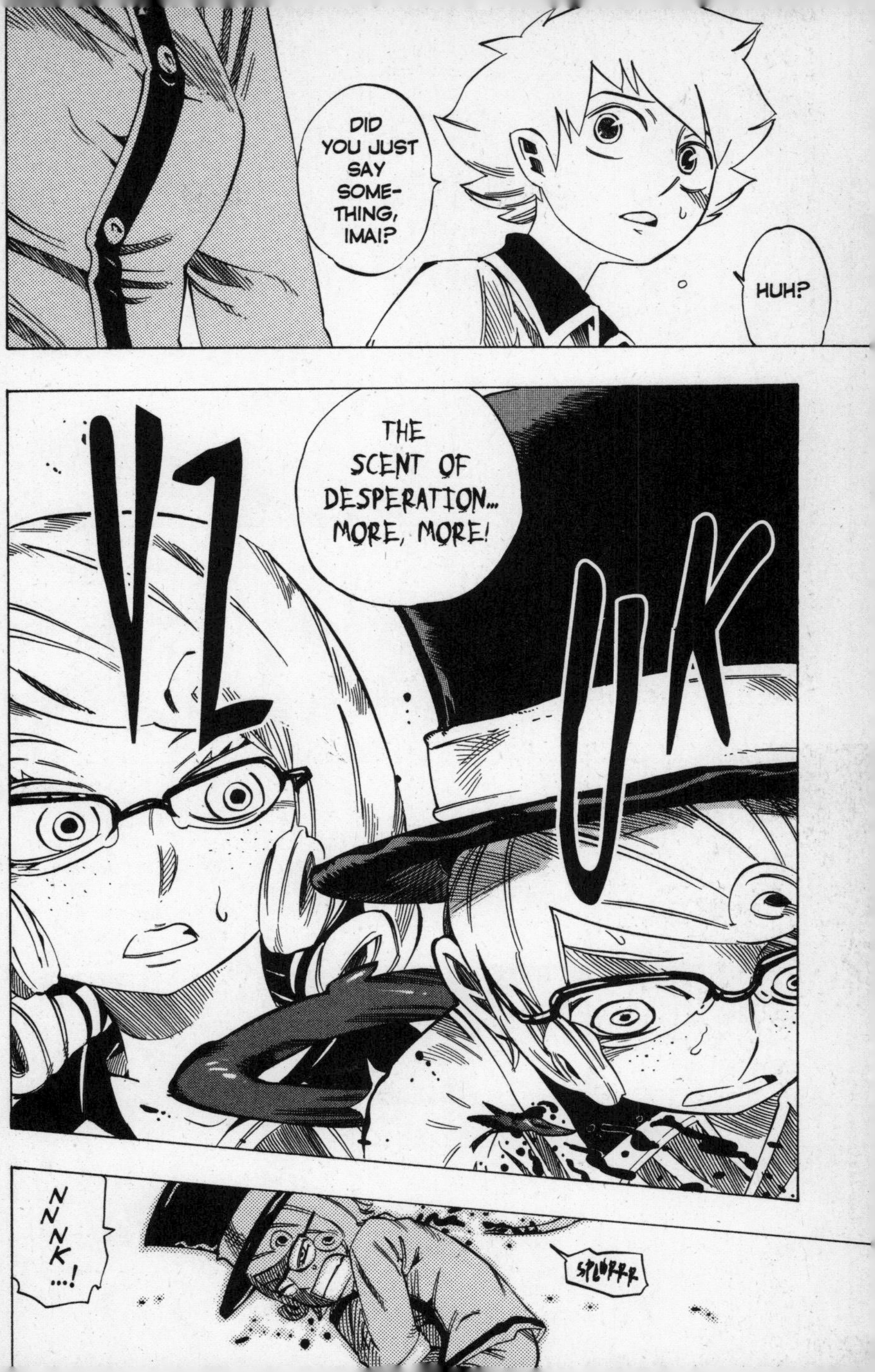
HUH?
DID YOU JUST SAY SOME-THING, IMAI?
THE SCENT OF DESPERATION... MORE, MORE!
VZ
UK
SPLURRR
NNNK...!

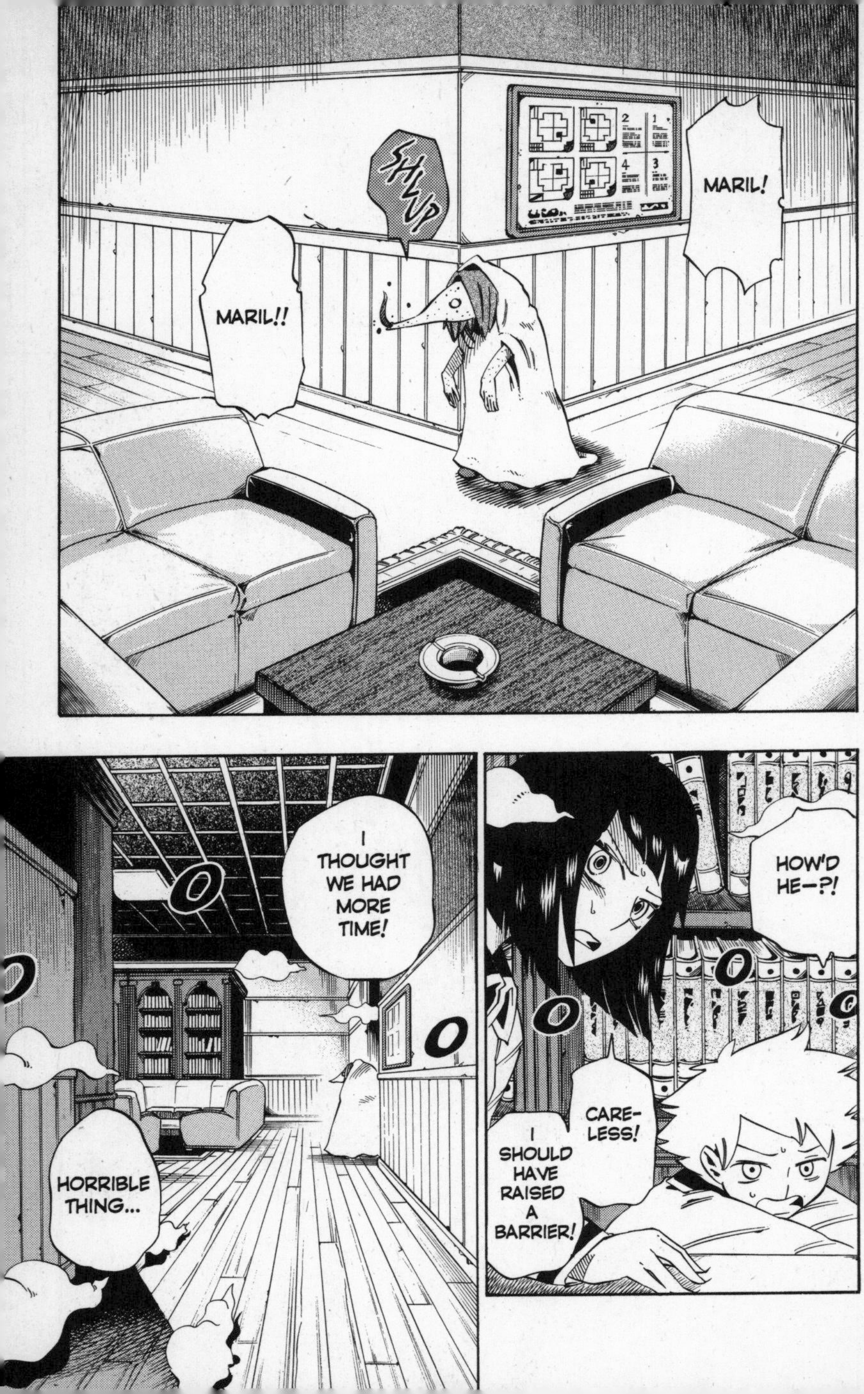
MARIL!
SHWP
MARIL!!
HOW'D HE—?!
CARE-LESS!
I SHOULD HAVE RAISED A BARRIER!
I THOUGHT WE HAD MORE TIME!
HORRIBLE THING...

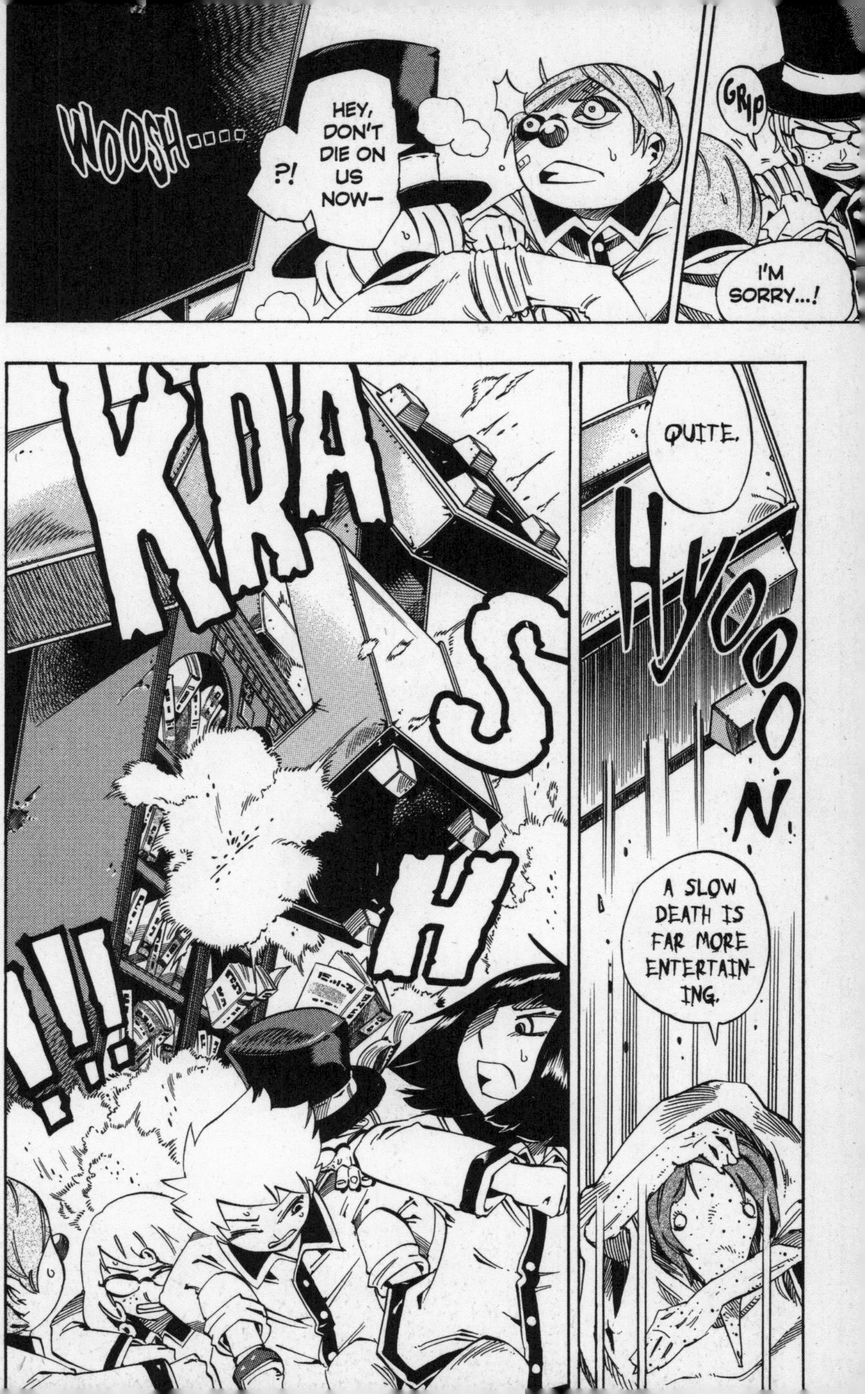
GRIP
I'M SORRY...!
HEY, DON'T DIE ON US NOW—
?!
WOOSH.....
QUITE.
HYOOON
A SLOW DEATH IS FAR MORE ENTERTAIN-ING.
KRASH
!!!

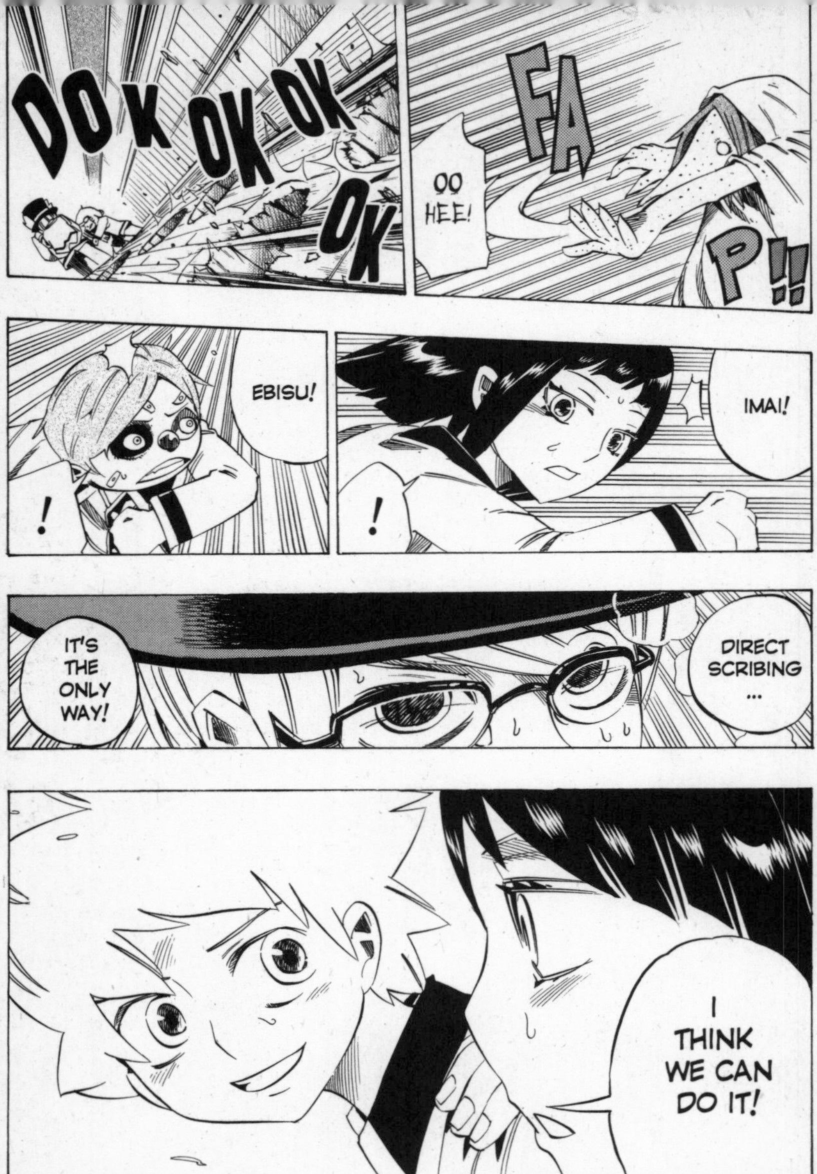
FA
P!!
OO HEE!
DOKOKOKOK
IMAI!
!
EBISU!
!
DIRECT SCRIBING ...
IT'S THE ONLY WAY!
I THINK WE CAN DO IT!

Q: I'VE SEEN PICTURES OF LITTLE TOMATO AND RIKOPIN MAN ON ROJI'S APRON AND THE COVER OF *JABIN*... ARE THESE BOTH CHARACTERS FROM THE *JABIN* MANGA "RIKOPIN MAN'S BIG ADVENTURE"? I WAS THINKING, MAYBE LITTLE TOMATO HAS SOME SORT OF RIKOPIN POWER AND WHEN SHE USES IT, SHE TURNS INTO RIKOPIN MAN...?
    -BUNNY-IN-GLASSES,
     MIYAGI PREFECTURE

A OOH, YOU'RE GOOD. I WAS WAITING FOR SOMEONE TO PICK UP ON THAT. I LIKE YOUR NAMES FOR THEM, TOO...

I'M SORRY! YOU'RE MORE THAN A CHARACTER IN A MANGA WITHIN A MANGA, HONEST!

ARTICLE 55
WINGS

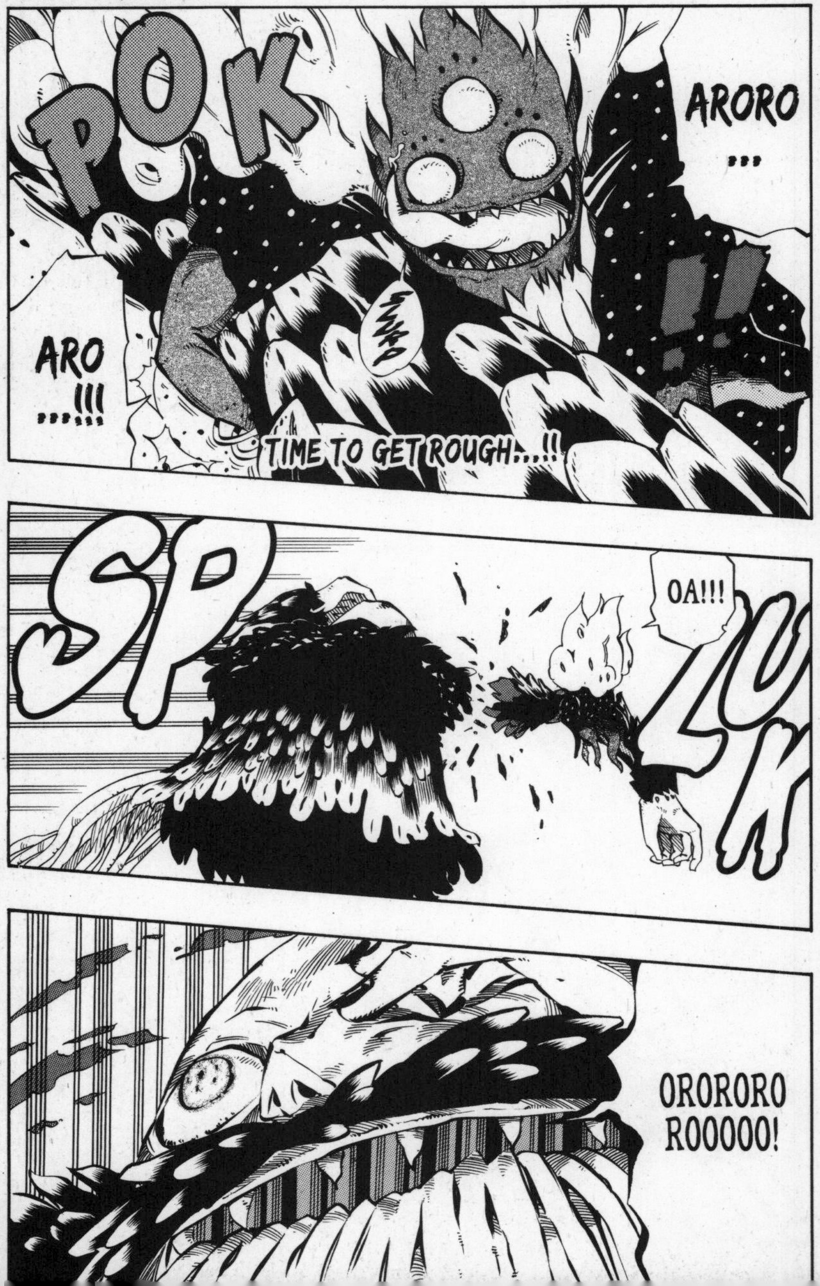
ARORO ...
!!
POK
TIME TO GET ROUGH...!!
ARO
!!!
...???
ZOK
OA!!!
SP
ORORORO ROOOOO!

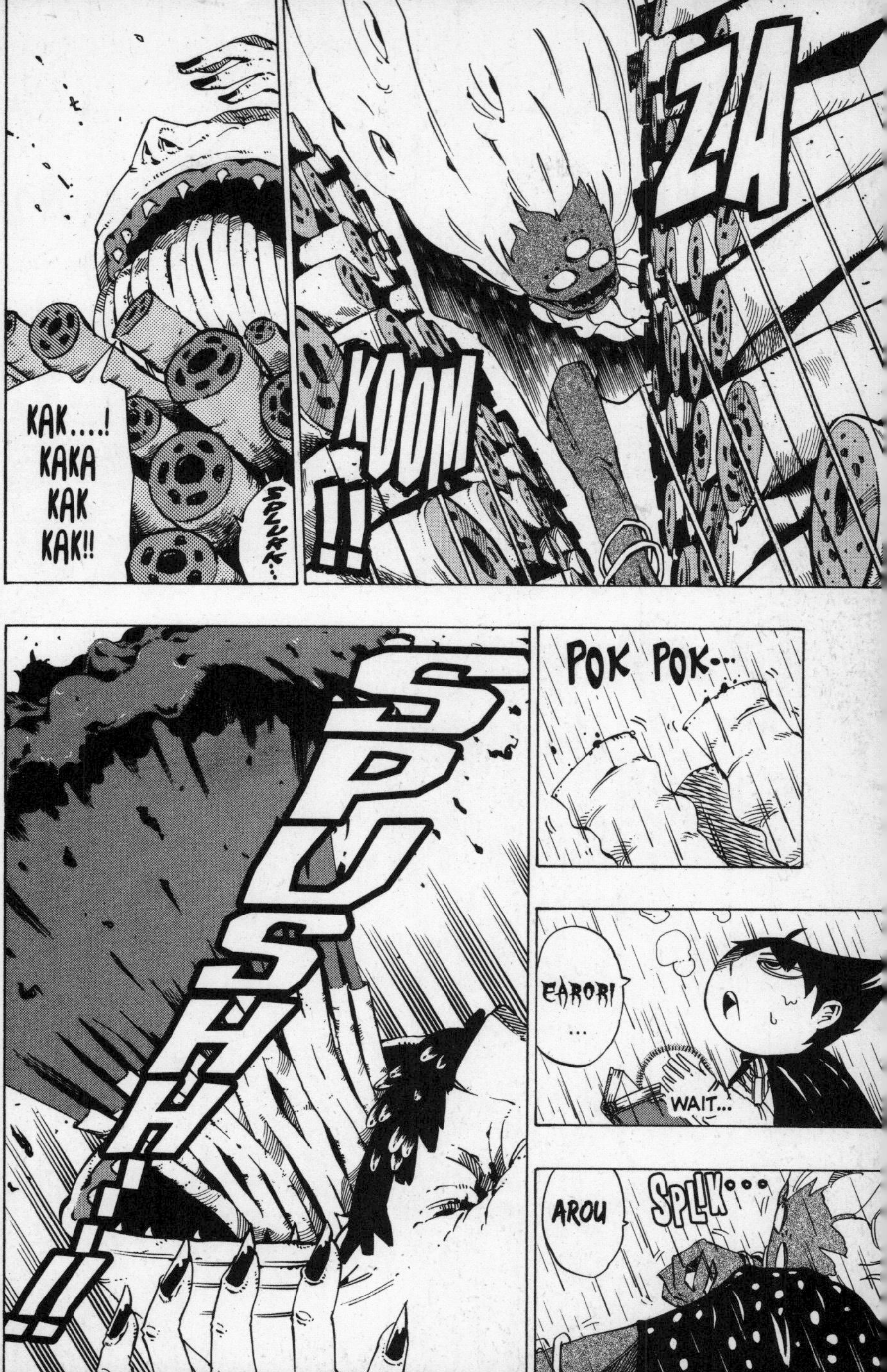
ZA
KOOM!!
KAK.....! KAKA KAK KAK!!
SPLURK...
POK POK...
EARORI ...
WAIT...
AROU
SPLIK...
SPPUSHHH...!!

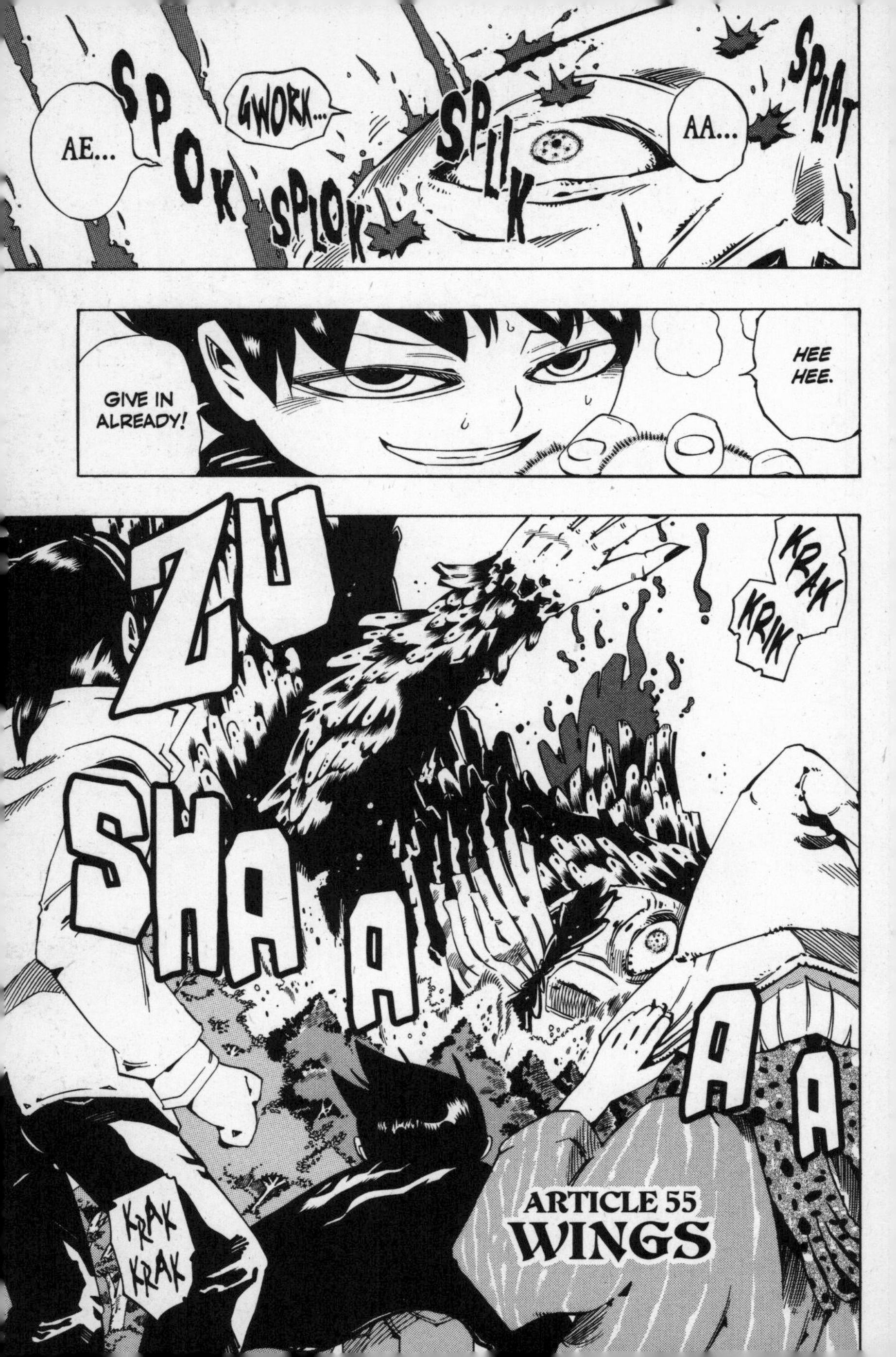
SPLAT
AA...
SPLIK
GWORK...
SPLOK
SPOK
AE...
HEE HEE.
GIVE IN ALREADY!
KRAK KRIK
ZU SHAAAA
ARTICLE 55
WINGS
KRAK KRAK

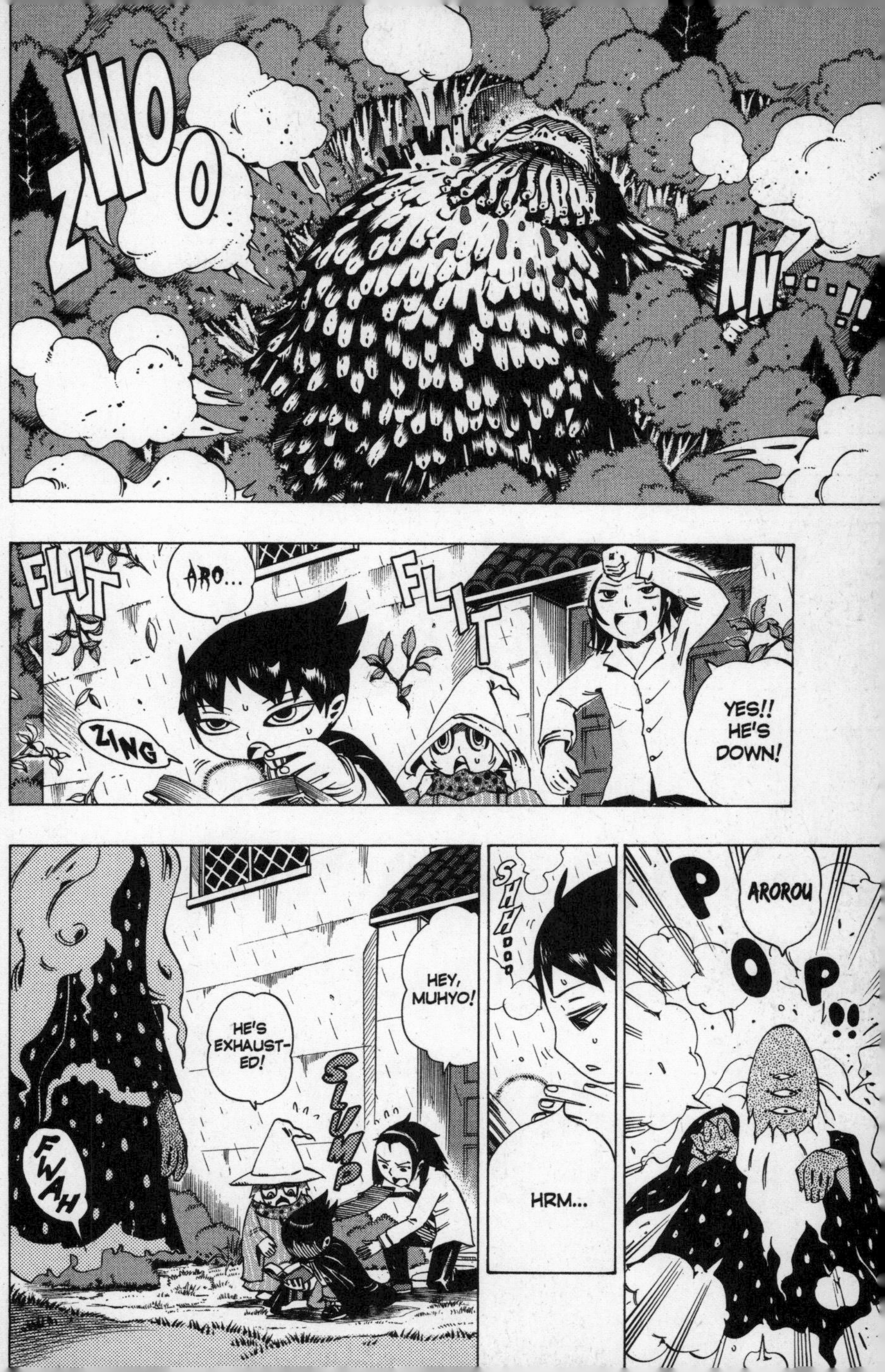

ZWOOO
NN...!!
YES!! HE'S DOWN!
FLIT
ARO...
FLIT
ZING
AROROU
POP!!
SHHHOOO
HRM...
HEY, MUHYO!
HE'S EXHAUST-ED!
SLUMP
FWAH

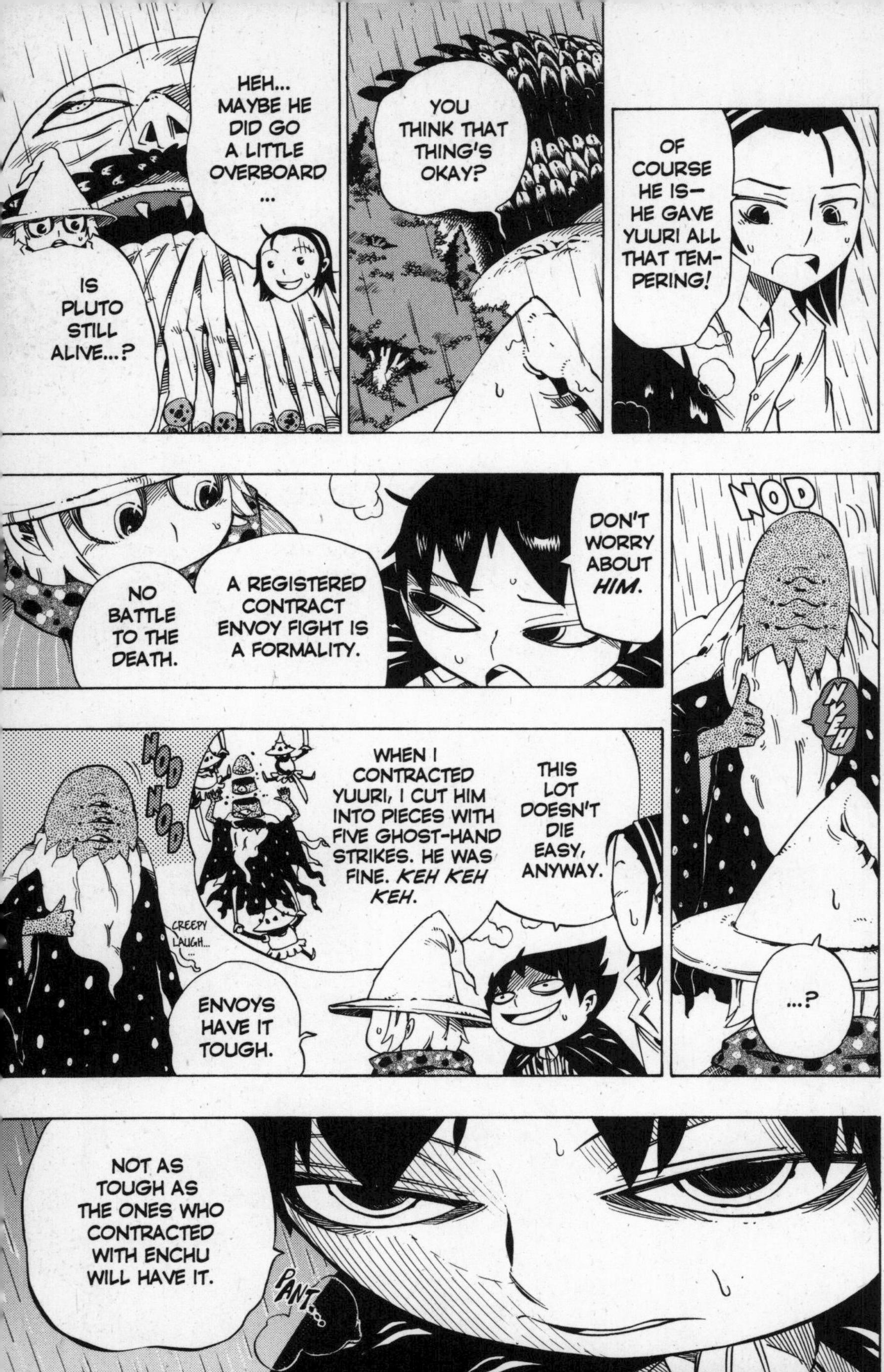
OF COURSE HE IS— HE GAVE YUURI ALL THAT TEMPERING!
YOU THINK THAT THING'S OKAY?
HEH... MAYBE HE DID GO A LITTLE OVERBOARD ...
IS PLUTO STILL ALIVE...?
NOD
NYEH
...?
DON'T WORRY ABOUT *HIM*.
A REGISTERED CONTRACT ENVOY FIGHT IS A FORMALITY.
NO BATTLE TO THE DEATH.
THIS LOT DOESN'T DIE EASY, ANYWAY.
WHEN I CONTRACTED YUURI, I CUT HIM INTO PIECES WITH FIVE GHOST-HAND STRIKES. HE WAS FINE. *KEH KEH KEH*.
NOD NOD
CREEPY LAUGH... ...
ENVOYS HAVE IT TOUGH.
NOT AS TOUGH AS THE ONES WHO CONTRACTED WITH ENCHU WILL HAVE IT.
PANT

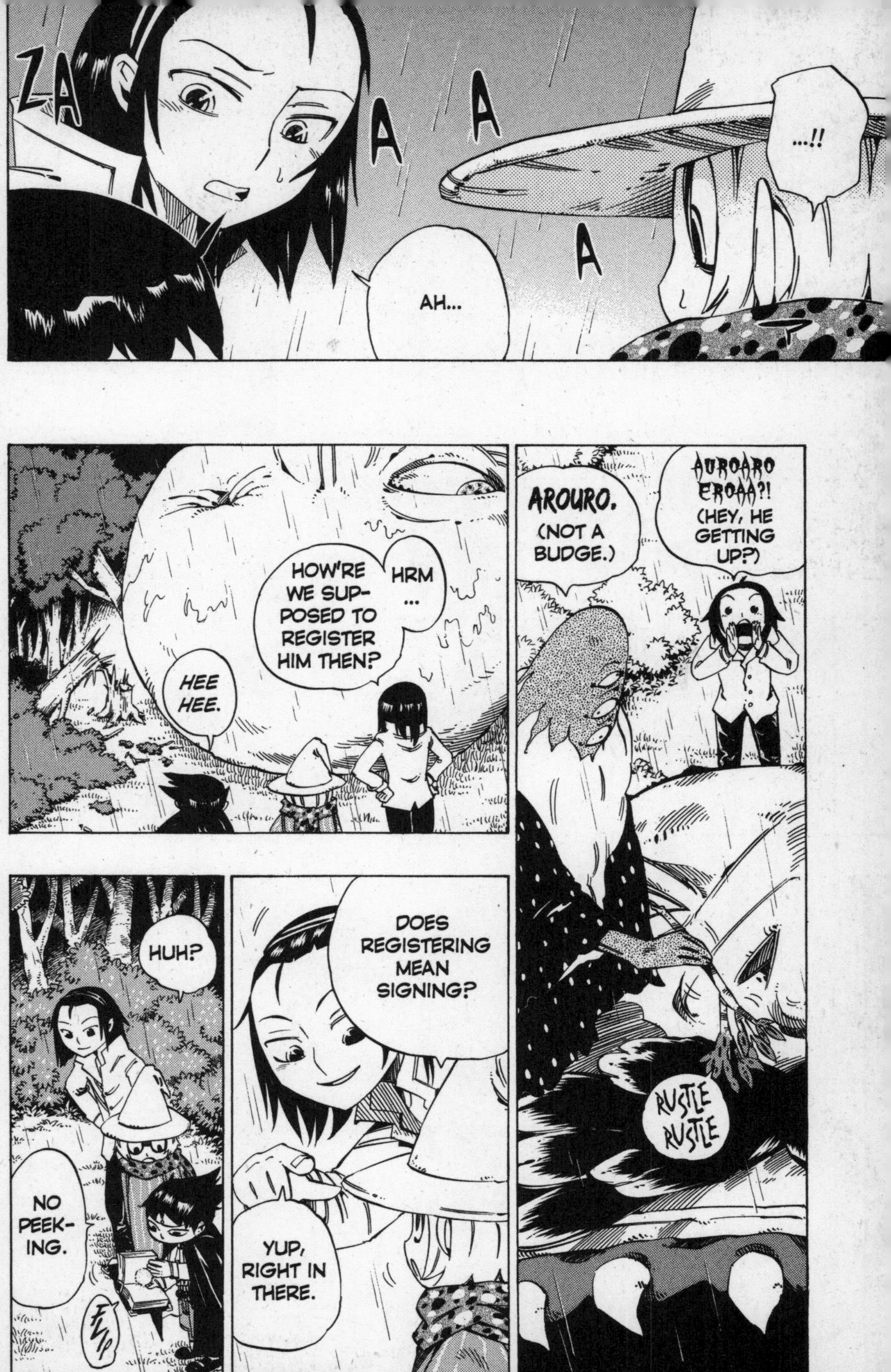
...!!
ZA A A A
AH...
AUROARO EROAA?! (HEY, HE GETTING UP?)
AROURO. (NOT A BUDGE.)
RUSTLE RUSTLE
HRM ...
HOW'RE WE SUP-POSED TO REGISTER HIM THEN?
HEE HEE.
DOES REGISTERING MEAN SIGNING?
YUP, RIGHT IN THERE.
HUH?
NO PEEK-ING.
FLIP

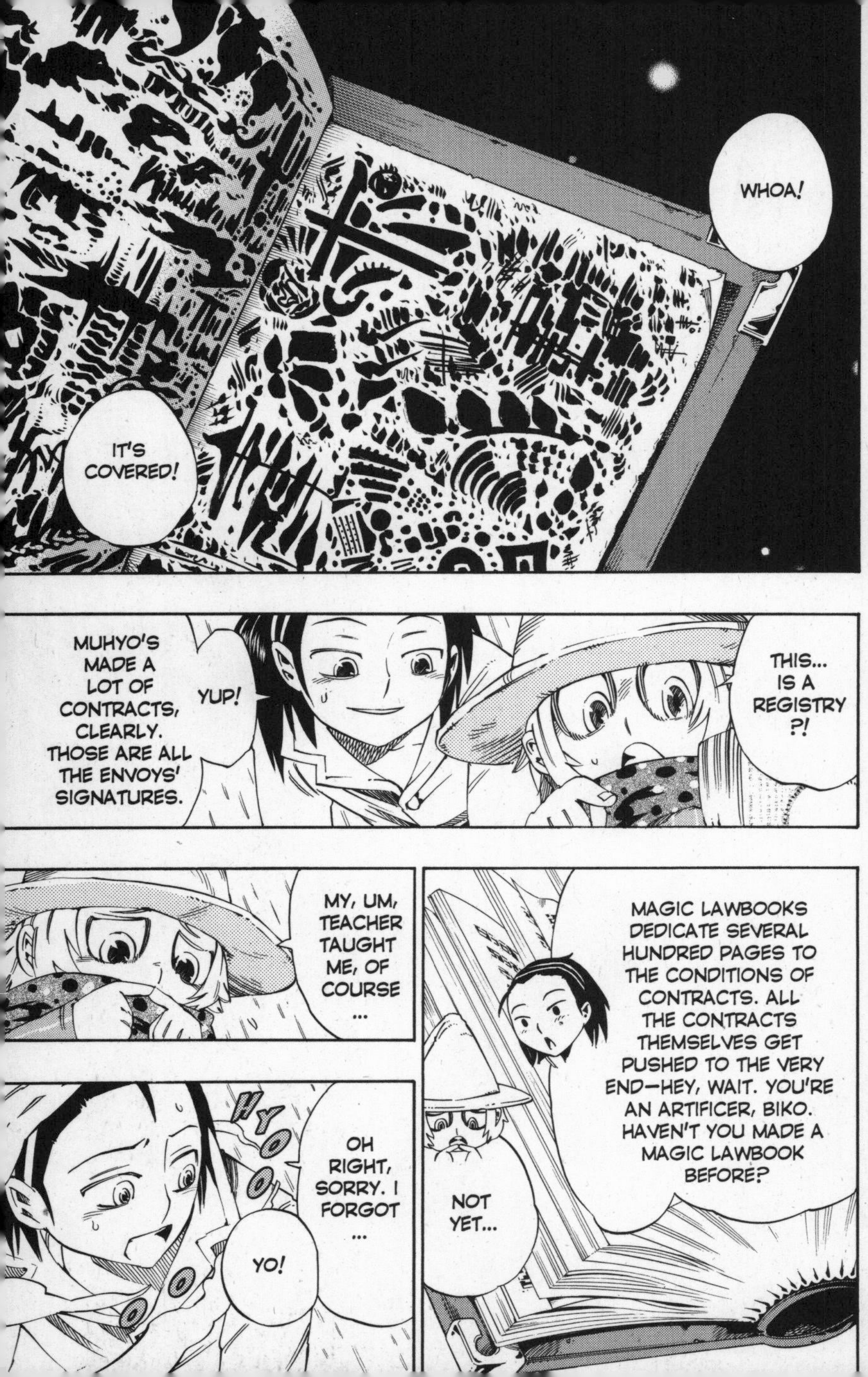
WHOA!
IT'S COVERED!
THIS... IS A REGISTRY ?!
YUP!
MUHYO'S MADE A LOT OF CONTRACTS, CLEARLY. THOSE ARE ALL THE ENVOYS' SIGNATURES.
MAGIC LAWBOOKS DEDICATE SEVERAL HUNDRED PAGES TO THE CONDITIONS OF CONTRACTS. ALL THE CONTRACTS THEMSELVES GET PUSHED TO THE VERY END—HEY, WAIT. YOU'RE AN ARTIFICER, BIKO. HAVEN'T YOU MADE A MAGIC LAWBOOK BEFORE?
NOT YET...
MY, UM, TEACHER TAUGHT ME, OF COURSE ...
OH RIGHT, SORRY. I FORGOT ...
YO!

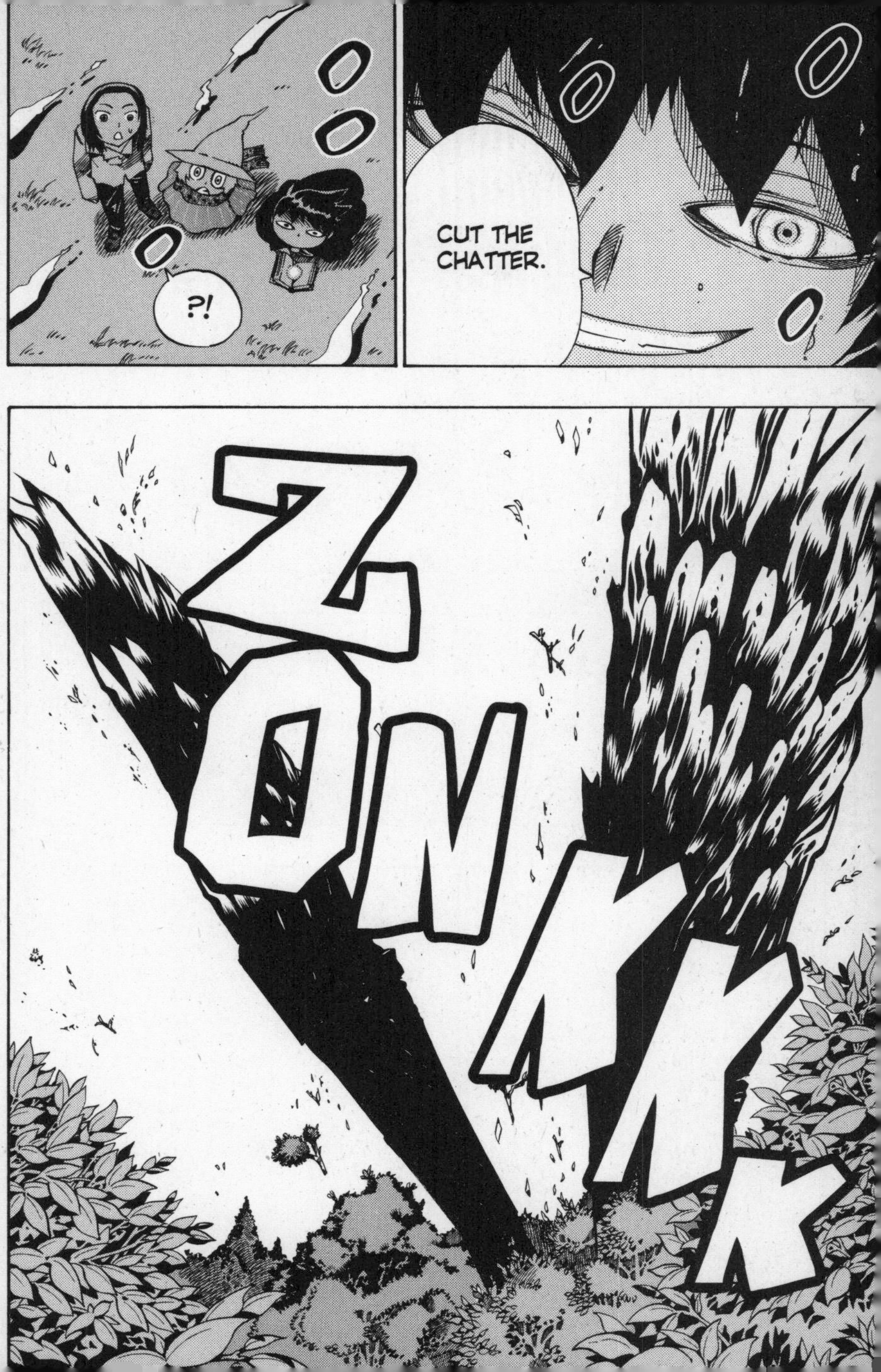
CUT THE CHATTER.
?!
ZONKK

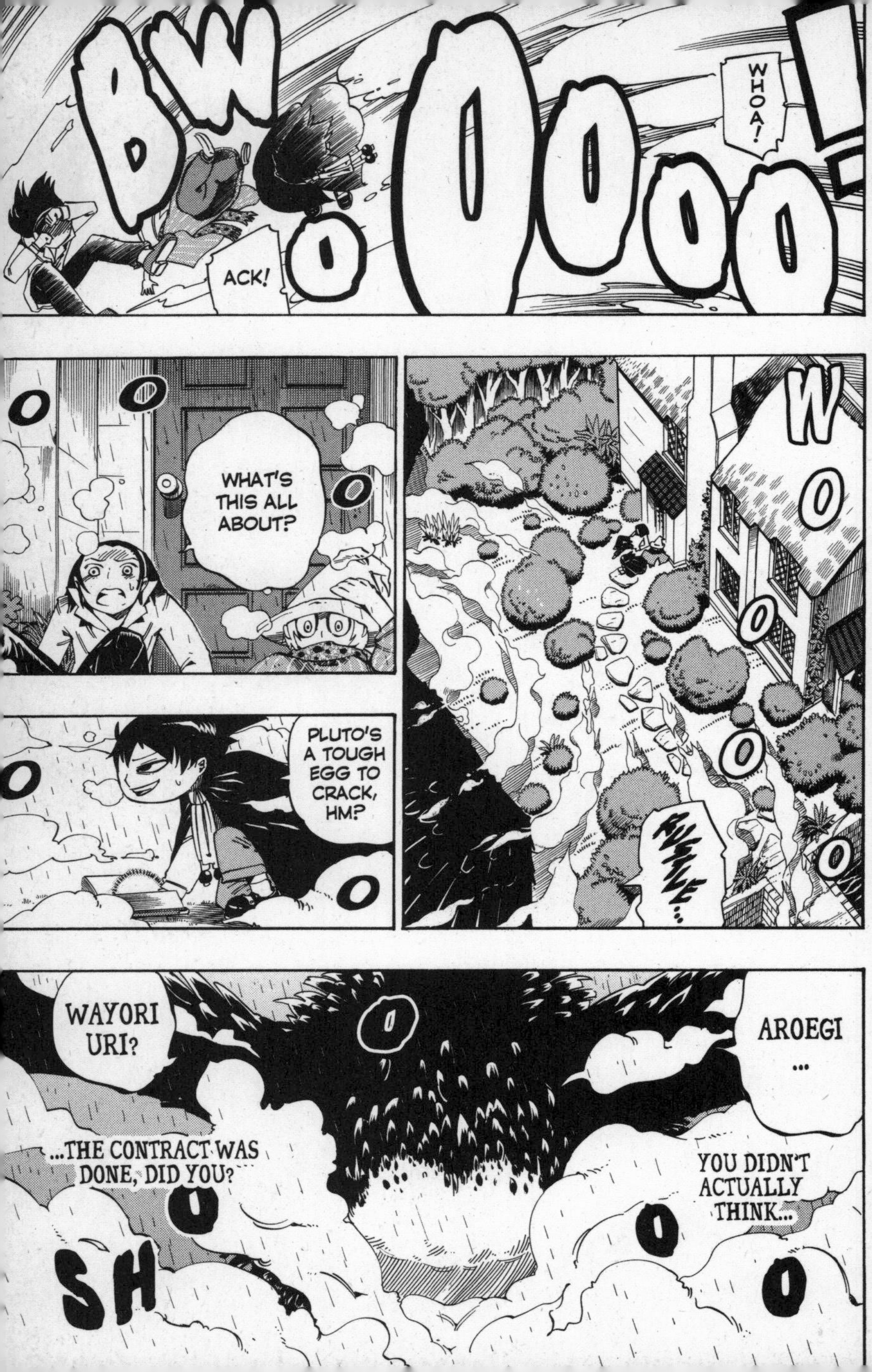
WHOA!
BWOOOOOO!
ACK!
WOOOOOO
RUSTLE...
WHAT'S THIS ALL ABOUT?
PLUTO'S A TOUGH EGG TO CRACK, HM?
AROEGI ...
WAYORI URI?
YOU DIDN'T ACTUALLY THINK...
...THE CONTRACT WAS DONE, DID YOU?
SHOOOOO

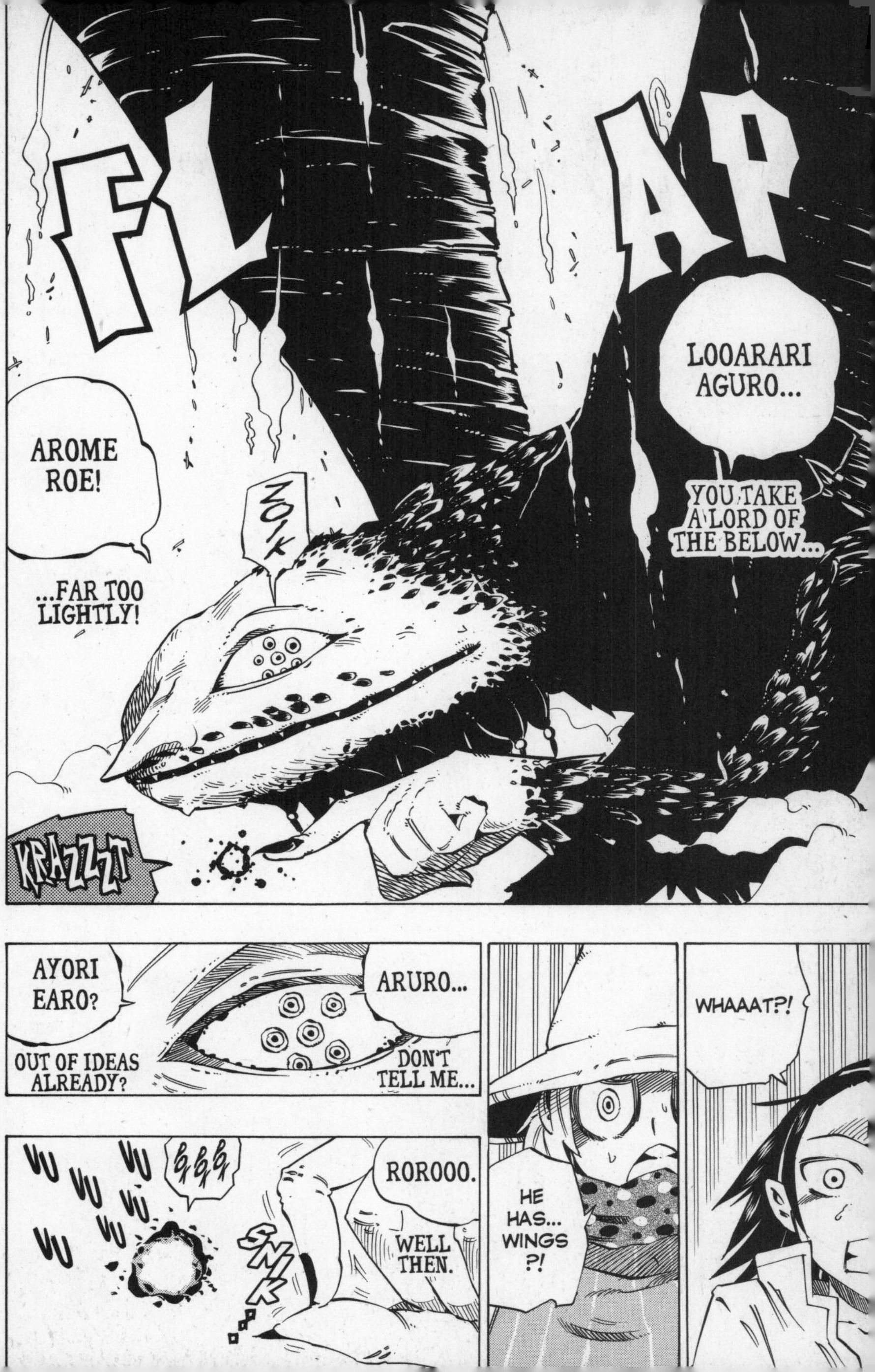
FLAP
LOOARARI AGURO...
YOU TAKE A LORD OF THE BELOW...
ZOIK
AROME ROE!
...FAR TOO LIGHTLY!
KRAZZZT
WHAAAT?!
HE HAS... WINGS?!
ARURO...
DON'T TELL ME...
AYORI EARO?
OUT OF IDEAS ALREADY?
RORROO.
WELL THEN.
SNIK
VU VU VU VU VU VU VU

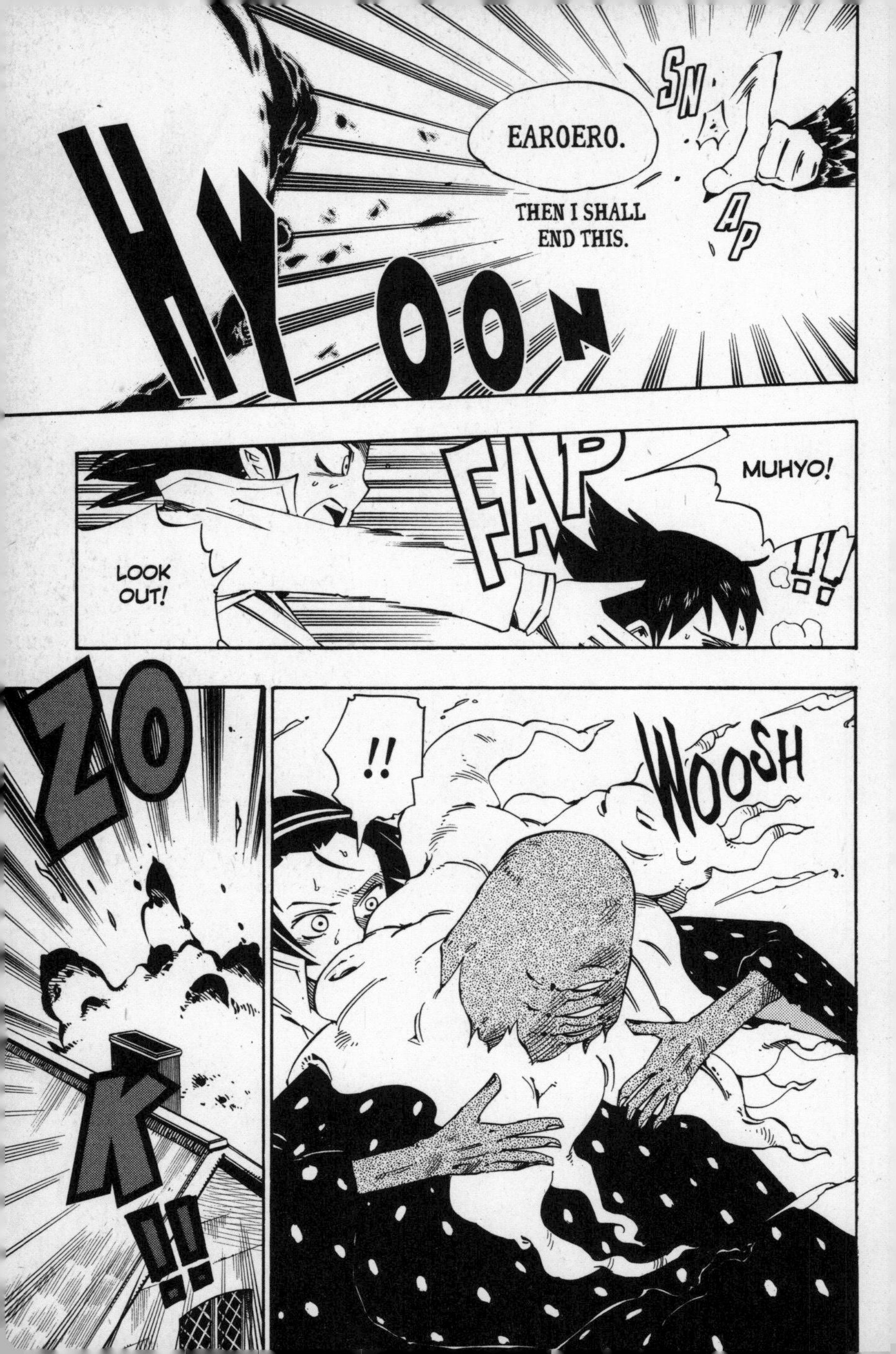
SNAP
EAROERO.
THEN I SHALL END THIS.
HYOON
MUHYO!
!!
FAP
LOOK OUT!
WOOSH
!!
ZOK!!

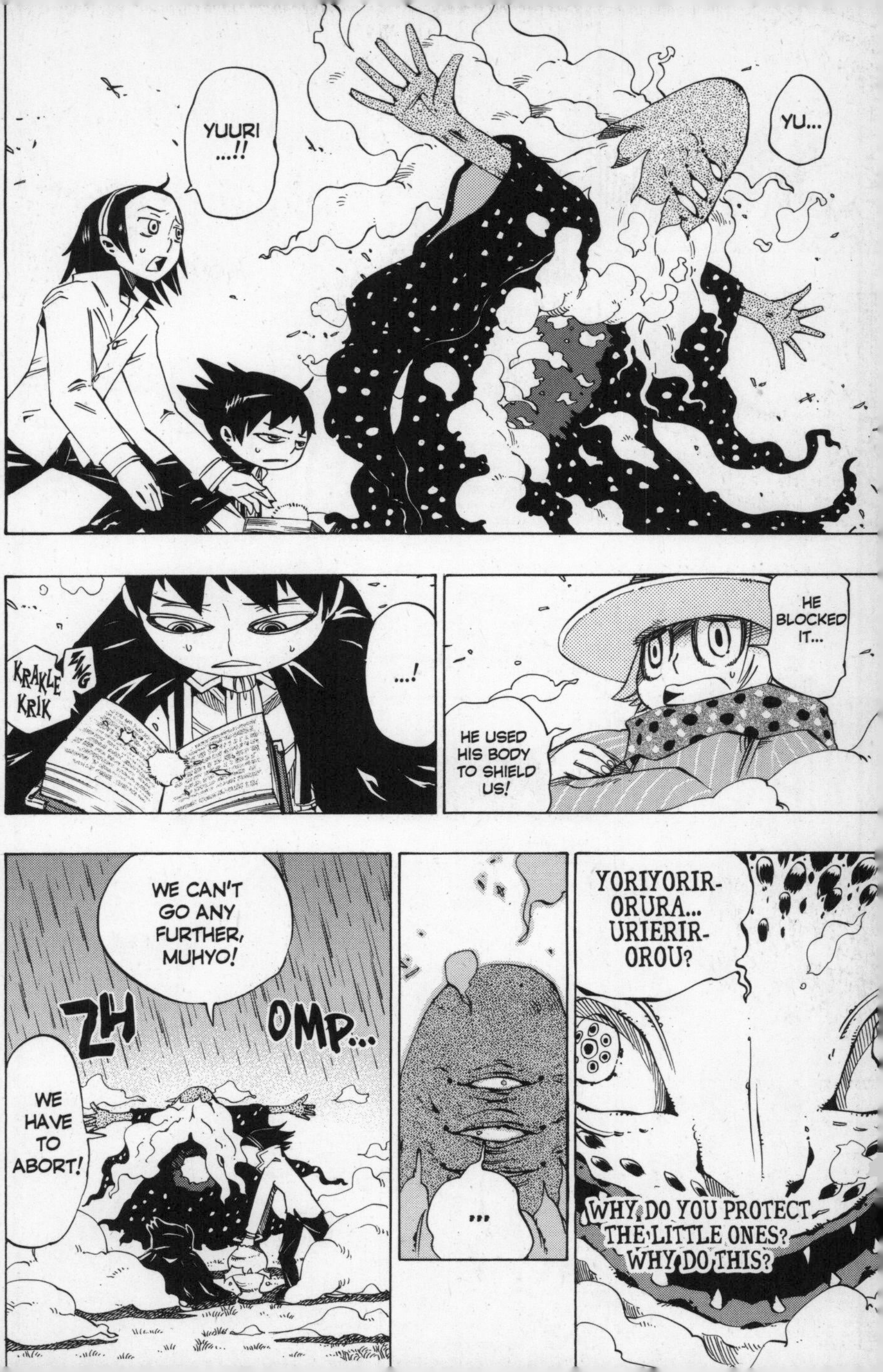
YU...
YUURI ...!!
HE BLOCKED IT...
HE USED HIS BODY TO SHIELD US!
...!
ZING
KRAKLE KRIK
YORIYORIR-ORURA... URIERIR-OROU?
WHY DO YOU PROTECT THE LITTLE ONES? WHY DO THIS?
...
WE CAN'T GO ANY FURTHER, MUHYO!
ZH OMP...
WE HAVE TO ABORT!

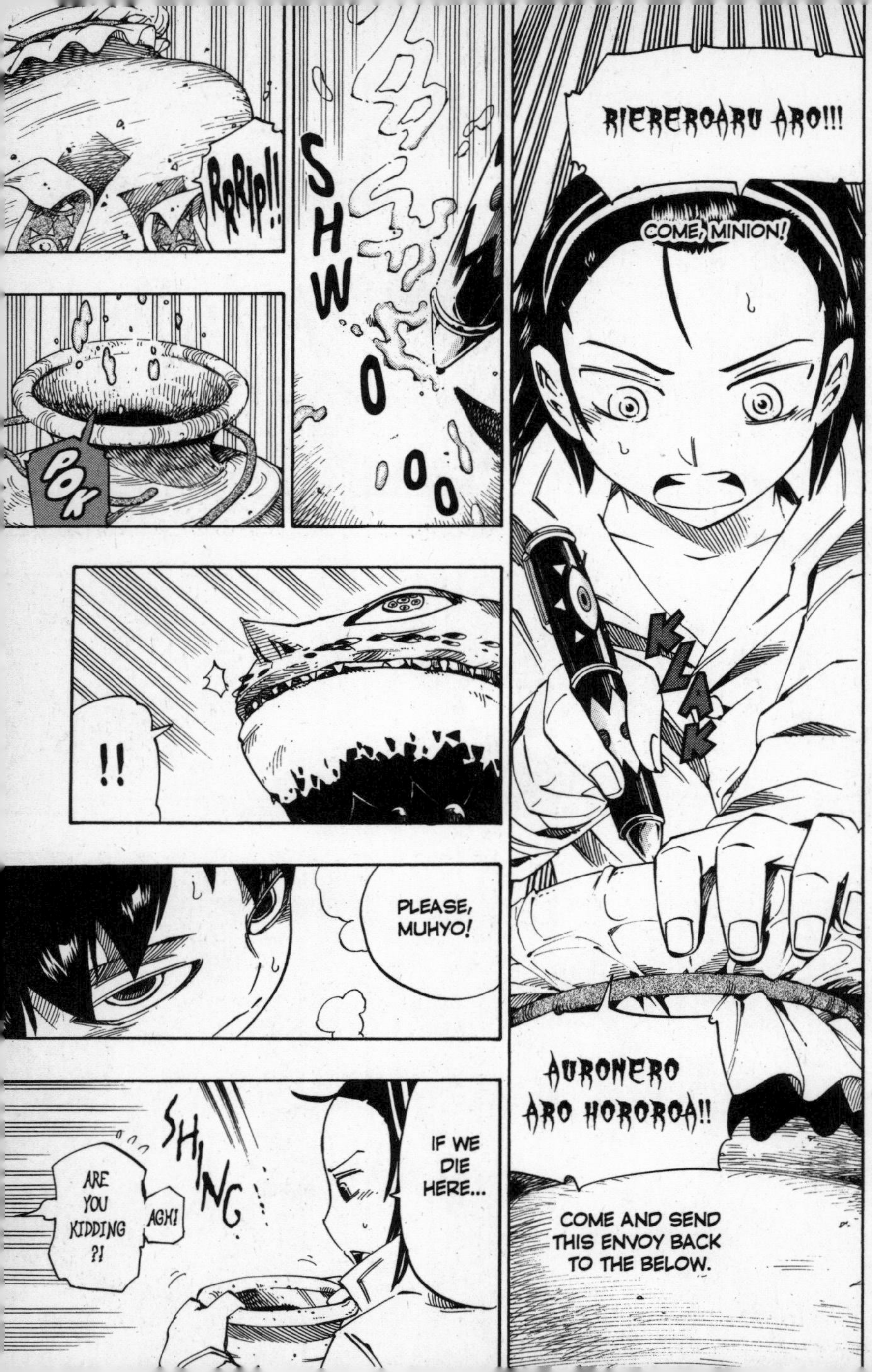
RIERERoARU ARO!!!
COME, MINION!
KLAK
AURONERO ARO HOROROA!!
COME AND SEND THIS ENVOY BACK TO THE BELOW.
SHWOOOO
RRRIP!!
POK
!!
PLEASE, MUHYO!
IF WE DIE HERE...
SHING
AGH!
ARE YOU KIDDING ?!

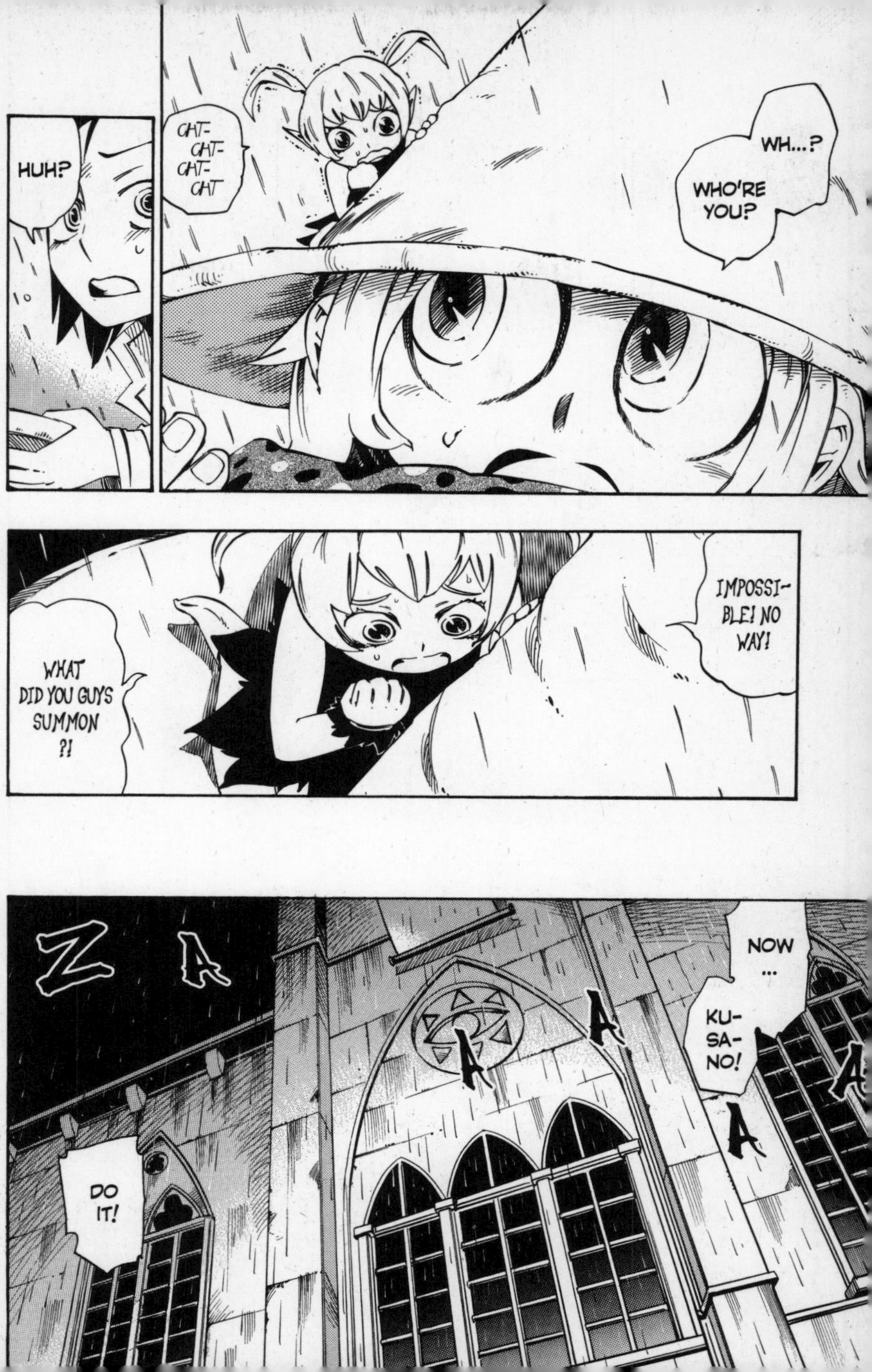
WH...?
WHO'RE YOU?
CHT-CHT-CHT-CHT
HUH?
IMPOSSI-BLE! NO WAY!
WHAT DID YOU GUYS SUMMON?!
NOW... KU-SA-NO!
ZAAAAAA
DO IT!

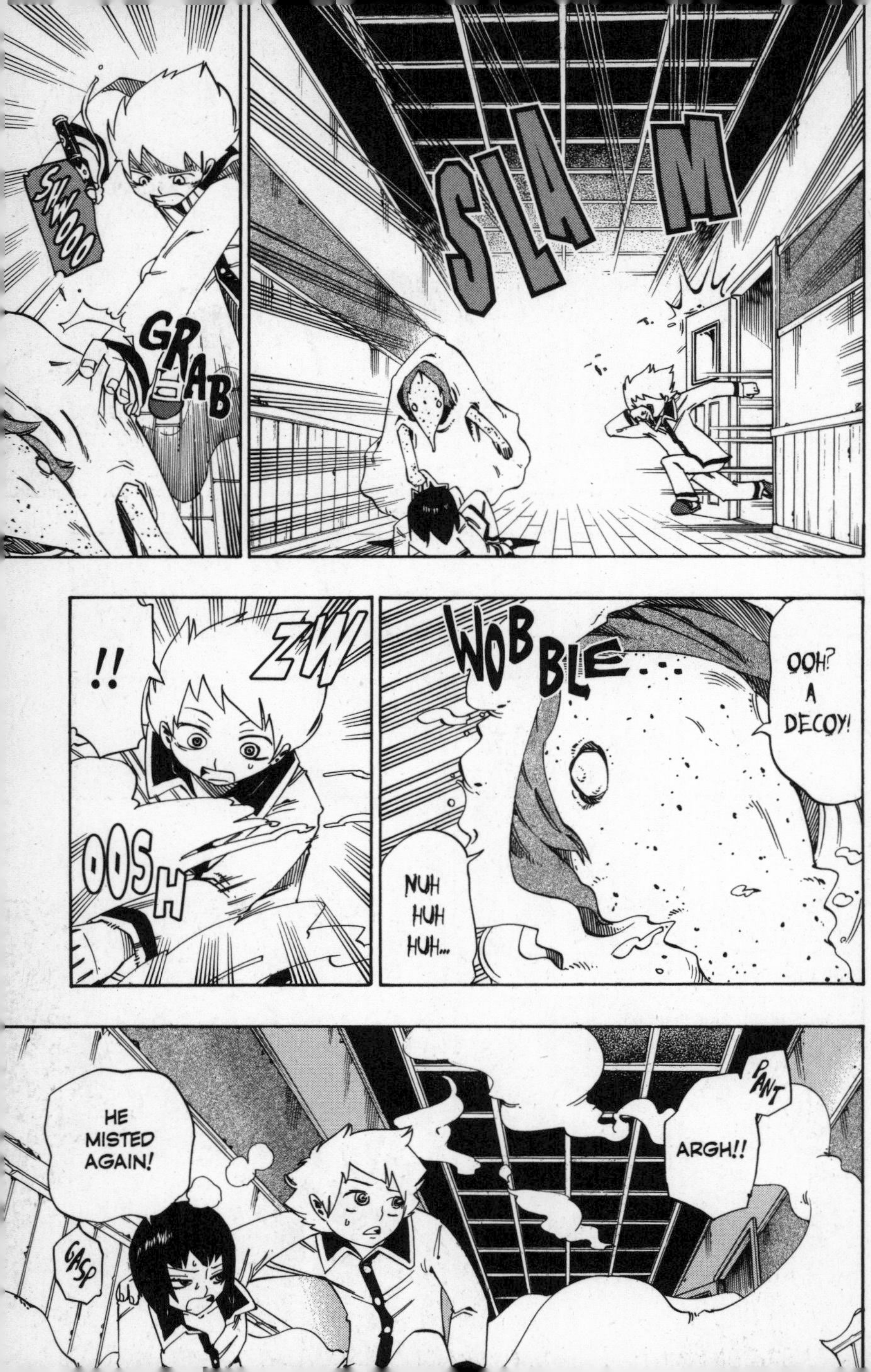
SLAM
SHWOOO
GRAB
OOH? A DECOY!
WOBBLE...
NUH HUH HUH...
ZW
!!
OOSH
PANT
ARGH!!
HE MISTED AGAIN!
GASP

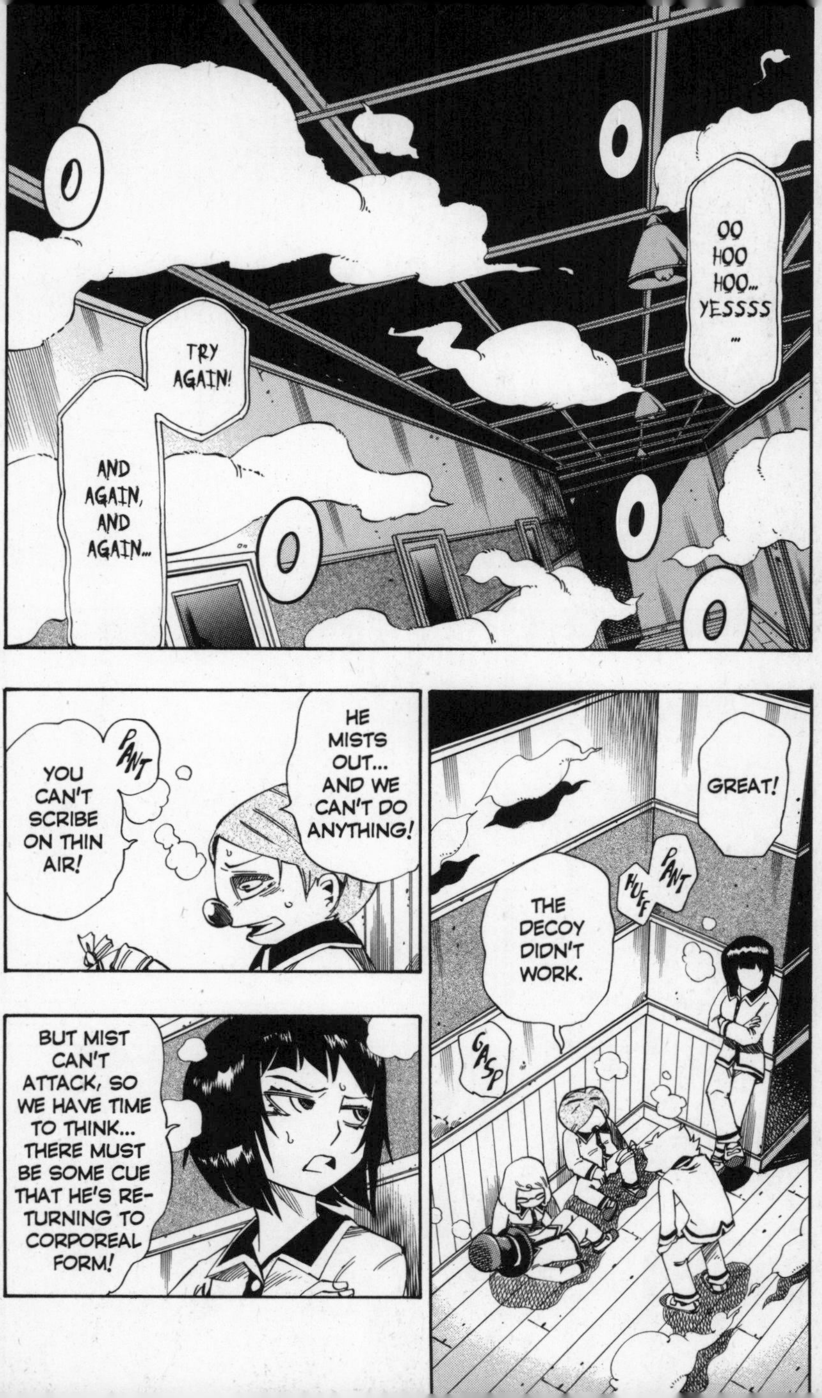

OO HOO HOO... YESSSS ...
TRY AGAIN!
AND AGAIN, AND AGAIN...
GREAT!
PANT
HUFF
THE DECOY DIDN'T WORK.
GASP
HE MISTS OUT... AND WE CAN'T DO ANYTHING!
PANT
YOU CAN'T SCRIBE ON THIN AIR!
BUT MIST CAN'T ATTACK, SO WE HAVE TIME TO THINK... THERE MUST BE SOME CUE THAT HE'S RE-TURNING TO CORPOREAL FORM!

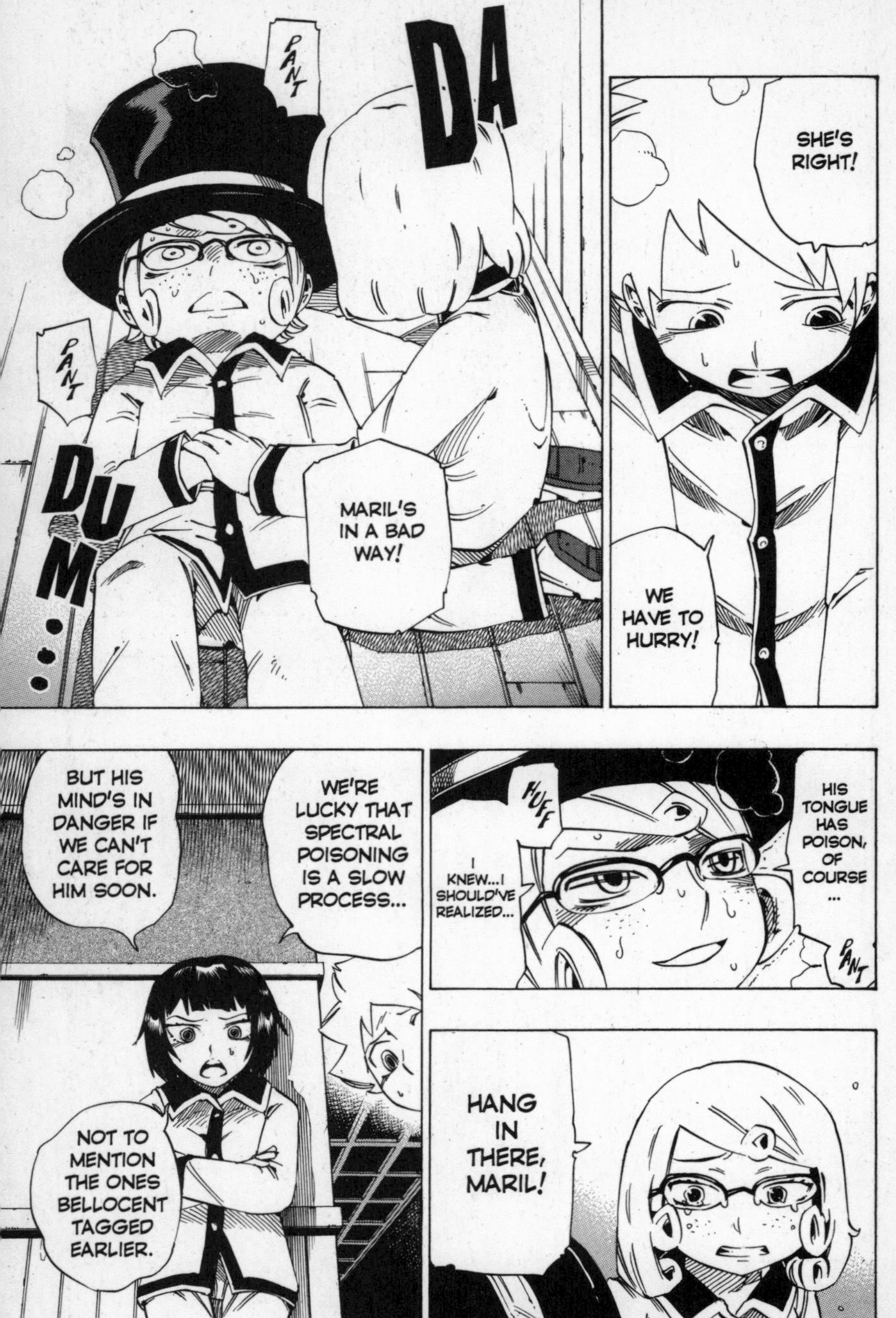
SHE'S RIGHT!
WE HAVE TO HURRY!
PANT
DA
MARIL'S IN A BAD WAY!
PANT
DUM...
HIS TONGUE HAS POISON, OF COURSE...
HUFF
I KNEW...I SHOULD'VE REALIZED...
PANT
WE'RE LUCKY THAT SPECTRAL POISONING IS A SLOW PROCESS...
BUT HIS MIND'S IN DANGER IF WE CAN'T CARE FOR HIM SOON.
HANG IN THERE, MARIL!
NOT TO MENTION THE ONES BELLOCENT TAGGED EARLIER.

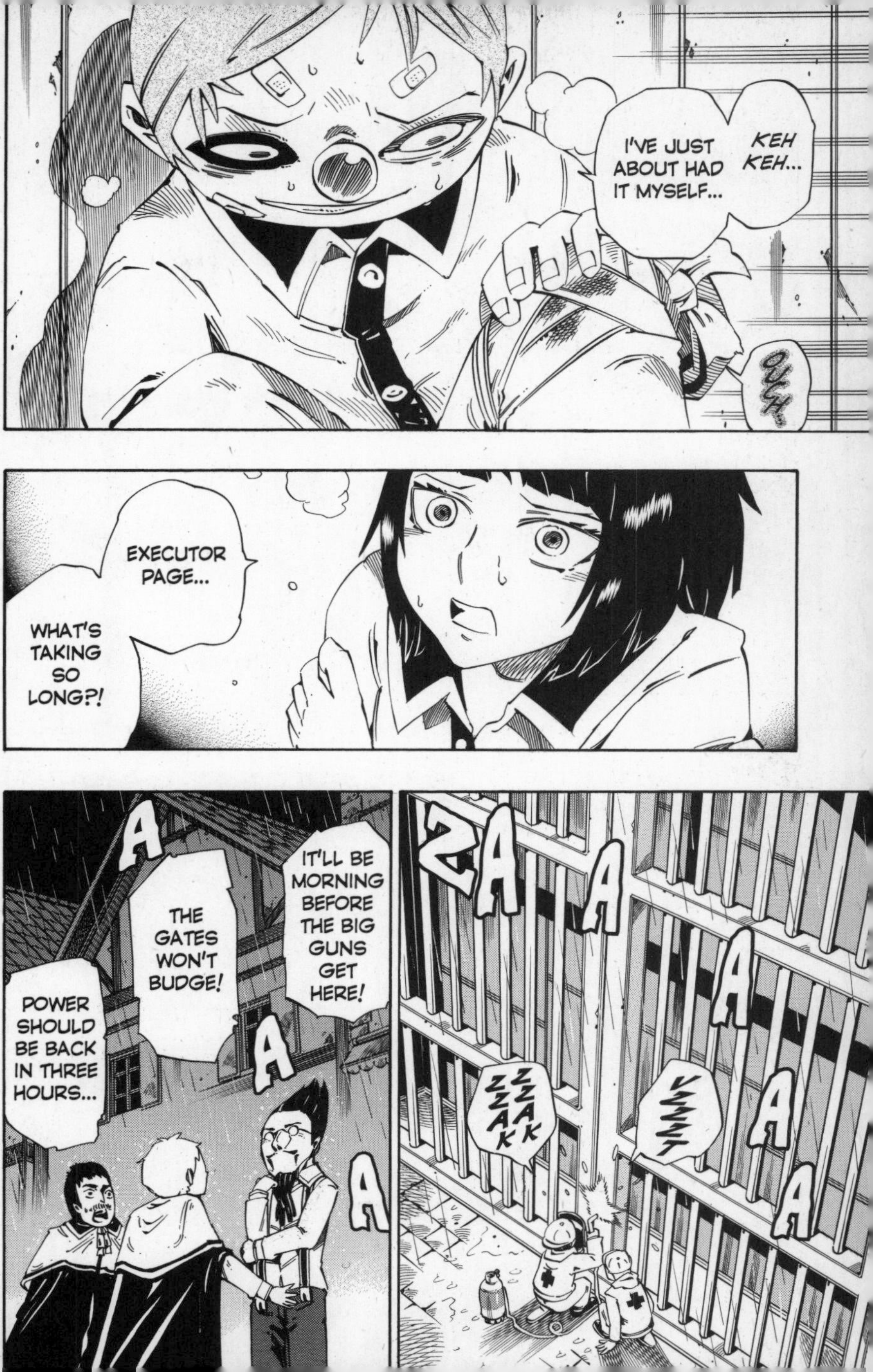
KEH KEH...
I'VE JUST ABOUT HAD IT MYSELF...
OUCH...
EXECUTOR PAGE...
WHAT'S TAKING SO LONG?!
ZAAAAAAA
VZZZT
ZZAK
ZZAK
AAAA
IT'LL BE MORNING BEFORE THE BIG GUNS GET HERE!
THE GATES WON'T BUDGE!
POWER SHOULD BE BACK IN THREE HOURS...

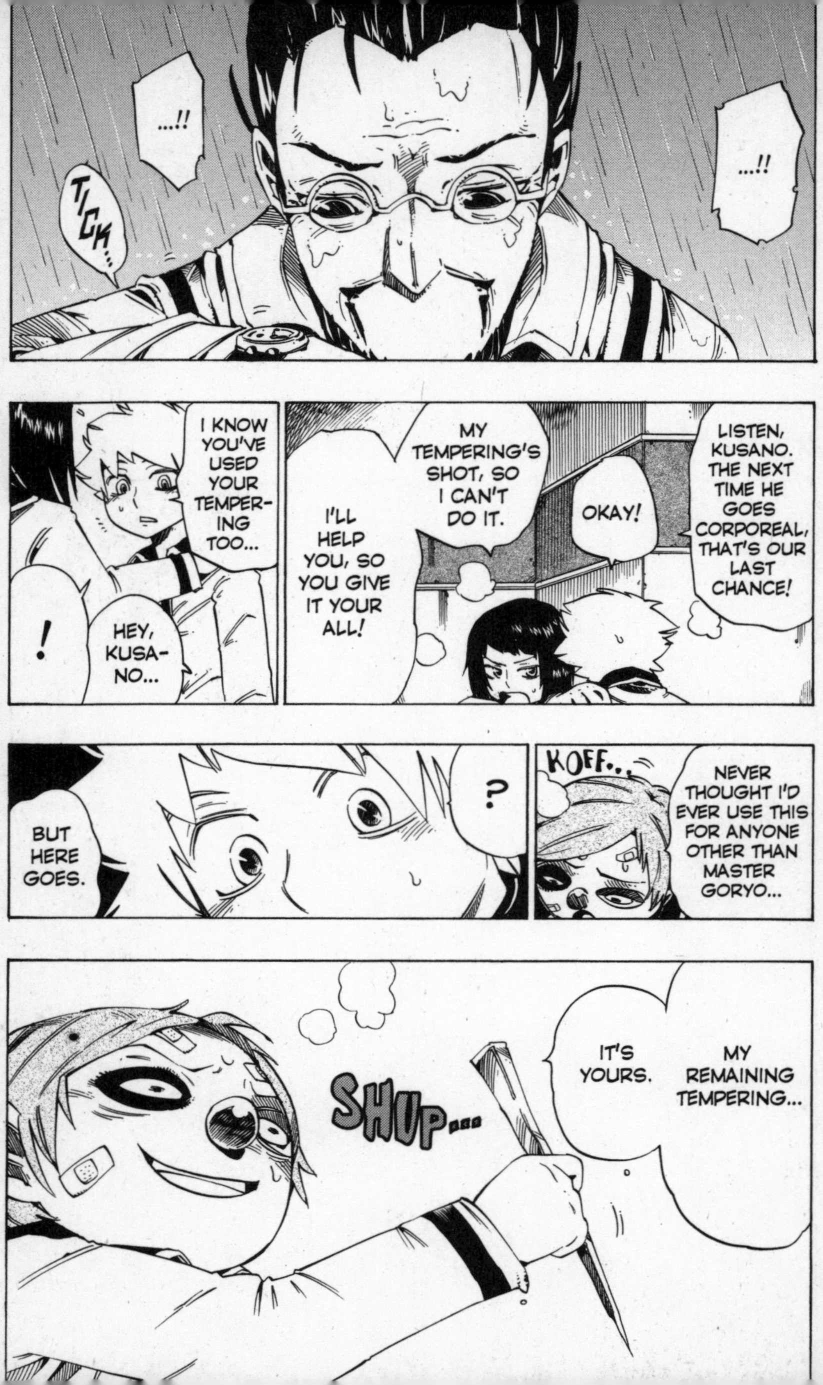
...!!
...!!
TICK...
LISTEN, KUSANO. THE NEXT TIME HE GOES CORPOREAL, THAT'S OUR LAST CHANCE!
OKAY!
MY TEMPERING'S SHOT, SO I CAN'T DO IT.
I'LL HELP YOU, SO YOU GIVE IT YOUR ALL!
I KNOW YOU'VE USED YOUR TEMPER-ING TOO...
HEY, KUSA-NO...
!
NEVER THOUGHT I'D EVER USE THIS FOR ANYONE OTHER THAN MASTER GORYO...
KOFF...
?
BUT HERE GOES.
MY REMAINING TEMPERING...
IT'S YOURS.
SHUP...

Q: I, LIKE NANA, AM AN E-CUP...AND I CAN NEVER FIND THINGS MY SIZE. WHERE DOES NANA BUY HER UNDERWEAR?

-I.M., KANAGAWA PREFECTURE

A: ER...HUH? UM, OKAY... LET'S ASK. *GULP*

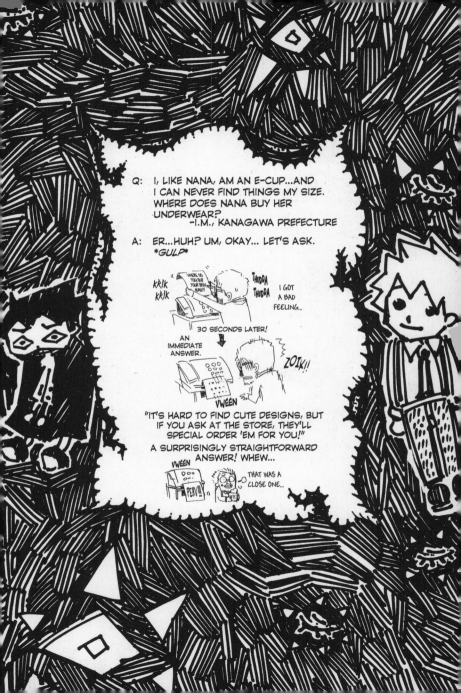

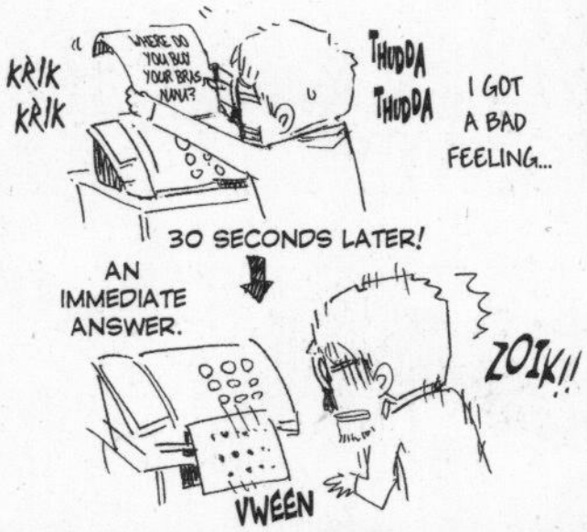
WHERE DO YOU BUY YOUR BRAS, NANA?
KRIK KRIK
THUDDA THUDDA
I GOT A BAD FEELING...
30 SECONDS LATER!
AN IMMEDIATE ANSWER.
ZOIK!!
VWEEN

"IT'S HARD TO FIND CUTE DESIGNS, BUT IF YOU ASK AT THE STORE, THEY'LL SPECIAL ORDER 'EM FOR YOU!"

A SURPRISINGLY STRAIGHTFORWARD ANSWER! WHEW...

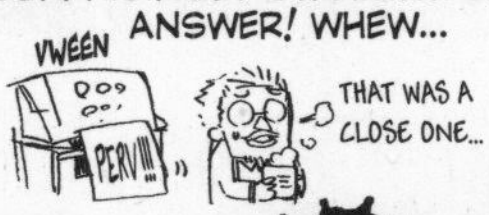
VWEEN
PERV!!!
THAT WAS A CLOSE ONE...

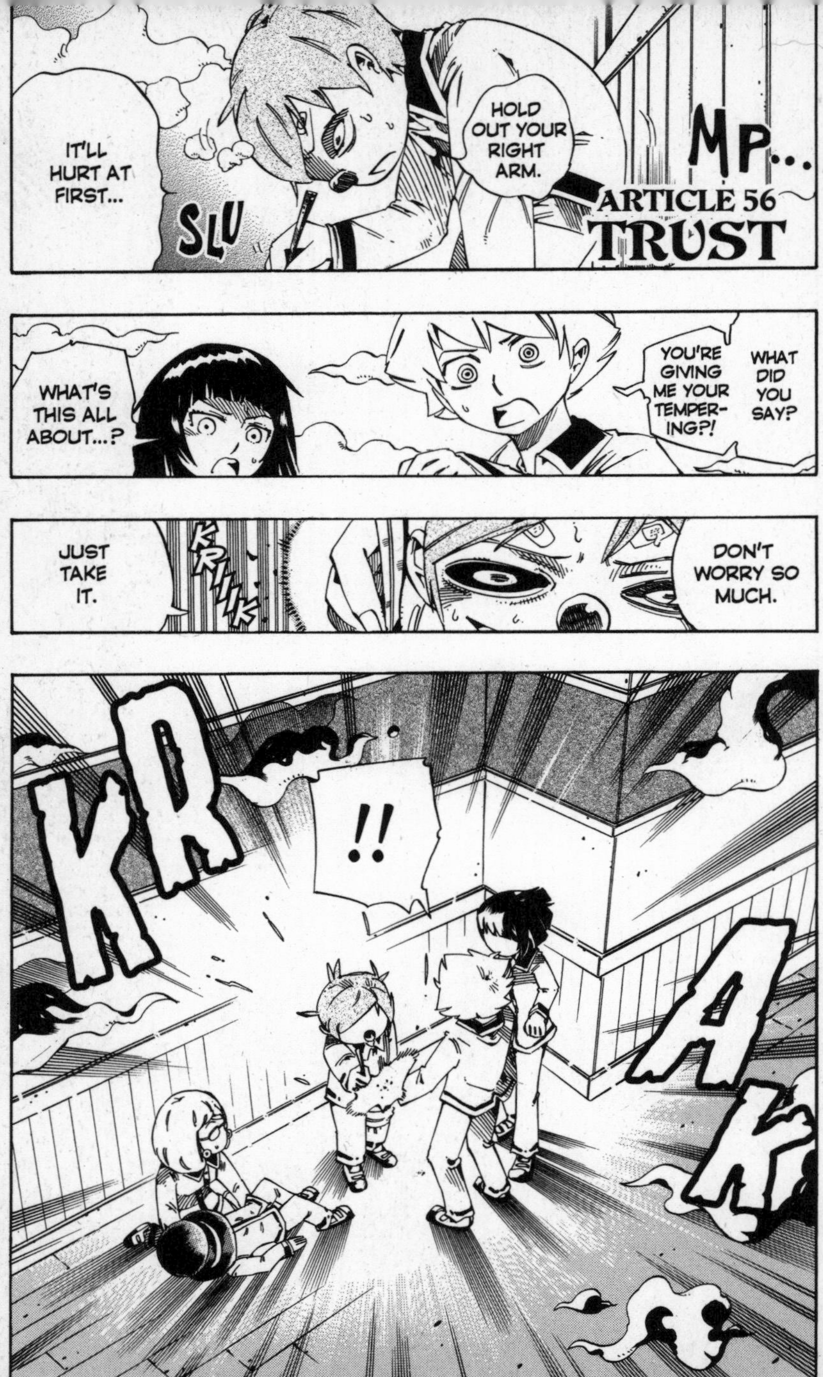
MP...
ARTICLE 56
TRUST
HOLD OUT YOUR RIGHT ARM.
SLU
IT'LL HURT AT FIRST...
WHAT DID YOU SAY?
YOU'RE GIVING ME YOUR TEMPER-ING?!
WHAT'S THIS ALL ABOUT...?
DON'T WORRY SO MUCH.
KRIIK
JUST TAKE IT.
!!
KRAK

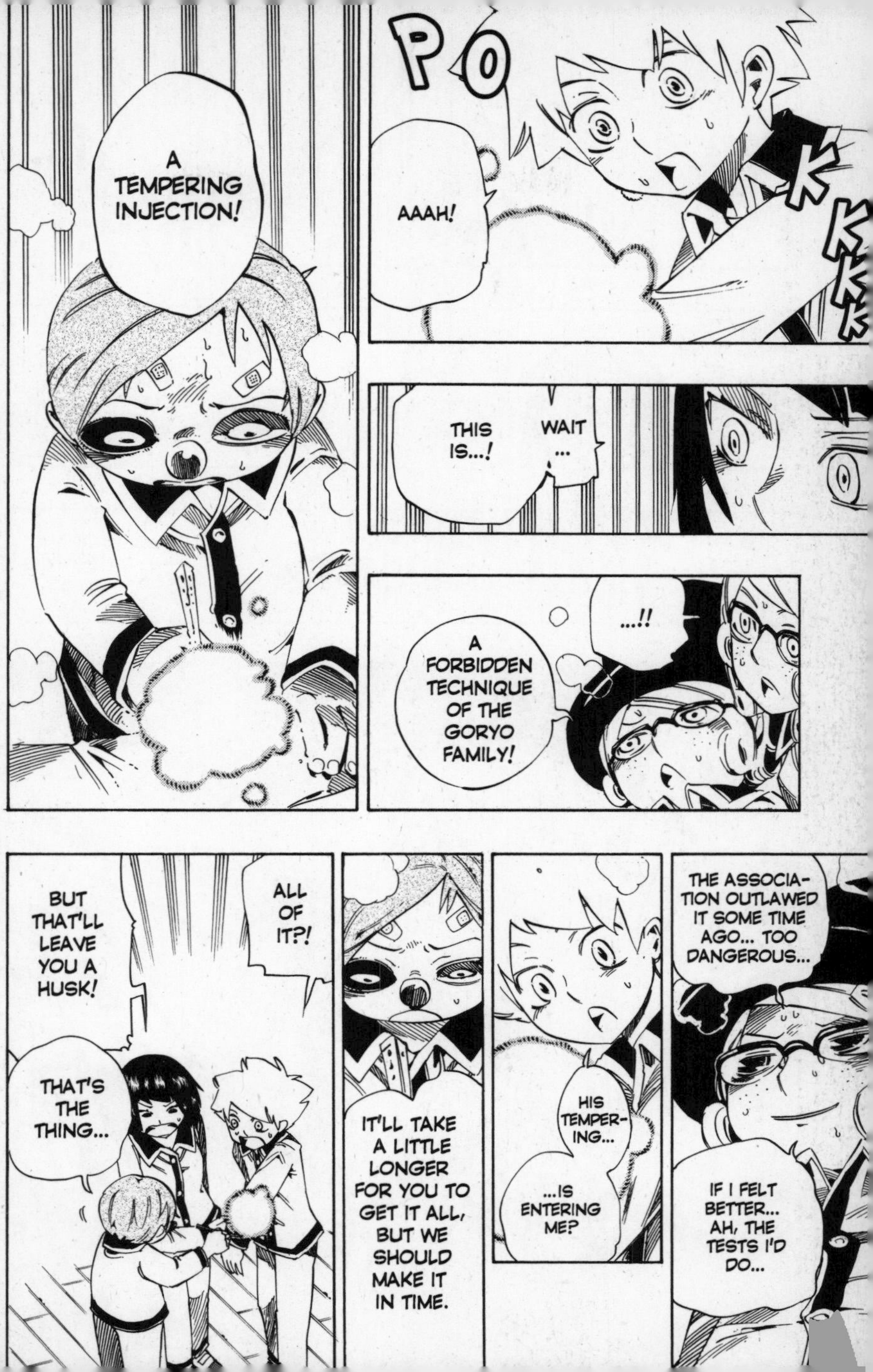
POKKKK
AAAH!
WAIT...
THIS IS...!
...!!
A FORBIDDEN TECHNIQUE OF THE GORYO FAMILY!
A TEMPERING INJECTION!
THE ASSOCIATION OUTLAWED IT SOME TIME AGO... TOO DANGEROUS...
IF I FELT BETTER... AH, THE TESTS I'D DO...
HIS TEMPERING...
...IS ENTERING ME?
IT'LL TAKE A LITTLE LONGER FOR YOU TO GET IT ALL, BUT WE SHOULD MAKE IT IN TIME.
ALL OF IT?!
BUT THAT'LL LEAVE YOU A HUSK!
THAT'S THE THING...

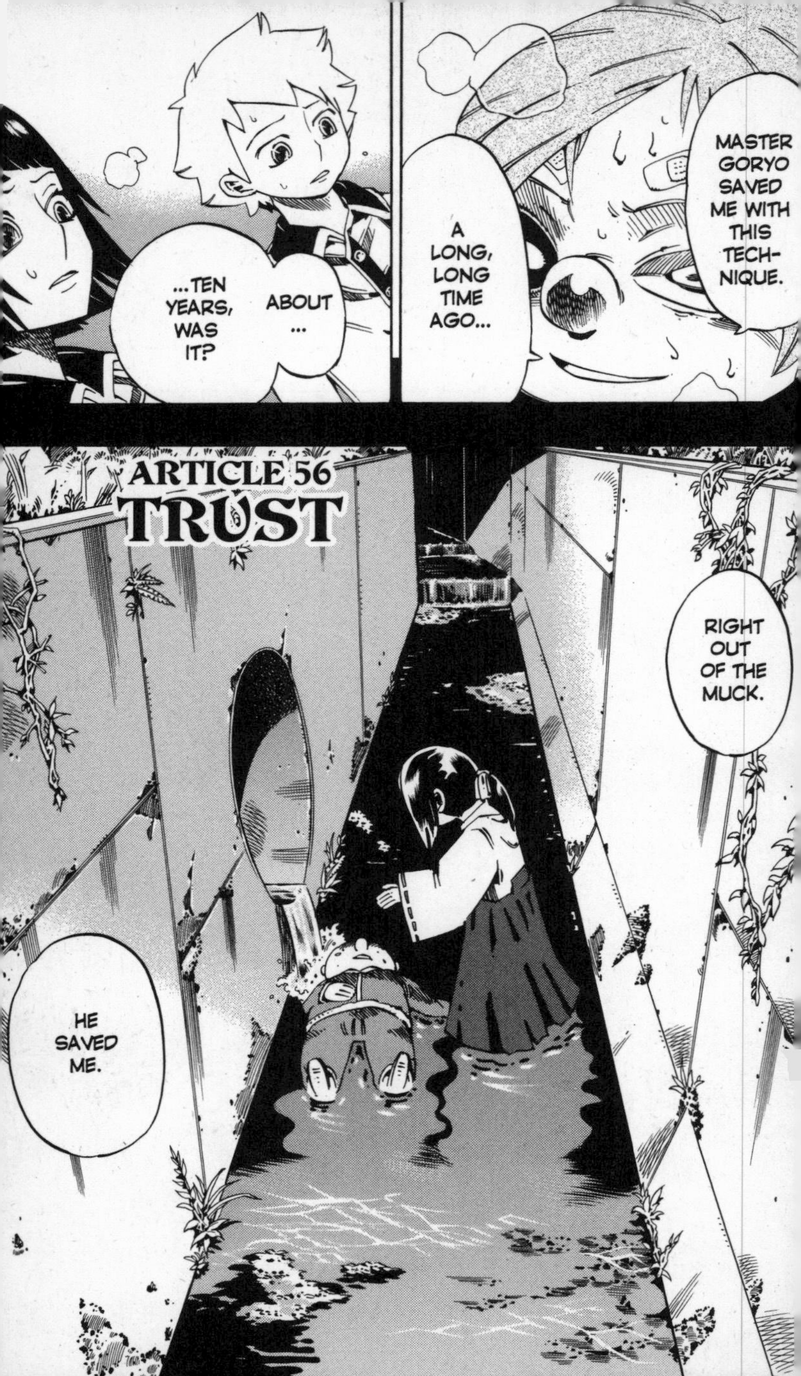
MASTER GORYO SAVED ME WITH THIS TECH-NIQUE.
A LONG, LONG TIME AGO...
ABOUT ...
...TEN YEARS, WAS IT?
ARTICLE 56
TRUST
RIGHT OUT OF THE MUCK.
HE SAVED ME.

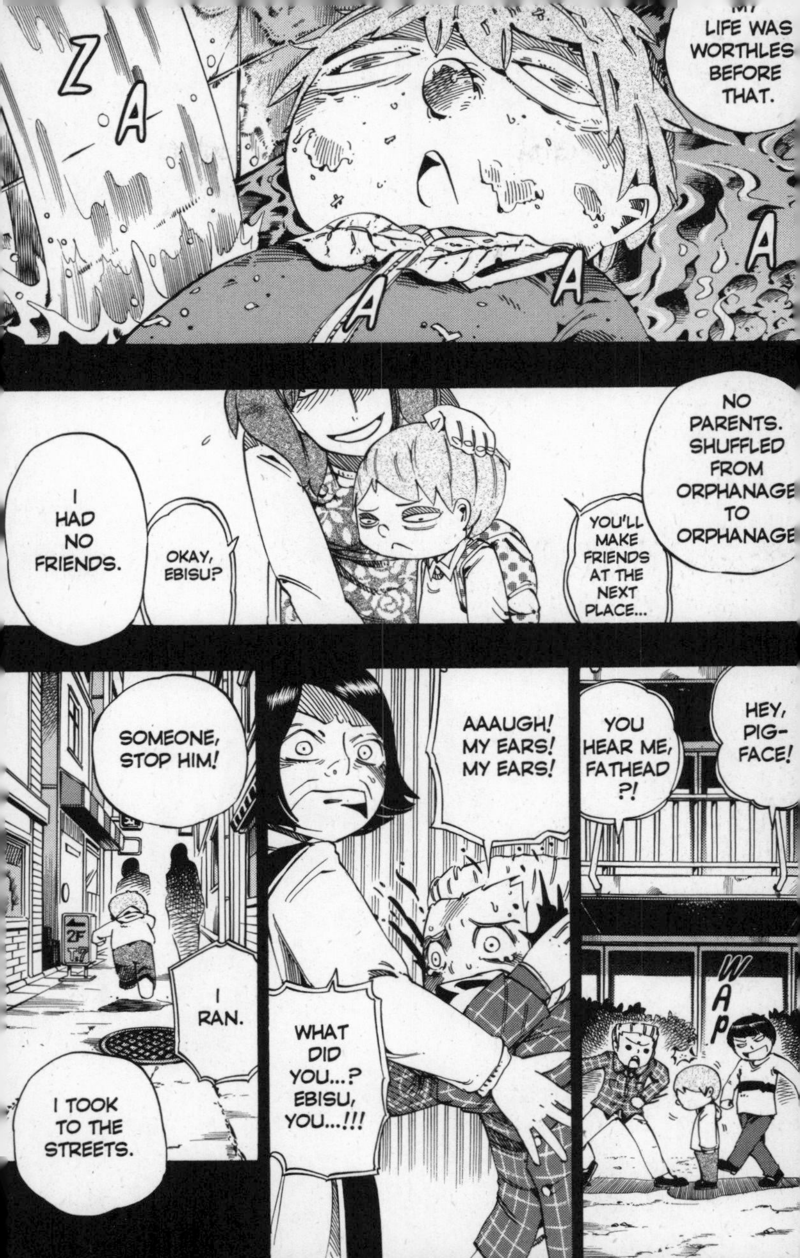
MY LIFE WAS WORTHLES BEFORE THAT.
ZAAAA
NO PARENTS. SHUFFLED FROM ORPHANAGE TO ORPHANAGE
YOU'LL MAKE FRIENDS AT THE NEXT PLACE...
OKAY, EBISU?
I HAD NO FRIENDS.
HEY, PIG-FACE!
YOU HEAR ME, FATHEAD?!
WAP
AAAUGH! MY EARS! MY EARS!
WHAT DID YOU...? EBISU, YOU...!!!
SOMEONE, STOP HIM!
I RAN.
I TOOK TO THE STREETS.

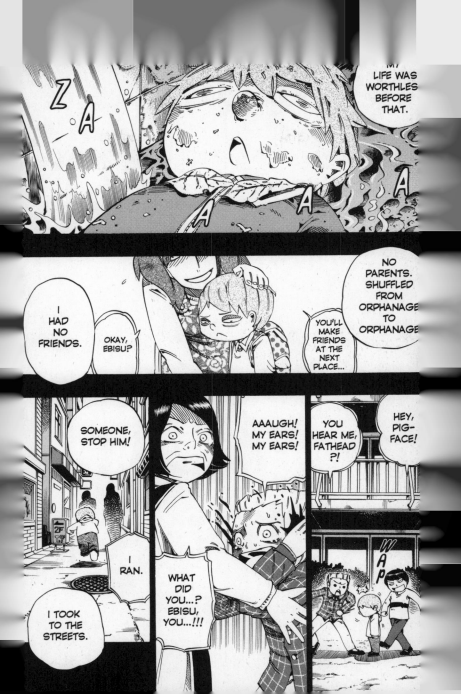

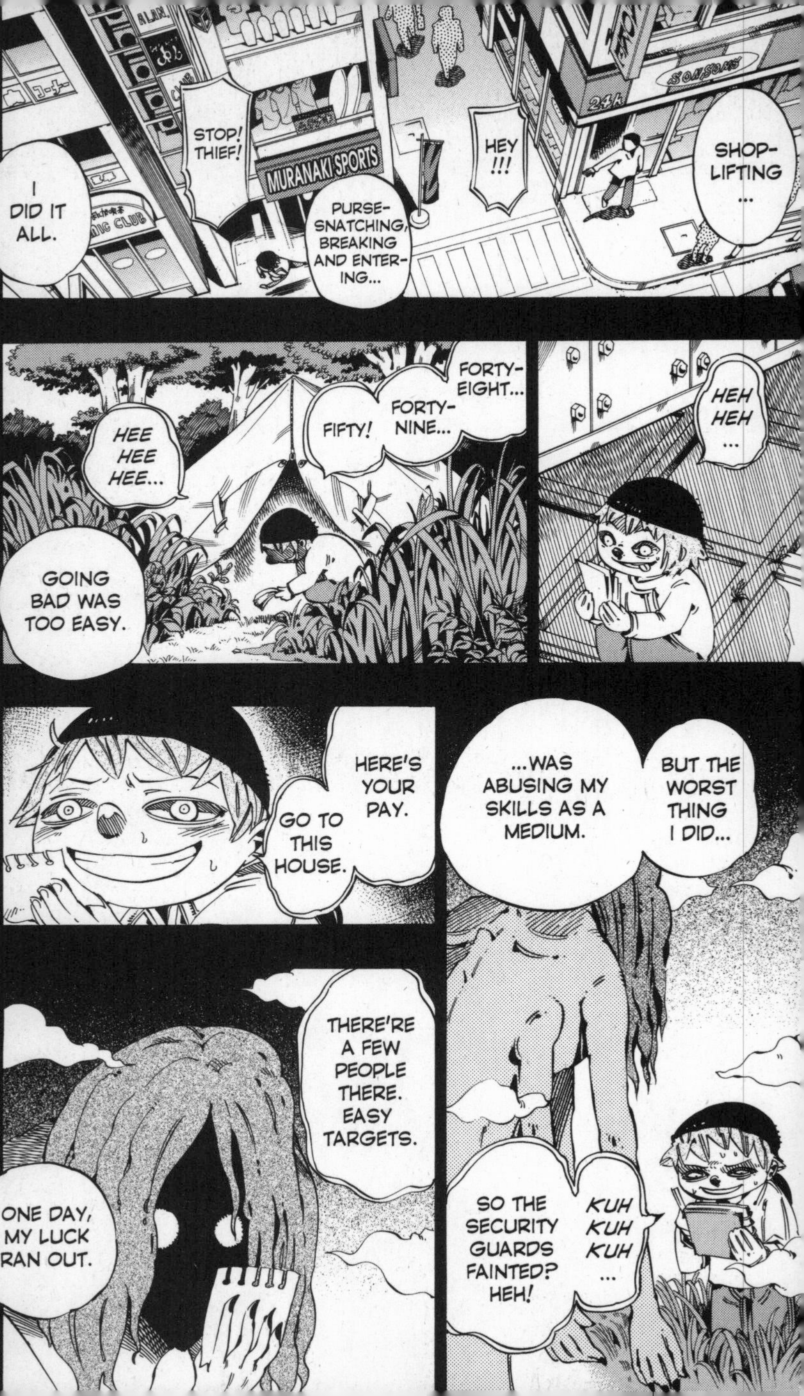
SHOP-LIFTING...
HEY!!!
STOP! THIEF!
MURANAKI SPORTS
PURSE-SNATCHING, BREAKING AND ENTERING...
I DID IT ALL.
HEH HEH ...
FORTY-EIGHT...
FORTY-NINE...
FIFTY!
HEE HEE HEE...
GOING BAD WAS TOO EASY.
BUT THE WORST THING I DID...
...WAS ABUSING MY SKILLS AS A MEDIUM.
KUH KUH KUH ...
SO THE SECURITY GUARDS FAINTED? HEH!
HERE'S YOUR PAY.
GO TO THIS HOUSE.
THERE'RE A FEW PEOPLE THERE. EASY TARGETS.
ONE DAY, MY LUCK RAN OUT.

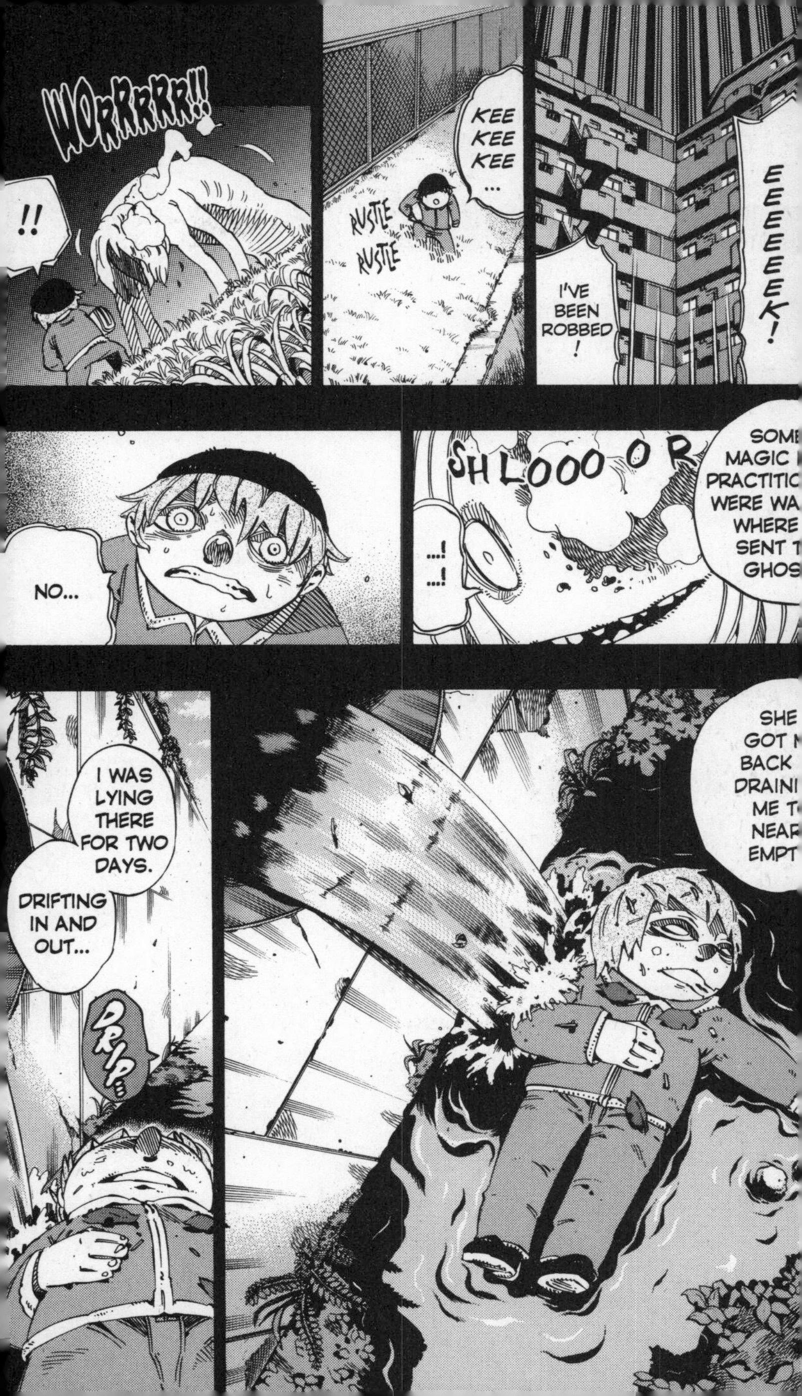

EEEEEEK!
I'VE BEEN ROBBED!
KEE KEE KEE ...
RUSTLE RUSTLE
WORRRRR!!
!!
SOME MAGIC PRACTITIC WERE WA WHERE SENT T GHOS
SHLOOO OR
..!! ..!!
NO...
SHE GOT BACK DRAINI ME T NEAR EMPT
I WAS LYING THERE FOR TWO DAYS.
DRIFTING IN AND OUT...
DRIP...

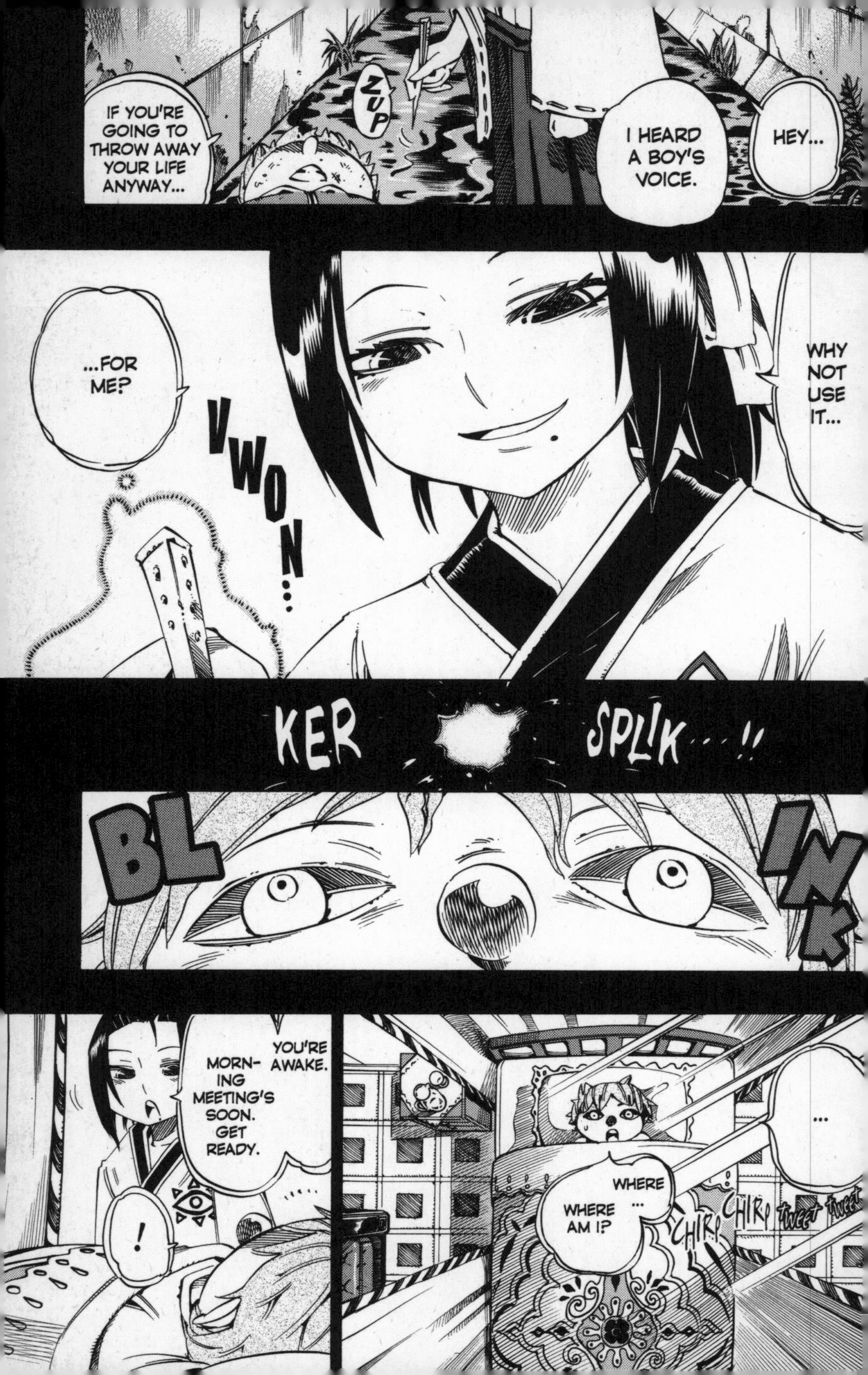
HEY...
I HEARD A BOY'S VOICE.
ZUP
IF YOU'RE GOING TO THROW AWAY YOUR LIFE ANYWAY...
WHY NOT USE IT...
VWON...
...FOR ME?
KER SPLIK...!!
BLINK
...
CHIRP CHIRP tweet tweet
WHERE... WHERE AM I?
YOU'RE AWAKE.
MORNING MEETING'S SOON. GET READY.
!

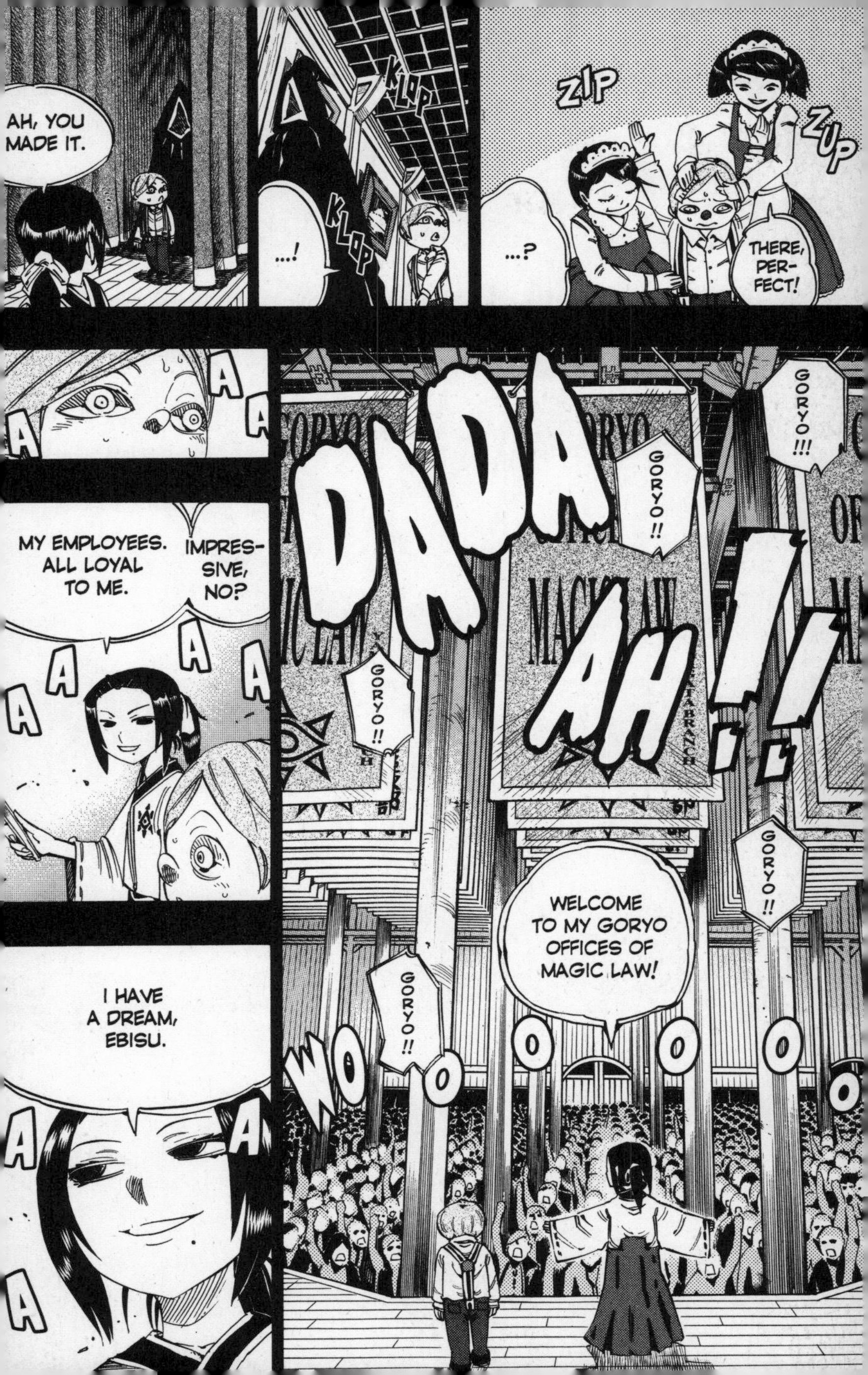
ZIP
ZUP
THERE, PER-FECT!
...?
KLOP
KLOP
...!
AH, YOU MADE IT.
GORYO!!!
DADA
AH!!
GORYO!!
GORYO!!
GORYO!!
WELCOME TO MY GORYO OFFICES OF MAGIC LAW!
GORYO!!
WOOOOOO
A A A
IMPRES-SIVE, NO?
MY EMPLOYEES. ALL LOYAL TO ME.
A A A A A
I HAVE A DREAM, EBISU.
A A A

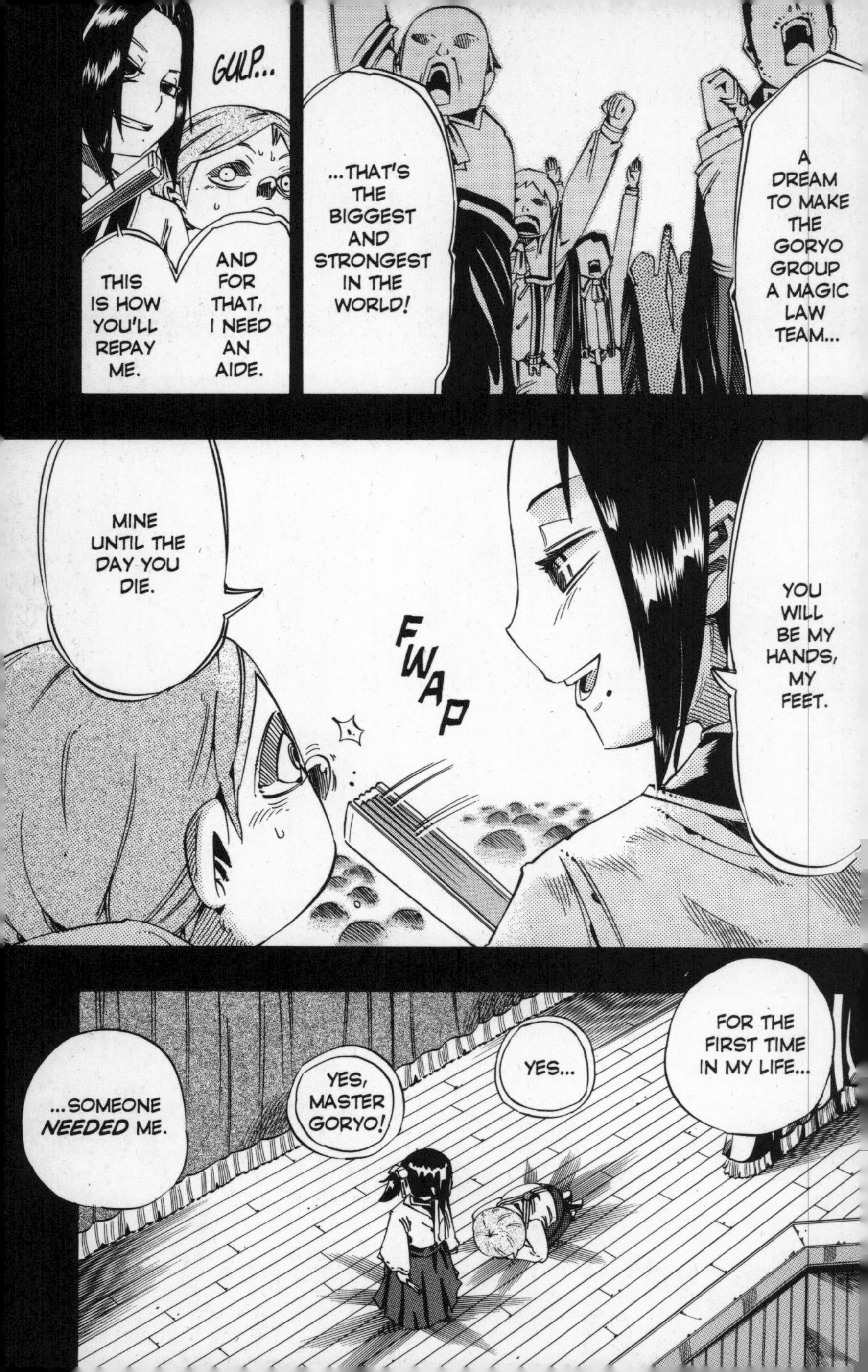
A DREAM TO MAKE THE GORYO GROUP A MAGIC LAW TEAM...
...THAT'S THE BIGGEST AND STRONGEST IN THE WORLD!
GULP...
AND FOR THAT, I NEED AN AIDE.
THIS IS HOW YOU'LL REPAY ME.
YOU WILL BE MY HANDS, MY FEET.
FWAP
MINE UNTIL THE DAY YOU DIE.
FOR THE FIRST TIME IN MY LIFE...
YES...
YES, MASTER GORYO!
...SOMEONE *NEEDED* ME.

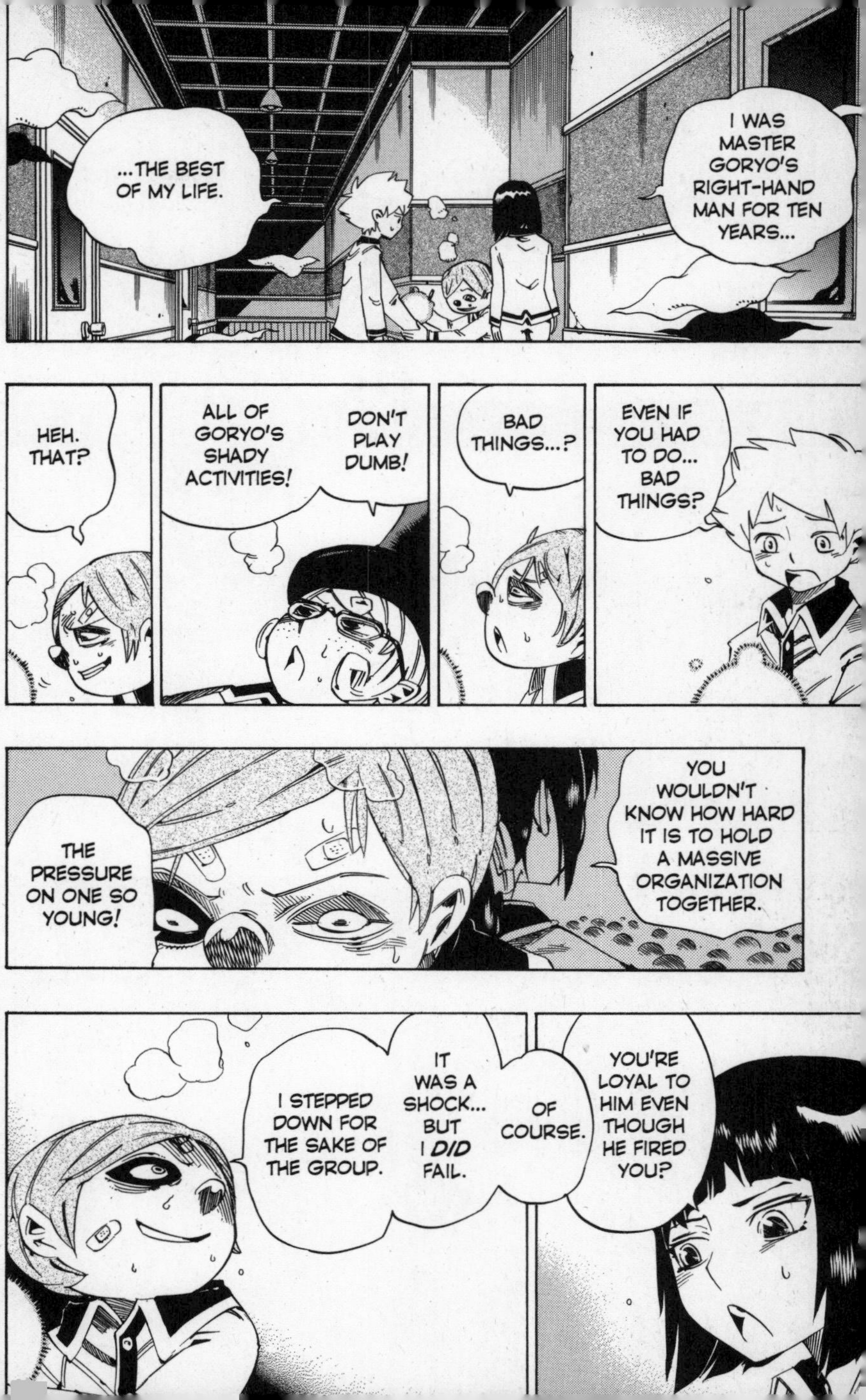
I WAS MASTER GORYO'S RIGHT-HAND MAN FOR TEN YEARS...
...THE BEST OF MY LIFE.
EVEN IF YOU HAD TO DO... BAD THINGS?
BAD THINGS...?
DON'T PLAY DUMB!
ALL OF GORYO'S SHADY ACTIVITIES!
HEH. THAT?
YOU WOULDN'T KNOW HOW HARD IT IS TO HOLD A MASSIVE ORGANIZATION TOGETHER.
THE PRESSURE ON ONE SO YOUNG!
YOU'RE LOYAL TO HIM EVEN THOUGH HE FIRED YOU?
OF COURSE.
IT WAS A SHOCK... BUT I *DID* FAIL.
I STEPPED DOWN FOR THE SAKE OF THE GROUP.

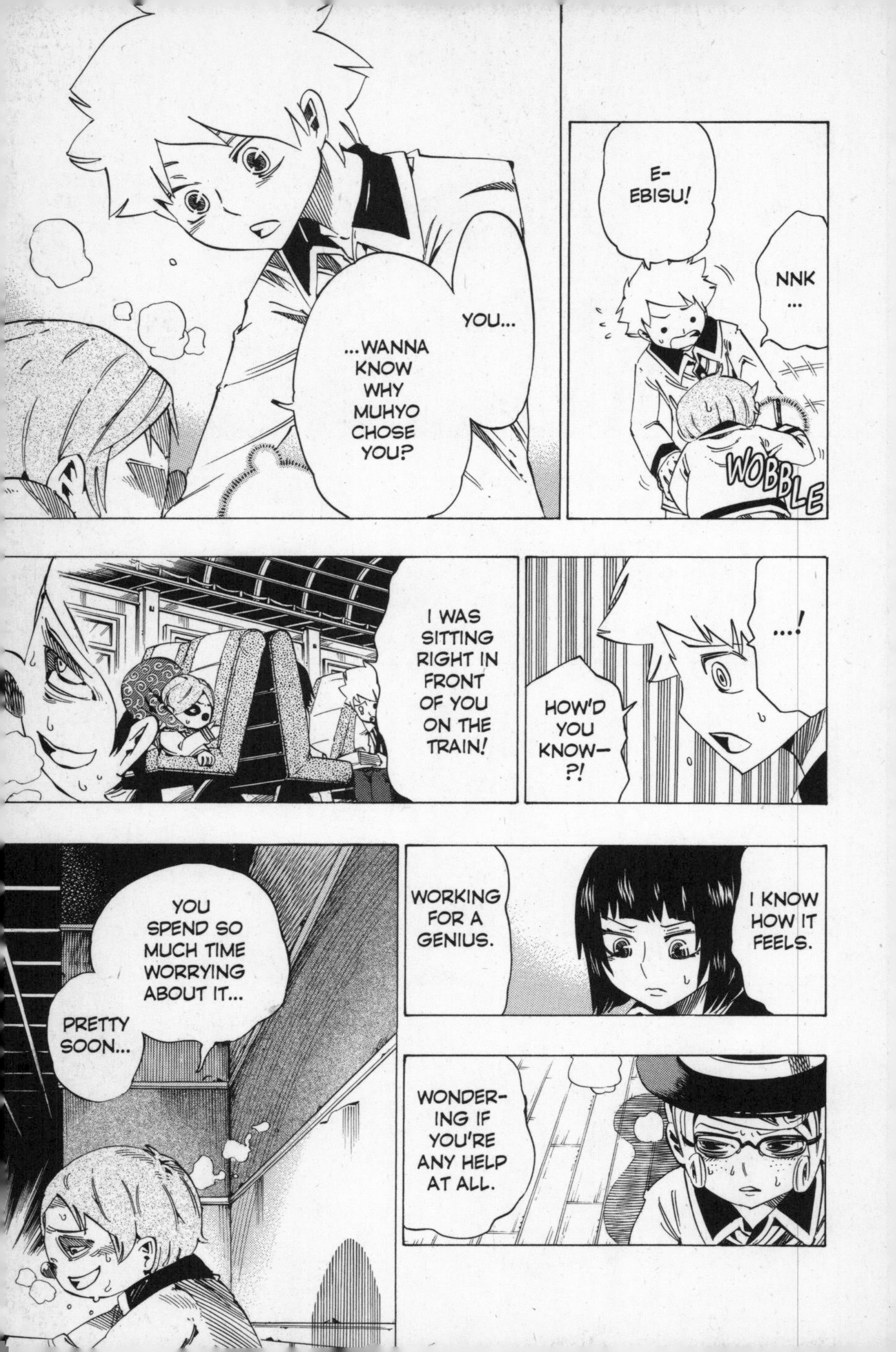
E-EBISU!
NNK...
WOBBLE
YOU...
...WANNA KNOW WHY MUHYO CHOSE YOU?
...!
HOW'D YOU KNOW—?!
I WAS SITTING RIGHT IN FRONT OF YOU ON THE TRAIN!
I KNOW HOW IT FEELS.
WORKING FOR A GENIUS.
WONDERING IF YOU'RE ANY HELP AT ALL.
YOU SPEND SO MUCH TIME WORRYING ABOUT IT...
PRETTY SOON...

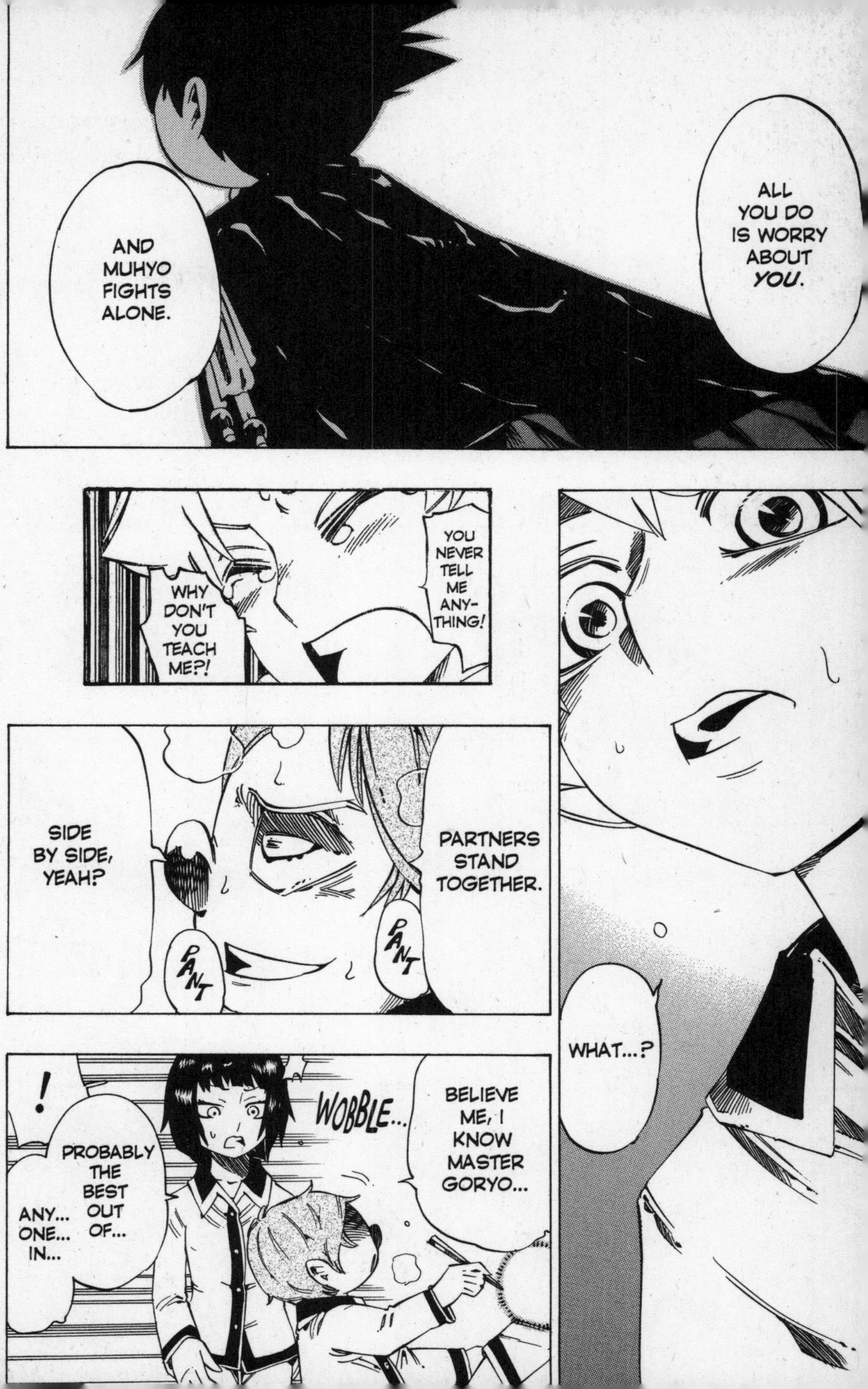
ALL YOU DO IS WORRY ABOUT *YOU*.
AND MUHYO FIGHTS ALONE.
WHAT...?
YOU NEVER TELL ME ANYTHING!
WHY DON'T YOU TEACH ME?!
PARTNERS STAND TOGETHER.
PANT
SIDE BY SIDE, YEAH?
PANT
BELIEVE ME, I KNOW MASTER GORYO...
WOBBLE...
PROBABLY THE BEST OUT OF...
ANY... ONE... IN...
!

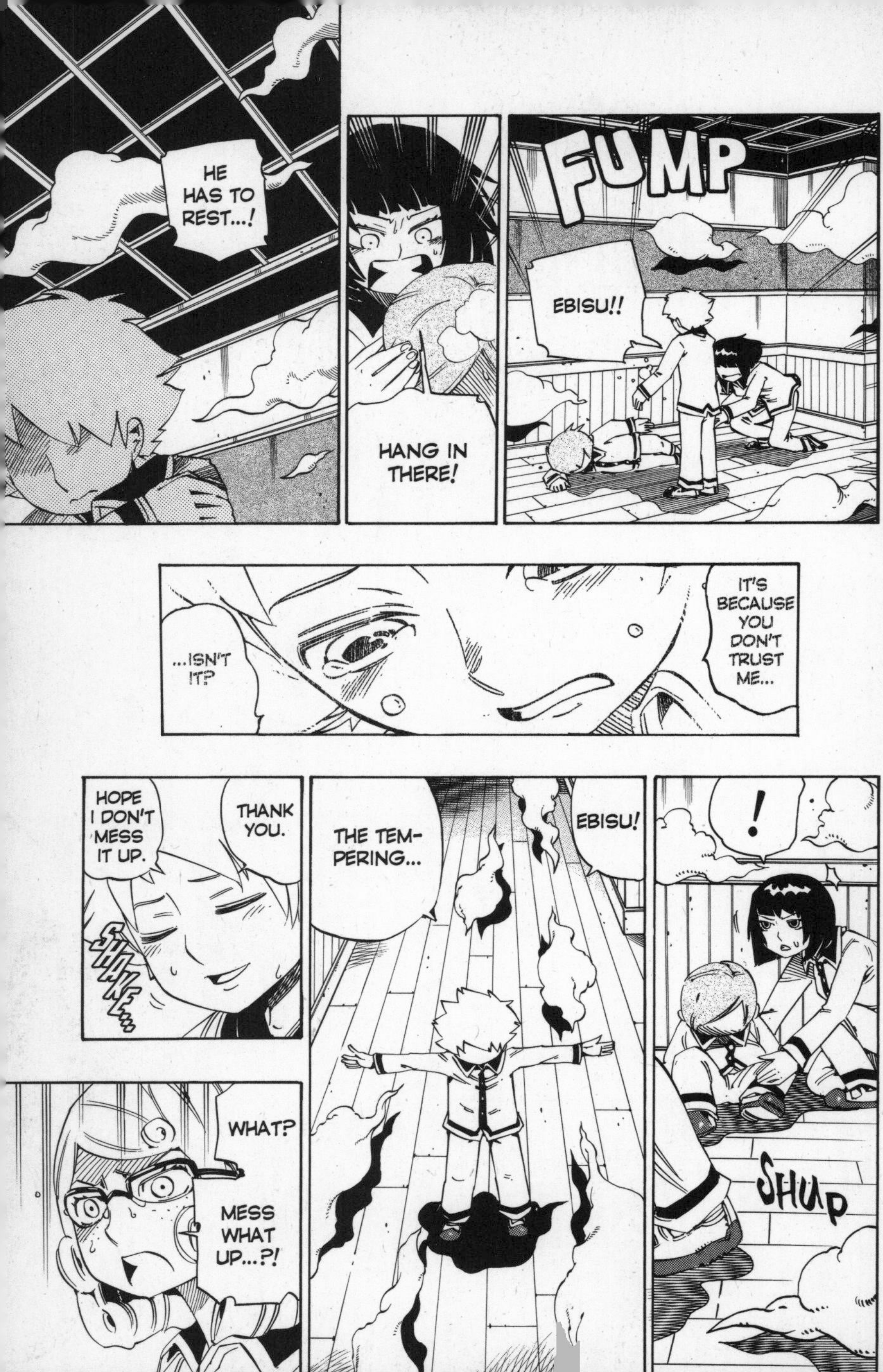
FUMP
EBISU!!
HANG IN THERE!
HE HAS TO REST...!
IT'S BECAUSE YOU DON'T TRUST ME...
...ISN'T IT?
!
SHUP
EBISU!
THE TEMPERING...
THANK YOU.
HOPE I DON'T MESS IT UP.
SHAKE...
WHAT?
MESS WHAT UP...?!

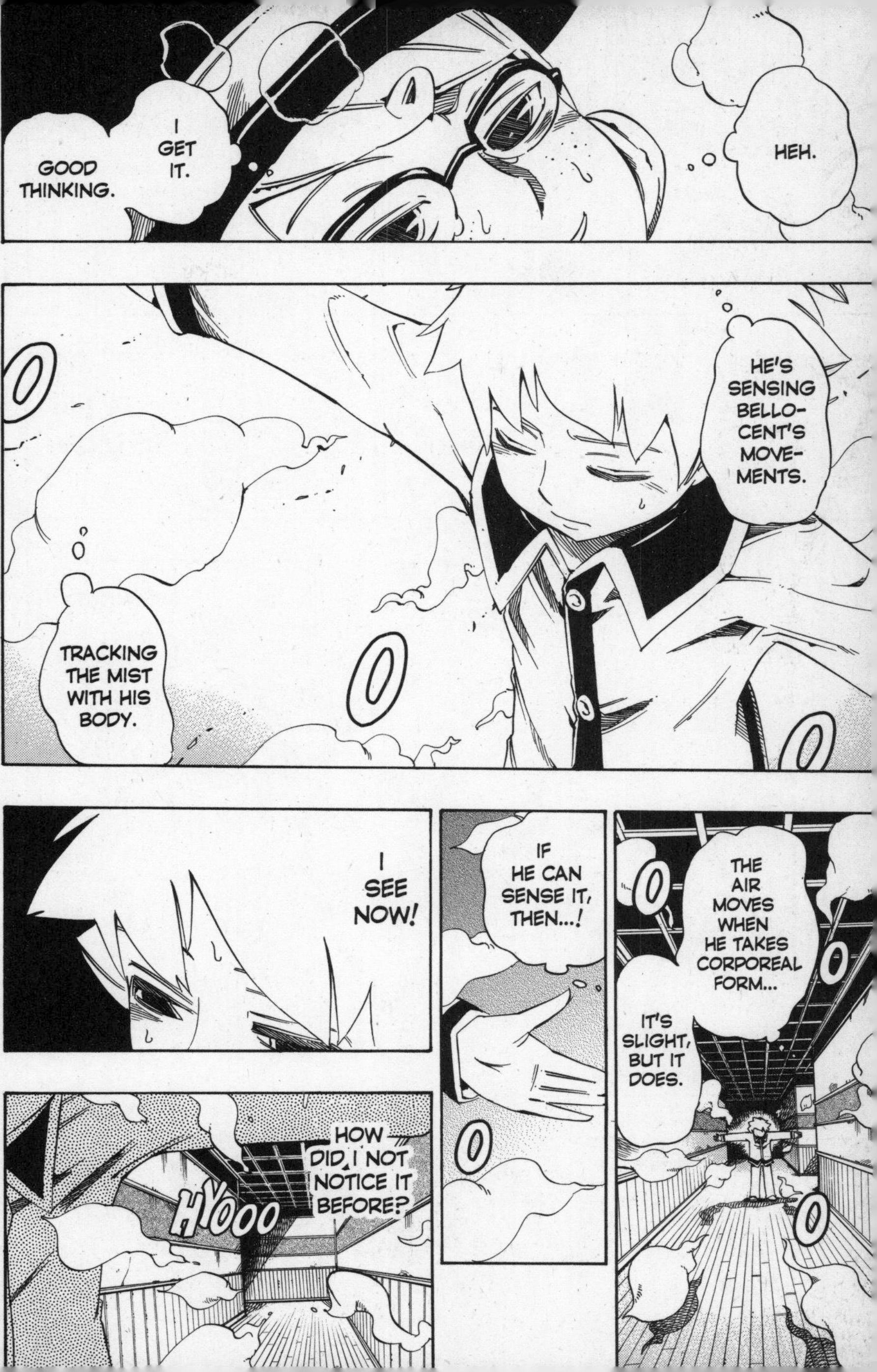
HEH.
I GET IT.
GOOD THINKING.
HE'S SENSING BELLOCENT'S MOVEMENTS.
TRACKING THE MIST WITH HIS BODY.
THE AIR MOVES WHEN HE TAKES CORPOREAL FORM...
IT'S SLIGHT, BUT IT DOES.
IF HE CAN SENSE IT, THEN...!
I SEE NOW!
HOW DID I NOT NOTICE IT BEFORE?
HYOOO

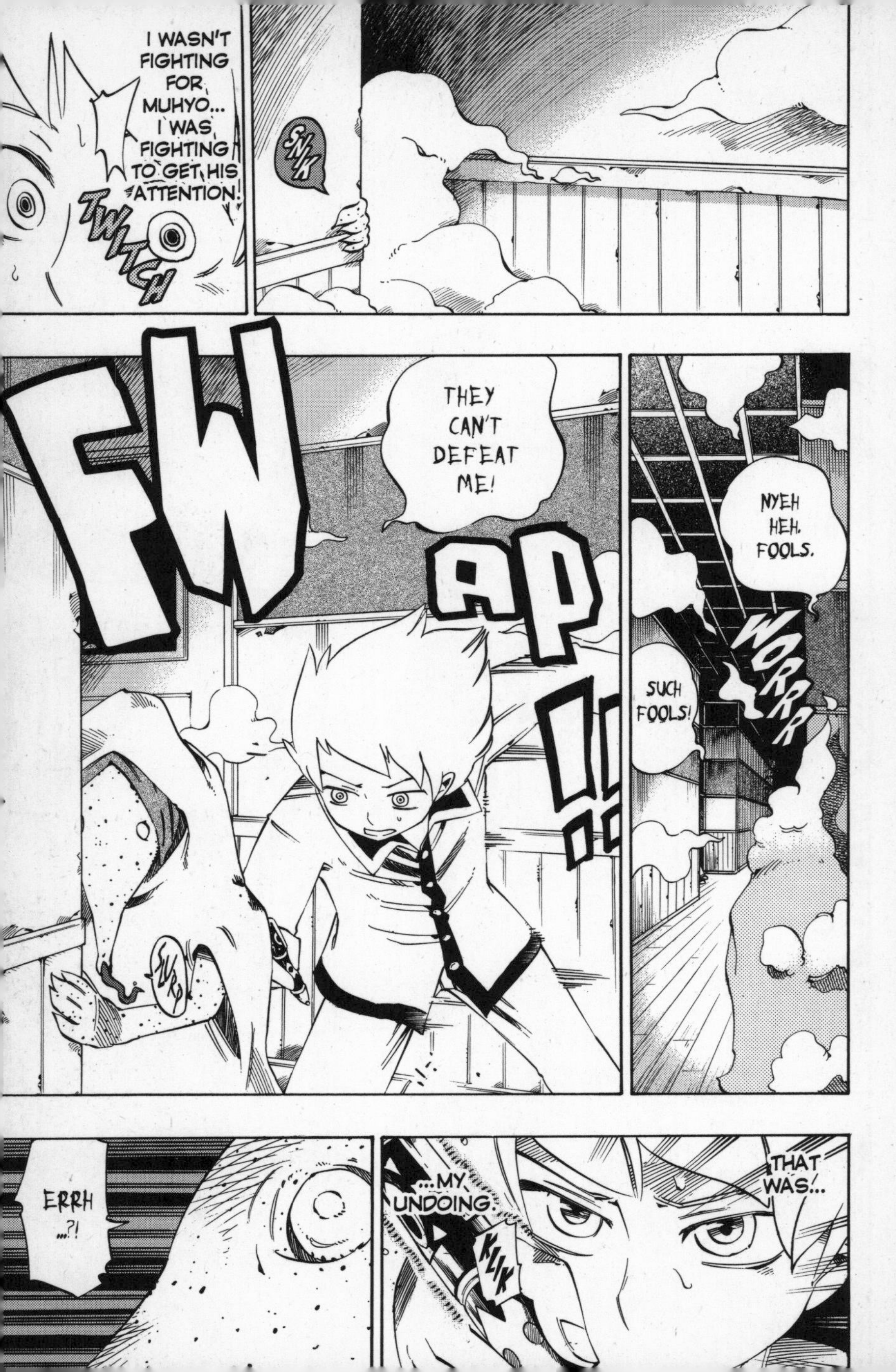
SNK
I WASN'T FIGHTING FOR MUHYO... I WAS FIGHTING TO GET HIS ATTENTION!
TWITCH
NYEH HEH. FOOLS.
WORRR
SUCH FOOLS!
FWAP!!
THEY CAN'T DEFEAT ME!
SLURP
THAT WAS...
...MY UNDOING.
KLIK
ERRH ...?!

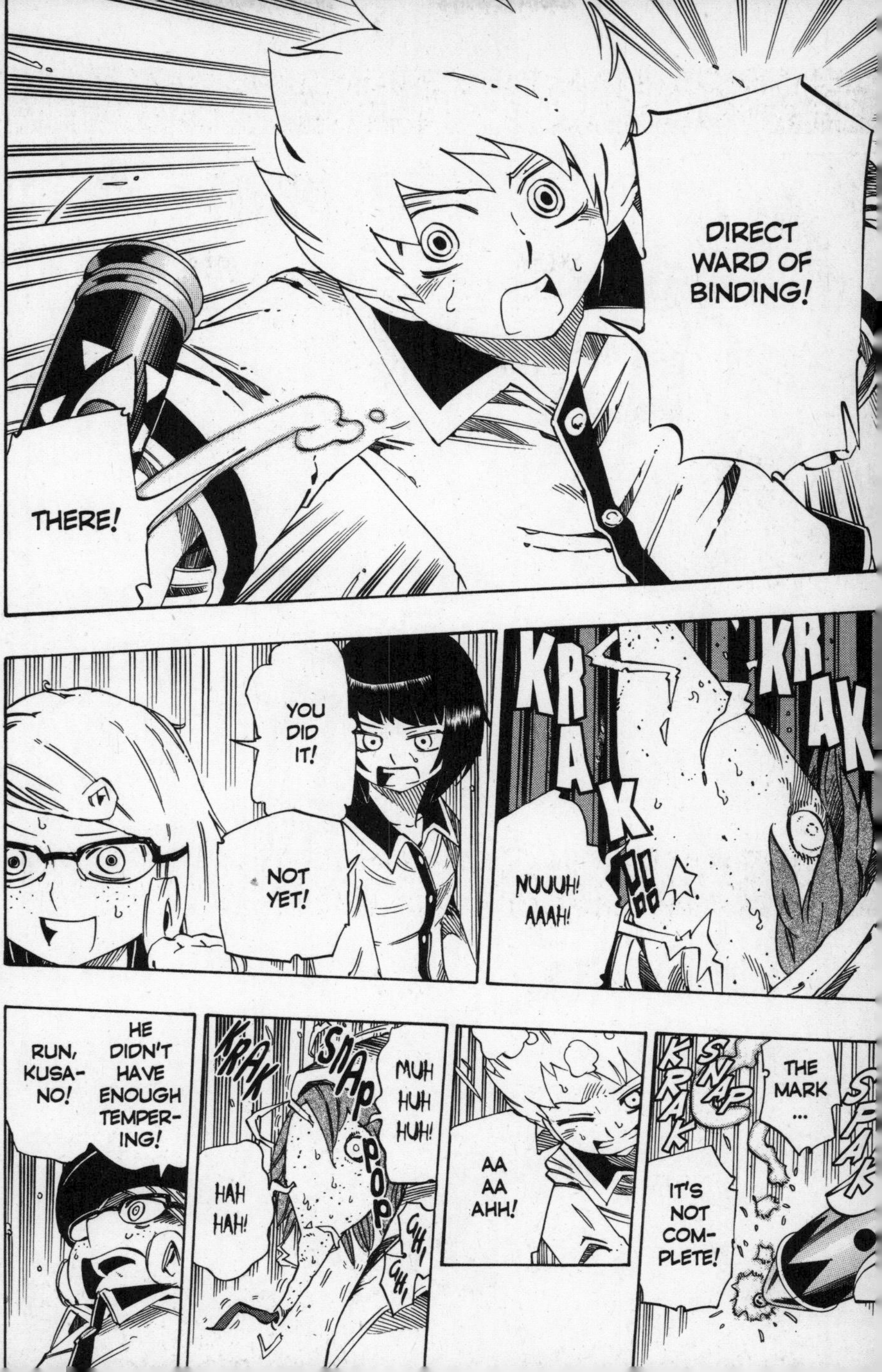
DIRECT WARD OF BINDING!
THERE!
KRAK
KRAK
NUUUH! AAAH!
YOU DID IT!
NOT YET!
THE MARK ...
SNAP
KRAK
SPAK
IT'S NOT COMPLETE!
AA AA AHH!
MUH HUH HUH!
SNAP
KRAK
POP
HAH HAH!
GH, GH,
HE DIDN'T HAVE ENOUGH TEMPERING!
RUN, KUSANO!

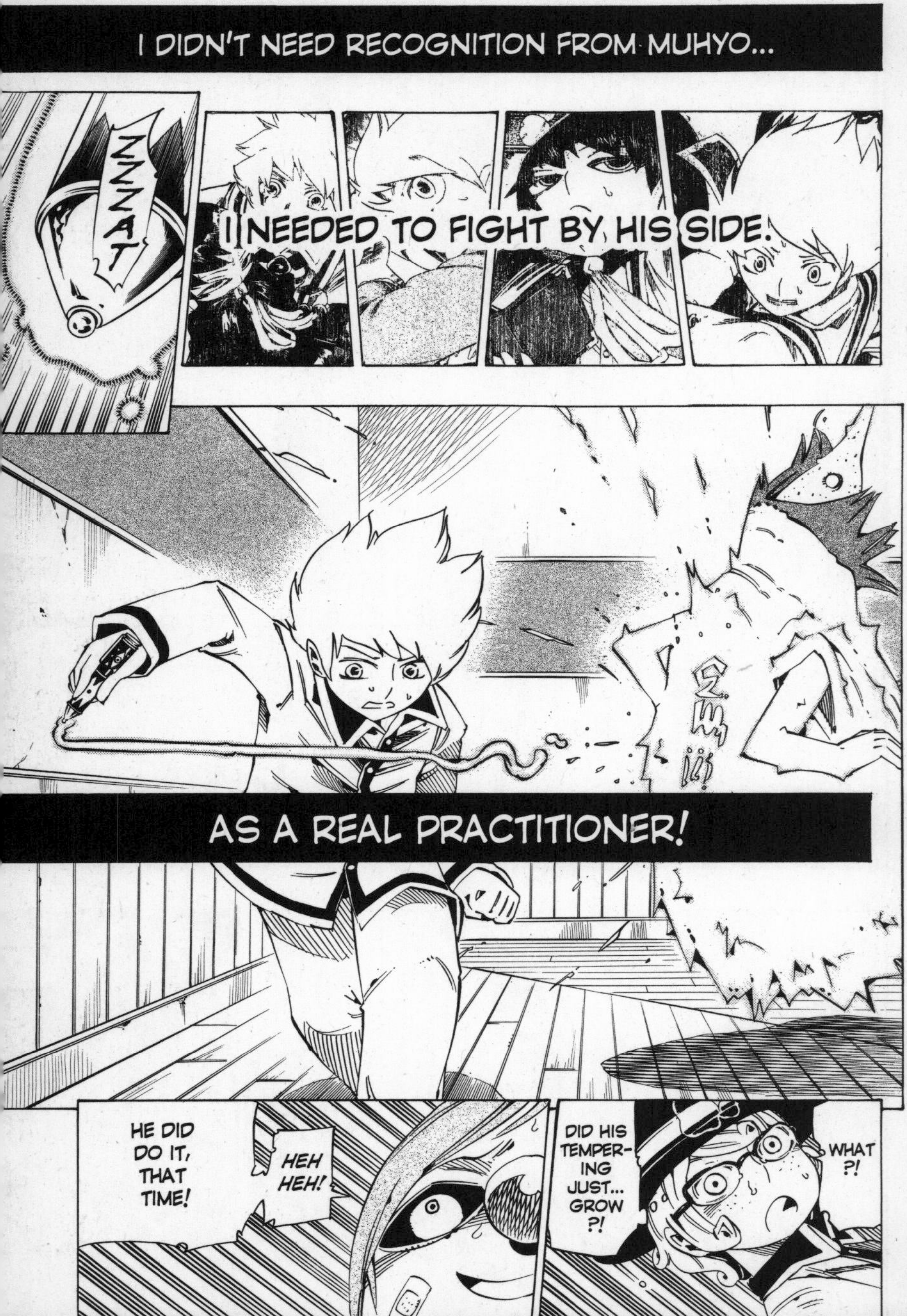
I DIDN'T NEED RECOGNITION FROM MUHYO...
I NEEDED TO FIGHT BY HIS SIDE.
ZZZAT
AS A REAL PRACTITIONER!
WHAT ?!
DID HIS TEMPERING JUST... GROW ?!
HEH HEH!
HE DID DO IT, THAT TIME!

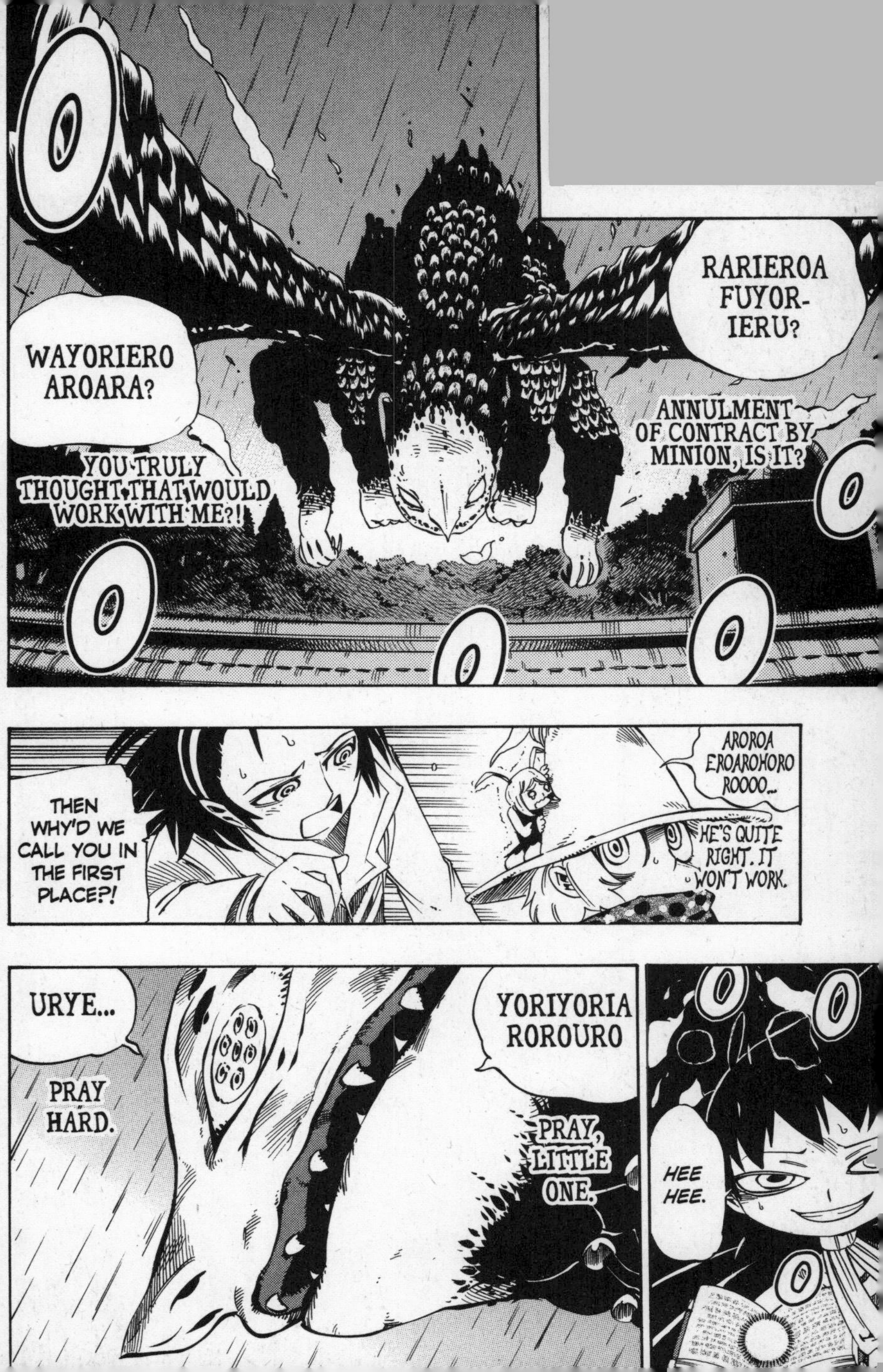
RARIEROA FUYOR-IERU?
ANNULMENT OF CONTRACT BY MINION, IS IT?
WAYORIERO AROARA?
YOU TRULY THOUGHT THAT WOULD WORK WITH ME?!
AROROA EROAROHORO ROOOO...
HE'S QUITE RIGHT. IT WON'T WORK.
THEN WHY'D WE CALL YOU IN THE FIRST PLACE?!
HEE HEE.
YORIYORIA ROROURO
PRAY, LITTLE ONE.
URYE...
PRAY HARD.

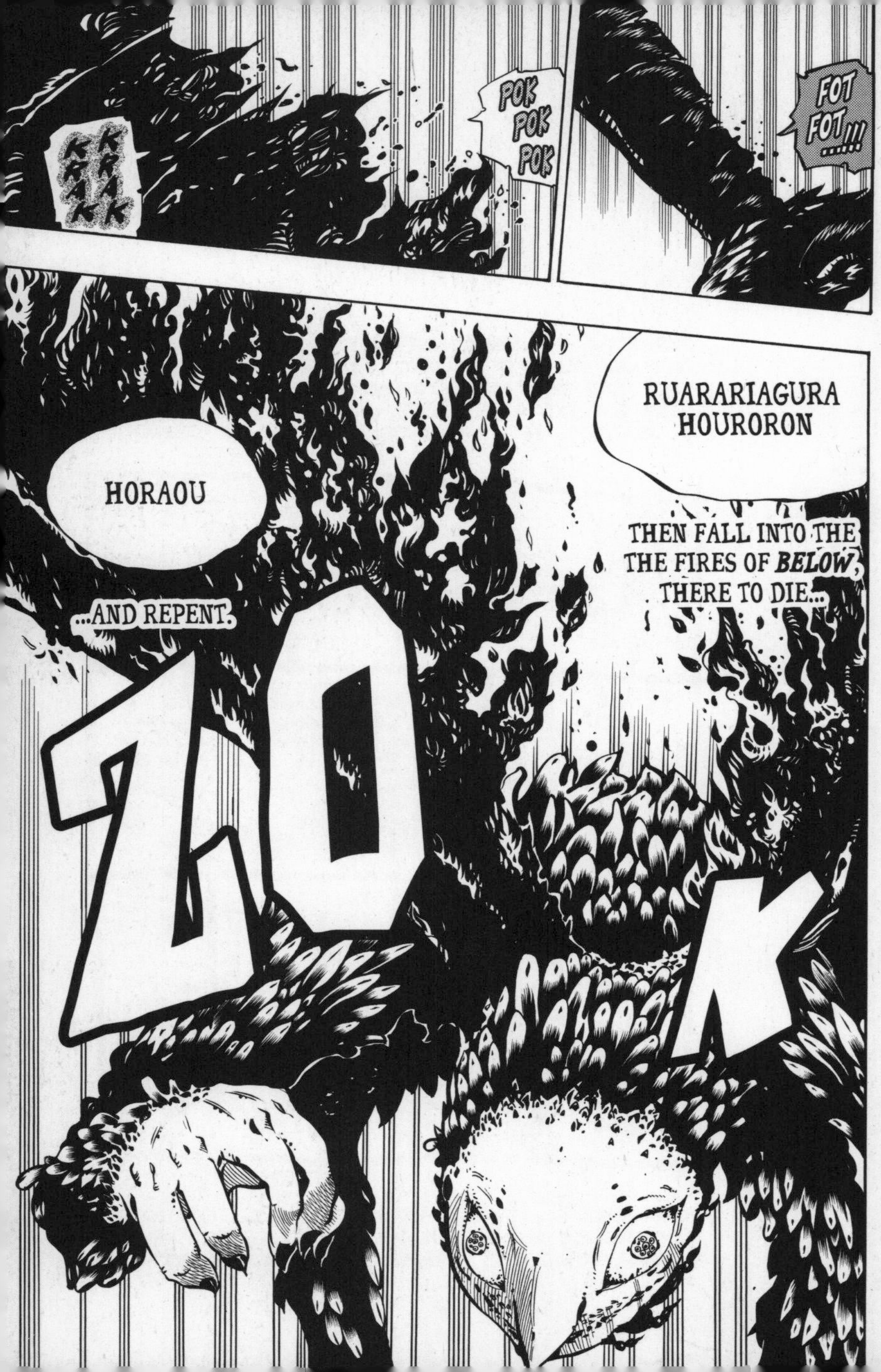
FOT FOT!!! ......
POK POK POK
KRAK KRAK
RUARARIAGURA HOUROROn
HORAOU
THEN FALL INTO THE THE FIRES OF *BELOW*, THERE TO DIE...
...AND REPENT.
ZOK

REGARDING THE QUESTIONS I RECEIVED IN THE LAST VOLUME: "WHY DID YOU START DRAWING MANGA?" "WHAT INFLUENCED YOU?" AND "WHAT DID YOU DO BEFORE YOU GOT SERIALIZED?" (FROM A.R., OITA PREFECTURE), I'D LIKE TO ANSWER QUESTION NUMBER TWO, "WHAT INFLUENCED YOU?" WITH...A MANGA!

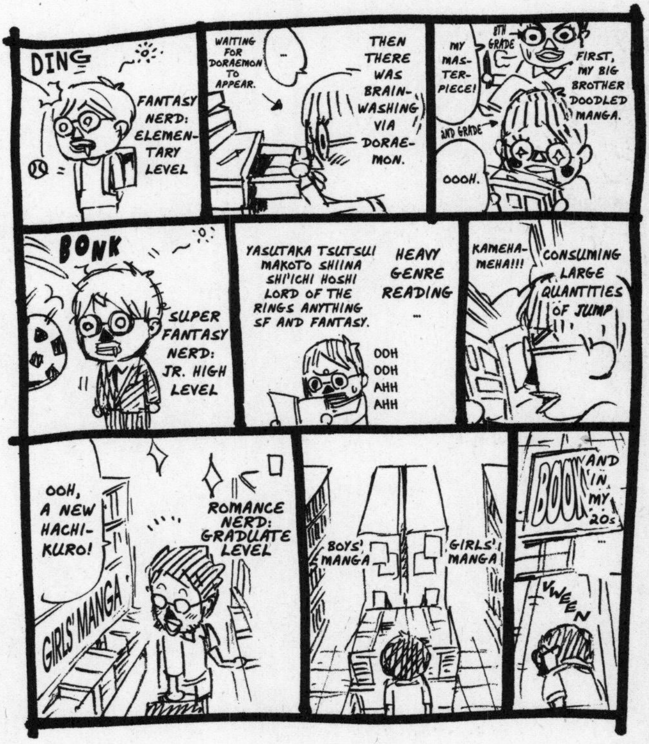
FIRST, MY BIG BROTHER DOODLED MANGA.
8TH GRADE
MY MASTERPIECE!
2ND GRADE
OOOH.
THEN THERE WAS BRAIN-WASHING VIA DORAEMON.
WAITING FOR DORAEMON TO APPEAR.
...
DING
FANTASY NERD: ELEMENTARY LEVEL
CONSUMING LARGE QUANTITIES OF JUMP
KAMEHAMEHA!!!
HEAVY GENRE READING
...
YASUTAKA TSUTSUI MAKOTO SHIINA SHI'ICHI HOSHI LORD OF THE RINGS ANYTHING SF AND FANTASY.
OOH OOH AHH AHH
BONK
SUPER FANTASY NERD: JR. HIGH LEVEL
AND IN MY 20s
...
BOOK
VWEEN
GIRLS' MANGA
BOYS' MANGA
ROMANCE NERD: GRADUATE LEVEL
OOH, A NEW HACHIKURO!
GIRLS' MANGA

FOR A WHILE, ALL I DID WAS READ. SOMEONE SUGGESTED SOME OLD CLASSICS, AND I WAS HOOKED. LATELY, I BARELY HAVE TIME TO READ MANGA. VERY STRESSFUL... I WANNA READ BOOKS, TOO!

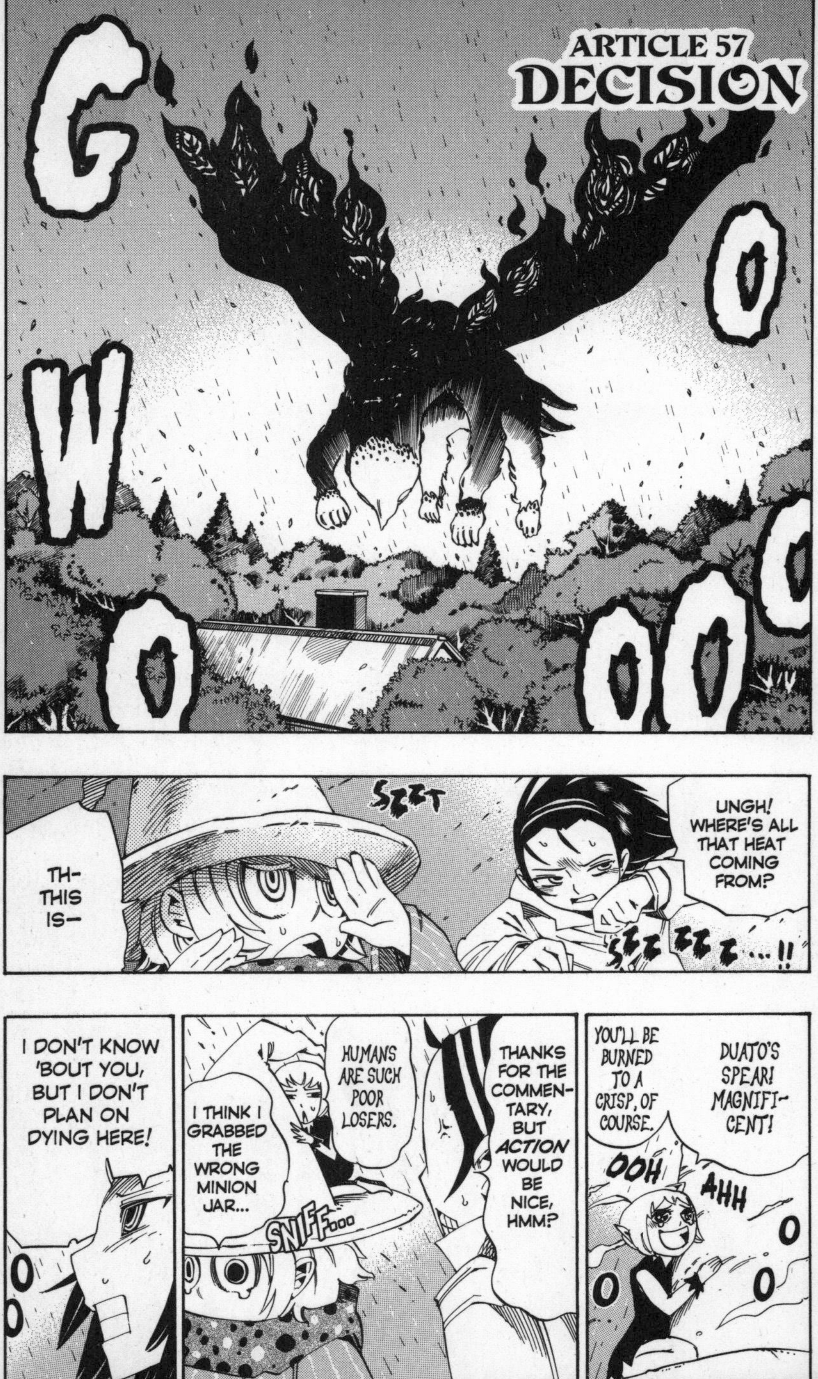
ARTICLE 57
DECISION
GWOOOOOO
UNGH! WHERE'S ALL THAT HEAT COMING FROM?
SZZT
SZZZZZZ...!!
TH- THIS IS—
DUATO'S SPEAR! MAGNIFICENT!
YOU'LL BE BURNED TO A CRISP, OF COURSE.
OOH
AHH
OO
THANKS FOR THE COMMENTARY, BUT *ACTION* WOULD BE NICE, HMM?
HUMANS ARE SUCH POOR LOSERS.
I THINK I GRABBED THE WRONG MINION JAR...
SNIFFooo
I DON'T KNOW 'BOUT YOU, BUT I DON'T PLAN ON DYING HERE!
OO

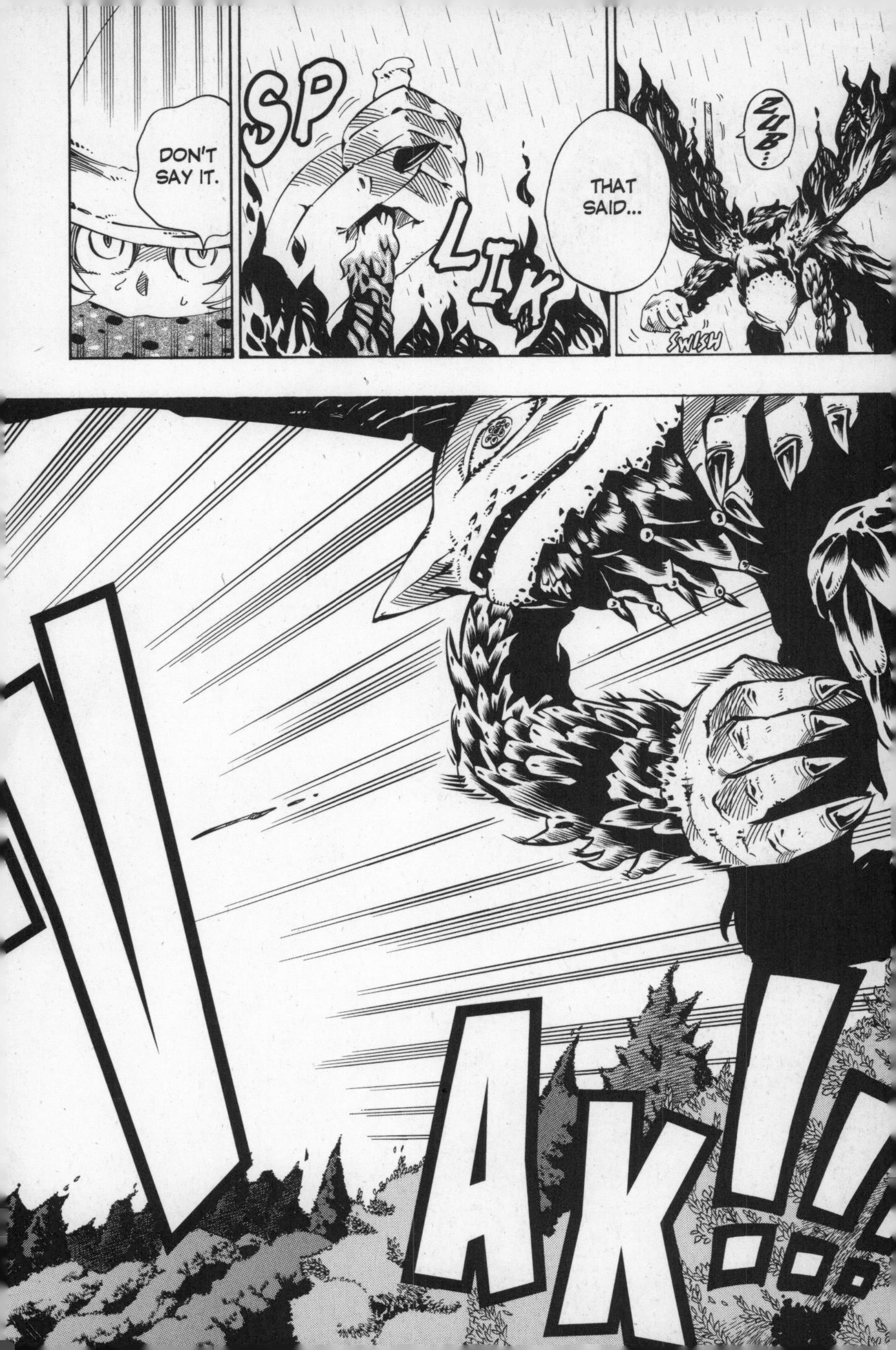
ZUB...
THAT SAID...
SWISH
SPLIK
DON'T SAY IT.
AK!!

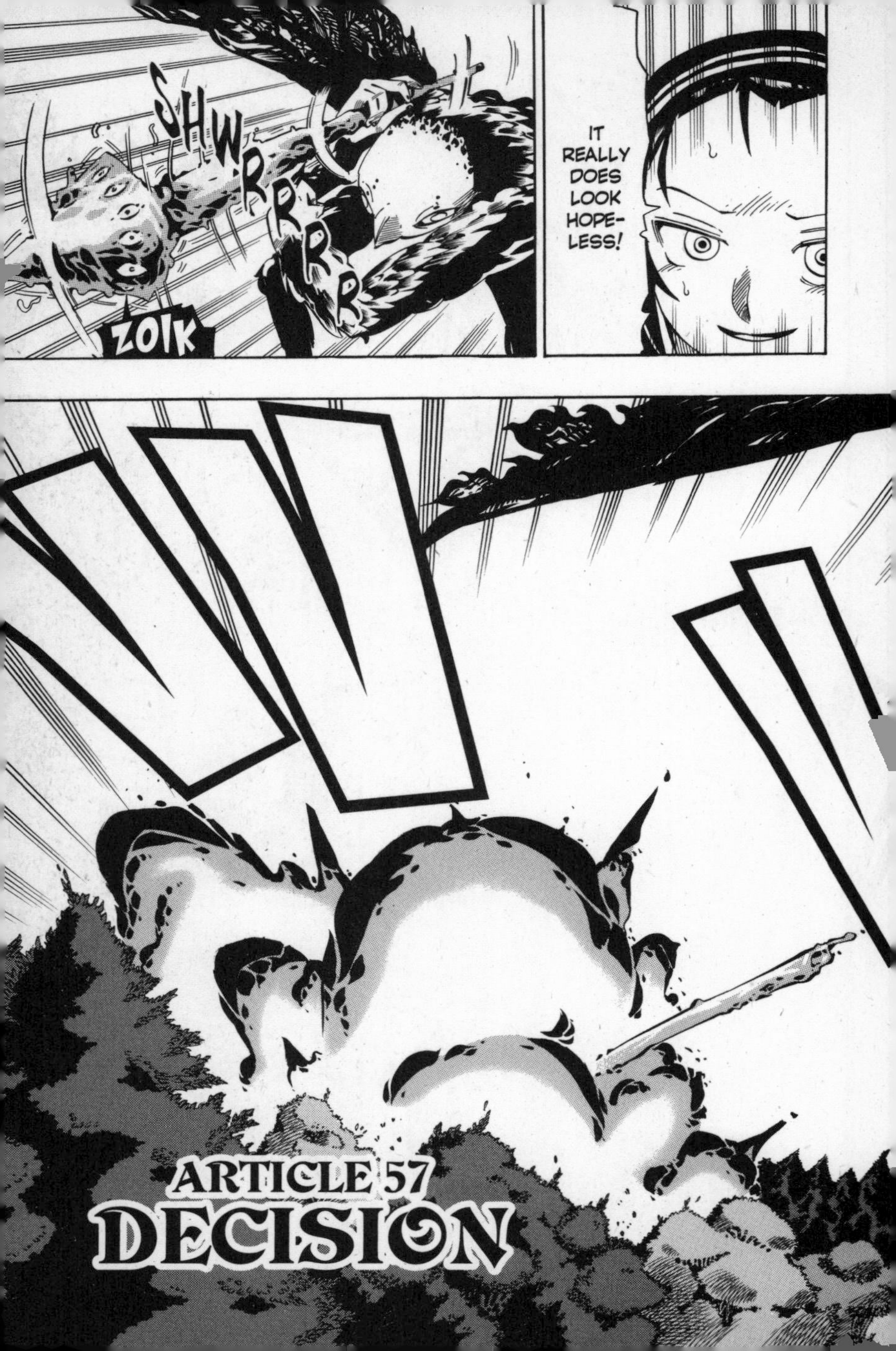

IT REALLY DOES LOOK HOPE-LESS!
SHWRRRRR
ZOIK
ARTICLE 57
DECISION

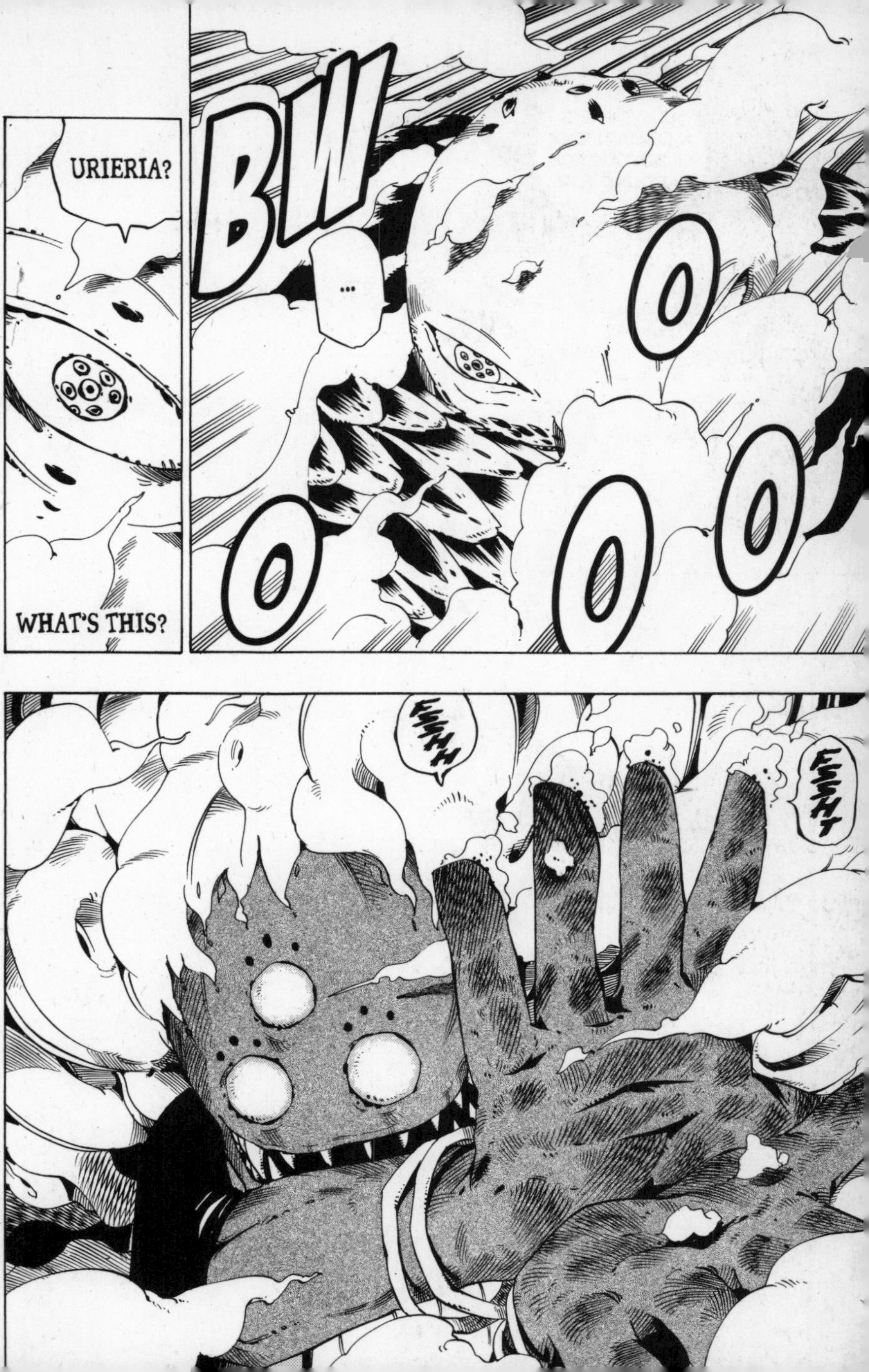
BWOOOO
...
URIERIA?
WHAT'S THIS?
EEEHHT
EEEHH

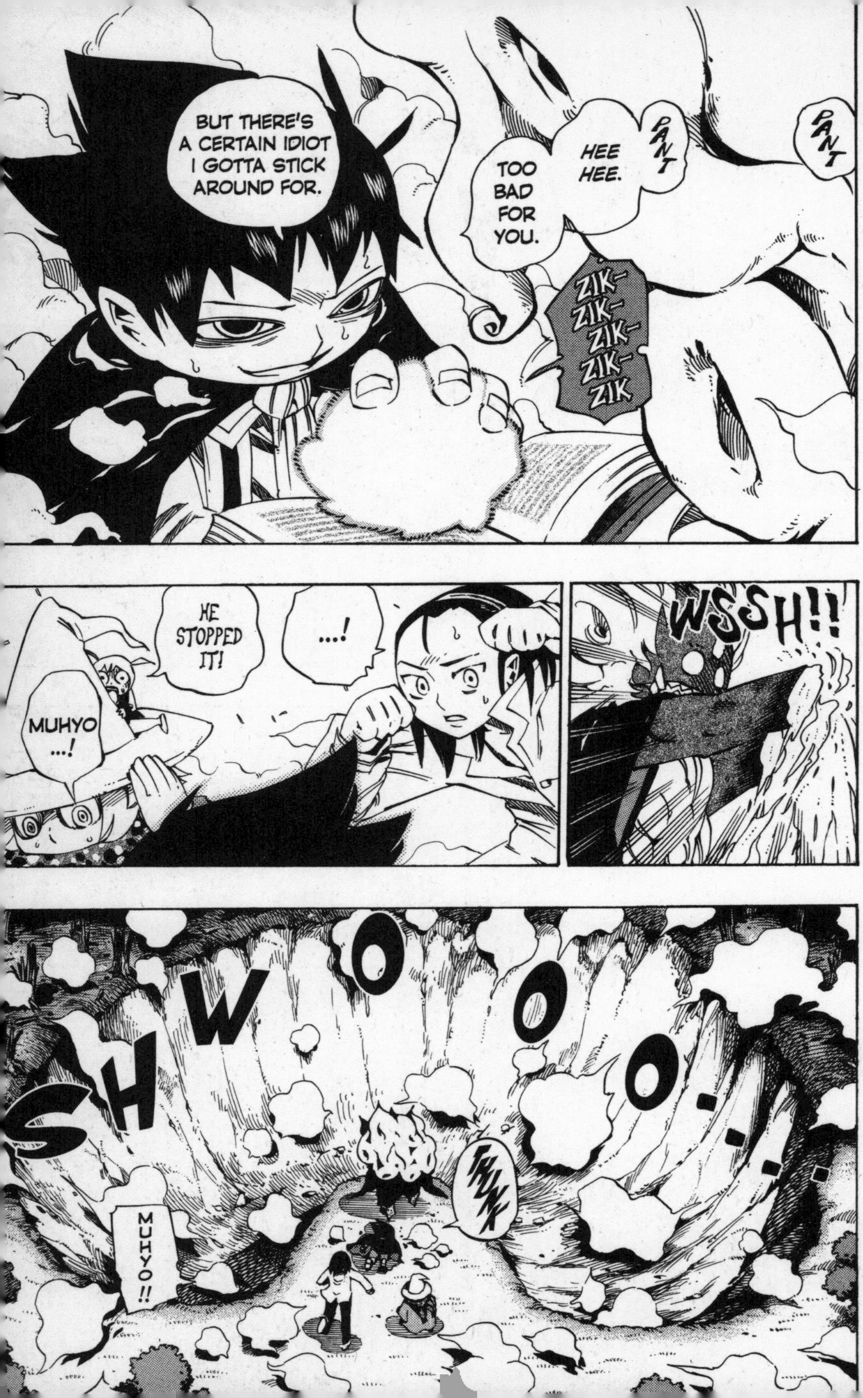
PANT
PANT
HEE HEE.
TOO BAD FOR YOU.
ZIK-ZIK-ZIK-ZIK-ZIK
BUT THERE'S A CERTAIN IDIOT I GOTTA STICK AROUND FOR.
WSSH!!
...!
HE STOPPED IT!
MUHYO ...!
SHWOOOO....
THUNK
MUHYO!!

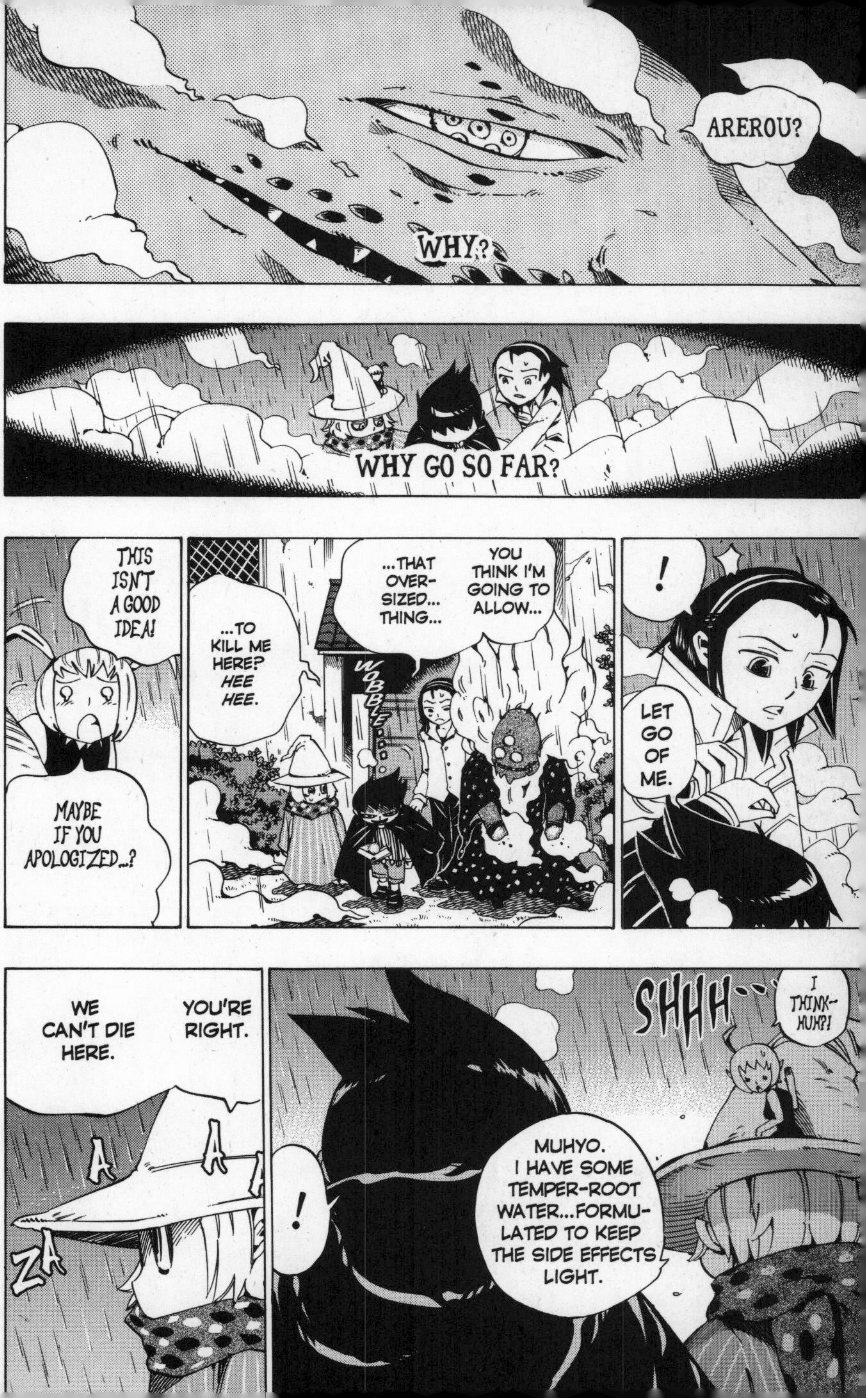
ARERO U?
WHY?
WHY GO SO FAR?
!
LET GO OF ME.
YOU THINK I'M GOING TO ALLOW...
...THAT OVER-SIZED... THING...
WOBBLE
...TO KILL ME HERE? HEE HEE.
THIS ISN'T A GOOD IDEA!
MAYBE IF YOU APOLOGIZED...?
I THINK-- HUH?!
SHHH...
MUHYO. I HAVE SOME TEMPER-ROOT WATER...FORMU-LATED TO KEEP THE SIDE EFFECTS LIGHT.
!
YOU'RE RIGHT.
WE CAN'T DIE HERE.
ZA A A A

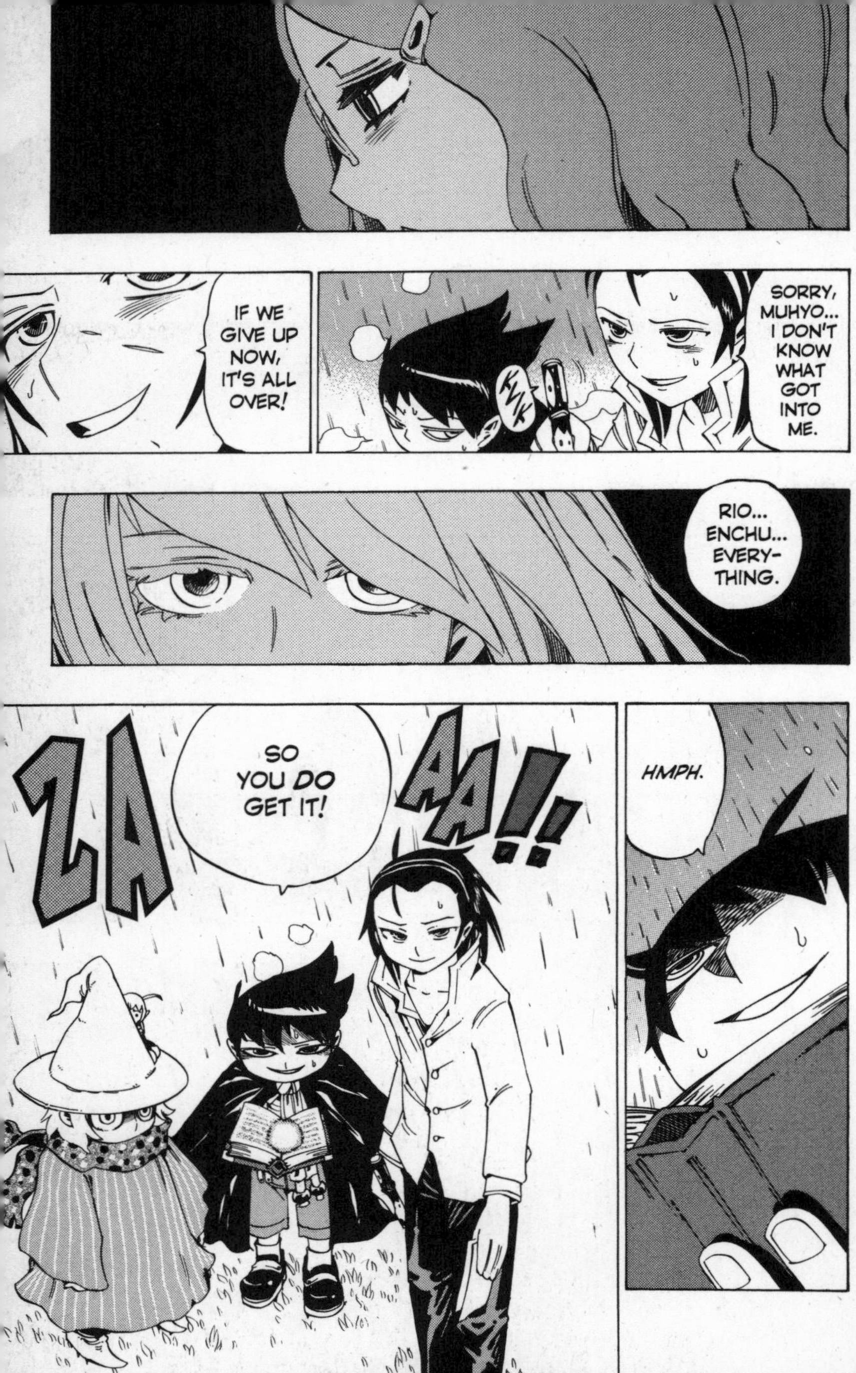
SORRY, MUHYO... I DON'T KNOW WHAT GOT INTO ME.
IF WE GIVE UP NOW, IT'S ALL OVER!
RIO... ENCHU... EVERYTHING.
HMPH.
SO YOU *DO* GET IT!
ZA AA!!

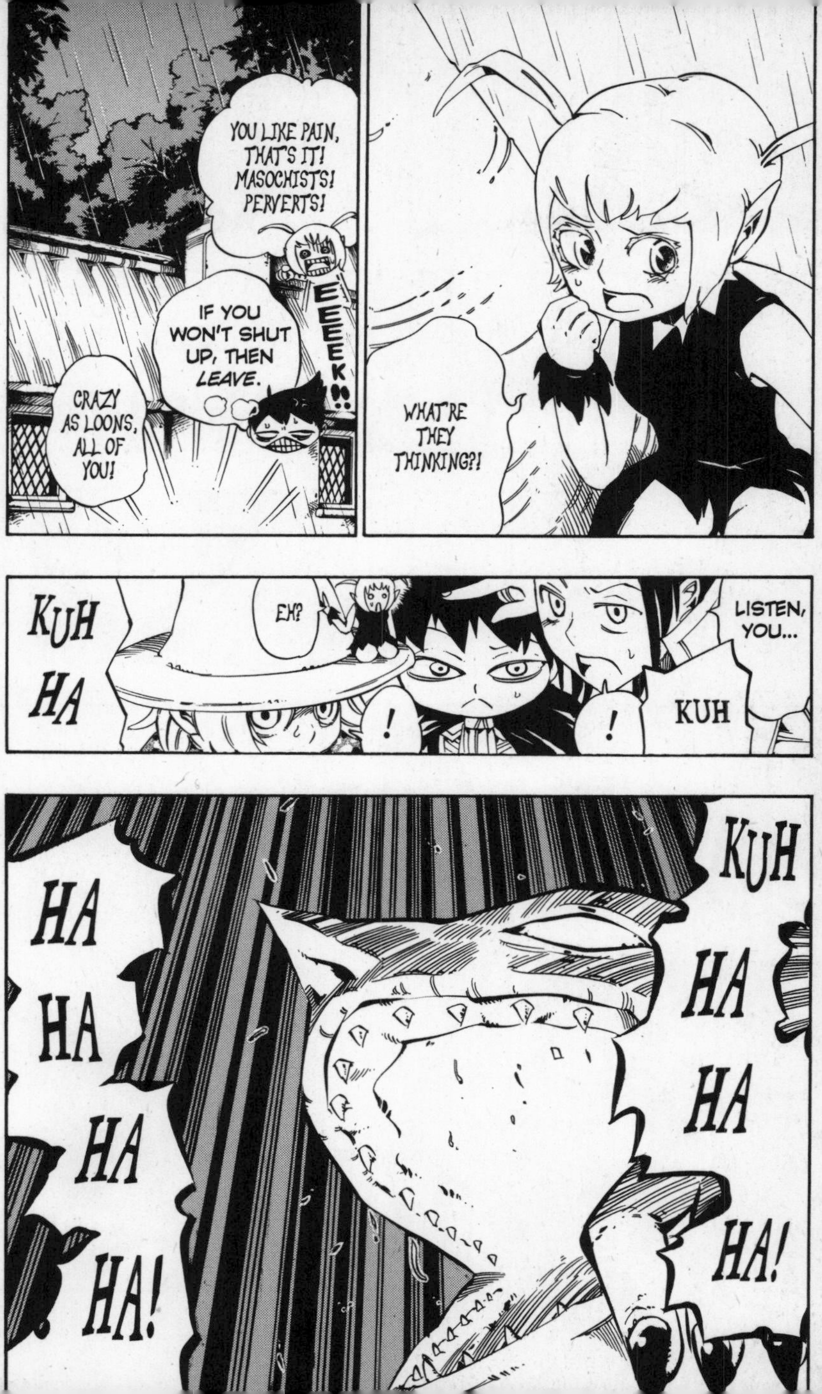
WHAT'RE THEY THINKING?!
YOU LIKE PAIN, THAT'S IT! MASOCHISTS! PERVERTS!
EEEEK!!
IF YOU WON'T SHUT UP, THEN LEAVE.
CRAZY AS LOONS, ALL OF YOU!
LISTEN, YOU...
KUH
!
!
EH?
KUH HA
KUH HA HA HA HA!
HA HA HA HA!

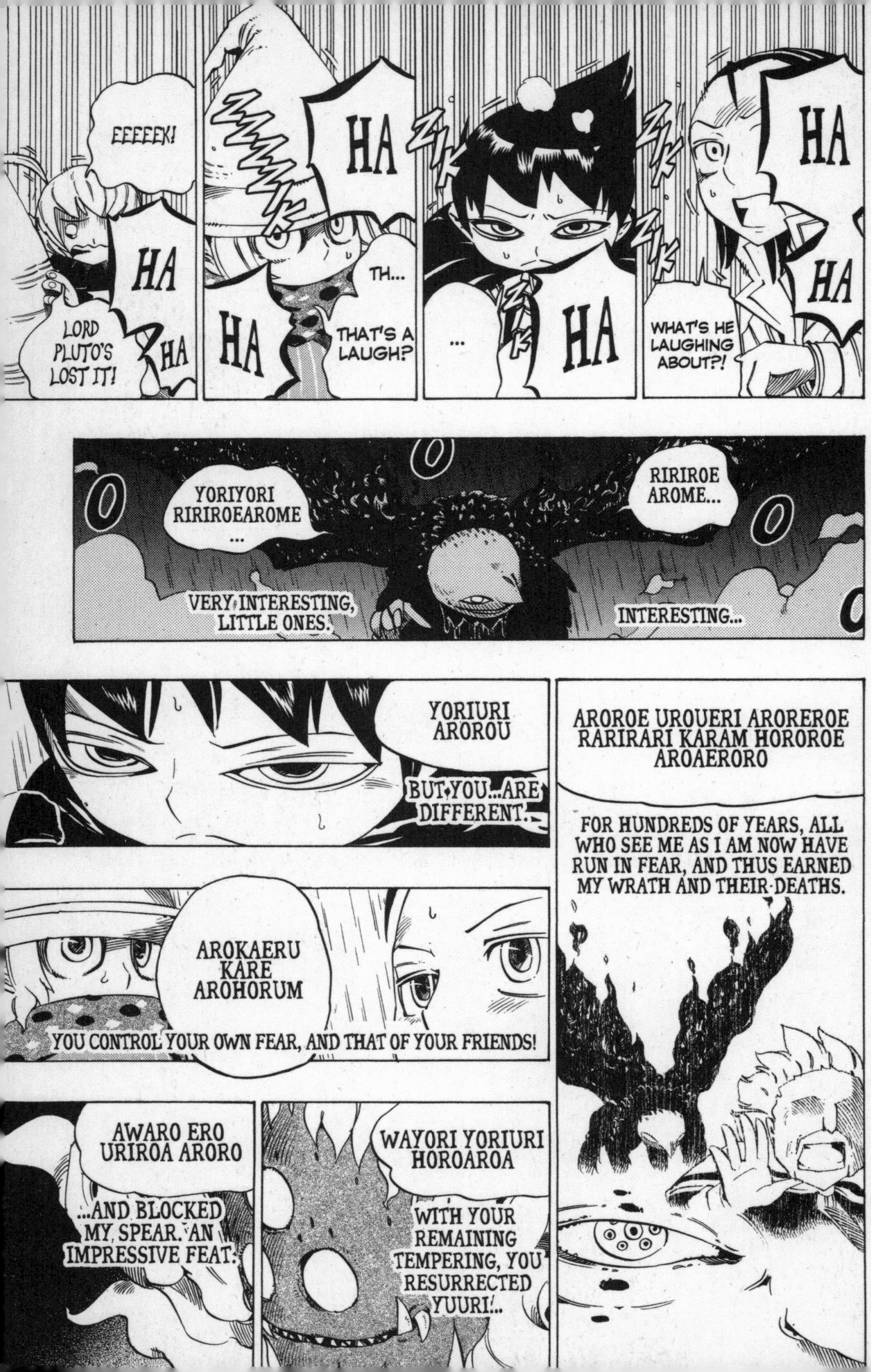
HA
HA
WHAT'S HE LAUGHING ABOUT?!
...
HA
HA
TH...
THAT'S A LAUGH?
HA
EEEEEK!
HA
HA
LORD PLUTO'S LOST IT!
RIRIROE AROME...
INTERESTING...
YORIYORI RIRIROEAROME ...
VERY INTERESTING, LITTLE ONES.
AROROE UROUERI ARORERO E RARIRARI KARAM HOROROE AROAERORO
FOR HUNDREDS OF YEARS, ALL WHO SEE ME AS I AM NOW HAVE RUN IN FEAR, AND THUS EARNED MY WRATH AND THEIR DEATHS.
YORIURI AROROU
BUT YOU...ARE DIFFERENT.
AROKAERU KARE AROHORUM
YOU CONTROL YOUR OWN FEAR, AND THAT OF YOUR FRIENDS!
WAYORI YORIURI HOROAROA
WITH YOUR REMAINING TEMPERING, YOU RESURRECTED YUURI...
AWARO ERO URIROA ARORO
...AND BLOCKED MY SPEAR. AN IMPRESSIVE FEAT.

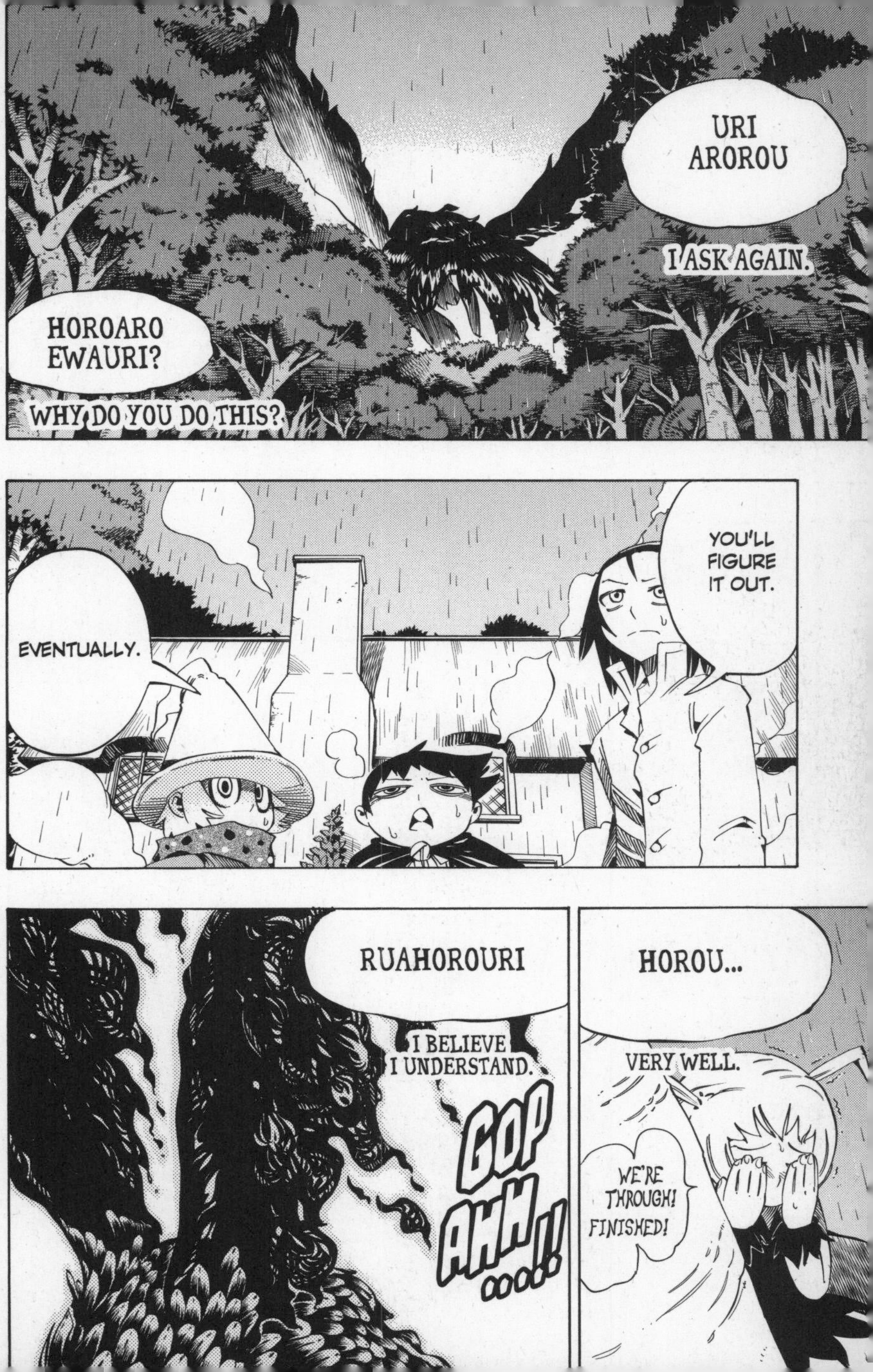
URI AROROU
I ASK AGAIN.
HOROARO EWAURI?
WHY DO YOU DO THIS?
YOU'LL FIGURE IT OUT.
EVENTUALLY.
HOROU...
VERY WELL.
WE'RE THROUGH! FINISHED!
RUAHOROURI
I BELIEVE I UNDERSTAND.
GOP AHH!!

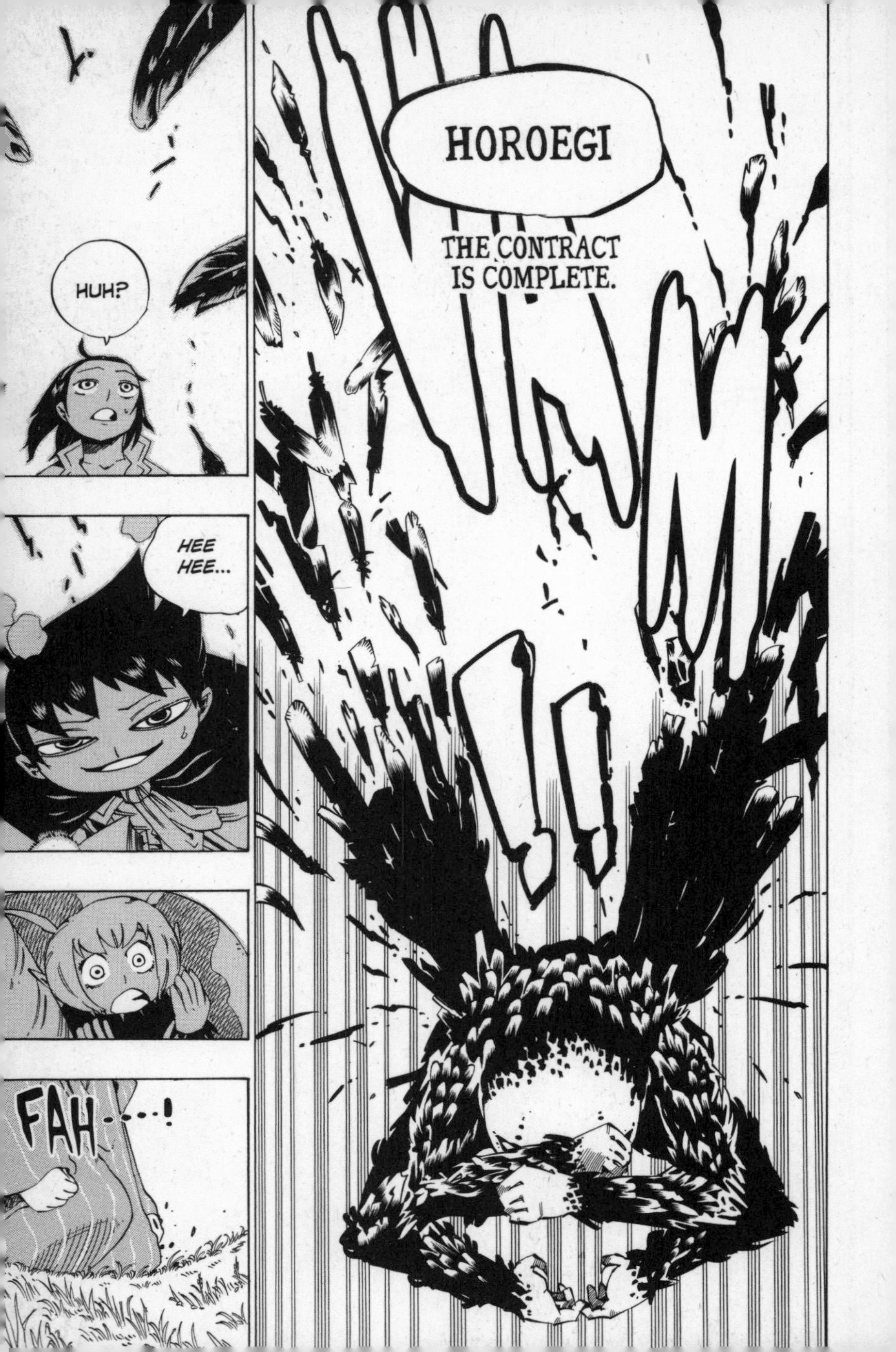
HOROEGI
THE CONTRACT IS COMPLETE.
HUH?
HEE HEE...
FAH---!

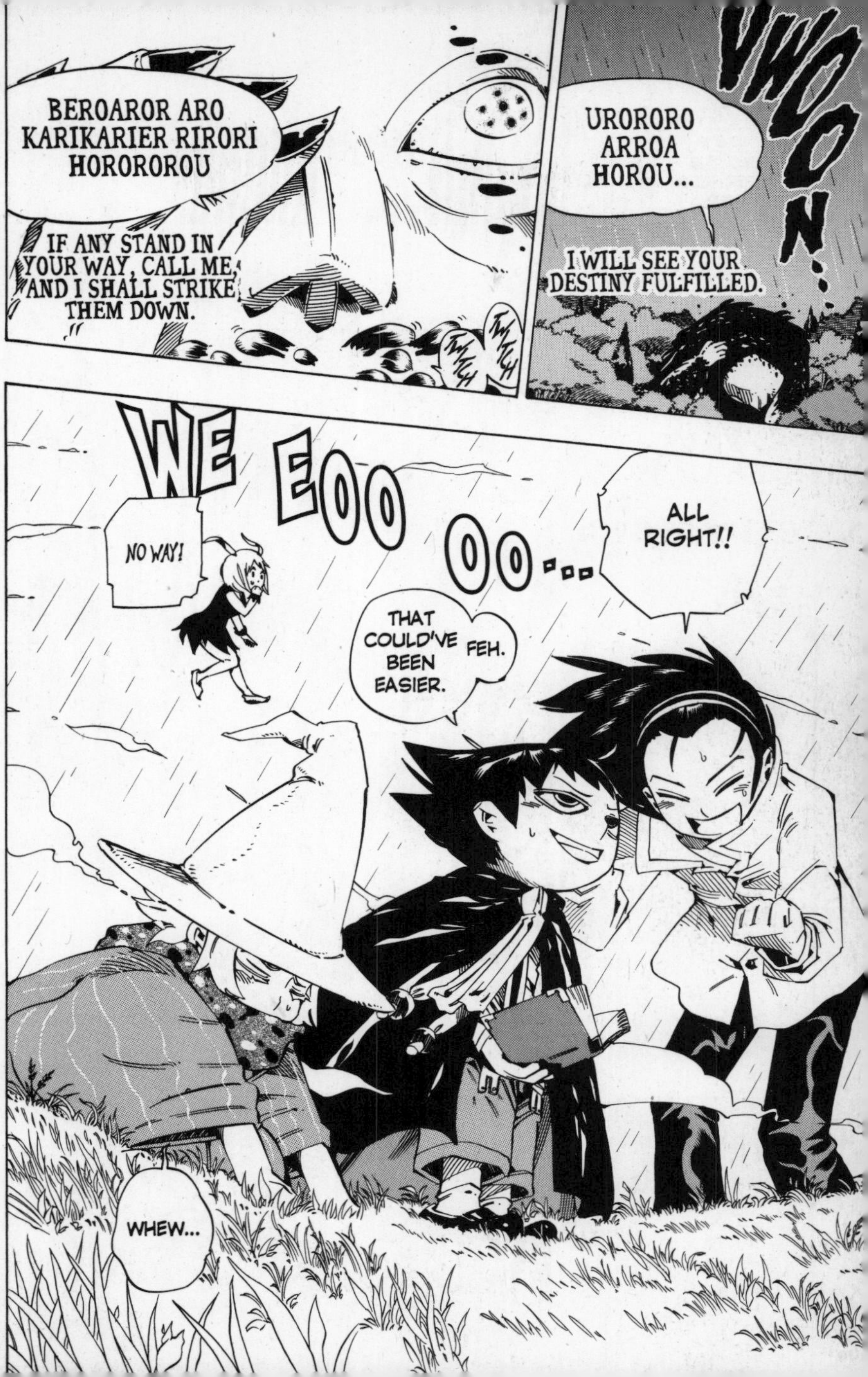
UROROROR ARROA HOROU...
I WILL SEE YOUR DESTINY FULFILLED.
VWOON...
BEROAROR ARO KARIKARIER RIRORI HORORORORU
IF ANY STAND IN YOUR WAY, CALL ME, AND I SHALL STRIKE THEM DOWN.
ALL RIGHT!!
WE EOO OO...
FEH.
THAT COULD'VE BEEN EASIER.
NO WAY!
WHEW...

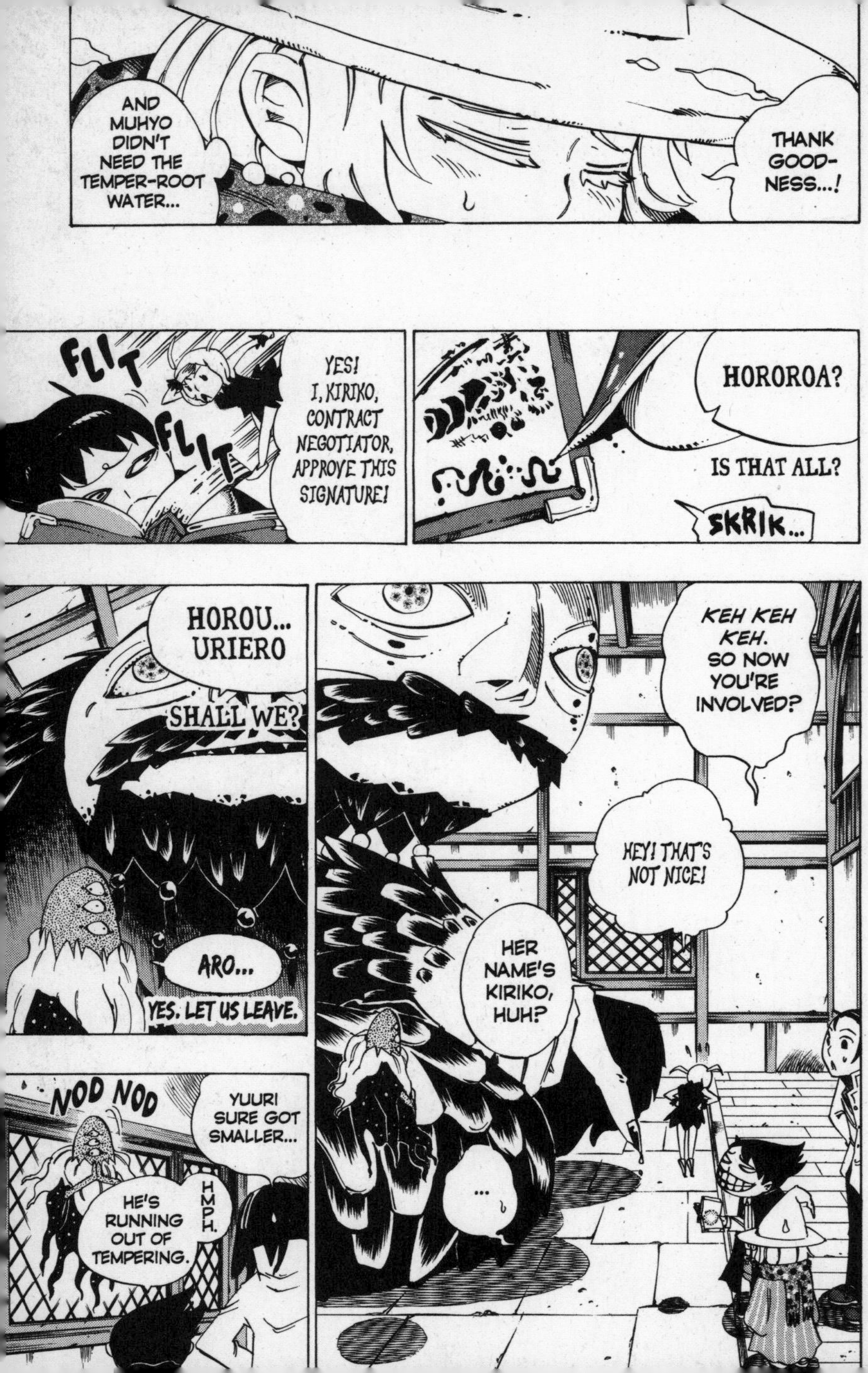
THANK GOODNESS...!
AND MUHYO DIDN'T NEED THE TEMPER-ROOT WATER...
HOROROA?
IS THAT ALL?
SKRIK...
YES! I, KIRIKO, CONTRACT NEGOTIATOR, APPROVE THIS SIGNATURE!
FLIT
FLIT
KEH KEH KEH. SO NOW YOU'RE INVOLVED?
HEY! THAT'S NOT NICE!
HER NAME'S KIRIKO, HUH?
...
HOROU... URIERO
SHALL WE?
ARO...
YES. LET US LEAVE.
YUURI SURE GOT SMALLER...
NOD NOD
HMPH.
HE'S RUNNING OUT OF TEMPERING.

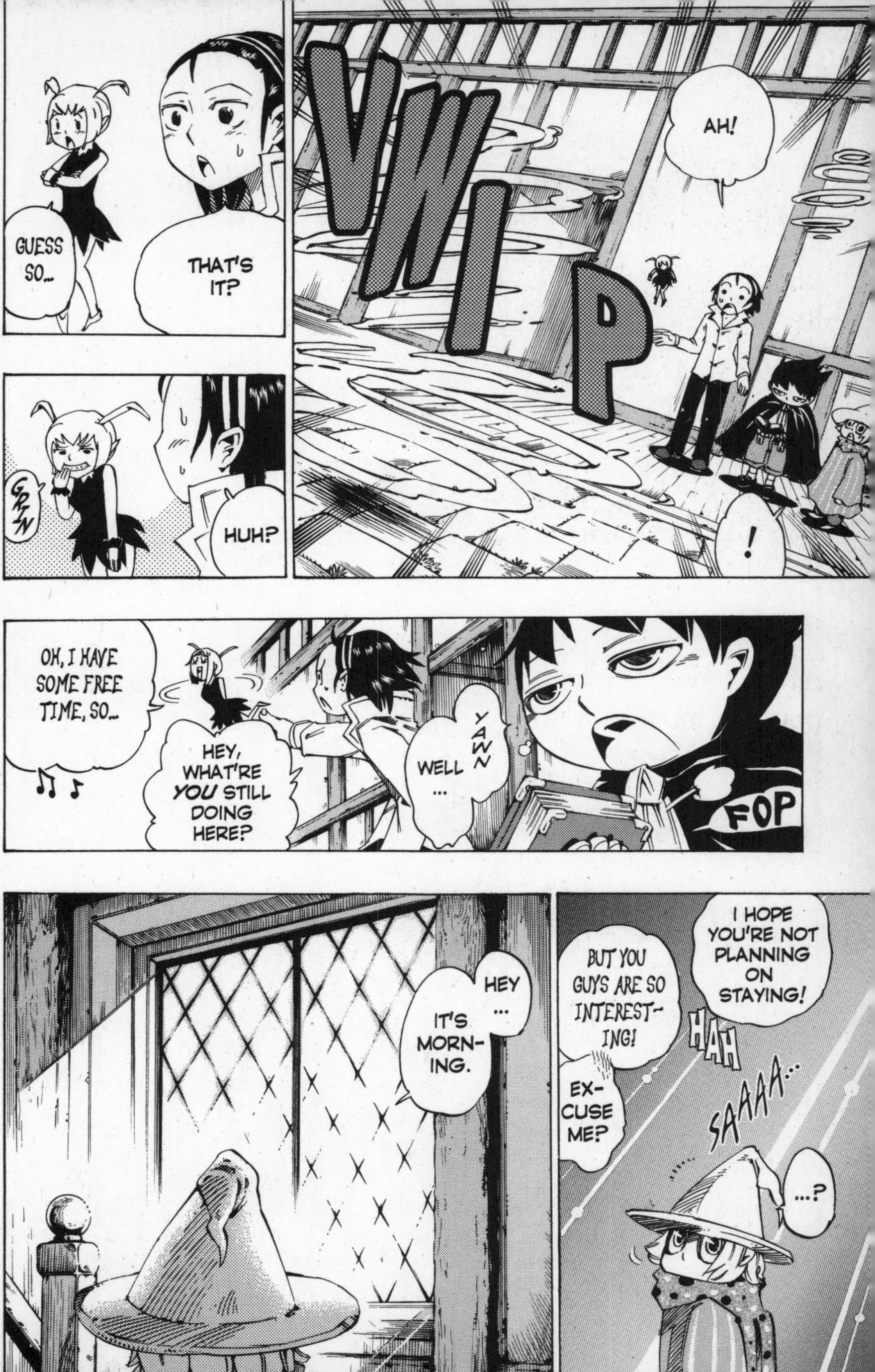
AH!
VWIP
!
THAT'S IT?
GUESS SO...
HUH?
GRIN
WELL ...
YAWN
FOP
HEY, WHAT'RE *YOU* STILL DOING HERE?
OH, I HAVE SOME FREE TIME, SO... ♫ ♪
I HOPE YOU'RE NOT PLANNING ON STAYING!
BUT YOU GUYS ARE SO INTEREST-ING!
HAH
EX-CUSE ME?
SAAAA...
...?
HEY ...
IT'S MORN-ING.

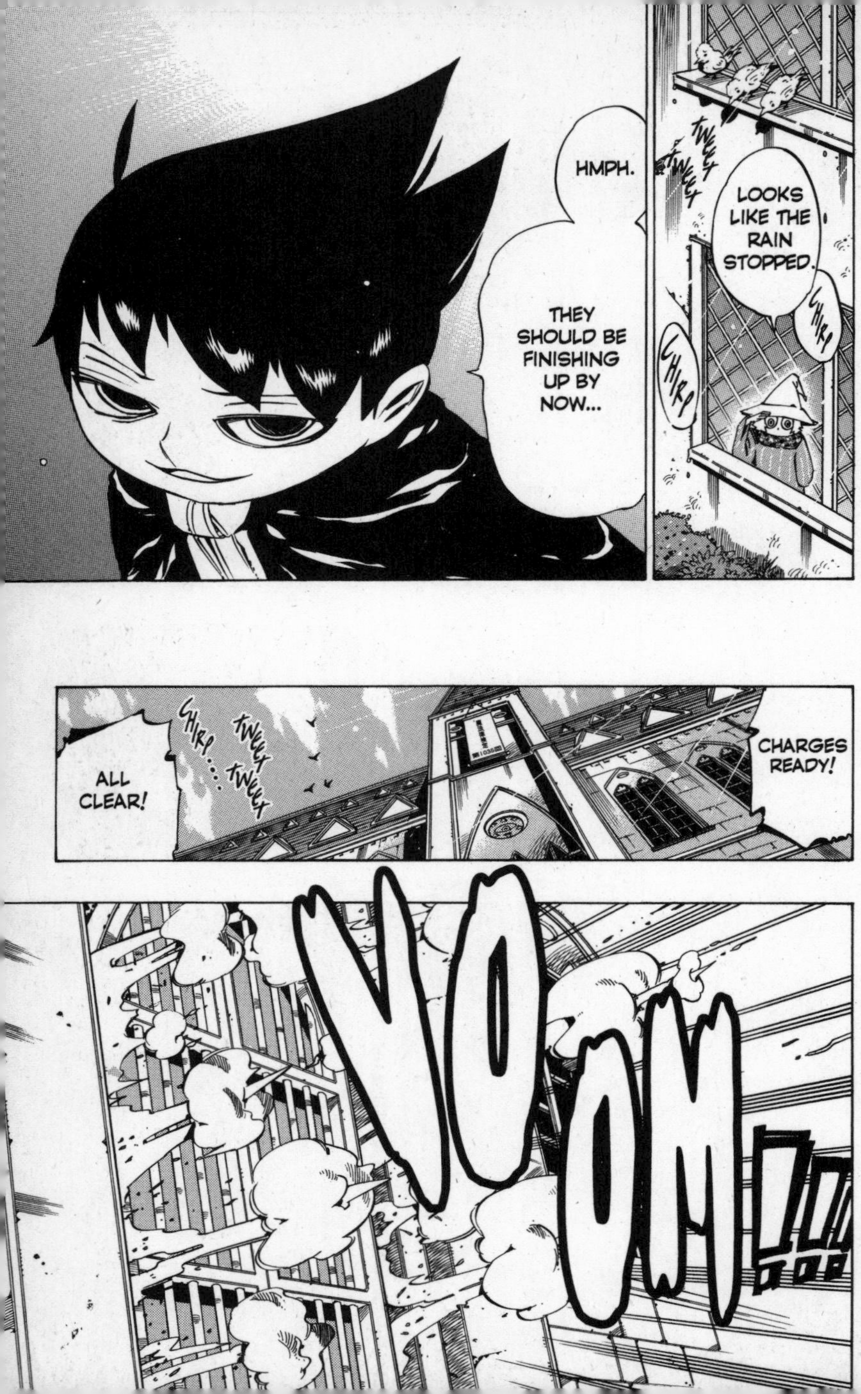
LOOKS LIKE THE RAIN STOPPED.
CHIRP
CHIRP
TWEEK TWEEK
HMPH.
THEY SHOULD BE FINISHING UP BY NOW...
CHARGES READY!
TWEEK TWEEK
CHIRP...
ALL CLEAR!
VOOM!!!

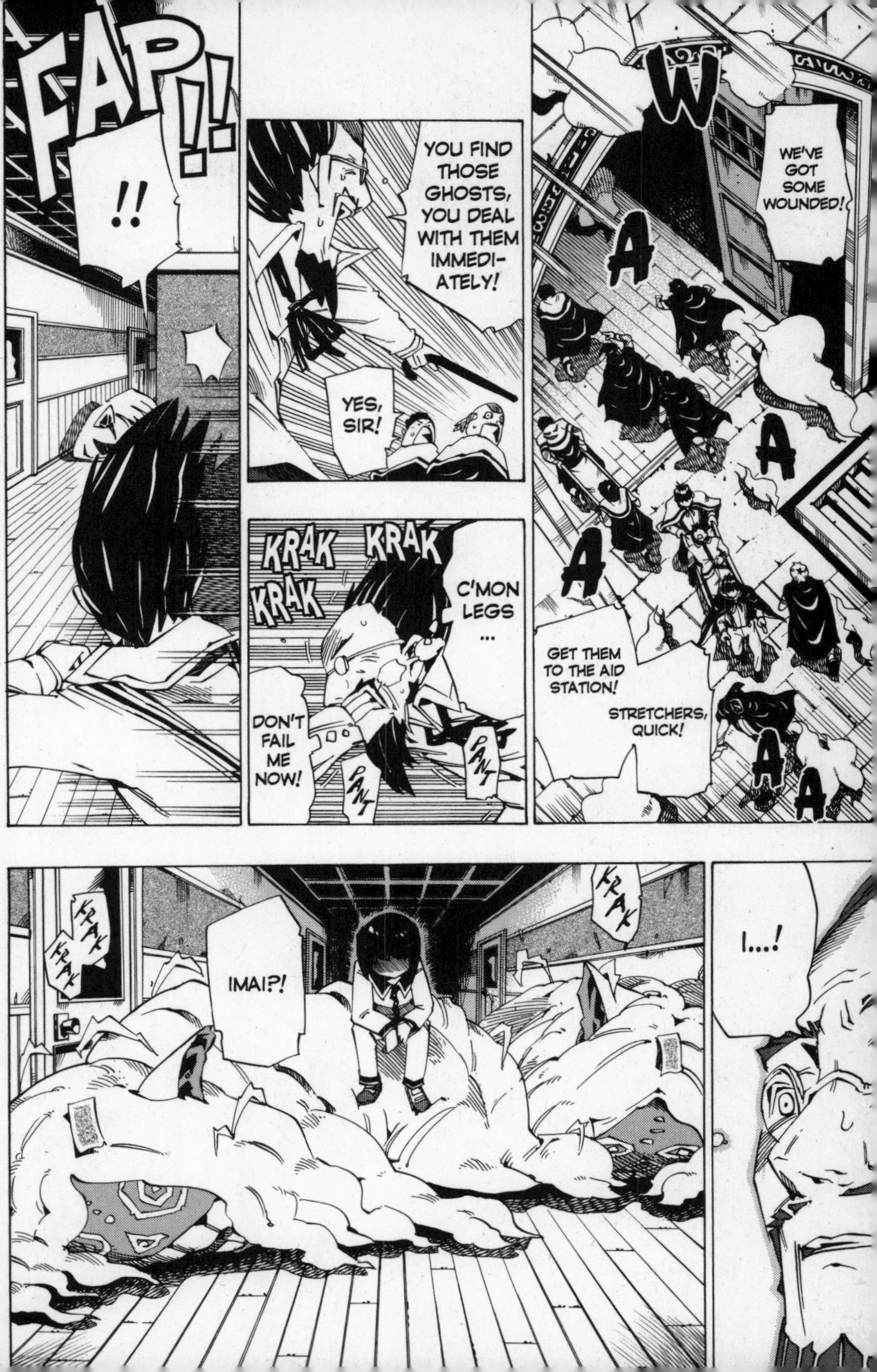
WAAAAAA
WE'VE GOT SOME WOUNDED!
GET THEM TO THE AID STATION!
STRETCHERS, QUICK!
YOU FIND THOSE GHOSTS, YOU DEAL WITH THEM IMMEDI-ATELY!
YES, SIR!
KRAK KRAK KRAK
C'MON LEGS...
DON'T FAIL ME NOW!
PANT PANT
FAP!!
!!
I...!
KRAK
KRAK KRAK
IMAI?!

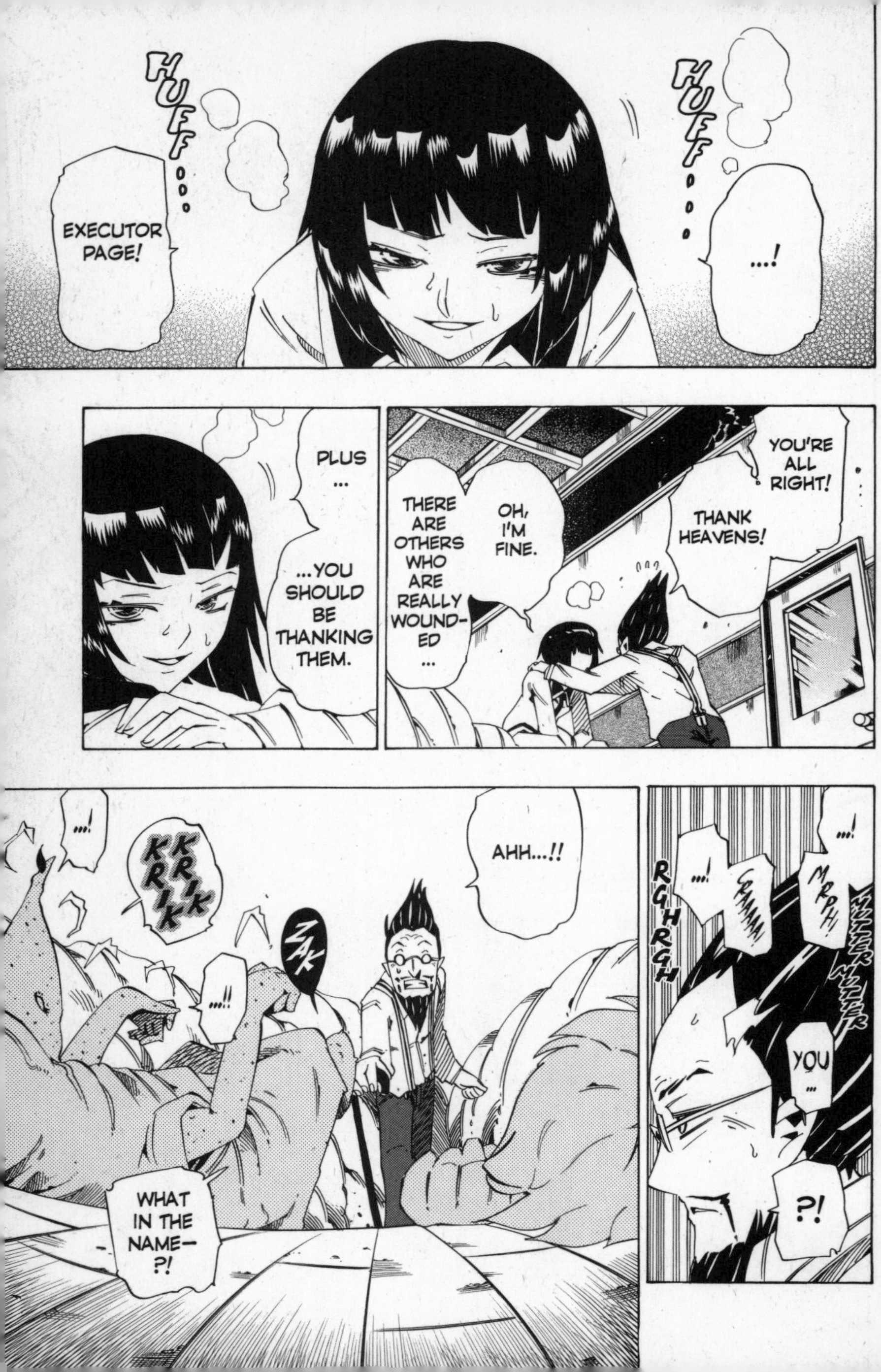

HUFF...
...!
HUFF...
EXECUTOR PAGE!
YOU'RE ALL RIGHT!
THANK HEAVENS!
OH, I'M FINE.
THERE ARE OTHERS WHO ARE REALLY WOUND-ED...
PLUS...
...YOU SHOULD BE THANKING THEM.
...!
MRPH!
MUTTER MUTTER
GRAAAAA!
...!
RGHRGH
YOU...
?!
AHH...!!
...!
KRIK KRIK
ZAK
...!!
WHAT IN THE NAME—?!

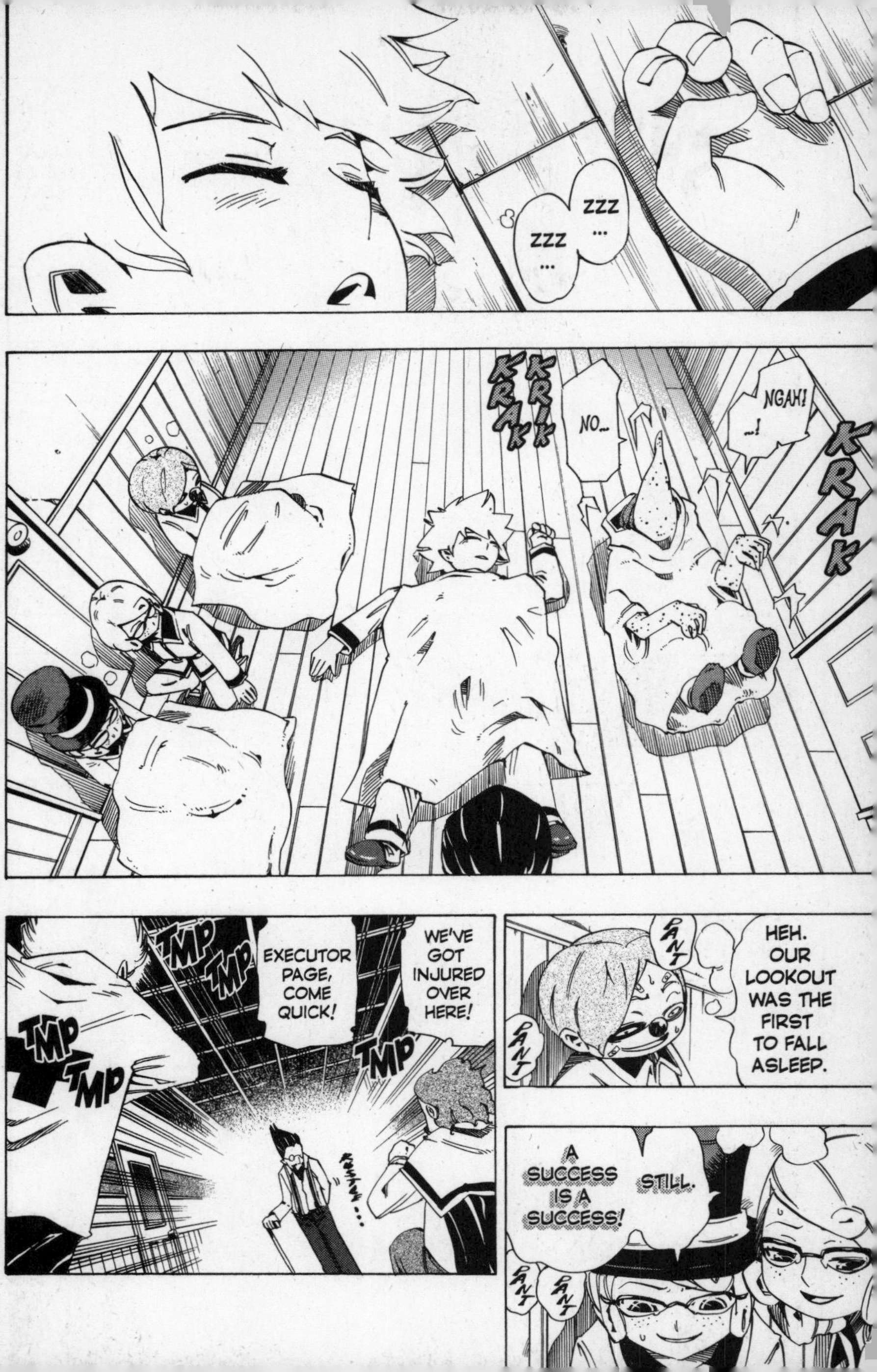
ZZZ...
ZZZ...
KRAK
NGAH! ...!
NO...
KRIK
KRAK
PANT
HEH. OUR LOOKOUT WAS THE FIRST TO FALL ASLEEP.
PANT
STILL.
A SUCCESS IS A SUCCESS!
PANT
PANT
WE'VE GOT INJURED OVER HERE!
EXECUTOR PAGE, COME QUICK!
TMP TMP
TMP
TMP TMP

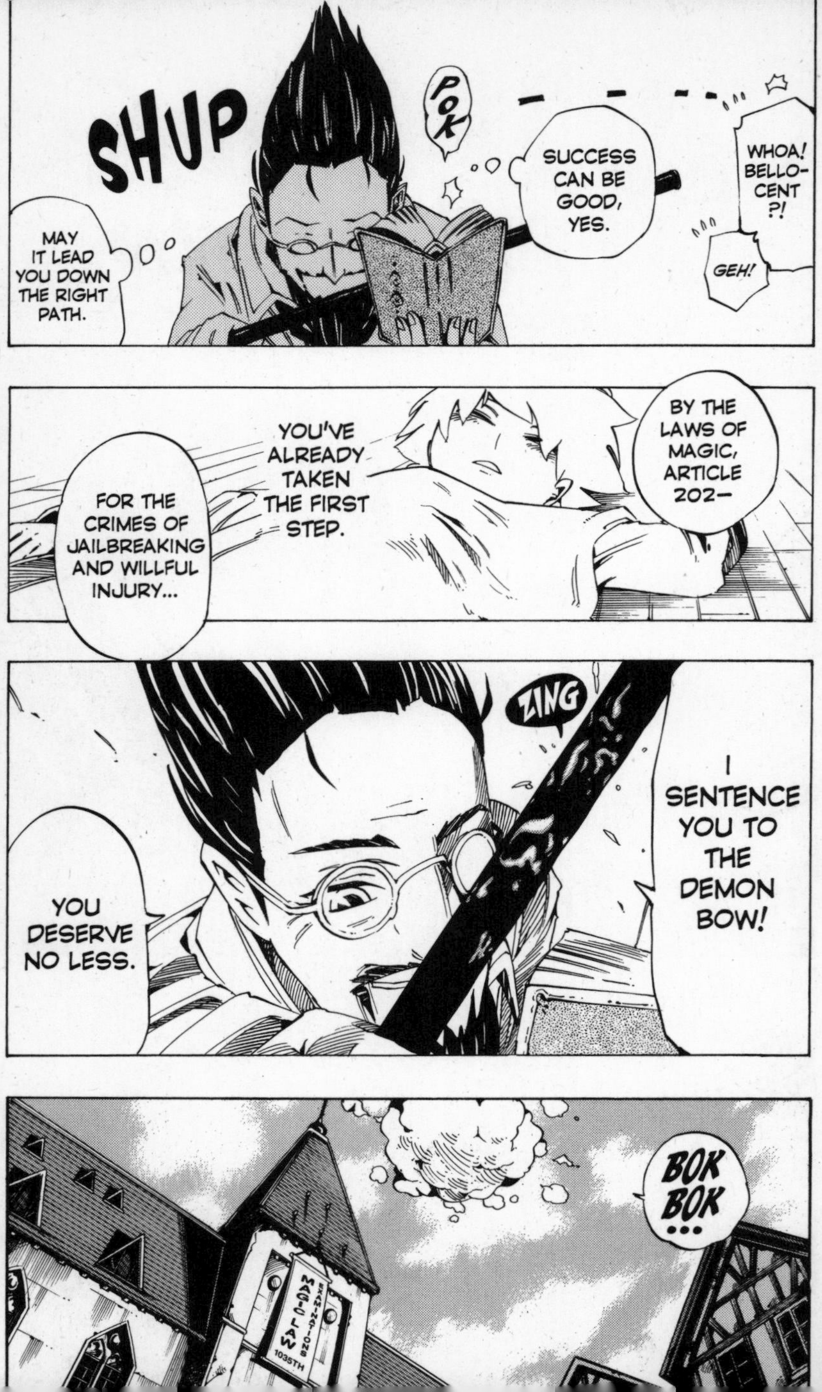
WHOA! BELLO-CENT ?!
GEH!
POK
SUCCESS CAN BE GOOD, YES.
SHUP
MAY IT LEAD YOU DOWN THE RIGHT PATH.
BY THE LAWS OF MAGIC, ARTICLE 202—
YOU'VE ALREADY TAKEN THE FIRST STEP.
FOR THE CRIMES OF JAILBREAKING AND WILLFUL INJURY...
ZING
I SENTENCE YOU TO THE DEMON BOW!
YOU DESERVE NO LESS.
BOK BOK...
MAGIC LAW EXAMINATIONS
1035TH

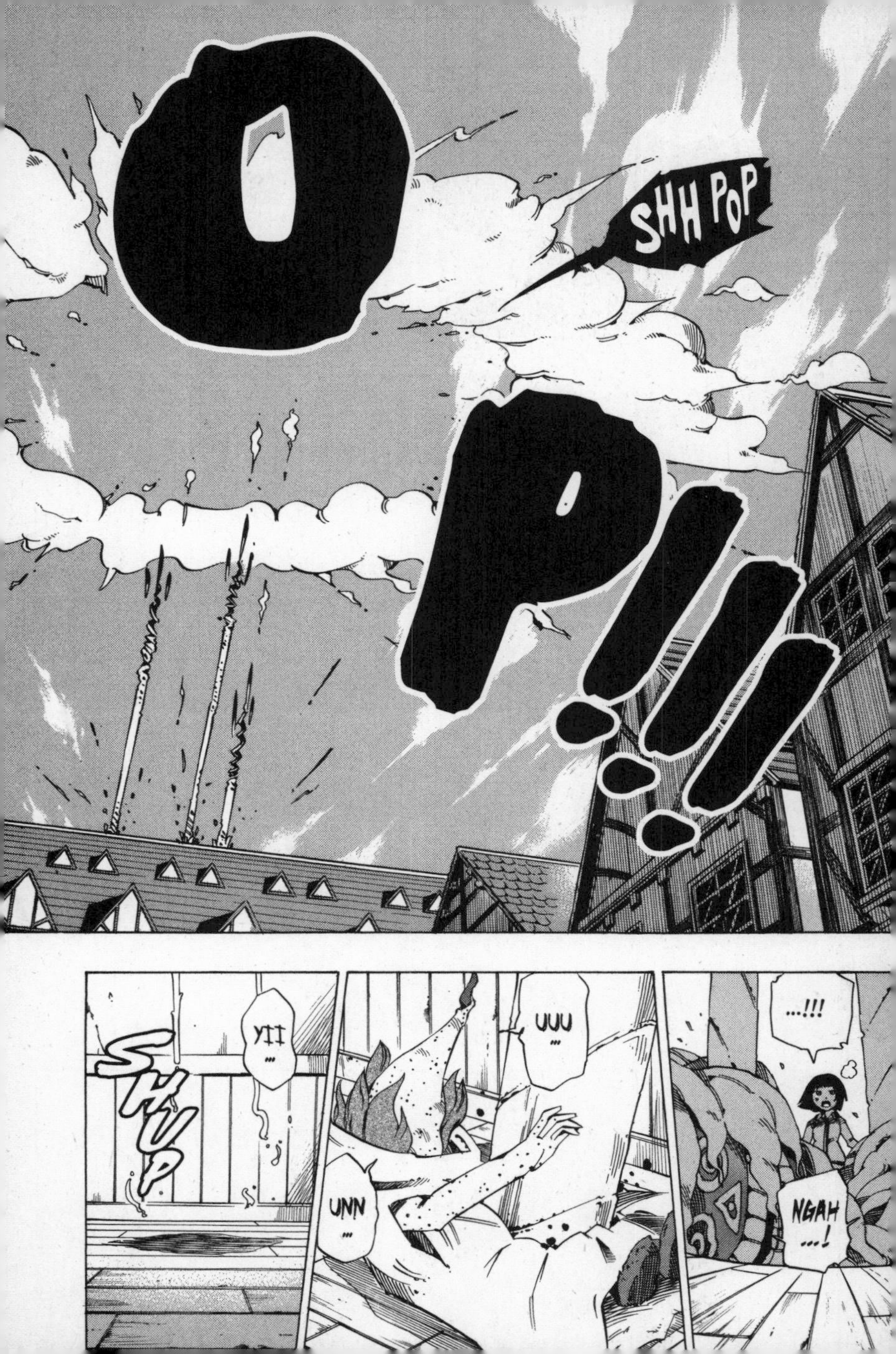
OP!!!
SHH POP
...!!!
NGAH ...!
UUU ...
UNN ...
YII ...
SHUP

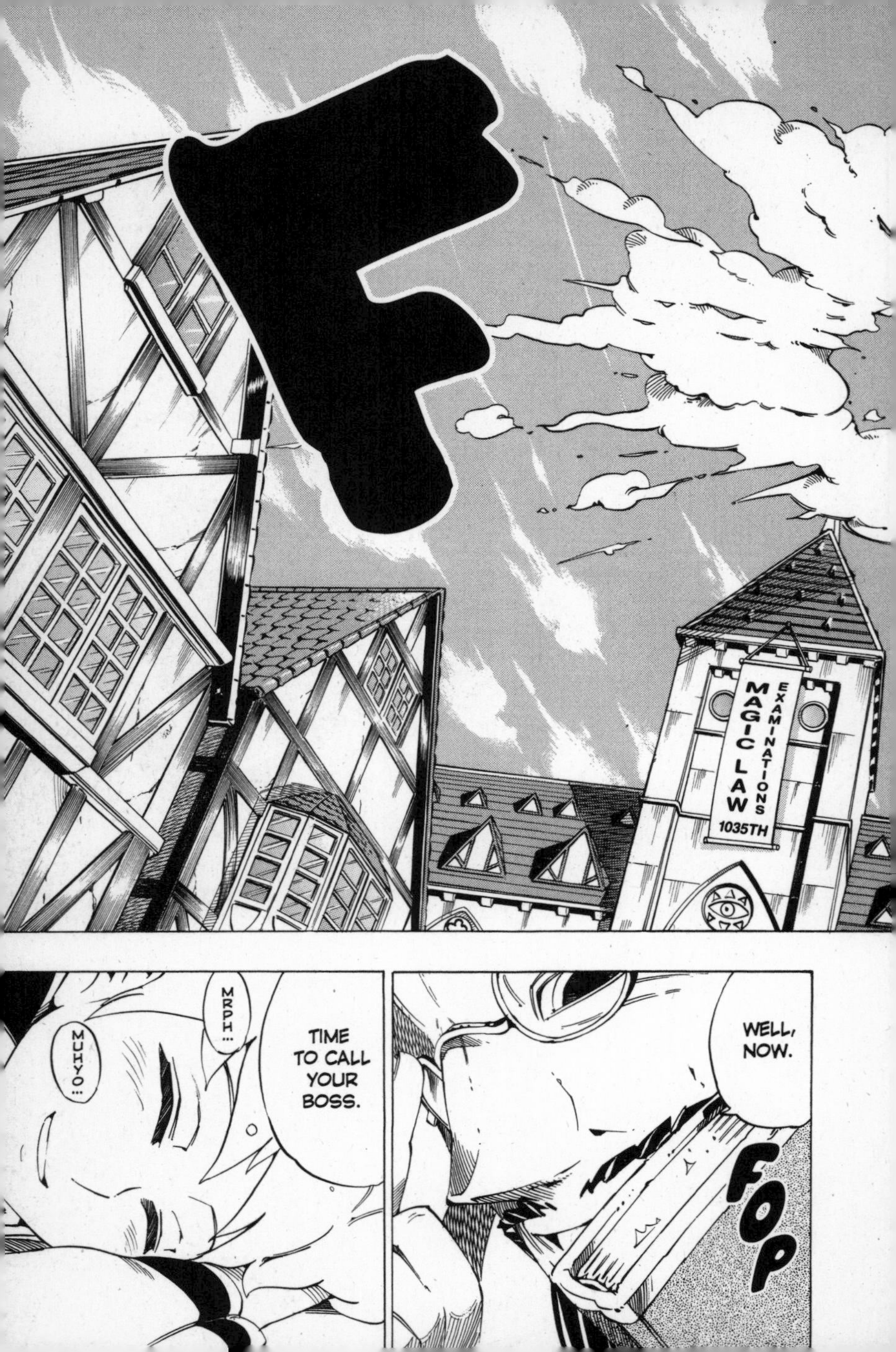
MAGIC LAW EXAMINATIONS
1035TH
WELL, NOW.
FOP
TIME TO CALL YOUR BOSS.
MRPH...
MUHYO...

KIRIKO
BIRTHDAY: UNKNOWN
HEIGHT: 20 CM

LIKES: SOFT THINGS
         TALKING (ESPECIALLY ABOUT
              RELATIONSHIPS)

TALENTS: RUNNING AWAY
          ZEROING IN ON
            HANDSOME GUYS
          SKIPPING WORK

NOT GOOD WITH: LABOR
                TAKING ORDERS
                HARD THINGS
                THE UNDERWORLD
                (WOULD LIKE TO
                 AVOID GOING HOME)

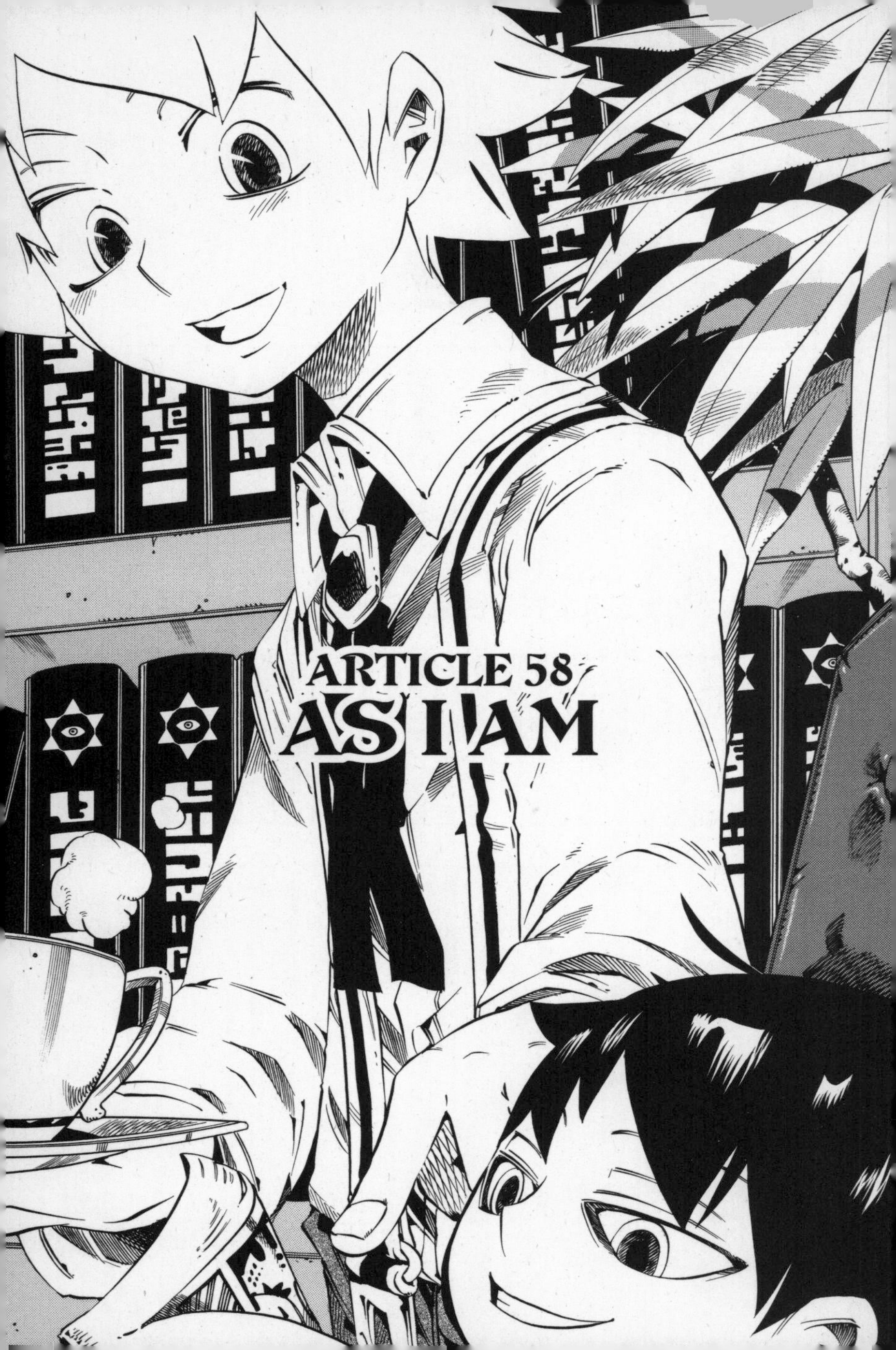
ARTICLE 58
AS I AM

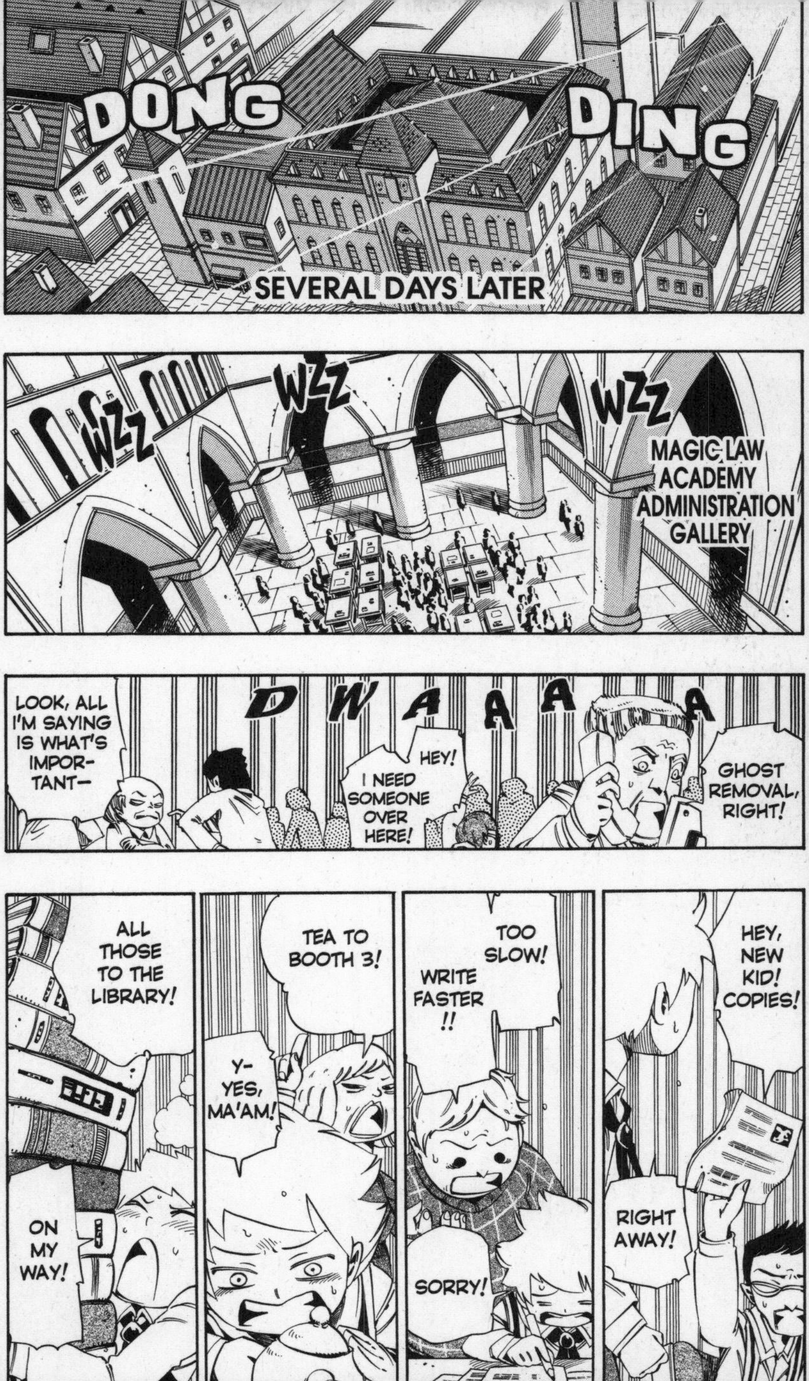
DING
DONG
SEVERAL DAYS LATER
WZZ
WZZ
WZZ
MAGIC LAW ACADEMY ADMINISTRATION GALLERY
DWAAAA
GHOST REMOVAL, RIGHT!
HEY! I NEED SOMEONE OVER HERE!
LOOK, ALL I'M SAYING IS WHAT'S IMPORTANT—
HEY, NEW KID! COPIES!
RIGHT AWAY!
TOO SLOW!
WRITE FASTER!!
SORRY!
TEA TO BOOTH 3!
Y-YES, MA'AM!
ALL THOSE TO THE LIBRARY!
ON MY WAY!

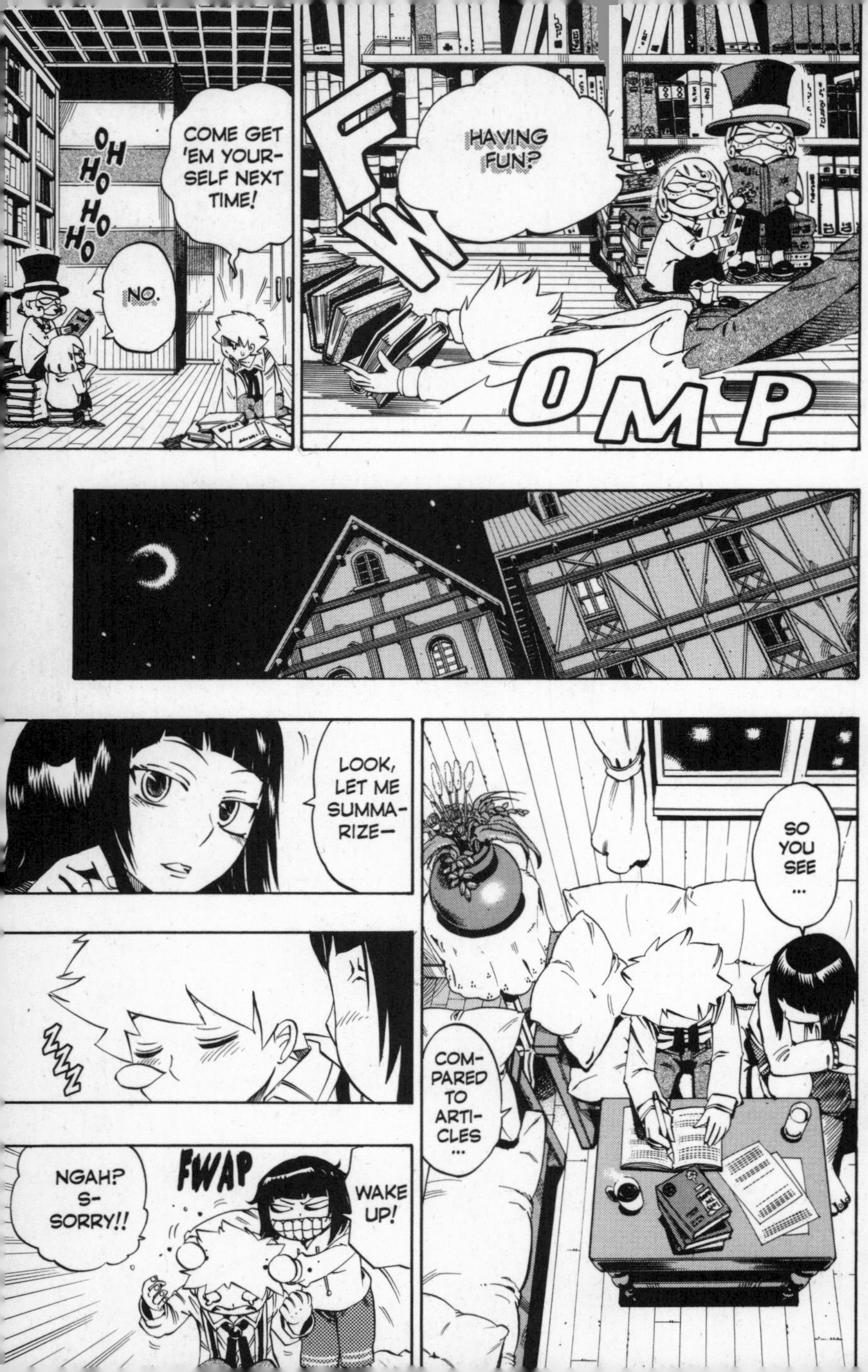

HAVING FUN?
FW
OMP
COME GET 'EM YOURSELF NEXT TIME!
OH HO HO HO HO
NO.
SO YOU SEE ...
COMPARED TO ARTICLES ...
LOOK, LET ME SUMMARIZE—
WAKE UP!
FWAP
NGAH? S-SORRY!!

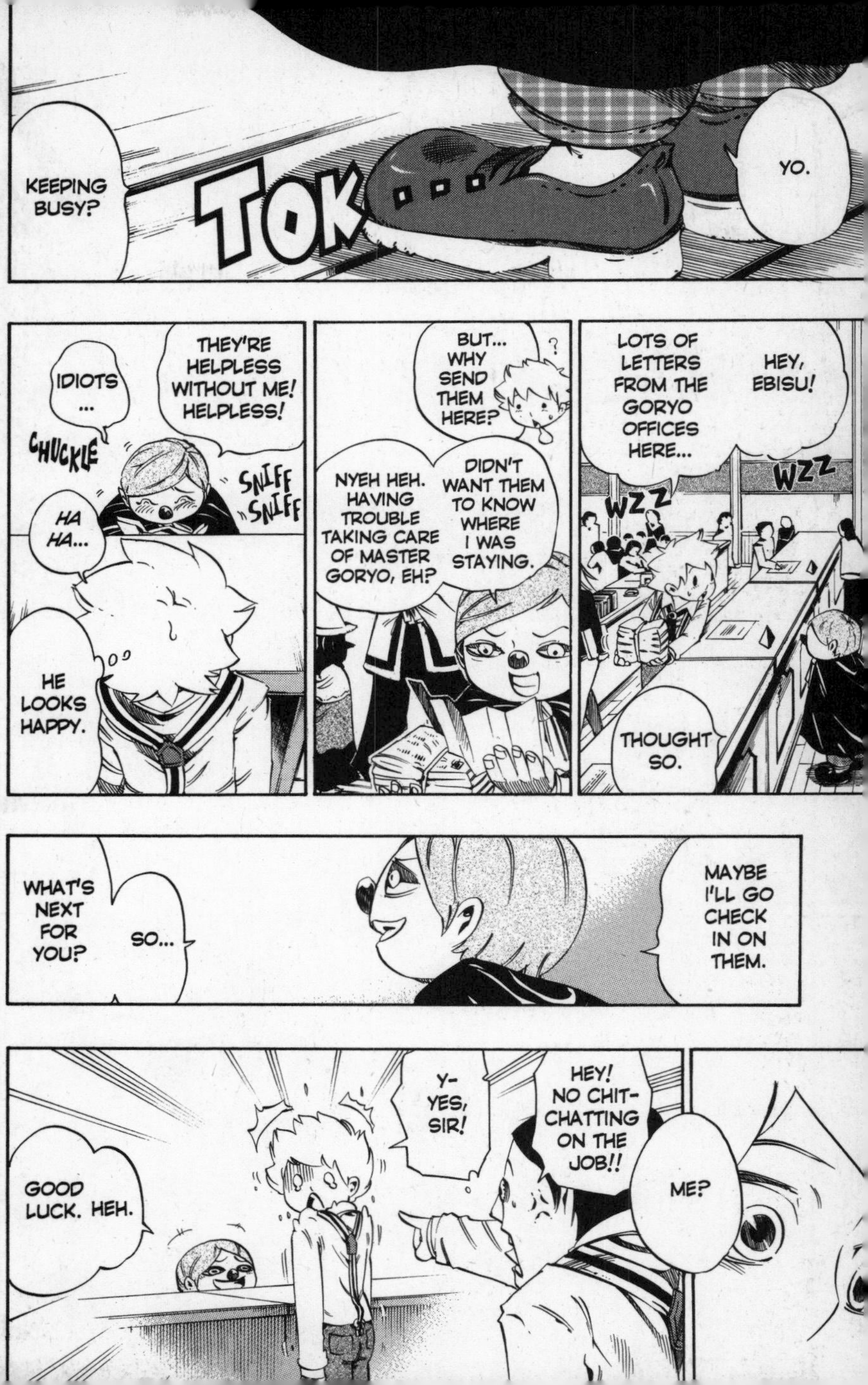
YO.
KEEPING BUSY?
TOK
HEY, EBISU!
LOTS OF LETTERS FROM THE GORYO OFFICES HERE...
WZZ
WZZ
THOUGHT SO.
BUT... WHY SEND THEM HERE?
DIDN'T WANT THEM TO KNOW WHERE I WAS STAYING.
NYEH HEH. HAVING TROUBLE TAKING CARE OF MASTER GORYO, EH?
THEY'RE HELPLESS WITHOUT ME! HELPLESS!
IDIOTS...
CHUCKLE
SNIFF SNIFF
HA HA...
HE LOOKS HAPPY.
MAYBE I'LL GO CHECK IN ON THEM.
SO...
WHAT'S NEXT FOR YOU?
ME?
HEY! NO CHIT-CHATTING ON THE JOB!!
Y-YES, SIR!
GOOD LUCK. HEH.

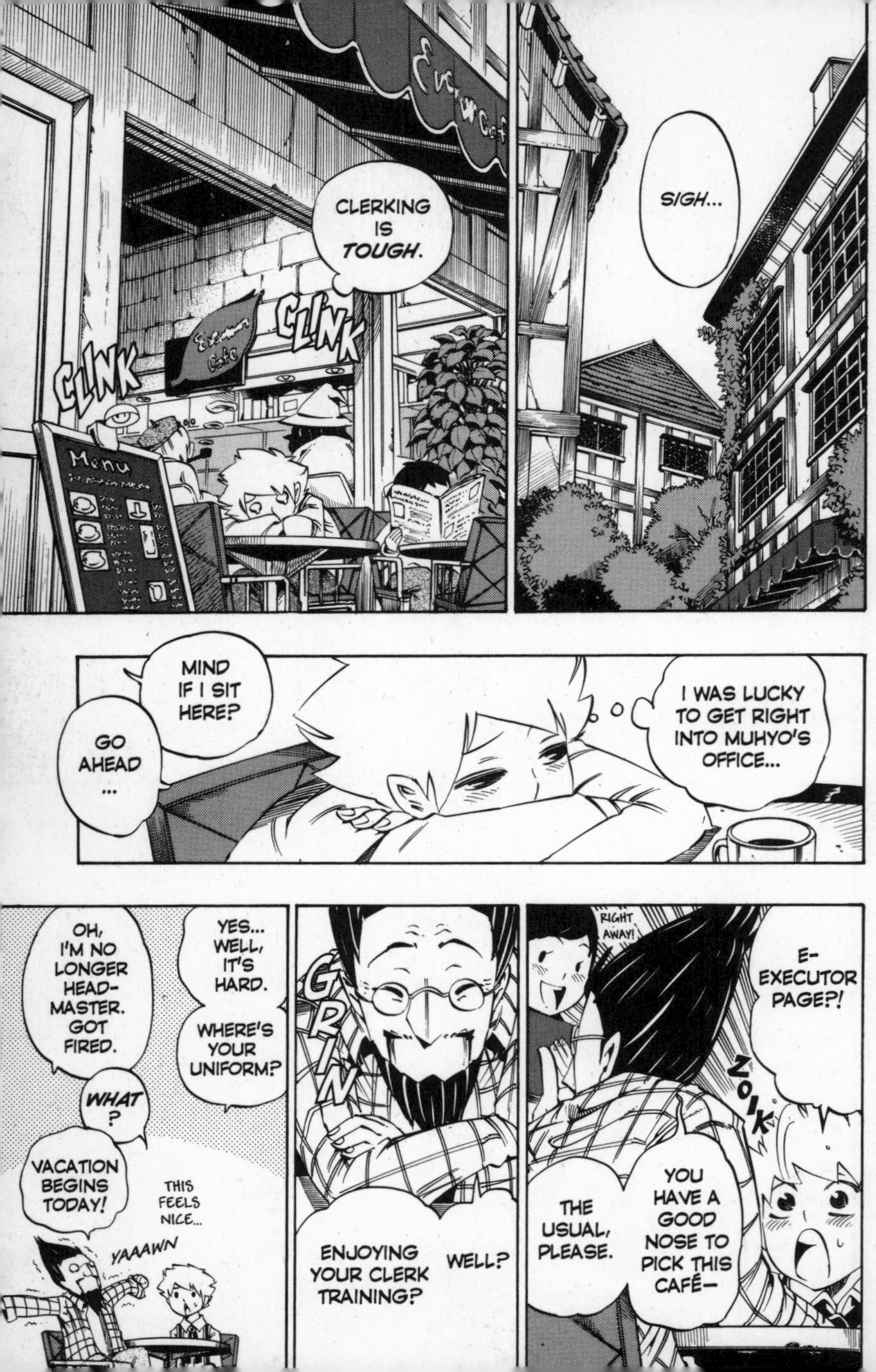
SIGH...
CLERKING IS TOUGH.
CLINK
CLINK
I WAS LUCKY TO GET RIGHT INTO MUHYO'S OFFICE...
MIND IF I SIT HERE?
GO AHEAD...
E-EXECUTOR PAGE?!
RIGHT AWAY!
ZOIK
YOU HAVE A GOOD NOSE TO PICK THIS CAFÉ—
THE USUAL, PLEASE.
GRIN
WELL?
ENJOYING YOUR CLERK TRAINING?
YES... WELL, IT'S HARD.
OH, I'M NO LONGER HEAD-MASTER. GOT FIRED.
WHERE'S YOUR UNIFORM?
WHAT?
VACATION BEGINS TODAY!
THIS FEELS NICE...
YAAAWN

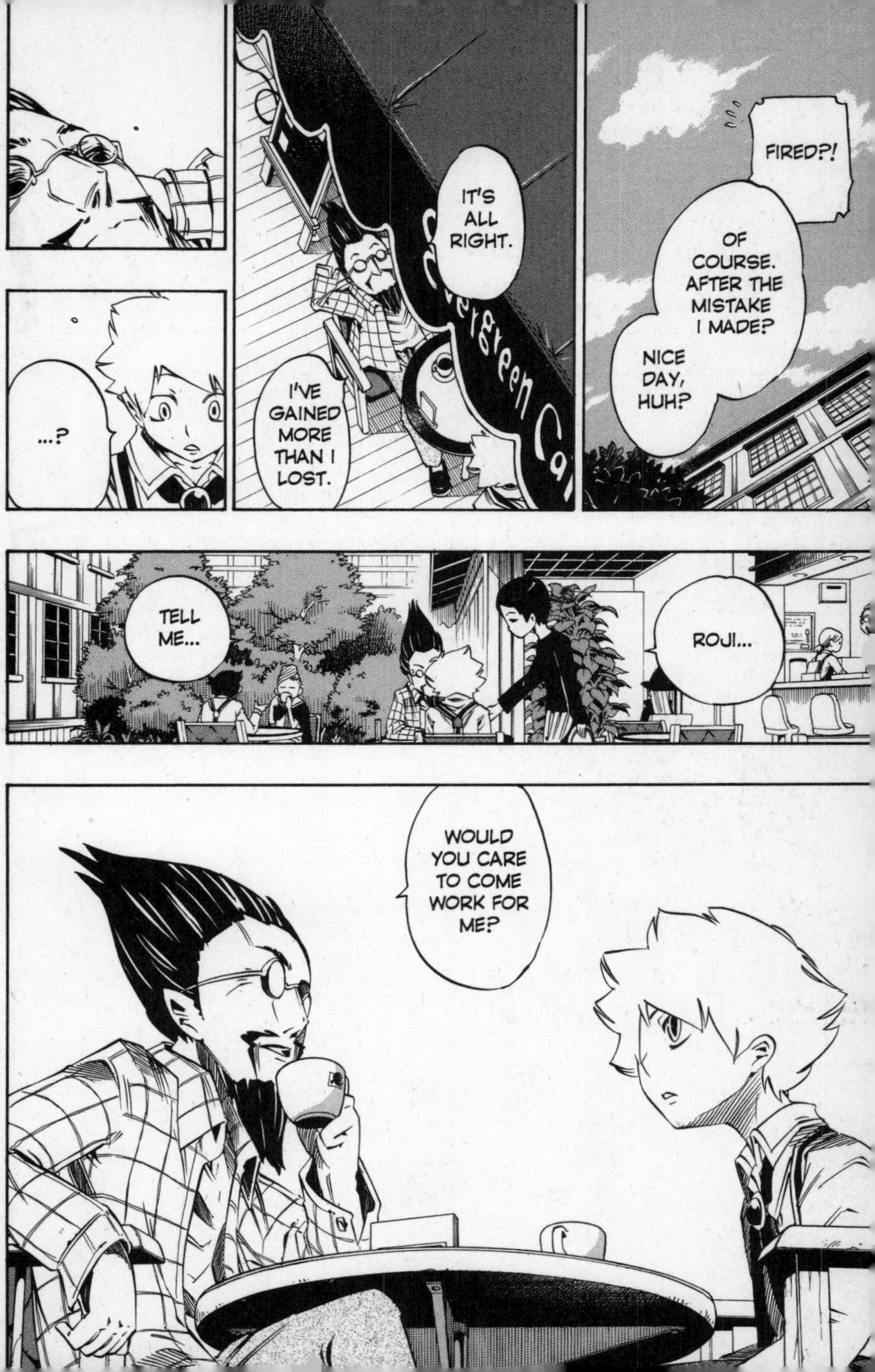
FIRED?!
OF COURSE. AFTER THE MISTAKE I MADE?
NICE DAY, HUH?
IT'S ALL RIGHT.
I'VE GAINED MORE THAN I LOST.
...?
ROJI...
TELL ME...
WOULD YOU CARE TO COME WORK FOR ME?

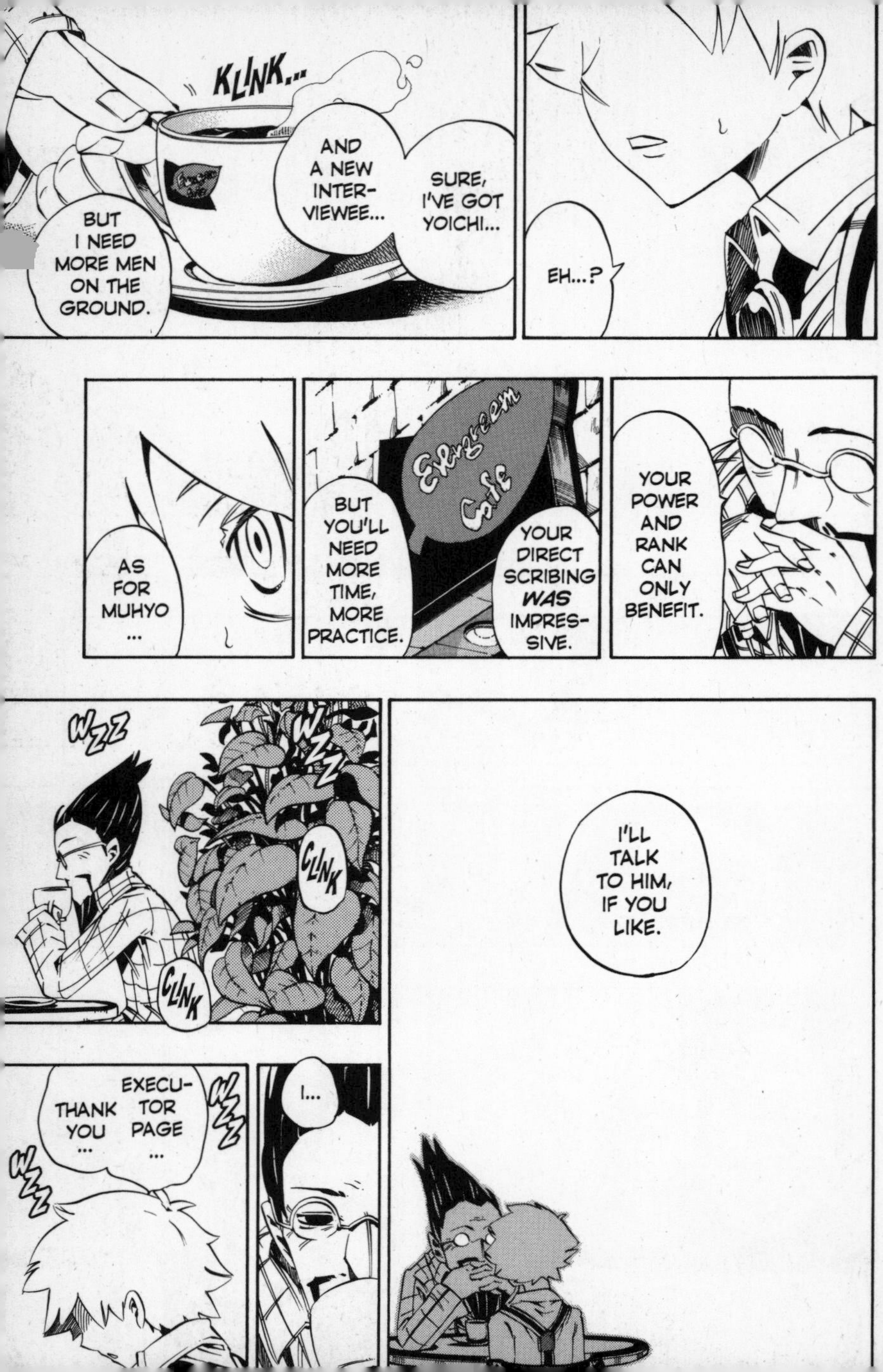
EH...?
KLINK...
SURE, I'VE GOT YOICHI...
AND A NEW INTER-VIEWEE...
BUT I NEED MORE MEN ON THE GROUND.
YOUR POWER AND RANK CAN ONLY BENEFIT.
Evergreem Cafe
YOUR DIRECT SCRIBING WAS IMPRES-SIVE.
BUT YOU'LL NEED MORE TIME, MORE PRACTICE.
AS FOR MUHYO ...
I'LL TALK TO HIM, IF YOU LIKE.
WZZ
WZZ
CLINK
CLINK
I...
WZZ
EXECU-TOR PAGE ...
THANK YOU ...
WZZ

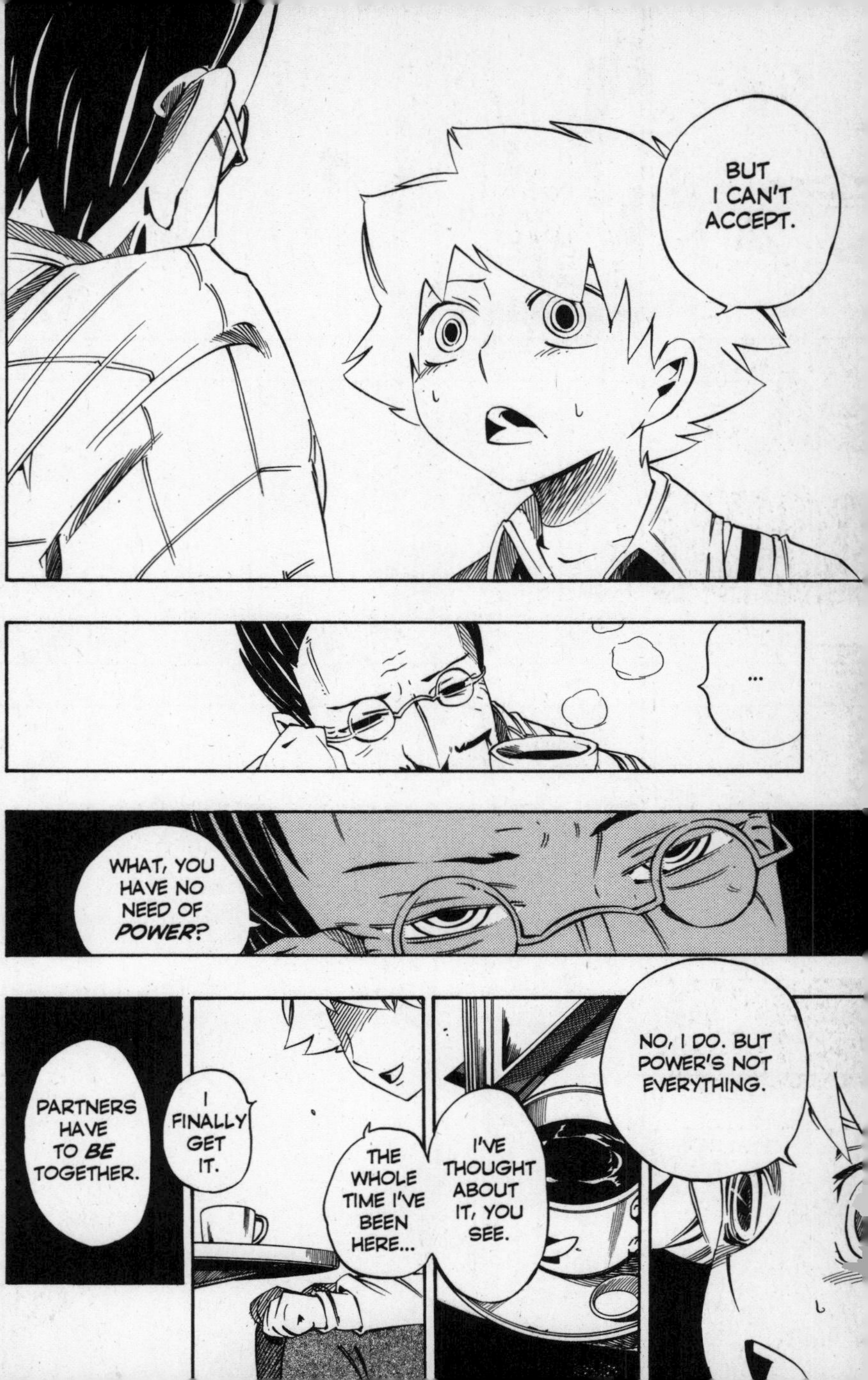
BUT I CAN'T ACCEPT.
...
WHAT, YOU HAVE NO NEED OF *POWER*?
NO, I DO. BUT POWER'S NOT EVERYTHING.
I'VE THOUGHT ABOUT IT, YOU SEE.
THE WHOLE TIME I'VE BEEN HERE...
I FINALLY GET IT.
PARTNERS HAVE TO *BE* TOGETHER.

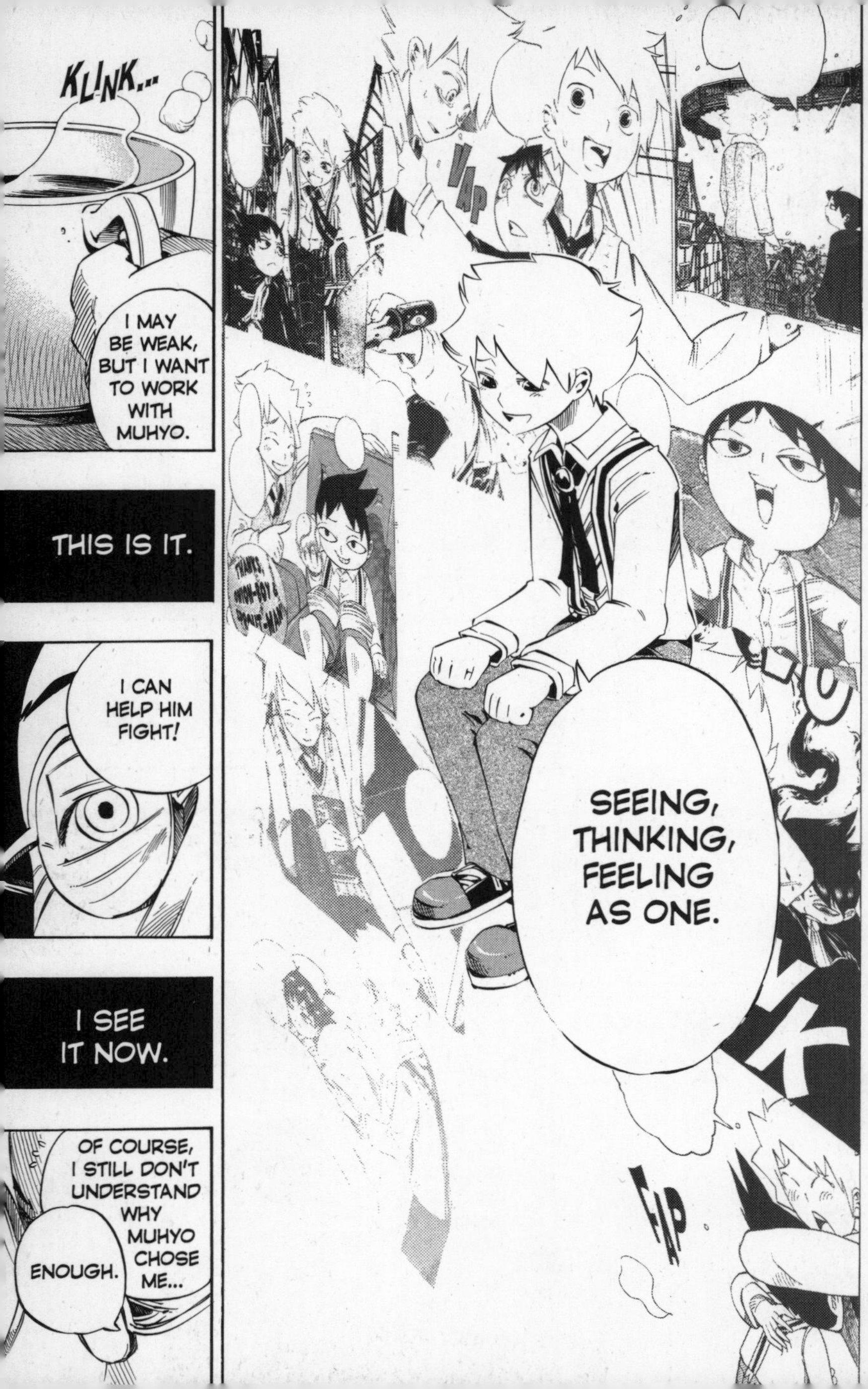
YAP
THANKS, ONION-BOY & DONUT-MAN!
SEEING, THINKING, FEELING AS ONE.
FAP
KLINK...
I MAY BE WEAK, BUT I WANT TO WORK WITH MUHYO.
THIS IS IT.
I CAN HELP HIM FIGHT!
I SEE IT NOW.
OF COURSE, I STILL DON'T UNDERSTAND WHY MUHYO CHOSE ME...
ENOUGH.

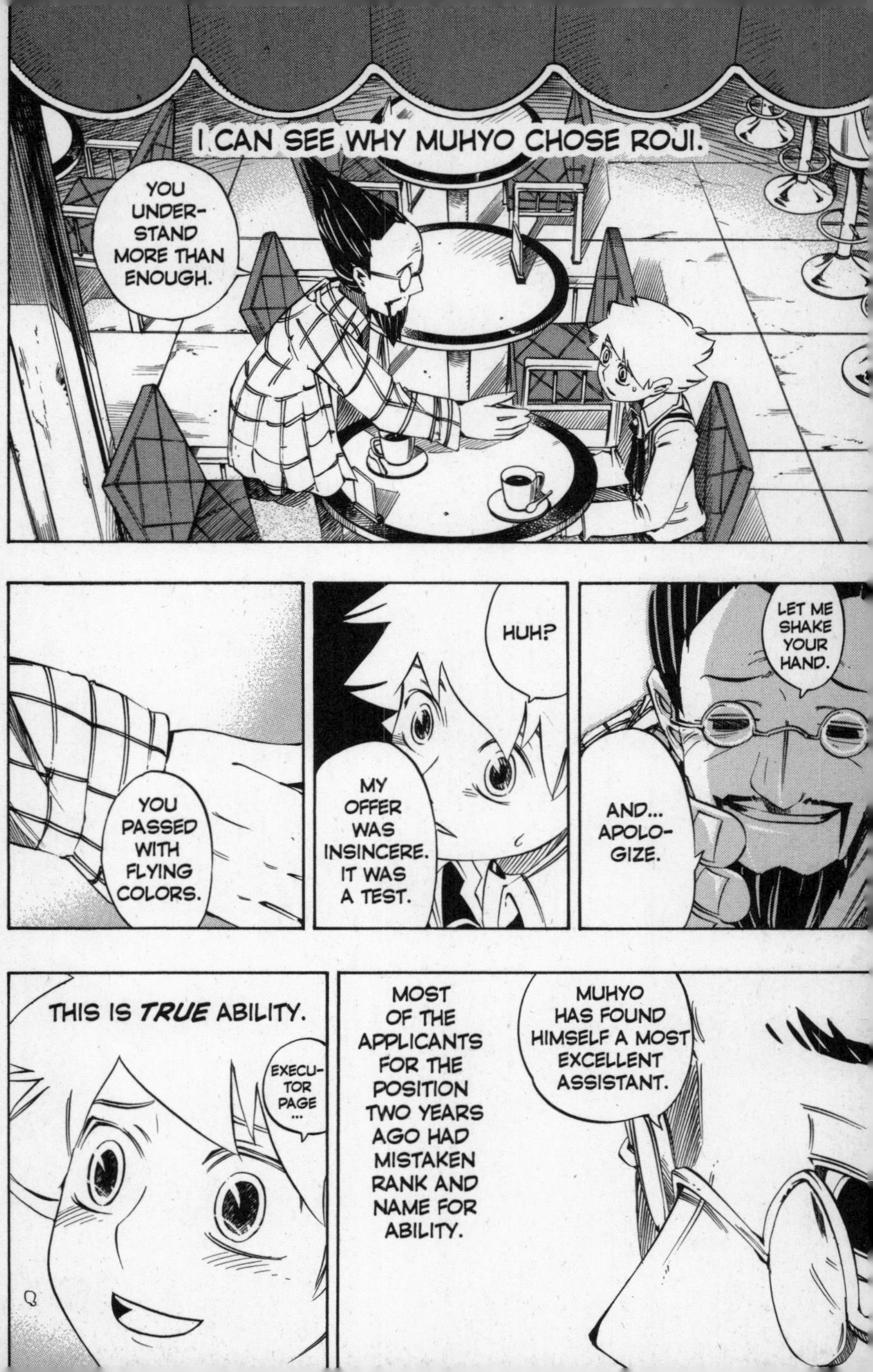
I CAN SEE WHY MUHYO CHOSE ROJI.
YOU UNDERSTAND MORE THAN ENOUGH.
LET ME SHAKE YOUR HAND.
AND... APOLOGIZE.
HUH?
MY OFFER WAS INSINCERE. IT WAS A TEST.
YOU PASSED WITH FLYING COLORS.
MUHYO HAS FOUND HIMSELF A MOST EXCELLENT ASSISTANT.
MOST OF THE APPLICANTS FOR THE POSITION TWO YEARS AGO HAD MISTAKEN RANK AND NAME FOR ABILITY.
THIS IS *TRUE* ABILITY.
EXECUTOR PAGE...

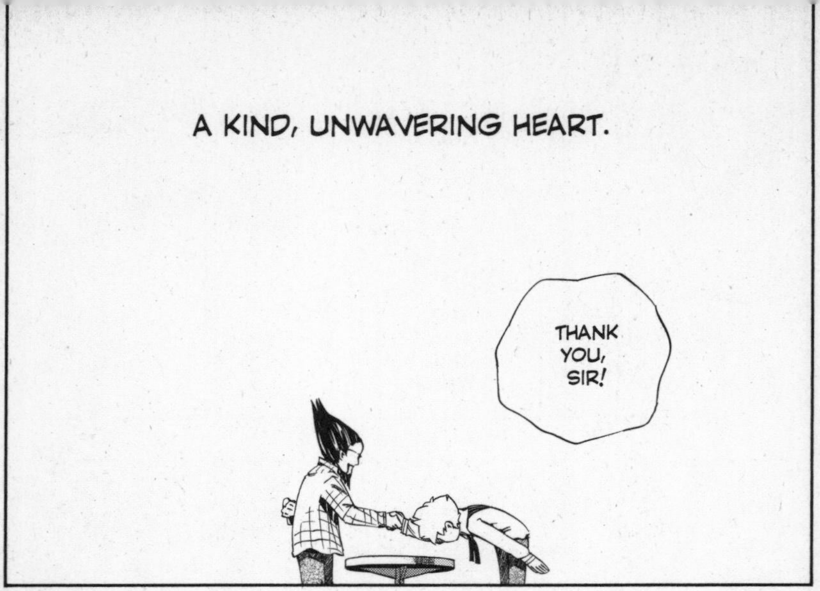
A KIND, UNWAVERING HEART.
THANK YOU, SIR!

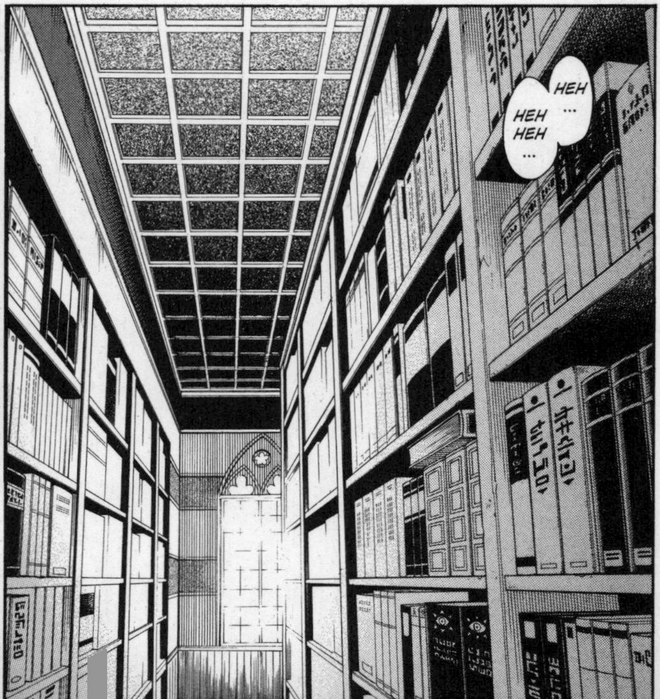
HEH ...
HEH HEH ...

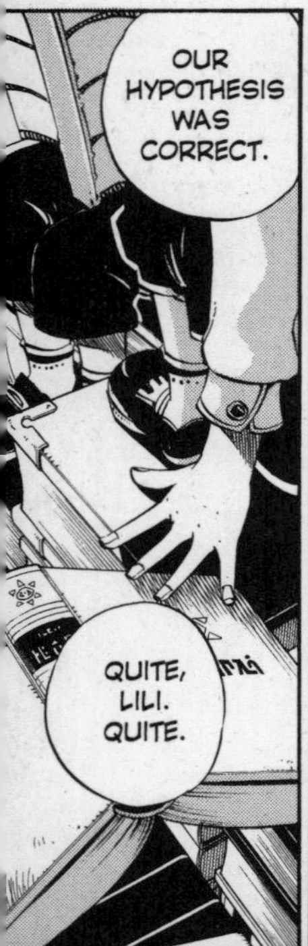
OUR HYPOTHESIS WAS CORRECT.
QUITE, LILI. QUITE.

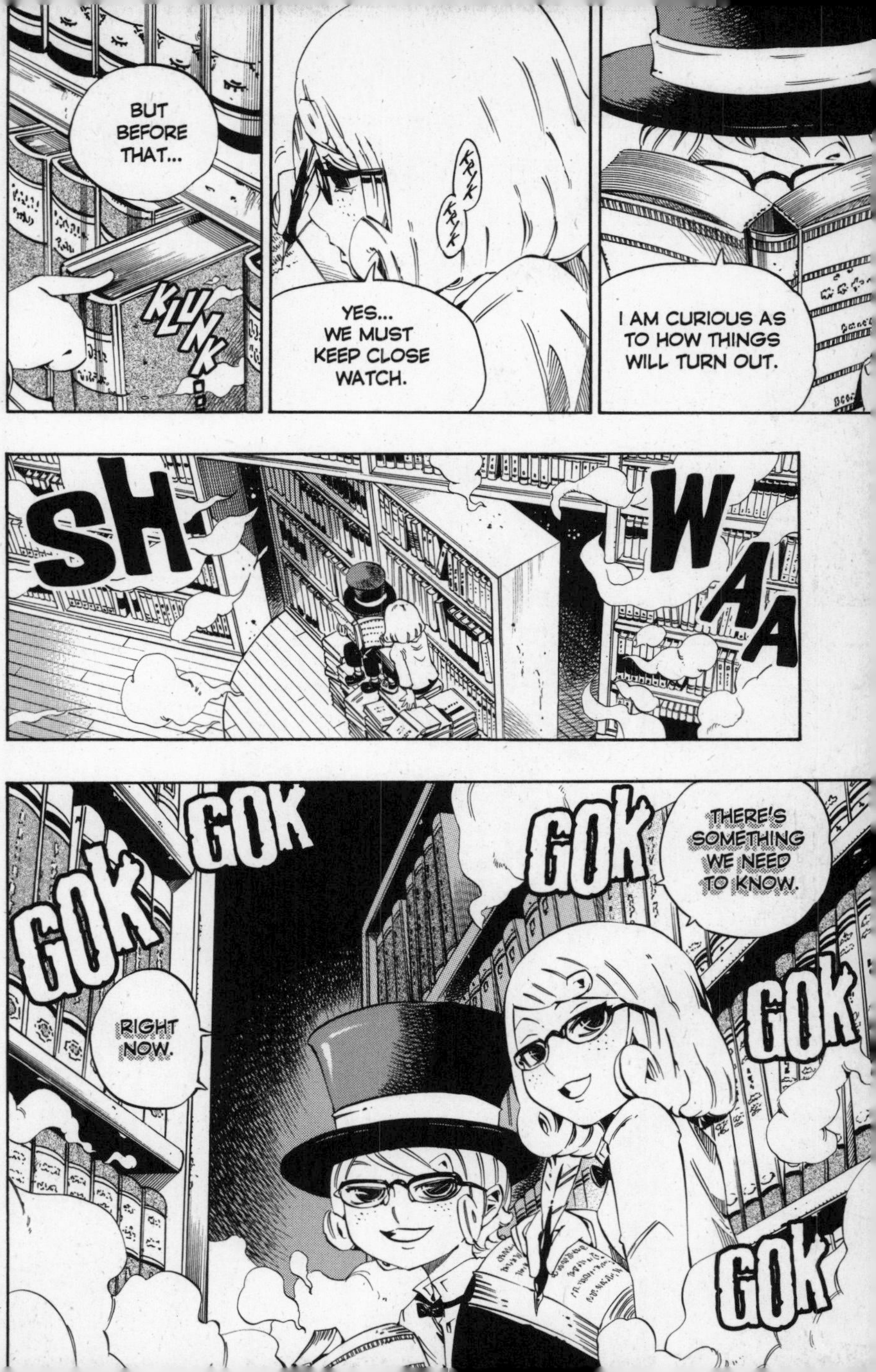
I AM CURIOUS AS TO HOW THINGS WILL TURN OUT.
TRIK TRIK TRIK
YES... WE MUST KEEP CLOSE WATCH.
BUT BEFORE THAT...
KLUNK
SHWAA
THERE'S SOMETHING WE NEED TO KNOW.
GOK
GOK
GOK
GOK
GOK
RIGHT NOW.

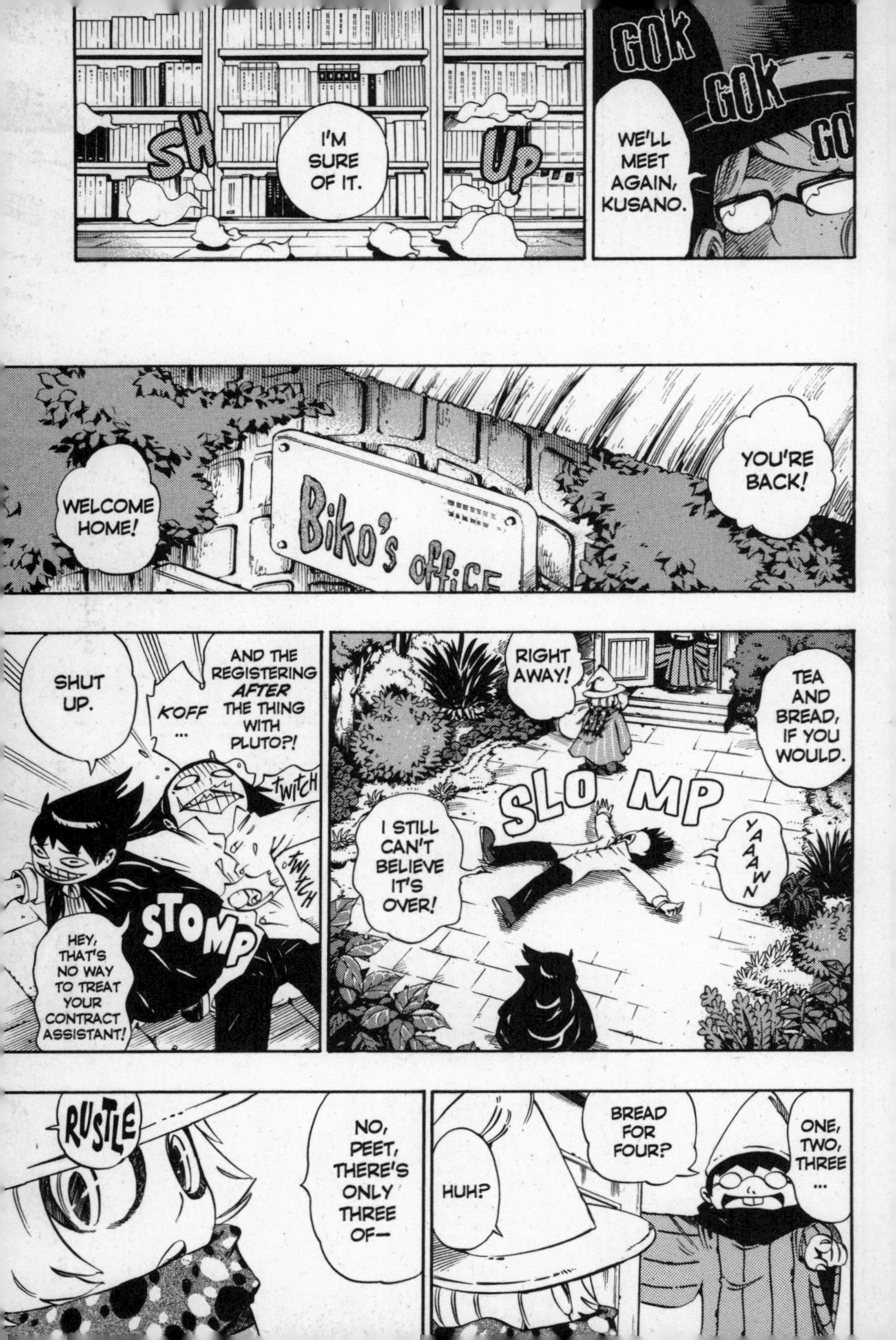
GOK
GOK
WE'LL MEET AGAIN, KUSANO.
I'M SURE OF IT.
SH UP
YOU'RE BACK!
Biko's office
WELCOME HOME!
TEA AND BREAD, IF YOU WOULD.
RIGHT AWAY!
YAAAWN
SLO MP
I STILL CAN'T BELIEVE IT'S OVER!
AND THE REGISTERING *AFTER* THE THING WITH PLUTO?!
SHUT UP.
KOFF ...
TWITCH
STOMP
HEY, THAT'S NO WAY TO TREAT YOUR CONTRACT ASSISTANT!
ONE, TWO, THREE ...
BREAD FOR FOUR?
HUH?
NO, PEET, THERE'S ONLY THREE OF—
RUSTLE

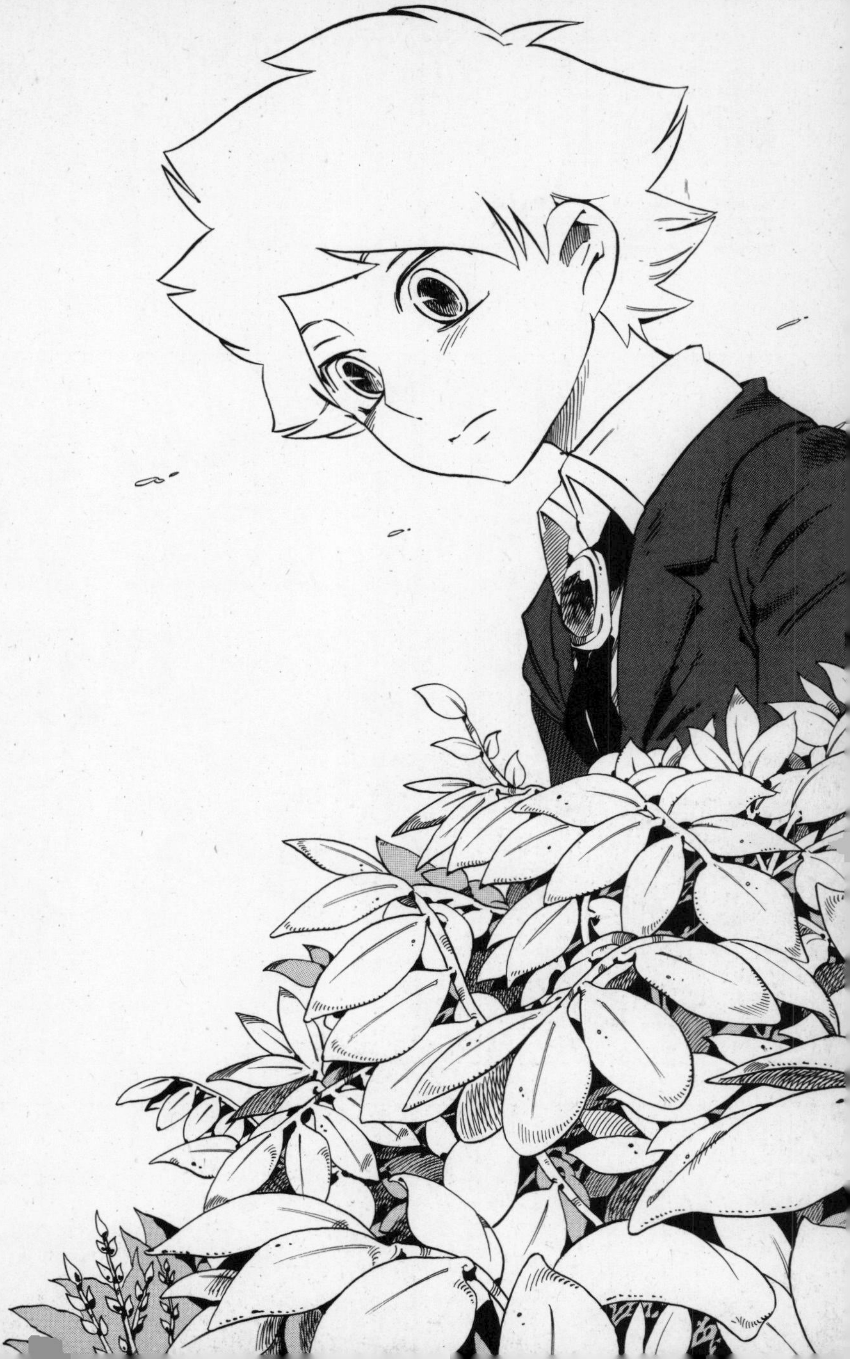

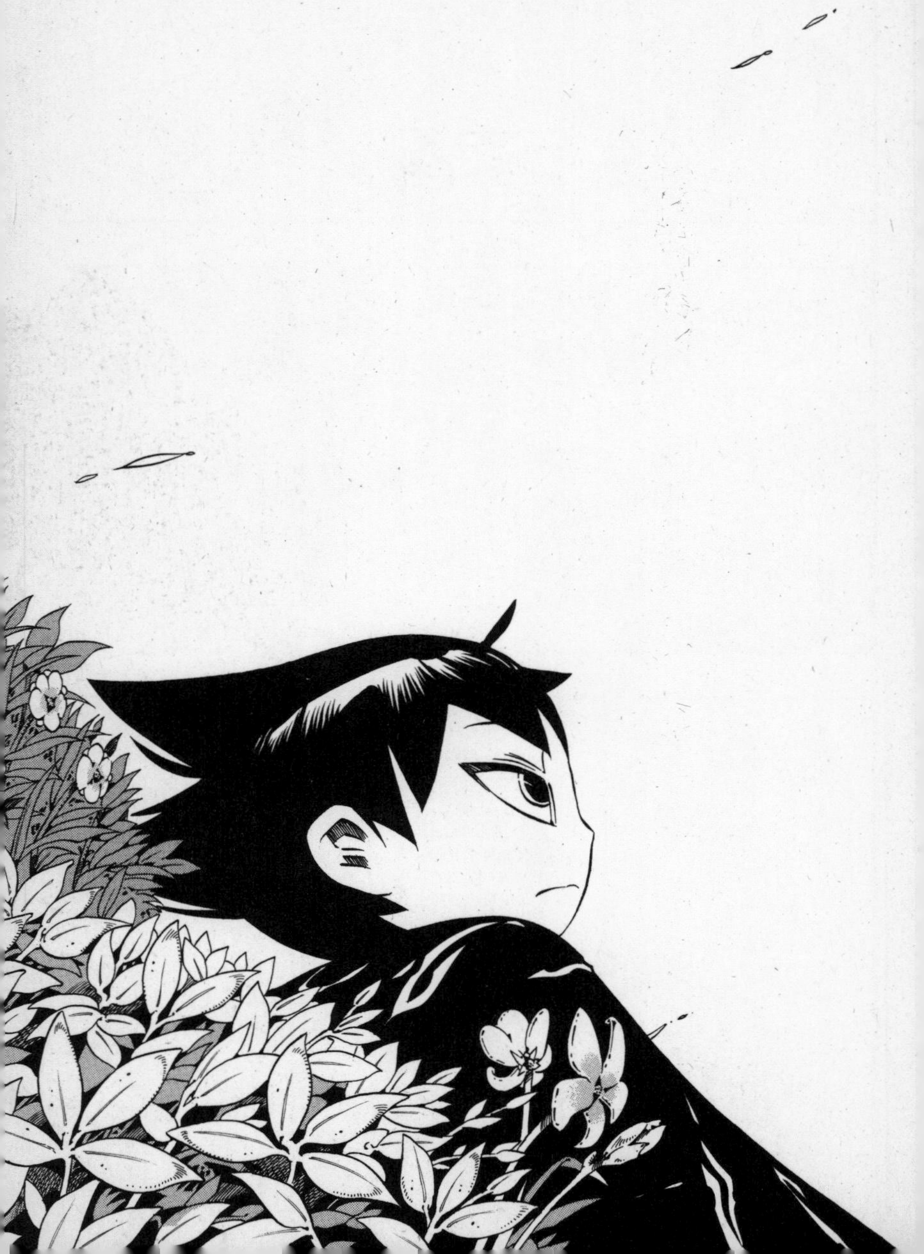

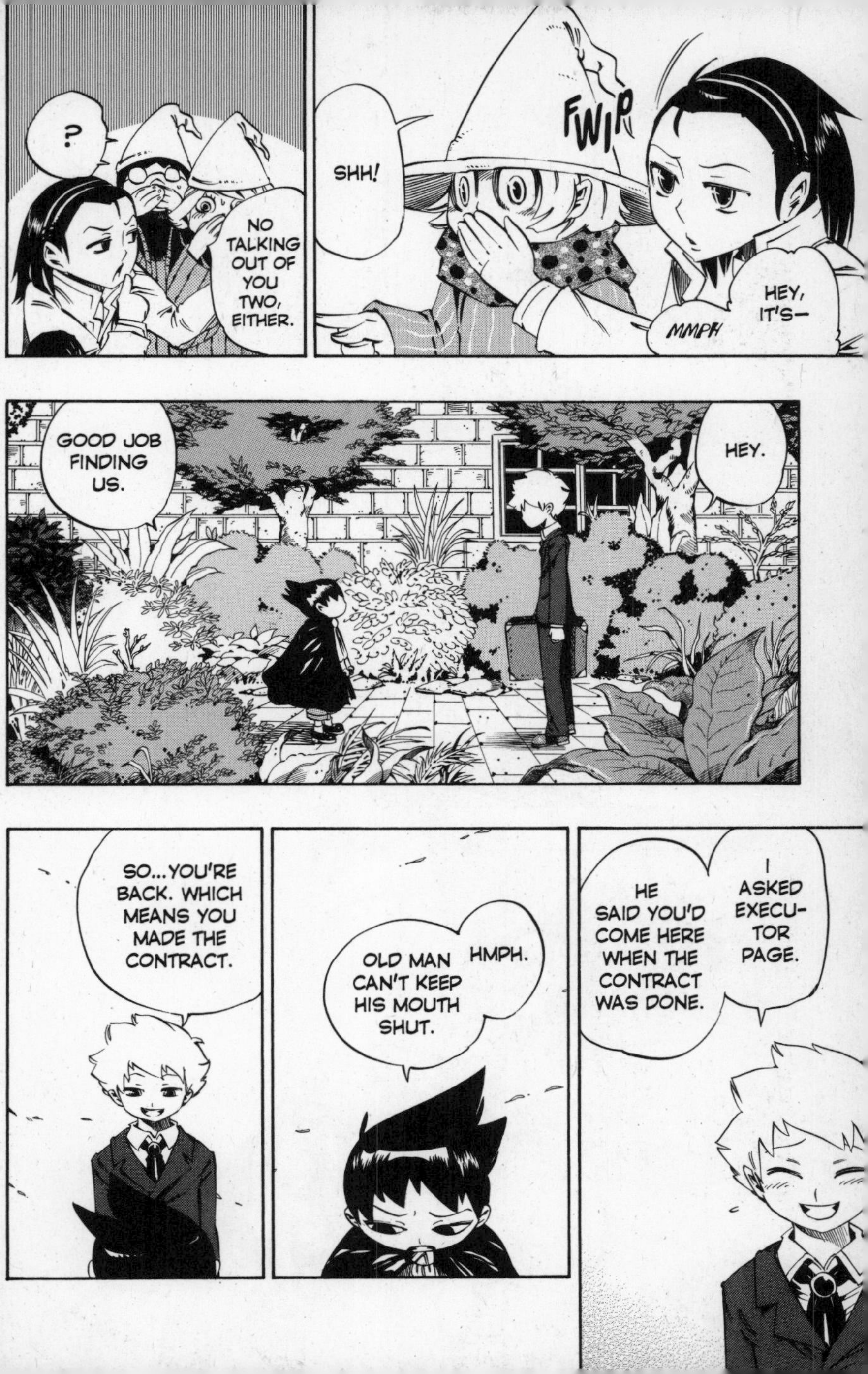
FWIP
SHH!
HEY, IT'S—
MMPH
?
NO TALKING OUT OF YOU TWO, EITHER.
HEY.
GOOD JOB FINDING US.
I ASKED EXECUTOR PAGE.
HE SAID YOU'D COME HERE WHEN THE CONTRACT WAS DONE.
HMPH.
OLD MAN CAN'T KEEP HIS MOUTH SHUT.
SO...YOU'RE BACK. WHICH MEANS YOU MADE THE CONTRACT.

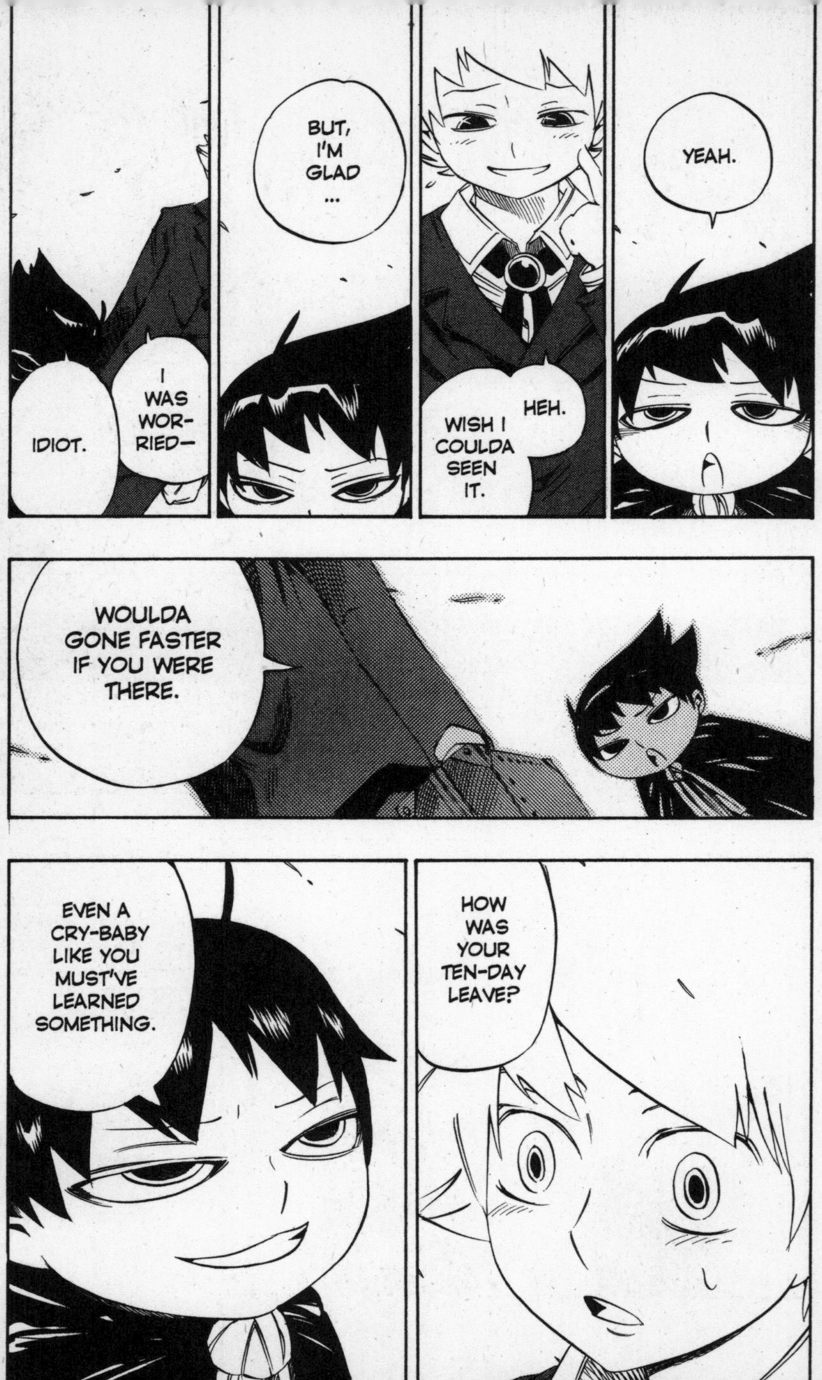
YEAH.
HEH.
WISH I COULDA SEEN IT.
BUT, I'M GLAD ...
I WAS WOR-RIED—
IDIOT.
WOULDA GONE FASTER IF YOU WERE THERE.
HOW WAS YOUR TEN-DAY LEAVE?
EVEN A CRY-BABY LIKE YOU MUST'VE LEARNED SOMETHING.

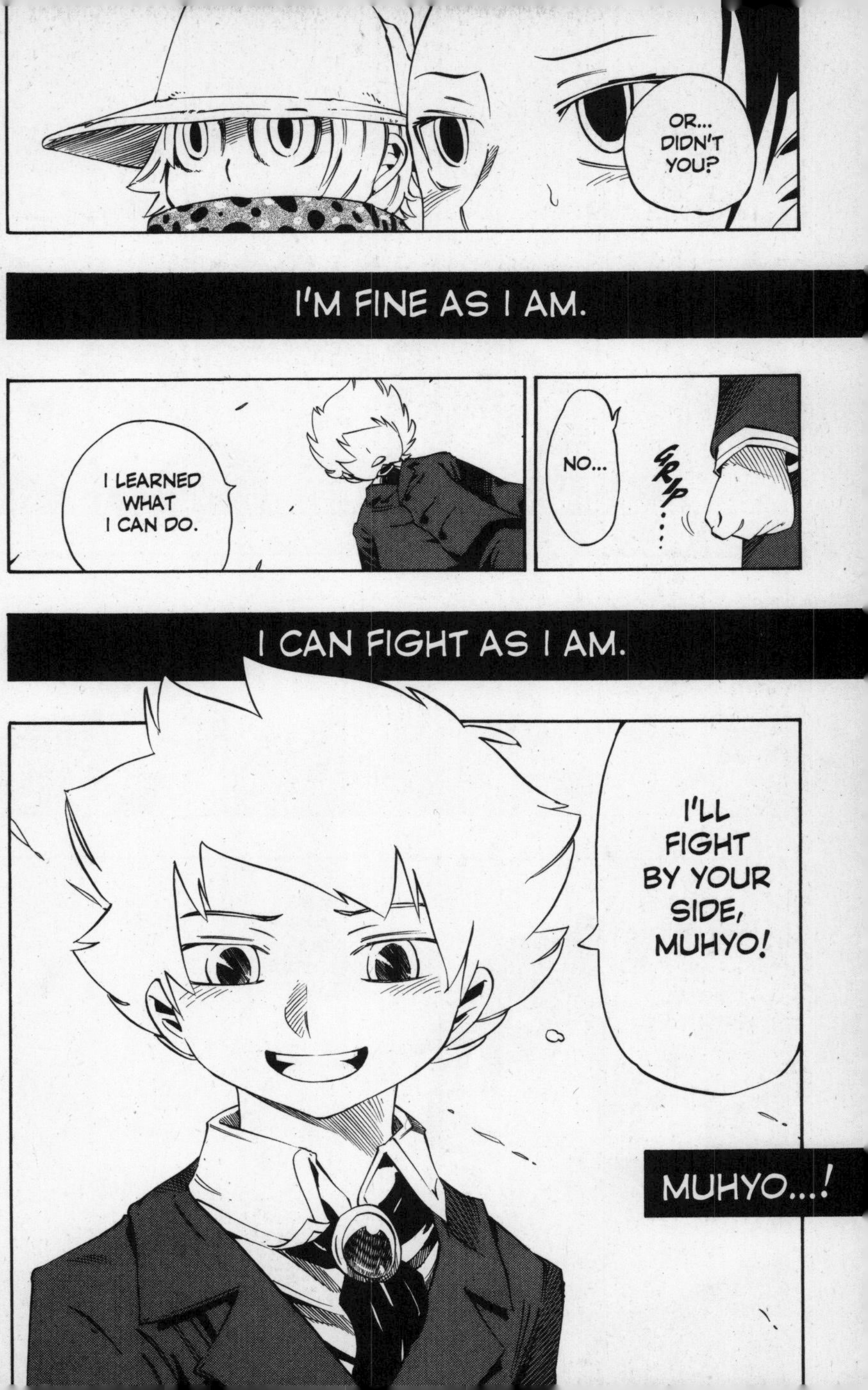
OR... DIDN'T YOU?
I'M FINE AS I AM.
NO...
GRIP...
I LEARNED WHAT I CAN DO.
I CAN FIGHT AS I AM.
I'LL FIGHT BY YOUR SIDE, MUHYO!
MUHYO...!

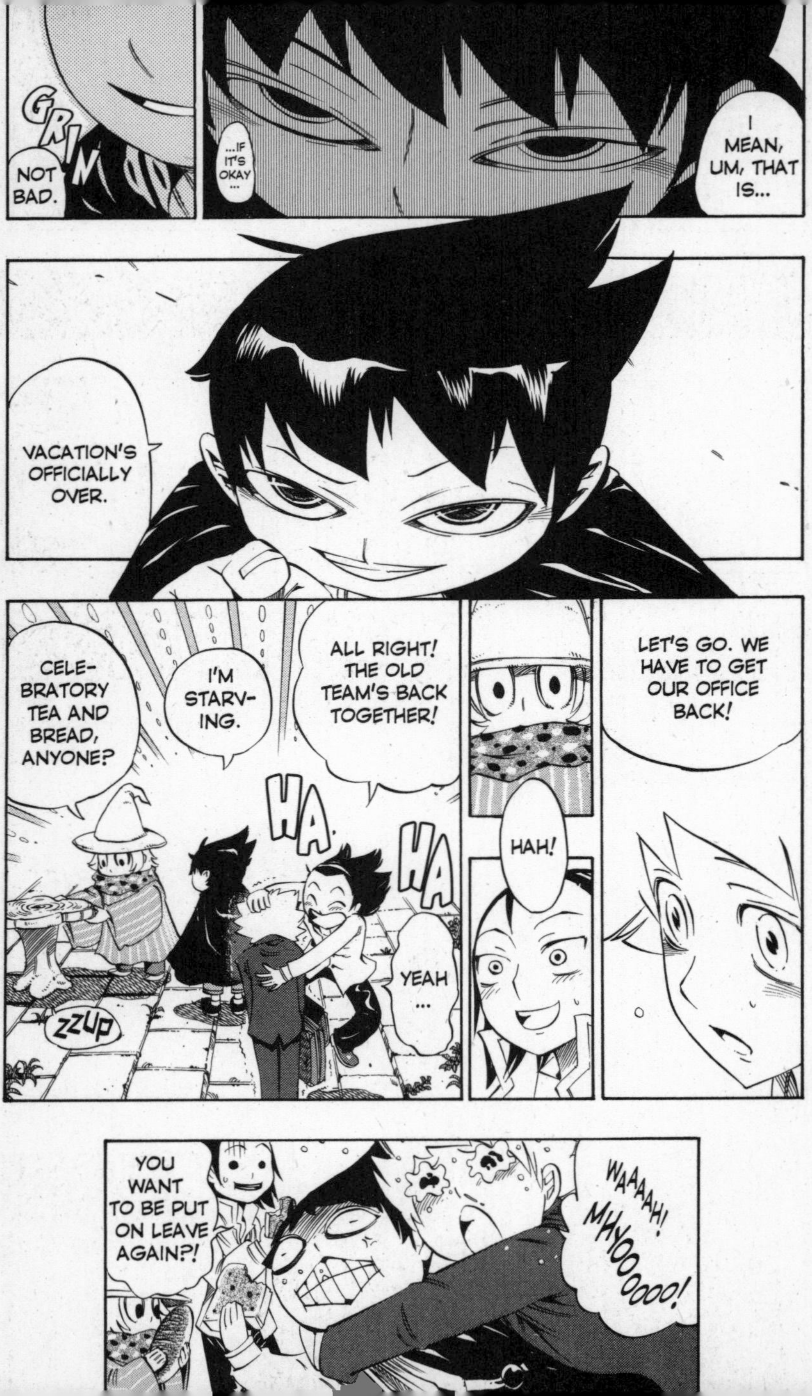
I MEAN, UM, THAT IS...
...IF IT'S OKAY...
GRIN
NOT BAD.
VACATION'S OFFICIALLY OVER.
LET'S GO. WE HAVE TO GET OUR OFFICE BACK!
HAH!
ALL RIGHT! THE OLD TEAM'S BACK TOGETHER!
I'M STARV-ING.
CELE-BRATORY TEA AND BREAD, ANYONE?
HA HA
YEAH...
ZZUP
WAAAAH!
MHYOOOOOO!
YOU WANT TO BE PUT ON LEAVE AGAIN?!

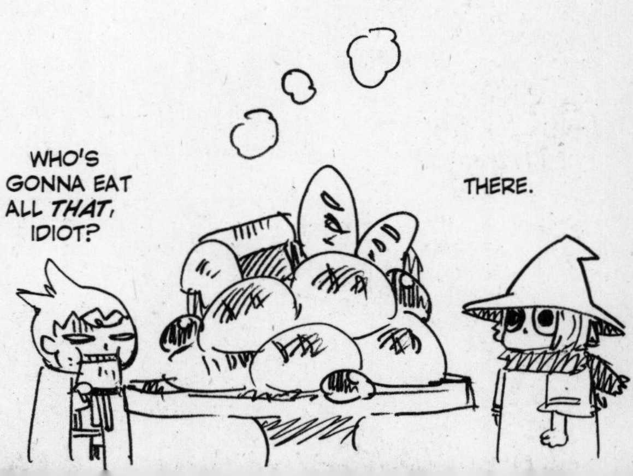
THERE.
WHO'S GONNA EAT ALL *THAT*, IDIOT?

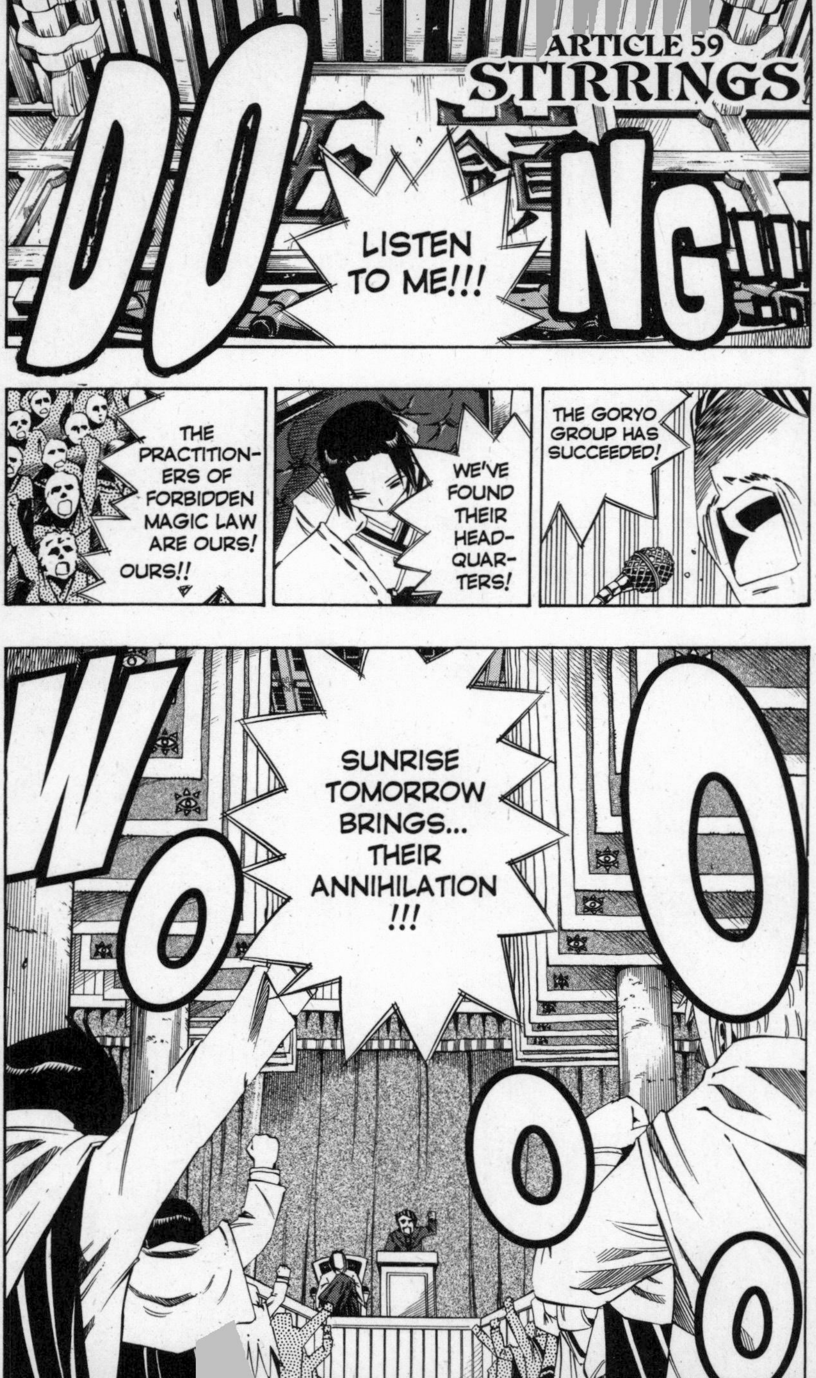
ARTICLE 59
STIRRINGS
DONG!!!
LISTEN TO ME!!!
THE GORYO GROUP HAS SUCCEEDED!
WE'VE FOUND THEIR HEADQUARTERS!
THE PRACTITIONERS OF FORBIDDEN MAGIC LAW ARE OURS!
OURS!!
SUNRISE TOMORROW BRINGS... THEIR ANNIHILATION!!!
WOOOO

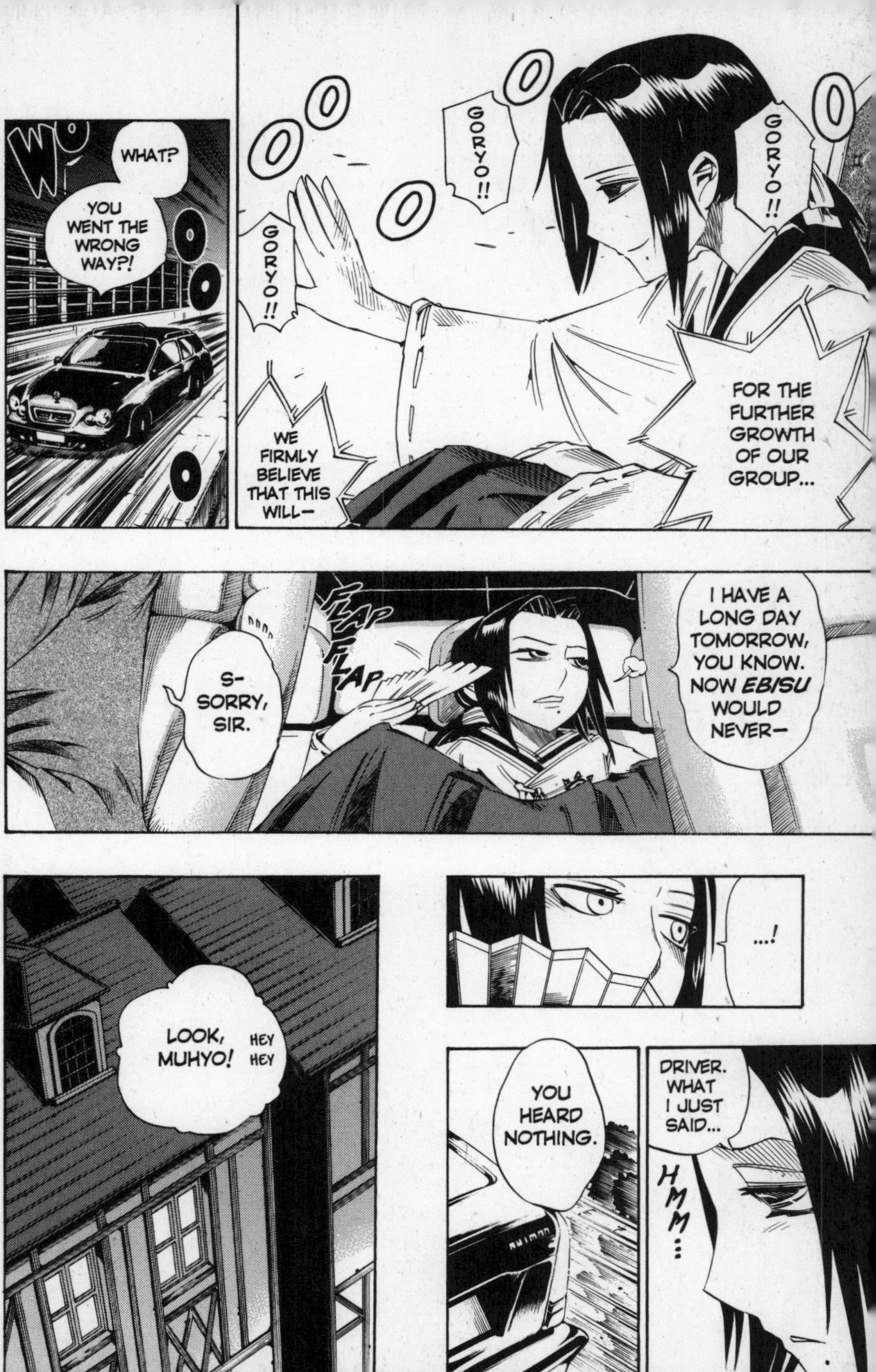
GORYO!!
GORYO!!
GORYO!!
FOR THE FURTHER GROWTH OF OUR GROUP...
WE FIRMLY BELIEVE THAT THIS WILL—
WHAT?
YOU WENT THE WRONG WAY?!
I HAVE A LONG DAY TOMORROW, YOU KNOW. NOW *EBISU* WOULD NEVER—
FLAP FLAP
S-SORRY, SIR.
...!
DRIVER. WHAT I JUST SAID...
YOU HEARD NOTHING.
HMM...
LOOK, MUHYO!
HEY HEY

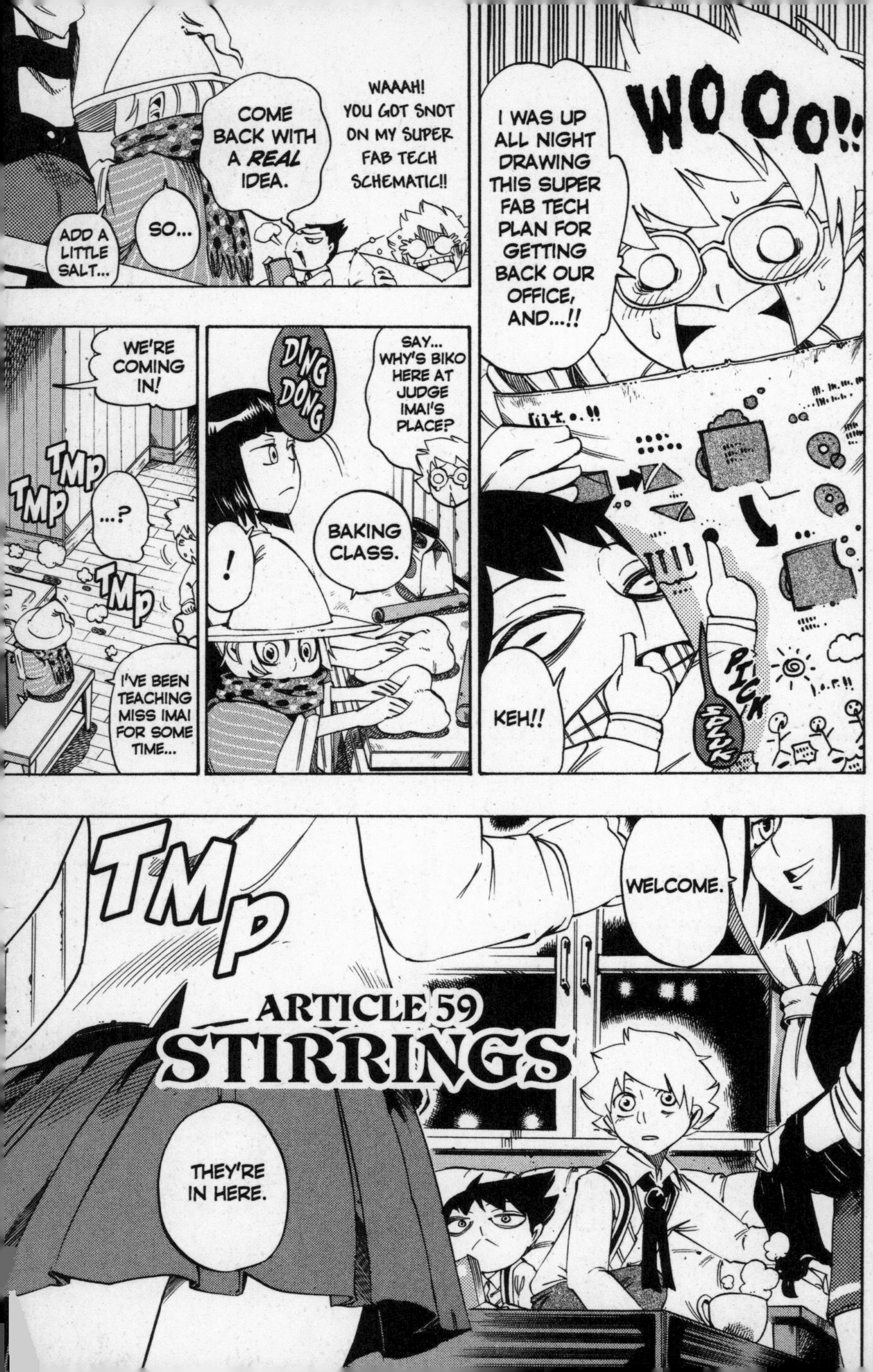
WOOOO!!
I WAS UP ALL NIGHT DRAWING THIS SUPER FAB TECH PLAN FOR GETTING BACK OUR OFFICE, AND...!!
PICK
SPLUK
KEH!!
WAAAH! YOU GOT SNOT ON MY SUPER FAB TECH SCHEMATIC!!
COME BACK WITH A *REAL* IDEA.
SO...
ADD A LITTLE SALT...
SAY... WHY'S BIKO HERE AT JUDGE IMAI'S PLACE?
DING DONG
BAKING CLASS.
!
WE'RE COMING IN!
TMP TMP
...?
TMP
I'VE BEEN TEACHING MISS IMAI FOR SOME TIME...
WELCOME.
TMP
ARTICLE 59
STIRRINGS
THEY'RE IN HERE.

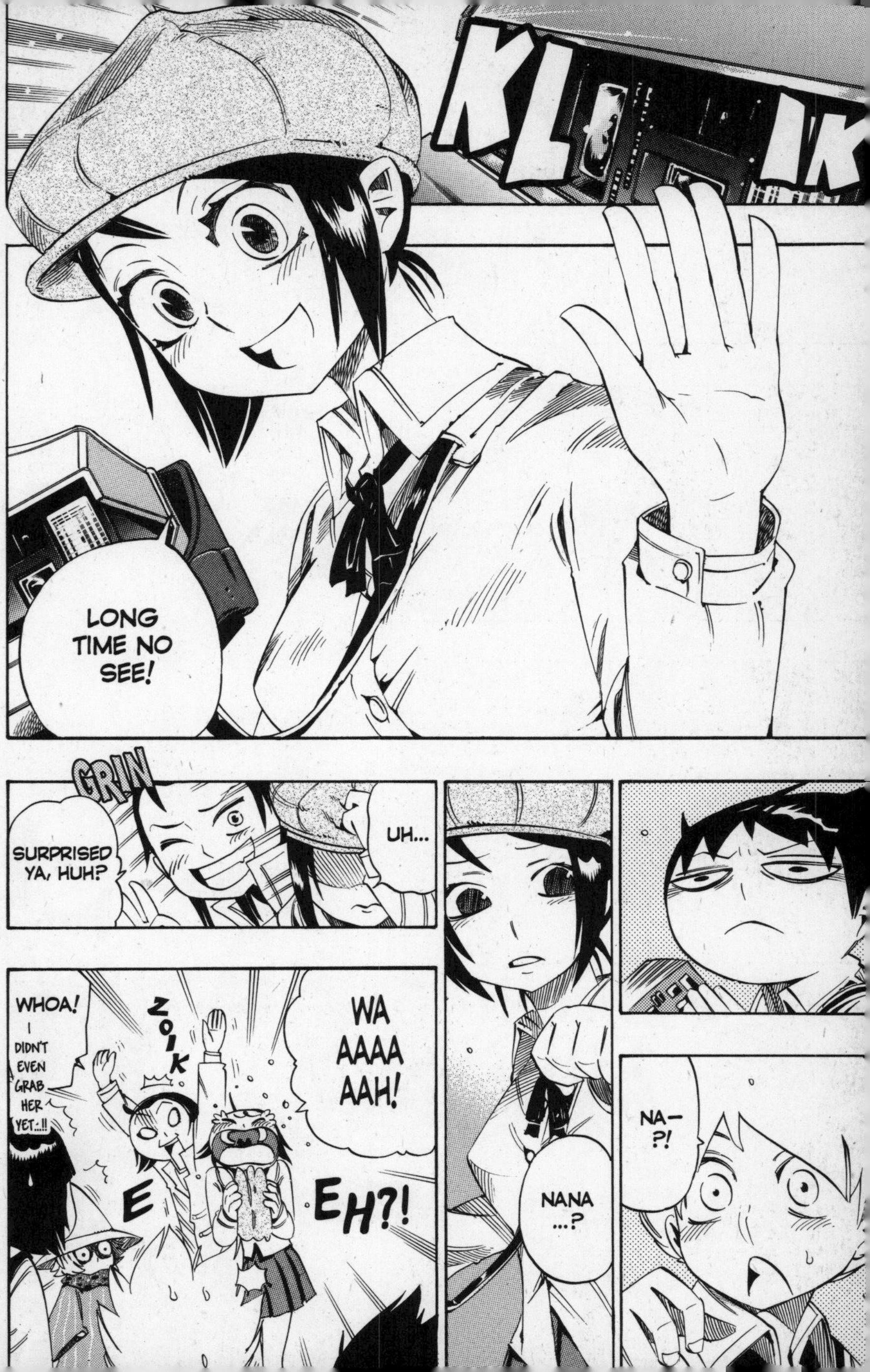
KL
IK
LONG TIME NO SEE!
NA— ?!
NANA ...?
UH...
GRIN
SURPRISED YA, HUH?
WA AAAA AAH!
ZOIK
WHOA! I DIDN'T EVEN GRAB HER YET...!!
EH?!
E

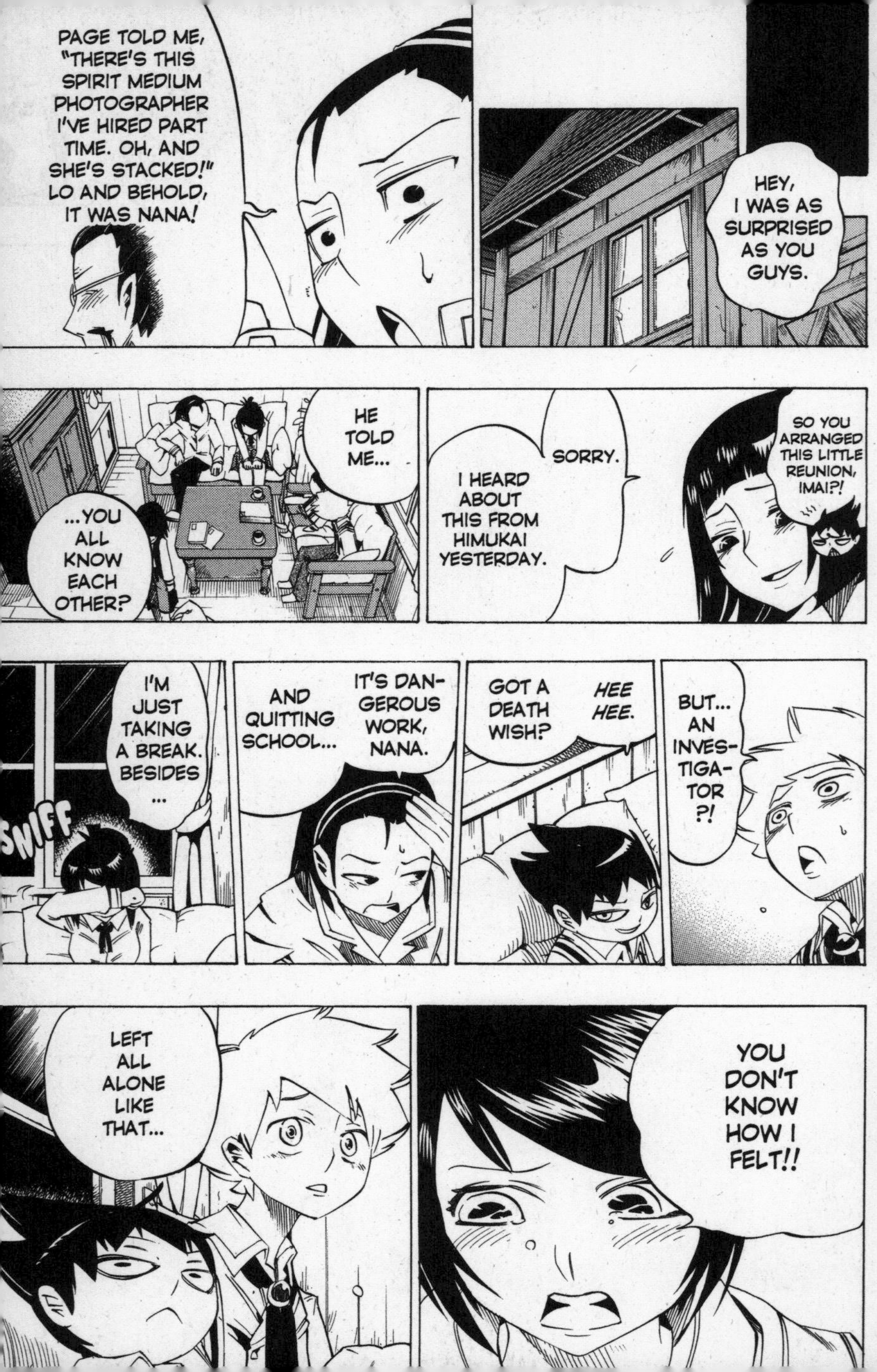
HEY, I WAS AS SURPRISED AS YOU GUYS.
PAGE TOLD ME, "THERE'S THIS SPIRIT MEDIUM PHOTOGRAPHER I'VE HIRED PART TIME. OH, AND SHE'S STACKED!" LO AND BEHOLD, IT WAS NANA!
SO YOU ARRANGED THIS LITTLE REUNION, IMAI?!
SORRY.
I HEARD ABOUT THIS FROM HIMUKAI YESTERDAY.
HE TOLD ME...
...YOU ALL KNOW EACH OTHER?
BUT... AN INVESTIGATOR?!
GOT A DEATH WISH?
HEE HEE.
IT'S DANGEROUS WORK, NANA.
AND QUITTING SCHOOL...
I'M JUST TAKING A BREAK. BESIDES...
SNIFF
YOU DON'T KNOW HOW I FELT!!
LEFT ALL ALONE LIKE THAT...

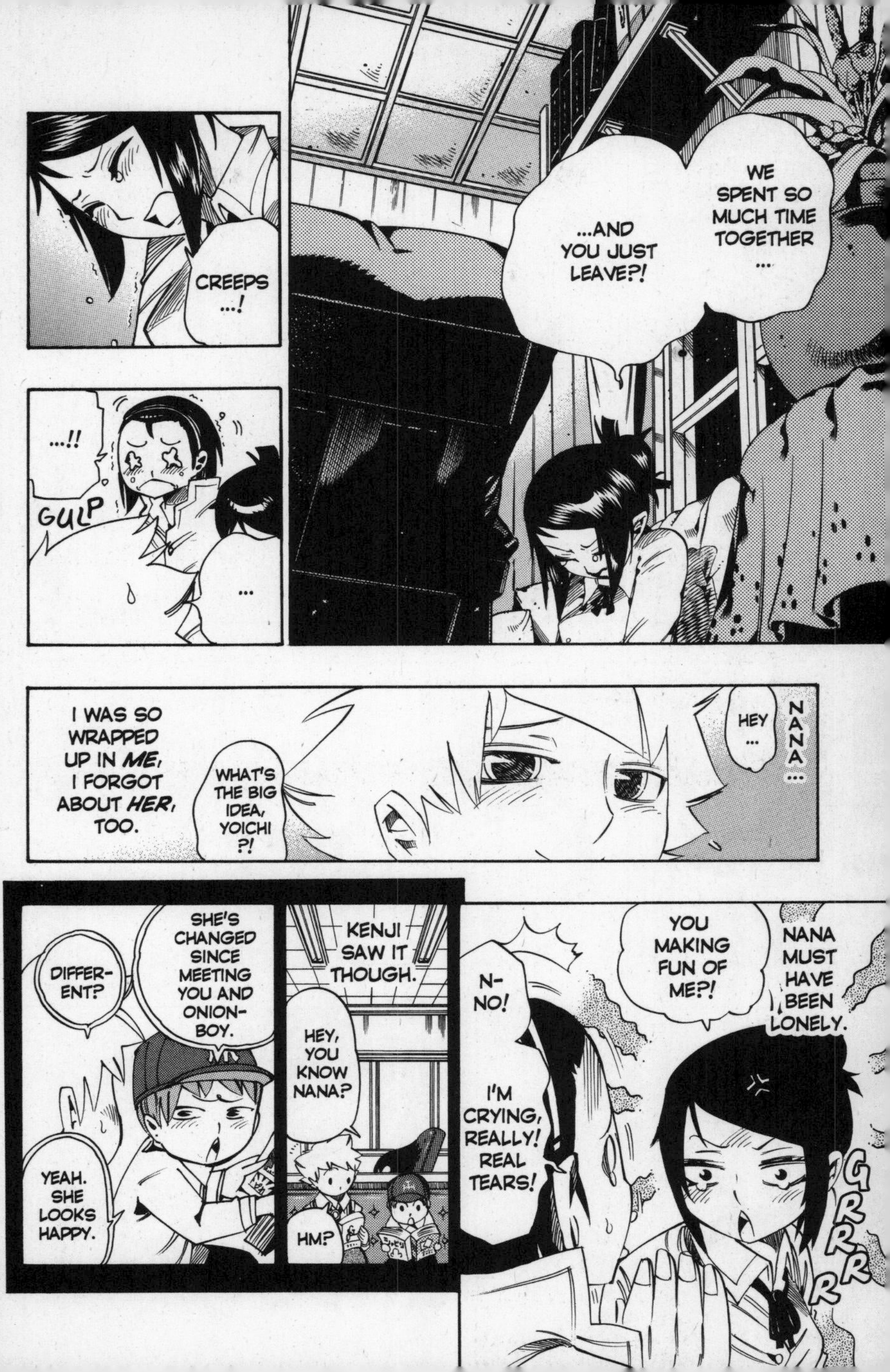
WE SPENT SO MUCH TIME TOGETHER ...
...AND YOU JUST LEAVE?!
CREEPS ...!
...!!
GULP
...
NANA ...
HEY ...
WHAT'S THE BIG IDEA, YOICHI ?!
I WAS SO WRAPPED UP IN *ME*, I FORGOT ABOUT *HER*, TOO.
NANA MUST HAVE BEEN LONELY.
YOU MAKING FUN OF ME?!
GRRRR
N-NO!
I'M CRYING, REALLY! REAL TEARS!
KENJI SAW IT THOUGH.
HEY, YOU KNOW NANA?
HM?
SHE'S CHANGED SINCE MEETING YOU AND ONION-BOY.
DIFFERENT?
YEAH. SHE LOOKS HAPPY.

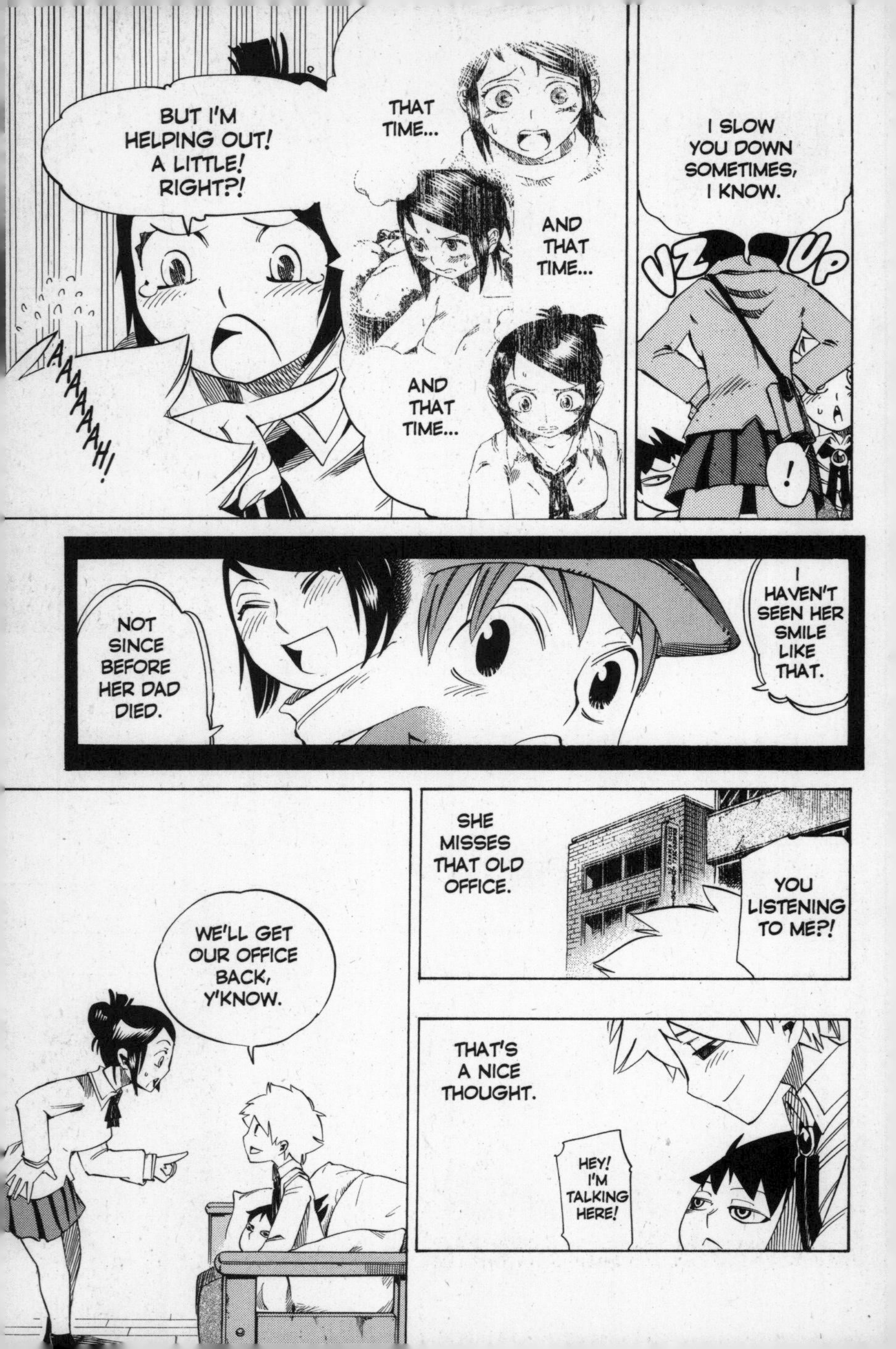
I SLOW YOU DOWN SOMETIMES, I KNOW.
VZ
UP
!
THAT TIME...
AND THAT TIME...
AND THAT TIME...
BUT I'M HELPING OUT! A LITTLE! RIGHT?!
AAAAAAAH!
I HAVEN'T SEEN HER SMILE LIKE THAT.
NOT SINCE BEFORE HER DAD DIED.
SHE MISSES THAT OLD OFFICE.
YOU LISTENING TO ME?!
THAT'S A NICE THOUGHT.
HEY! I'M TALKING HERE!
WE'LL GET OUR OFFICE BACK, Y'KNOW.

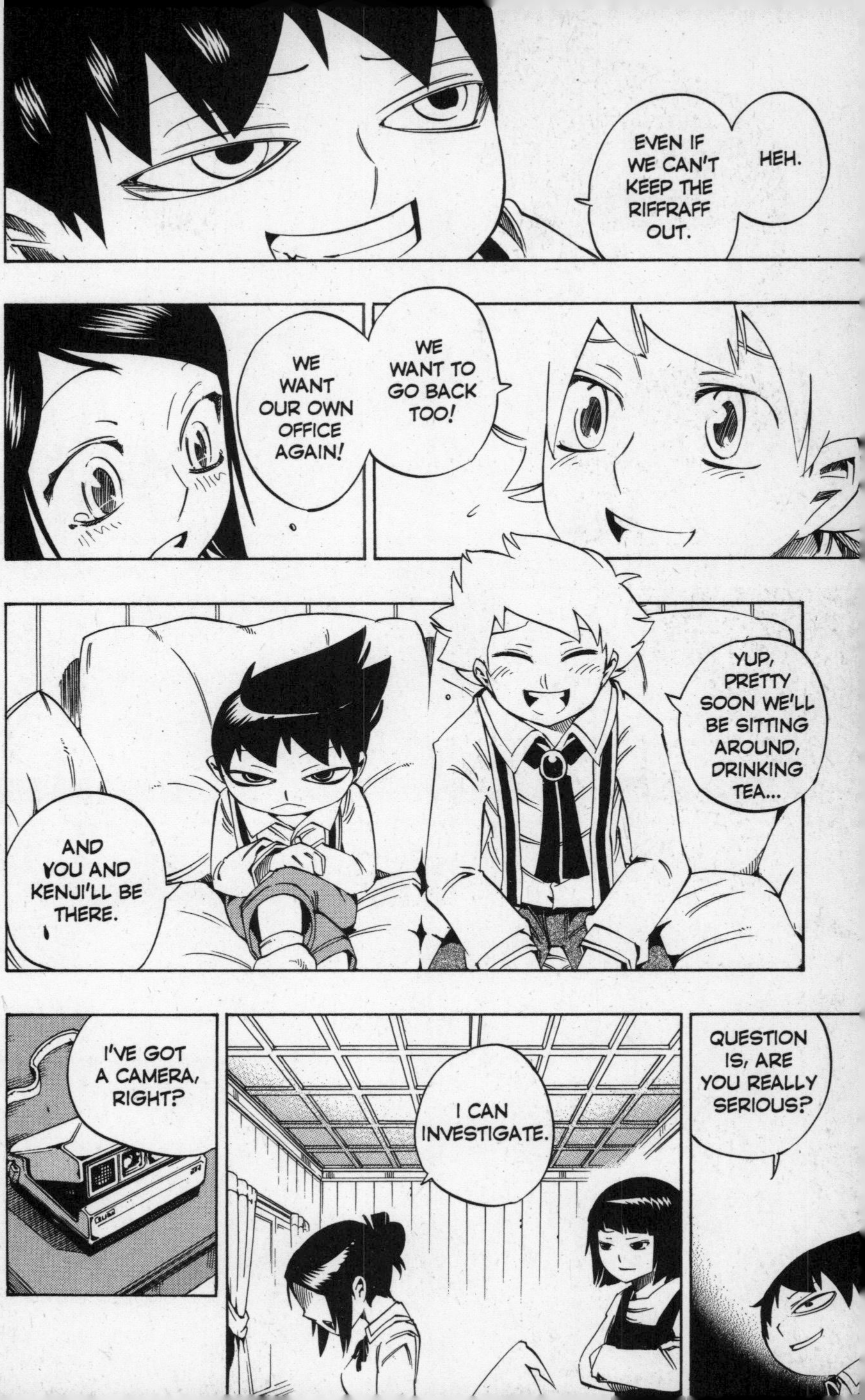
HEH.
EVEN IF WE CAN'T KEEP THE RIFFRAFF OUT.
WE WANT TO GO BACK TOO!
WE WANT OUR OWN OFFICE AGAIN!
YUP, PRETTY SOON WE'LL BE SITTING AROUND, DRINKING TEA...
AND YOU AND KENJI'LL BE THERE.
QUESTION IS, ARE YOU REALLY SERIOUS?
I CAN INVESTIGATE.
I'VE GOT A CAMERA, RIGHT?

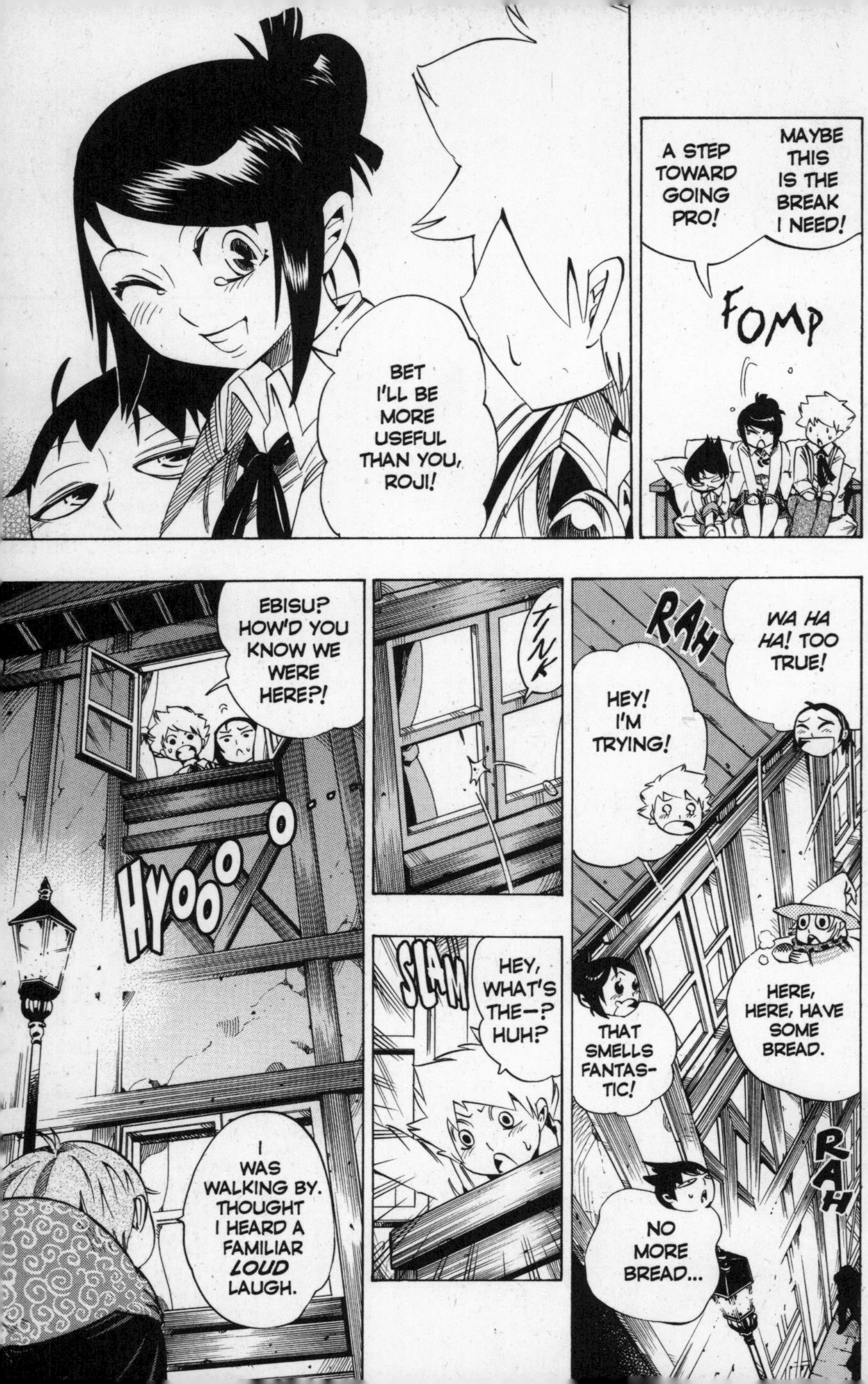

MAYBE THIS IS THE BREAK I NEED!
A STEP TOWARD GOING PRO!
FOMP
BET I'LL BE MORE USEFUL THAN YOU, ROJI!
RAH
WA HA HA! TOO TRUE!
HEY! I'M TRYING!
HERE, HERE, HAVE SOME BREAD.
THAT SMELLS FANTAS-TIC!
RAH
NO MORE BREAD...
TINK
SLAM
HEY, WHAT'S THE—? HUH?
EBISU? HOW'D YOU KNOW WE WERE HERE?!
HYOOO
I WAS WALKING BY. THOUGHT I HEARD A FAMILIAR LOUD LAUGH.

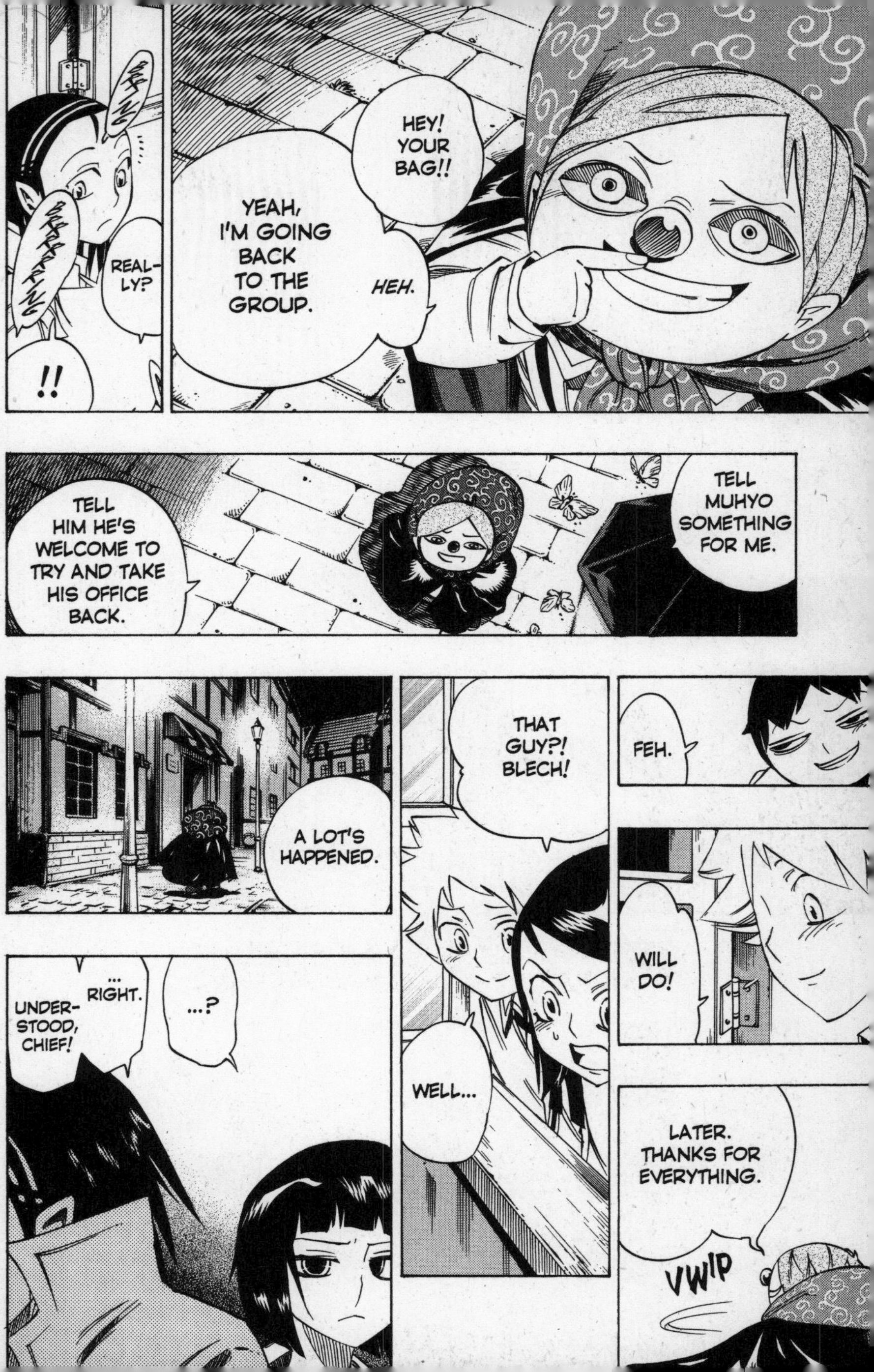
HEY! YOUR BAG!!
YEAH, I'M GOING BACK TO THE GROUP.
HEH.
REAL-LY?
!!
TELL MUHYO SOMETHING FOR ME.
TELL HIM HE'S WELCOME TO TRY AND TAKE HIS OFFICE BACK.
FEH.
WILL DO!
LATER. THANKS FOR EVERYTHING.
VWIP
THAT GUY?! BLECH!
WELL...
A LOT'S HAPPENED.
...?
... RIGHT.
UNDER-STOOD, CHIEF!

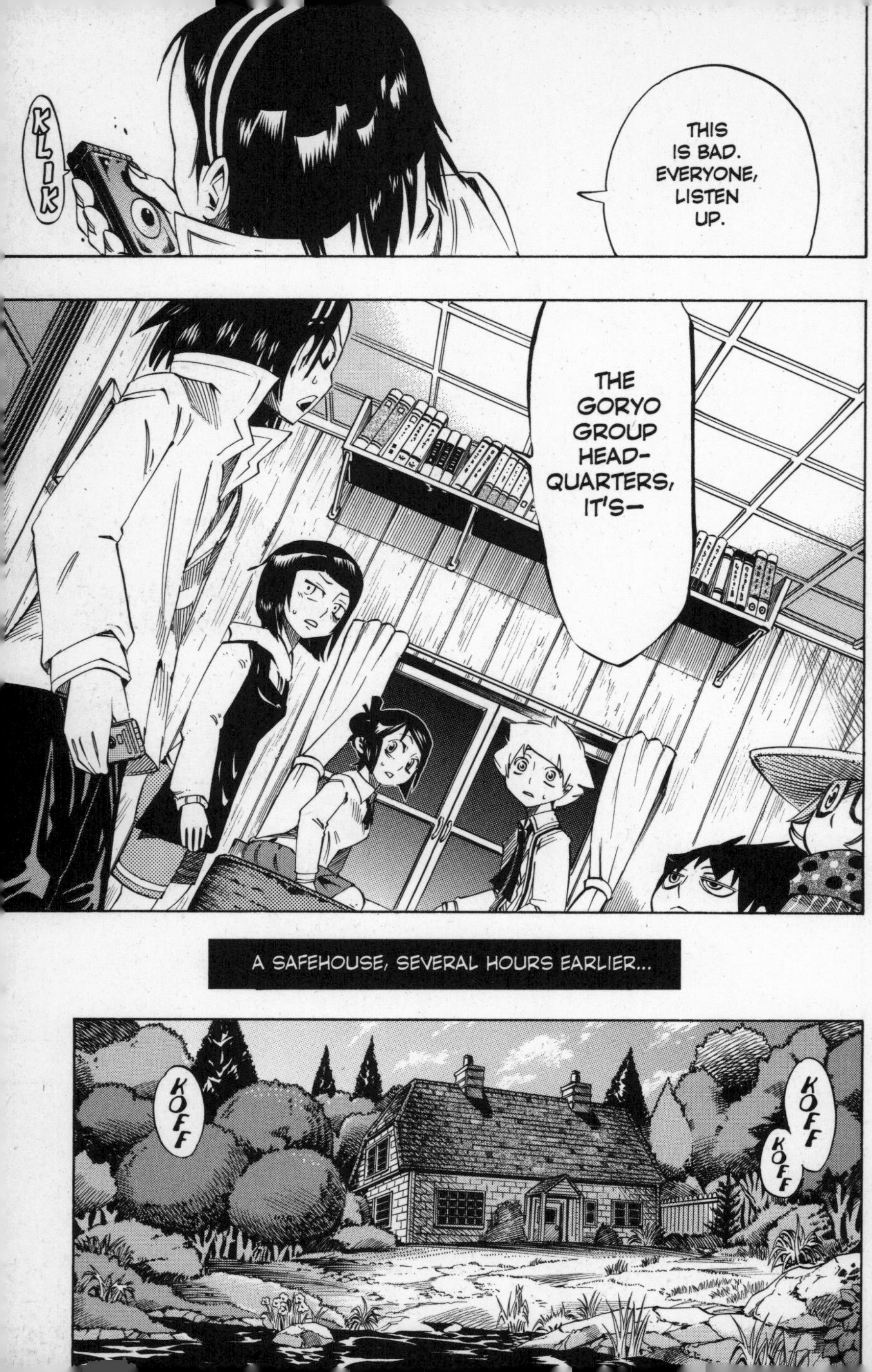
THIS IS BAD. EVERYONE, LISTEN UP.
KLIK
THE GORYO GROUP HEAD-QUARTERS, IT'S—
A SAFEHOUSE, SEVERAL HOURS EARLIER...
KOFF
KOFF
KOFF

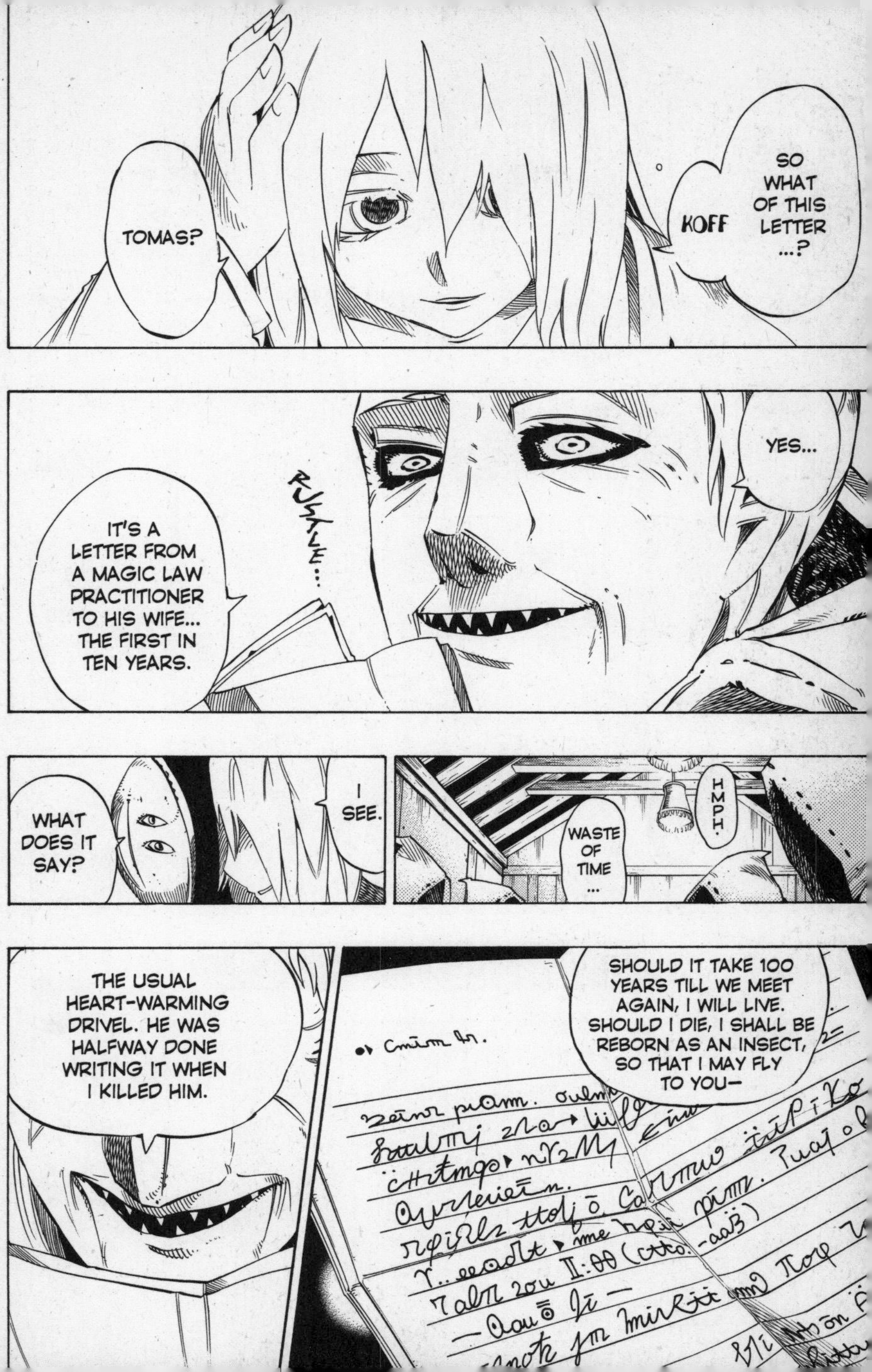
KOFF
SO WHAT OF THIS LETTER ...?
TOMAS?
YES...
RUSTLE...
IT'S A LETTER FROM A MAGIC LAW PRACTITIONER TO HIS WIFE... THE FIRST IN TEN YEARS.
HMPH.
WASTE OF TIME ...
I SEE.
WHAT DOES IT SAY?
SHOULD IT TAKE 100 YEARS TILL WE MEET AGAIN, I WILL LIVE. SHOULD I DIE, I SHALL BE REBORN AS AN INSECT, SO THAT I MAY FLY TO YOU—
THE USUAL HEART-WARMING DRIVEL. HE WAS HALFWAY DONE WRITING IT WHEN I KILLED HIM.

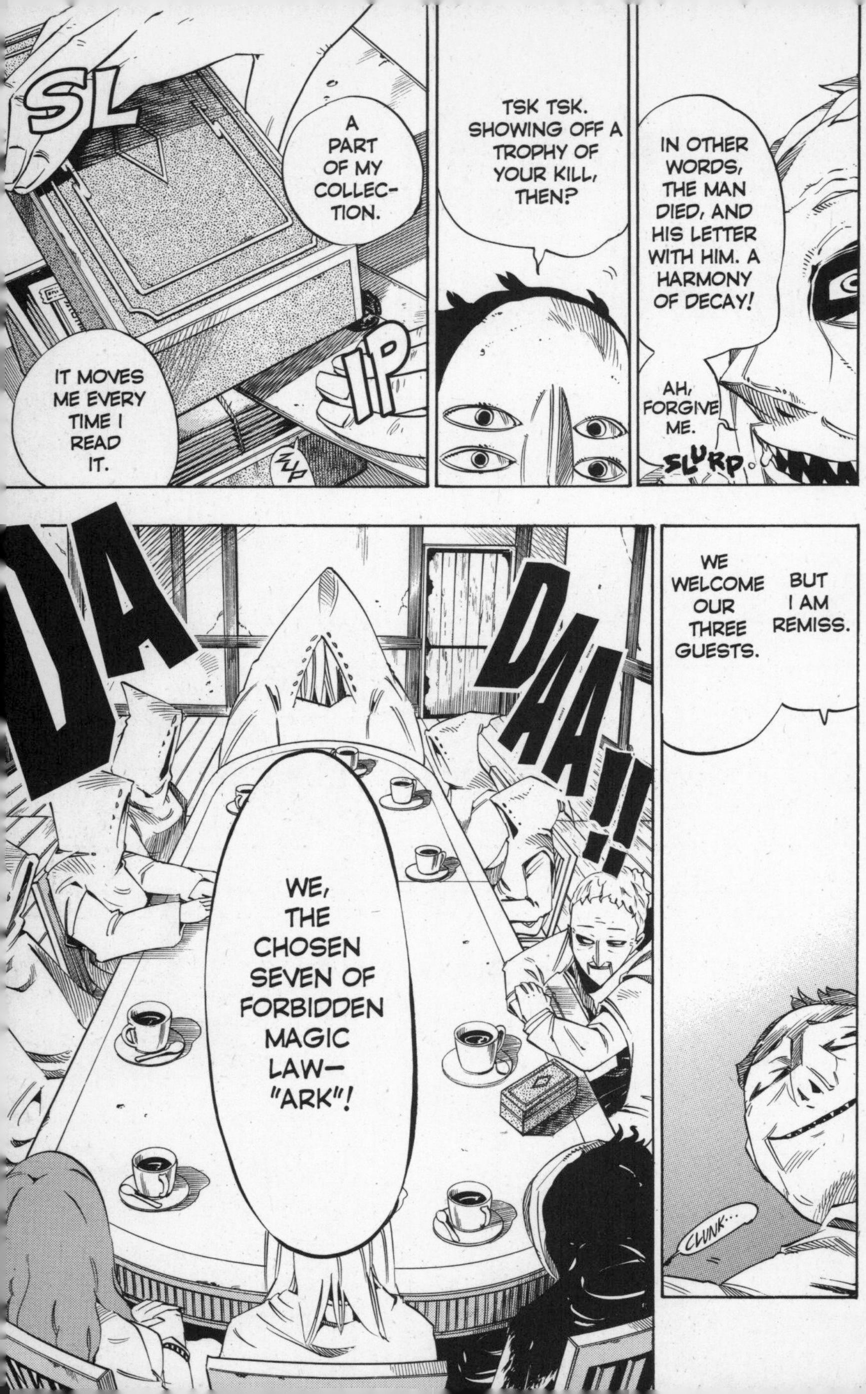
IN OTHER WORDS, THE MAN DIED, AND HIS LETTER WITH HIM. A HARMONY OF DECAY!
AH, FORGIVE ME.
SLURP
TSK TSK. SHOWING OFF A TROPHY OF YOUR KILL, THEN?
SL
IP
A PART OF MY COLLEC- TION.
IT MOVES ME EVERY TIME I READ IT.
BUT I AM REMISS.
WE WELCOME OUR THREE GUESTS.
CLUNK...
DA
DAA!!
WE, THE CHOSEN SEVEN OF FORBIDDEN MAGIC LAW— "ARK"!

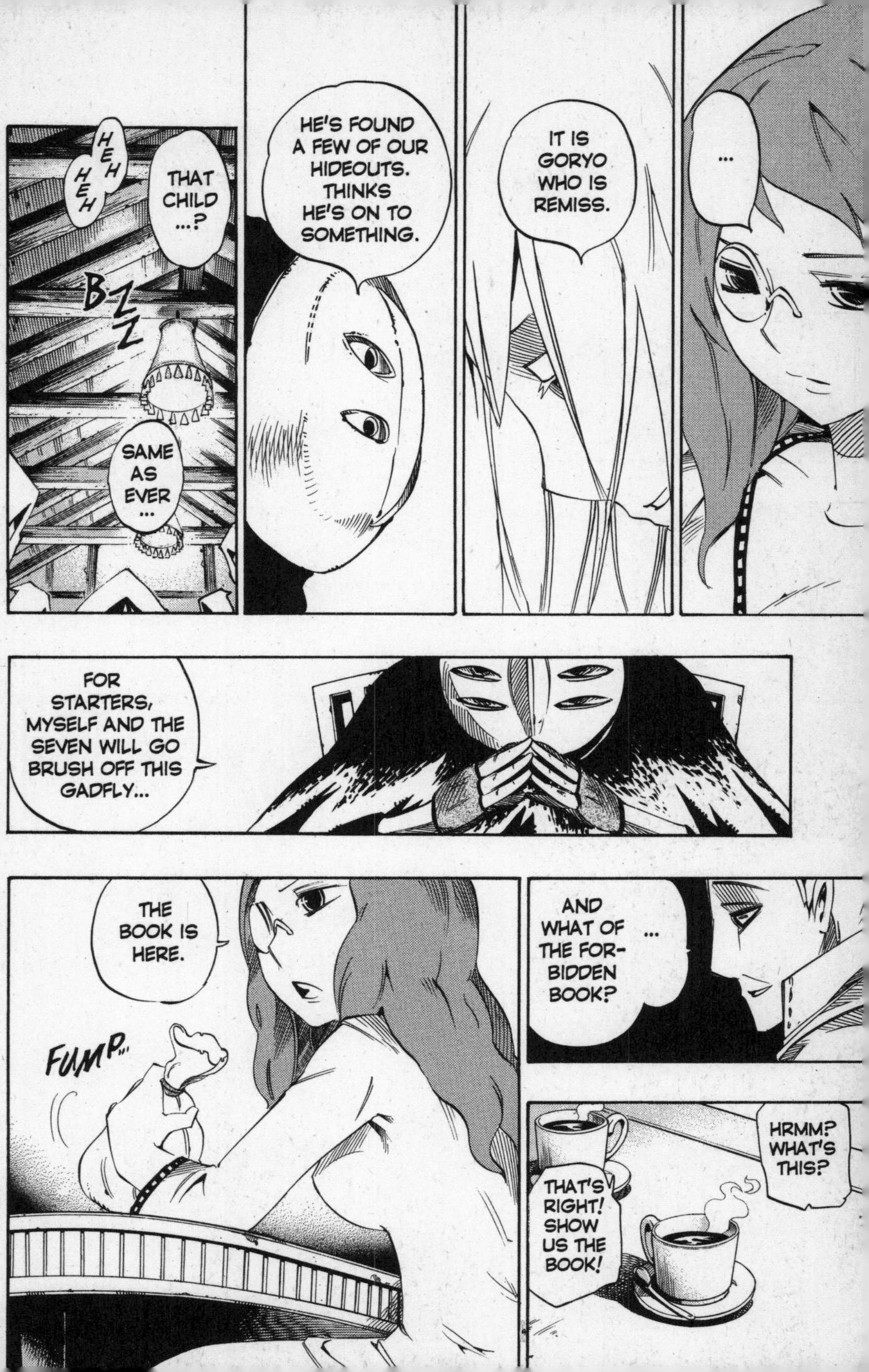
...
IT IS GORYO WHO IS REMISS.
HE'S FOUND A FEW OF OUR HIDEOUTS. THINKS HE'S ON TO SOMETHING.
THAT CHILD ...?
HEH HEH
BZZ
SAME AS EVER ...
FOR STARTERS, MYSELF AND THE SEVEN WILL GO BRUSH OFF THIS GADFLY...
AND WHAT OF THE FOR-BIDDEN BOOK? ...
HRMM? WHAT'S THIS?
THAT'S RIGHT! SHOW US THE BOOK!
THE BOOK IS HERE.
FUMP...

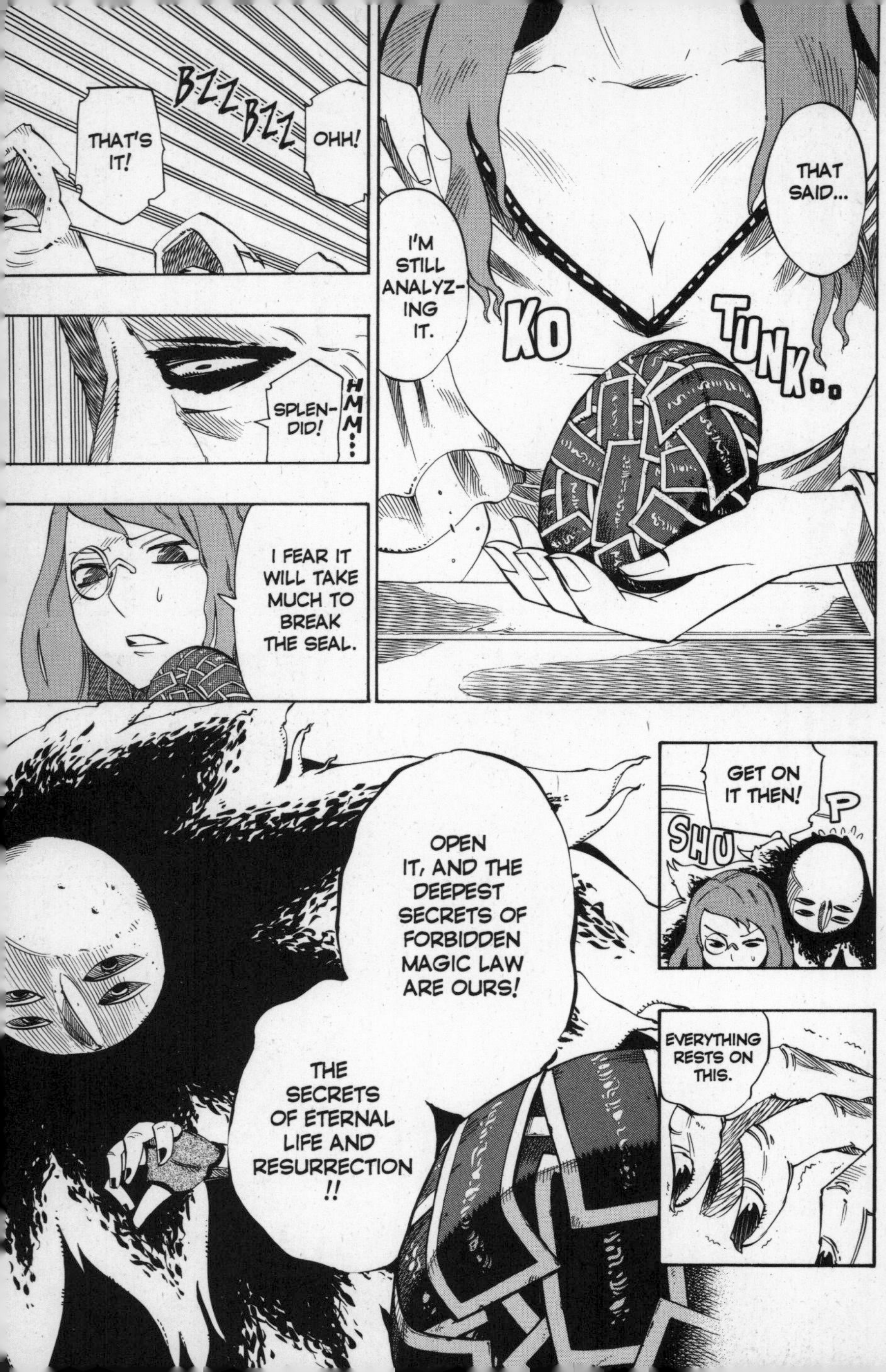
THAT SAID...
I'M STILL ANALYZING IT.
KO TUNK..
OHH!
BZZ BZZ
THAT'S IT!
HMM...
SPLENDID!
I FEAR IT WILL TAKE MUCH TO BREAK THE SEAL.
GET ON IT THEN!
SHU P
EVERYTHING RESTS ON THIS.
OPEN IT, AND THE DEEPEST SECRETS OF FORBIDDEN MAGIC LAW ARE OURS!
THE SECRETS OF ETERNAL LIFE AND RESURRECTION!!

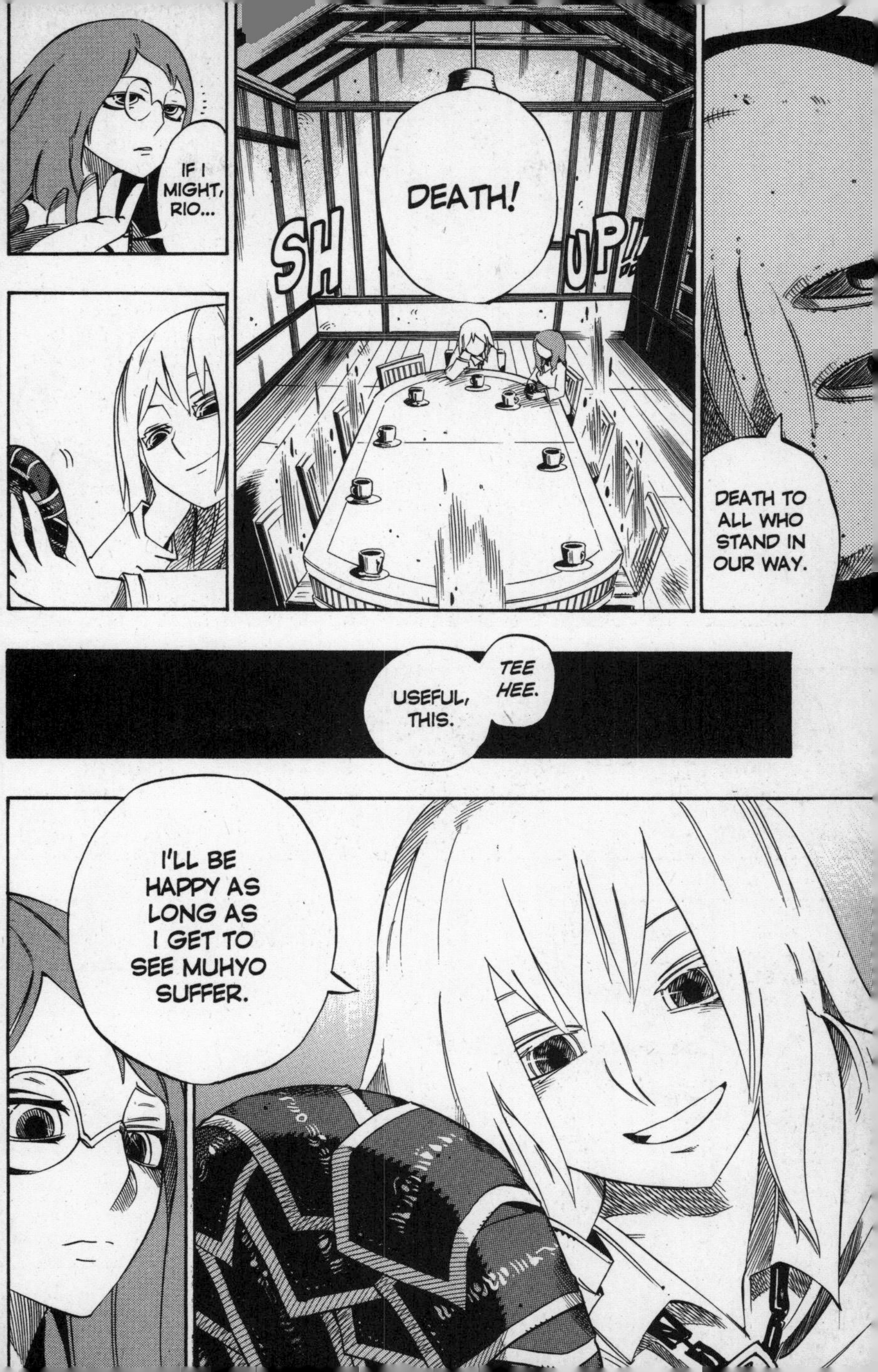
DEATH TO ALL WHO STAND IN OUR WAY.
SH
DEATH!
UP!!
IF I MIGHT, RIO...
TEE HEE.
USEFUL, THIS.
I'LL BE HAPPY AS LONG AS I GET TO SEE MUHYO SUFFER.

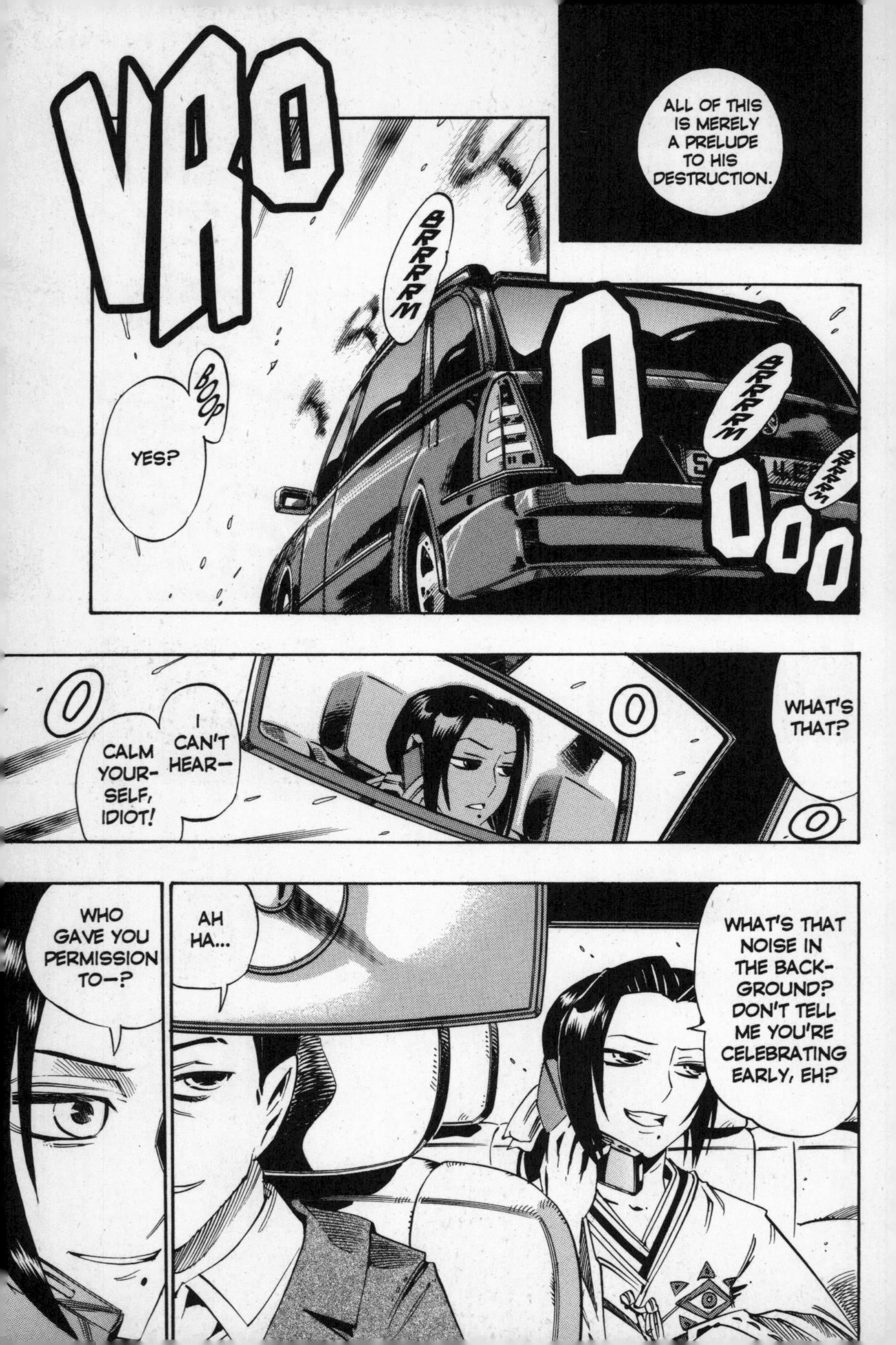
ALL OF THIS IS MERELY A PRELUDE TO HIS DESTRUCTION.
VROOOOOO
BRRRRM
BRRRRM
BRRRRM
BOOP
YES?
WHAT'S THAT?
I CAN'T HEAR—
CALM YOURSELF, IDIOT!
WHAT'S THAT NOISE IN THE BACKGROUND? DON'T TELL ME YOU'RE CELEBRATING EARLY, EH?
AH HA...
WHO GAVE YOU PERMISSION TO—?

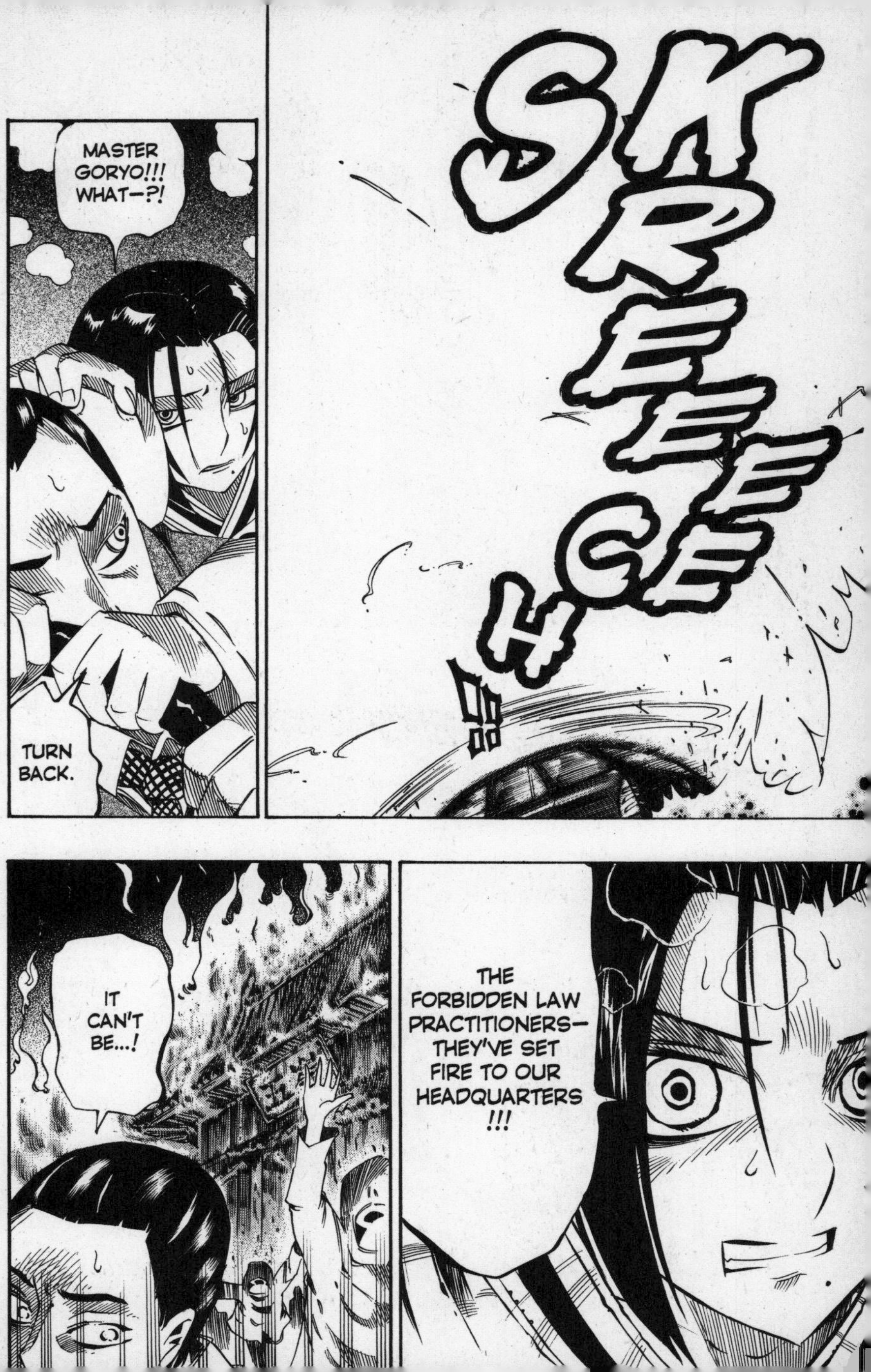
SKREEEECH
MASTER GORYO!!! WHAT—?!
TURN BACK.
THE FORBIDDEN LAW PRACTITIONERS— THEY'VE SET FIRE TO OUR HEADQUARTERS !!!
IT CAN'T BE...!

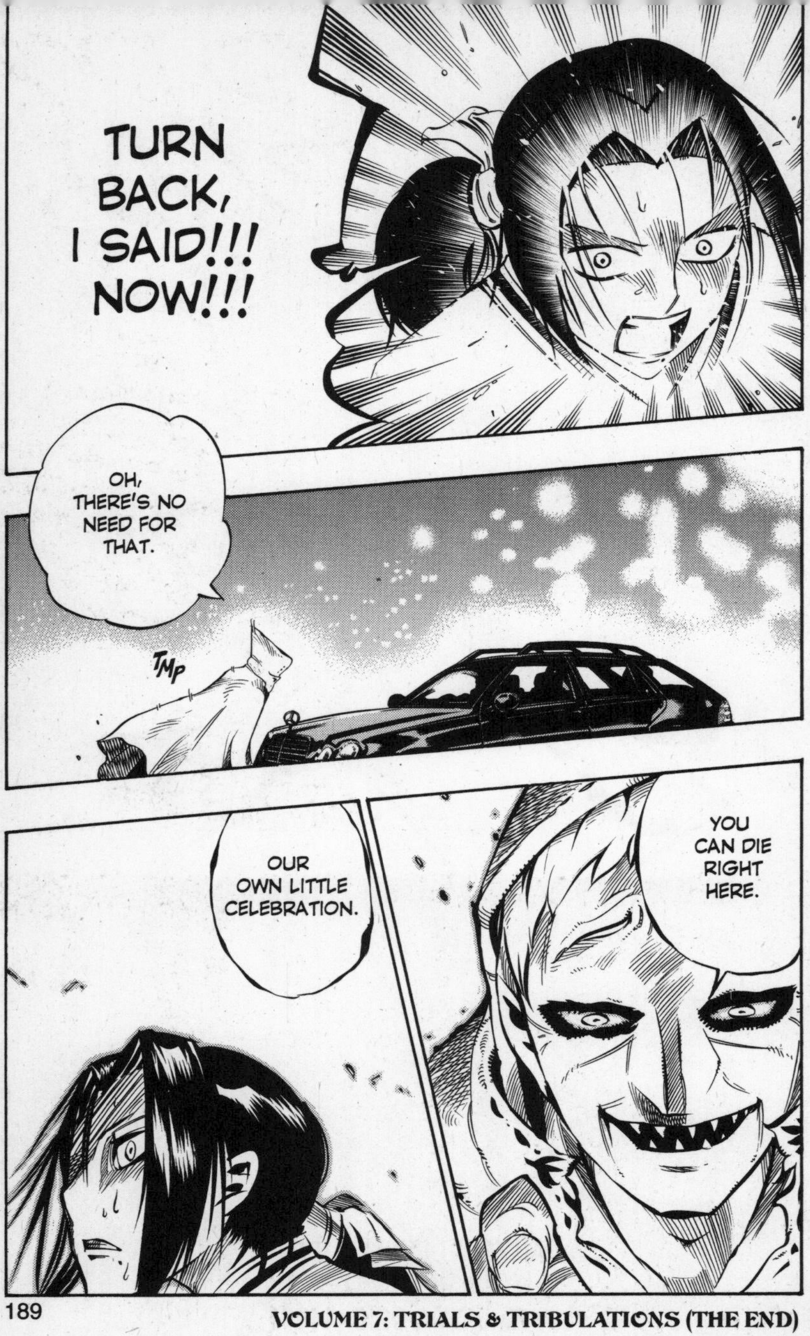
TURN BACK, I SAID!!! NOW!!!
OH, THERE'S NO NEED FOR THAT.
TMP
YOU CAN DIE RIGHT HERE.
OUR OWN LITTLE CELEBRATION.

VOLUME 7: TRIALS & TRIBULATIONS (THE END)

In The Next Volume...

When a forbidden magic law practitioner takes Goryo
prisoner, will Muhyo and the gang be able to save him before
he turns into a ghost?

Available December 2008!

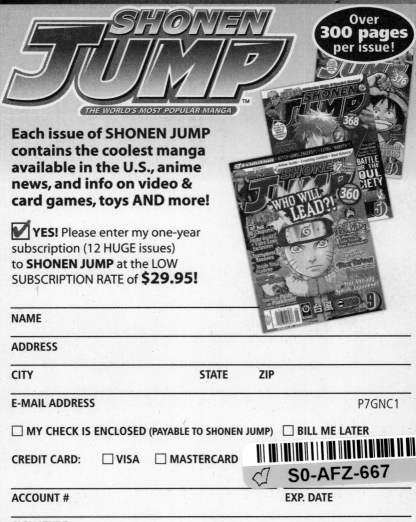